MAIL O
MADE EASY

Here's what they said about the last edition:

"Leslie Geddes-Brown's definitive guide to mail order gift buying is… invaluable all year round."
You magazine, Mail on Sunday.

•

"One indispensable guide rounds up every telephone number you need to procure." *Harpers and Queen*

•

"Leslie Geddes-Brown's new book…lists mail order sources for just about any Christmas essential and could save you having to leave the house at all…it's a marvellous source for telephone shoppers." *The Times*

•

"Pressed for time? **Christmas Made Easy** is the book for you…" *Daily Mail*

•

"Try reading **Christmas Made Easy** by the guru of shopaholics, Leslie Geddes-Brown." *Country Life*

•

"An invaluable source of inspirational presents for birthdays, christenings and weddings too."
The Independent.

MAIL ORDER MADE EASY

LESLIE GEDDES-BROWN

First published in Great Britain in 1996 by Metro Books
under the title *Christmas Made Easy*.

This edition published in 1998 by
Columbine Press Limited,
42 Canonbury Square,
London N1 2AW
E-mail: dovebooks@aol.com
Website: www.g-vis.co.uk/MailOrderMadeEasy

All rights reserved: no part of this publication may be
reproduced, stored in a retrieval system, or transmitted in
any form or by any means, electronic, mechanical,
photocopying or otherwise without the prior written
consent of the publisher.

© 1998 Leslie Geddes-Brown

Leslie Geddes-Brown is hereby identified as the author of this work
in accordance with Section 77 of the Copyright, Designs
and Patents Act 1988

ISBN 1 902563 00 X

Typeset by Pat Jacobs
Printed in Great Britain by Biddles Limited

Illustrations by Michael Hill

Dedicated to all my dogs

CONTENTS

INTRODUCTION		**11**
1.	**GENERAL**	**15**
2.	**CLOTHES AND ACCESSORIES**	**23**
	Women's clothes	23
	Men's clothes	42
	Children's clothes	49
	Accessories	57
	Jewellery	73
3.	**HOUSE AND GARDEN**	**80**
	Art and replicas	80
	Home	91
	Garden	142
4.	**FOOD AND DRINK**	**168**
	General	168
	Breads, cakes and puddings	176
	Cheese	186
	Confectionery	190
	Fish	194
	Fruit and vegetables	202
	Hampers	203
	Meat, game and poultry	208
	Oils, sauces, herbs and spices	222
	Miscellaneous	231
	Drink	234

8   MAIL ORDER MADE EASY

5.   LUXURIES   248

Scent, aromatics and cosmetics	248
Flowers	259
Cigars	260

6.   BOOKS, CDs, CASSETTES, VIDEOS, STATIONERY   263

7.   MOTHER AND BABY   273

8.   SPECIAL INTERESTS AND SPORT   291

Enthusiasms	291
Activities	304
Equipment	306

9.   ANIMALS   312

10.   PRESENTS   318

General	318
Toys	324
Stocking Fillers	342
Teenagers	344
Problem People	346
Personalised	348
Charities	353

11.   CELEBRATIONS   360

Cards and wrappings	360
Decorations	362
Christmas	367
Creating an atmosphere	367

12.	LEGAL	369
13.	INDEX OF SUPPLIERS	373

While every effort has been made to ensure that all prices and details in this book are correct at time of going to press, the publishers do not hold themselves responsible for any consequences that might arise from errors or omissions.

INTRODUCTION

When I was first asked to write a book about mail order in 1996, I had dabbled in the subject personally and had written quite a bit about it as editor of the shopping pages on the *Mail on Sunday's You Magazine*. There, dealing with a huge nation-wide readership of around six million, I felt I had to produce ideas which could be as easily bought in Penzance or Aberdeen as in London. Having lived for a long time in Yorkshire and County Durham, I knew how infuriating it was when shopping writers could see no further than the metropolis. So, it was either the High Street stores which, though worthy, could be so middle-of-the-road that they were dull, dull, dull – or mail order.

I was lucky that Britain in the nineties was the launching pad for mail order as it ought to be. All sorts of factors were – and are – at work to make it so. The recession had sent a lot of independent shops to the wall and bright young couples to the country where they had to create their own employment from scratch. Many women were too busy working to have time for all but the most enjoyable shopping and others were looking for a less stressful life. At the same time, people both wanted and needed something a little bit different. This might be organic meat, pushed by the BSE scare and a fear of additives, or it might be aromatic oils and candles to soothe the spirits. People had enthusiasms, be it for croquet or poetry, which the big stores ignored. All were suddenly available through the post.

Then there were all the technology aids: what could be easier than to fax your order and credit card number one evening and have a parcel delivered the next day? Or to get more information from a net site which filled out the paper catalogue? There were fast couriers to zing the goods to you from Devon or Argyll, insulated polystyrene boxes and ice blocks to keep food and flowers super fresh.

My first mail order book, commissioned by a clever publisher, simply dealt with Christmas. I found that it was possible to order absolutely everything except fresh vegetables for the holiday through the post and ran through a series of radio and TV interviews proving just that. This was easy because, researching the book, I actually followed my own advice. For three years now I have had my entire Christmas holiday food brought to my doorstep – goose, ham, stuffing, pudding, pre-Christmas meals and post-Christmas meals – leaving the supermarkets to heave and pullulate without me. I have sent presents by post – cakes, silk scarves, decoy ducks, silverware and scent – with just a phone call. My wrapping paper has come in the mail, as has the Christmas tree and other greenery.

Now I am a total convert to mail order not just at Christmas but all the year round which is why I have changed the book's title from Christmas Made Easy to Mail Order Made Easy. Many of the companies I started with are still here because their wares are not confined to Christmas. You can buy delicious food and drink, presents, cookware and clothes all the year round. Christmas still figures in my new chapter called Celebrations but I have widened it out to include ideas for wedding and Christening presents, birthday and anniversary gifts and, of course, little thank-you tokens.

I have also introduced a new chapter which was not relevant for Christmas. This is Mother and Baby, written by Pat Jacobs, who has two children of her own and knows all about the subject. No one needs the help of mail order more than women who are pregnant with all the discomforts which go with that, or

INTRODUCTION

those learning to be mothers for the first time and desperate for goods like cots or high chairs which are virtually impossible to lug about the High Street with a baby in tow.

Otherwise, I have combined in one chapter all food and drink suppliers rather than separate those companies which provide food for presents – hampers, chocolates and the like. With imagination, most food can be sent as a gift and some presents awarded to yourself. The Little Red Barn, a newcomer here, makes the most delicious brownies. They work as presents but I'd hate to be without them myself.

HOW TO USE THE BOOK

The chapters are divided into simple categories but, as some firms sell anything they feel like, I have cross-referenced subjects where necessary. The first, general, chapter is for companies which sell so many different items that they defy categorisation.

Each listing has a section given to detailed facts – price range, returns policy, phone and fax numbers. This is intended as a guide only. Inevitably, firms move premises, telephone numbers change, prices move up and down with inflation and availability, yet I think it's important for mail order shoppers to have some idea of price. Sometimes firms have no stated refund policy – this may not be sinister, they may never have been asked. In the final chapter of the book, I deal with the legal side of mail order but, when in doubt, find out about returns, damage etc simply by asking. Mail order firms would be nowhere without the telephone and most are charming to deal with.

In the various interviews I did with radio and TV I was surprised how nervous people are about mail order. Shoppers who will happily buy shrink-wrapped objects from the supermarket shelves worry that they will be ripped off when they buy from a picture and description in a catalogue. I suppose there are sharks out there but I've never come across one. I've been delighted when things have gone right and, when things have gone wrong (a courier lost an entire pack of kippers) the kipper smoker immediately sent another without charge.

It's quite hard to get the best from mail order without a credit card. There are a few, tiny firms which still have not signed up for the facility and, for them, you will have to send a cheque (which can take a few days to clear) or a postal order. Most firms, however, take credit cards and are fully supplied with faxes and answer phones which means they can deal with your order almost immediately. Many state that goods may take 28 days to arrive, but that's generally to give them legal protection against glitches. Others offer next day delivery for an extra fee.

Since I began to write about mail order, the website and the e-mail have become important. E-mail allows you to send letters and orders from your computer to the firm's computer but it's still considered risky to give your credit card number over cyber space. The boffins are working at changing this.

Surprisingly, international mail order is still in its infancy. America, France and Germany all have up-and-running mail order networks but most seem uninterested in crossing frontiers. And, inevitably, there will be other omissions in the book. Though I seem to have endlessly scavenged the magazines, papers and advertisements for ideas, some will have eluded me. As in the past, I rely on you to make suggestions of firms which should be in but are omitted. Several in this new book come from helpful readers.

Chapter One

GENERAL CATALOGUES

These firms either supply virtually everything you can need, such as those from London's mega stores, or they are so idiosyncratic that they cannot be pigeonholed. Usually this is because items are chosen at random by the owner. If you like the style, you'll probably enjoy everything that's listed.

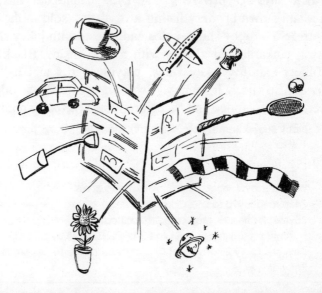

GENERAL CATALOGUES - LISTINGS

Barclay & Bodie You will often find this firm featured in the papers. It's because they come up with such original ideas such as the famous toyboy ironing cover and the hottie like a pair of breasts. Not all is naughty: the blue and white china and vine leaf plates from Italy are beautiful, as are the French fabric-design trays. A red and blue umbrella really does stand up to the description "The smartest umbrella in town."

16 MAIL ORDER MADE EASY

Barclay & Bodie Ltd, 7 & 9 Blenheim Terrace, London NW8 0EH
Tel: 0171 372 5705 **Fax:** 0171 328 4266
Price range: £4.50 to £85. Catalogue free.
Payment: cheque, major credit cards.
Postage & packing: £4.75. Next day delivery add £5.25.
Overseas rates on application.
Delivery: allow 28 days.
Refunds: yes, if returned within 14 days, excluding mono-
grammed items.
Specials: gift service.

Black Sheep Brewery

A lads' catalogue, this, from Masham's own brewery listing just what is sold in the visitor centre. So – rugby shirts, polos and sweats with jokey slogans, mugs, tankards and glasses with more slogans, Black Sheep brollies, soft toys, key rings, playing cards and a "Baa...r Towel." So kitsch, it's funny. Also hampers for Eew...ltide, with beer, chutney, fudge and sheep droppings (actually mints).

Black Sheep Brewery plc, Wellgarth, Masham, Ripon, North
Yorkshire HG4 4EN
Tel: 01765 689227 **Fax:** 01765 689746
E-mail: visitor.centre@blacksheep.co.uk.
Website: www.visitor.centre@blacksheep.co.uk
Price range: 99p to £60. Catalogue free.
Payment: cheque, major credit/debit cards.
Postage & packing: from £1 to £5, or £5.95/£6.95 by courier.
Delivery: allow 28 days. Last Christmas orders by 15 December.
Refunds: yes.

First Impressions

The name reflects the fact that items in this catalogue are either copied from antiques or stamped in the antique dies. There are perfume bottles and atomisers plus syringes for transferring the scent, silver photo frames, desk sets, clocks and trinket boxes. Though people don't realise it, the firm has a shop where you can look at the full range.

First Impressions, Lewes Road, Forest Row, East Sussex RH18 5AA
Tel: 01342 826620 **Fax:** 01342 822289
E-mail: 101576.3372@compuserve.com

Price range: £2 to £45. Catalogue free.
Payment: major credit/debit cards.
Postage & packing: £2.95 for orders under £25, free thereafter.
Delivery: despatched within 24 hours. Last Christmas orders by last posting date.
Refunds: yes.

Fortnum & Mason Though much of the catalogue is full of Fortnum's celebrated hampers, bowls of caviar, boxes of rare varieties of apples and their Winter Fruits selection of crystallised fruits, there's much more. It includes amber for necklaces and earrings, a huge range of French perfumes and the company's own English lavender. Children are offered old-fashioned clothes, toy chess sets and clever fluffy toys. Grannies might appreciate a silver tea strainer. For Christmas there are excellent candles and crackers.

Fortnum & Mason, 181 Piccadilly, London W1A 1ER
Tel: 0171 465 8666
Fax: 0171 437 3278
Price range: £7.50 to £2,000. Catalogue £3 by post in UK.
Payment: cheque, major credit cards, FM account.
Postage & packing: chart in catalogue.
Delivery: allow 28 days. Last Christmas orders by 8 December.
Refunds: by arrangement.

The General Trading Company For nearly 80 years it has been a bastion in Sloane Square. Today, its fame is worldwide, though it's hard to put a finger on what exactly it sells. "Stylish, well-made and timeless" is their description. The range certainly doesn't rely too much on fashion, which can become so quickly dated – more, perhaps, objects which have withstood fashion to stand as classics in their own right. This doesn't mean that the company ignores trends – there's a lot of East-meets-West objects currently – but none will date when the fashion passes. They have notable wedding present and other gift lists.

The General Trading Company, Catalogue Dept, 144 Sloane Street, London SW1X 9BL

Tel: 0171 730 0411 ext. 243 **Fax:** 0171 823 4624

E-mail: catalogue@general-trading.co.uk

Website: http://www.general-trading.co.uk

Price range: £1 to £10,000. Catalogue £2.

Payment: cheque, postal order,, major credit cards.

Postage & packing: £6.50 by 48-hour Datapost in UK. Last Christmas orders 19 December.

Refunds: yes, if returned in perfect condition within 28 days.

Goodwood Festival of Speed Collection

One of the best-marketed sets of goods connected with this grand house and its events calendar. The Festival of Speed goods are black and white, usually incorporating the chequered finishing flag. Baseball caps, sweatshirts, children's T-shirts, bumbags and mugs are included. Extremely stylish, very dashing.

Festival of Speed Merchandise, Mail Order Dept, Goodwood House, Goodwood, Chichester, West Sussex PO18 0PX

Tel: 01243 755000 **Fax:** 01243 755005

Price range: 50p to £70. Catalogue free.

Payment: cheque, major credit/debit cards.

Postage & packing: £2.90 per order.

Delivery: allow 28 days. Last Christmas orders by 11 December.

Refunds: yes, if faulty, otherwise exchange.

Goodwood Racing Colours Collection

The Racing Colours (for Glorious Goodwood) goods are based on the Richmond scarlet and yellow colours and an old Stubbs painting in the house. There are brilliant panamas, cufflinks, umbrellas and braces, Racing Colours socks, travel rugs, bridge cards and chocolates.

GENERAL 19

Racecourse Merchandise, Racing Colours Dept, Goodwood Racecourse, Goodwood, Chichester, West Sussex PO18 0PS
Tel: 01243 755022 **Fax:** 01243 755025
Price range: 50p to £95. Catalogue free.
Payment: cheque, major credit/debit cards.
Postage & packing: £2.90 per order.
Delivery: allow 28 days. Last Christmas orders by 11 December.
Refunds: yes, if faulty, otherwise exchange.

The Green Shop Everything you need around you in the greenest possible way. Casein paints, made with milk and pigments to dilute with water, bleaches and strippers without violent solvents to catch your breath. There are rainwater recycling systems, compost bins and even kit to harness wind power. The baby section includes reusable nappies, baby shampoos and creams.

The Green Shop, Bisley, Stroud, Gloucestershire GL6 7BX
Tel: 01452 770629/770272 **Fax:** 01452 770043
Price range: 70p to £2,000. Catalogue free.
Payment: major credit cards.
Postage & packing: according to weight.
Delivery: normally within 1 week, but allow 2.
Refunds: yes, in all valid cases.

Harrods Four times a year Harrods produces a glossy catalogue featuring some of the best goods it has to offer and these can be mail-ordered. They range from designs by top fashion names such as Thierry Mugler and Cartier to Theo Fennell's cult jewellery, pure silk pyjamas and cashmere sweaters. There are hampers, drinks and cakes from the famous food hall and the Harrods teddy bear and watch which are regularly updated. The formal children's party clothes, in sumptuous fabrics like black velvet, are delightful.

Harrods Ltd, Knightsbridge, London SW1X 7XL
Tel: 0171 730 1234, Tel orders: 0800 376 1234.
Fax: 0171 581 0470
Price range: £1.50 to £12,000. Catalogue free to account customers, otherwise there will be a charge.

Payment: cheque, Harrods card, major credit cards.
Postage & packing: generally £5 in UK.
Delivery: 2-3 days in London area, 5-7 elsewhere in UK. Last Christmas orders by 10 December.
Refunds: yes, if returned within 28 days.

Hitchcocks' by Post

The firm has two shops in Bath and Alresford and their mail order catalogue concentrates on textiles, jewellery and automata, generally by named designers. Robert Race's weird animals – a domestic cat which becomes a tiger and a series of gawky birds are made of driftwood, pebbles and finds on beaches. Ian McKay uses driftwood for moving ships and fish. The jewellery and scarves are bold and distinctive in design – no department store blandness in this catalogue.

Hitchcocks' by Post, 10 Chapel Row, Bath BA1 1HN
Tel/Fax: 01225 330646
Price range: £5.95 to £150. Catalogue free.
Payment: cheque, major credit/debit cards.
Postage & packing: £1.50 per order in UK.
Delivery: allow 28 days.
Refunds: yes.

The House of Bruar

Hot off the press, the firm which specialises in all things Scottish launched its mail order catalogue in September. It has taken founders Mark and Linda Birkbeck three years to develop a catalogue for the range of tweeds, luggage, cashmere and foods. Brands like Timberland, Musto, Johnstons of Elgin and Mackintosh are included.

The House of Bruar, by Blair Atholl, Perthshire PH18 5TW
Tel: 01796 483236 **Fax:** 01796 483218
Price range: £4.95 to £249.95. Catalogue free.
Payment: cheque, major credit cards.
Postage & packing: £4.95.
Delivery: normally 10 days but allow 28.
Refunds: yes, prepaid envelope included.

GENERAL

The House of Henry I can't quite get to grips with the logic behind this selection but I like what they have. In general there are transparent plastic bags, purses and shower curtains with integral flowers, fruit and even golden fish, garden accessories and bird feeders, and ever-useful sausage draught excluders. One, I see, has a picture of the liner, Normandie. It should have been the cult Titanic.

The House of Henry Ltd, The Barns, Pitchbury Farm, Church Lane, Churchill, North Somerset BS25 5QW

Tel: 01934 853153 **Fax:** 01934 853231

E-mail: houseofhenry@compuserve.com

Price range: £9.50 to £325. Catalogue £1 refunded with order.

Payment: Mastercard, Visa, Switch.

Postage & packing: included in UK.

Delivery: within 15 days. Last Christmas orders by 11 December.

Refunds: yes, if returned within 14 days.

L.L. Bean This classic American catalogue seems to cater for your every need. It specialises in tough outdoor clothes for men and women. There are padded parkas, multi-pocketed jackets which professional photographers love, cotton sweatshirts and turtlenecks plus shoes to take you from mountain to board-room. But there's also a range of kitbags, tents, cycles, canoes and hammocks. In addition to the general catalogue there are others devoted solely to furnishings, travel, fly-fishing and clothes for men, women and children.

L.L. Bean, Freeport, Maine 04033-0001, USA

Tel: free UK order/catalogue request line 0800 962954, queries 0800 891297 **Fax:** 00 1 207 552 4080

Website: http://www.llbean.com

Price range: $12 to $899. Catalogue free.

Payment: international money order, Mastercard, Visa, Amex, JCB.

Postage & packing: surface $15 to $60, airmail $20 to $80, express $35 to $125.

Delivery: surface 8-12 weeks, airmail 2-3 weeks, express 1-2 weeks.

Refunds: yes.

Layden Designs

Layden Designs Sellers of Takeradi, a compulsive African game which involves each player stacking wooden bricks with one hand only, trying to build as high as possible before it collapses. It's thought that the idea originated with RAF flyers based at Takoradi station during the war. There is more to it, however, in that each of the forty-eight bricks is made of a different timber, from English oak to Lebanon cedar, jarrah from Australia to afromosia found in central Africa. It teaches children about woods and looks most handsome.

> **Layden Designs**, Arbour Hill, Patrick Brompton, Bedale, North Yorkshire DL8 1JX
>
> **Tel:** 01677 450642 **Fax:** 01677 450766
>
> **Price:** £45. Details of game free on request.
>
> **Payment:** cheque, postal order.
>
> **Postage & packing:** £4 for 1 set, £5 for 2, £6 for 3, free thereafter.
>
> **Delivery:** allow 10 days. Next day delivery at extra cost.
>
> **Refunds:** by arrangement.
>
> **Specials:** a royalty is paid to a disabled charity. Presentation box included.

Natural Collection

Natural Collection The more you read about what scientists are doing to our foods, our homes and the environment, the more alarming it becomes. Several firms have sprung to the rescue with lists which are both eco-friendly and likely to improve our health. This list has clothes from organically grown cotton, water filters and Ecover cleaning products, unbleached bed linen and now a range of natural foods. If you need convincing, read some of the books they list.

> **Natural Collection**, Eco House, 19a Monmouth Place, Bath BA1 2AY
>
> **Tel:** 01225 442288 **Fax:** 01225 469673
>
> **E-mail:** naturalcollection@ecotrade.co.uk
>
> **Price range:** £1.25 to £249.99. Catalogue free.
>
> **Payment:** cheque, major credit/debit cards.
>
> **Postage & packing:** £1.75 for orders up to £5, £3.50 to £100, free thereafter. Overseas add 20% surcharge.
>
> **Delivery:** within 5 working days.
>
> **Refunds:** yes.
>
> **Specials:** gift-wrapping £2.50, gift cards £1.50.

Chapter Two

CLOTHES AND ACCESSORIES

WOMEN

A few years ago, no one would have suggested that women would buy high fashion clothes by mail order. This barrier has now crumbled completely – not only for high quality classics like cashmere sweaters, silk shirts or wonderful pashmina throws which are expensive but not difficult to pick off the page – but also for hats, shoes and even ballgowns. This has been achieved by cleverly photographed catalogues, detailed descriptions and sizing and, very important, a returns policy which asks you to treat the clothes as though they were on appro. If you can cope with sending bulky parcels back, there are huge advantages. New clothes can be tried on with shoes, bags, coats, underwear to suit, rather than in a sweaty changing room. You can make sure of your back view, how the garment copes when you sit down, stride out or get into the car. You can check for minute details. You can even get family approval without dragging everyone around the shops.

WOMEN'S CLOTHES - LISTINGS

The Alpaca Collection Alpaca is the Andes answer to the cashmere goat of India. Its wool is incredibly light to wear while being warmer and softer than sheep's wool. The company has had alpaca made into a range of knits for men and women. Designed in Italy, some, like the Picasso, are quite wild and colourful but others are simple and neutral. Go for grey, currently fashionable but never out of date.

The Alpaca Collection, 14 Waterloo Park, Bidford-on-Avon, Warwickshire B50 4JH

Tel: 01789 778004 **Fax:** 01789 778119

E-mail: alpacacollection@compuserve.com

Price range: £35 to £139. Catalogue free.

Payment: cheque, Mastercard, Visa.

Postage & packing: £4 including insurance.

Delivery: usually ex stock. 24-hour delivery available. Last Christmas orders by 22 December.

Refunds: yes, if returned unworn in original condition within 14 days.

Artigiano The reason that mainstream Italian clothes are more effortlessly stylish than British ones is the colouring. In this range, you will find a near-black navy range, cream, beiges and camel suits, jackets, dresses and knitwear which comes from honey to amber. Apart from the odd scarlet, everything here is in the best neutral tradition. Sizes go up to 20.

Artigiano, P O Box 1, Yarmouth, Isle of Wight PO41 0US

Tel: 01983 531881 **Fax:** 01983 531726

E-mail: orders@artigiano.com

Website: http://www.artigiano.com

Price range: £25 to £180. Catalogue free.

Payment: cheque, major credit/debit cards.

Postage & packing: £3.95 in UK. Express delivery £5 extra

Delivery: usually within 48 hours, or 24 hours by express.

Refunds: yes, if returned in original condition within 14 days.

Bathrobe Company This range of bathrobes is made from thick, cotton towelling in strong designs like Aztec geometrics, musical notes and jigsaw patterns. They are generally brilliantly coloured and good for holidays or weekend homes. There is a current trend for wearing nightclothes and lingerie designs in the evening and these chunky robes are warm and comforting for casual breakfasts or firelit TV watching.

Bathrobe Company of Covent Garden, Springcroft, The Common, Chelsworth, Suffolk IP7 7HY

Tel/Fax: 01449 740069

Price range: £115 to £175. Catalogue free.

CLOTHES AND ACCESSORIES

Payment: Mastercard, Visa, Amex.

Postage & packing: £8.50 in UK. Overseas rates on application.

Delivery: Next day delivery available on request. Handcrafted, so early ordering recommended at Christmas.

Refunds: by arrangement.

Specials: made to measure service on request.

Born for Loden Since Douglas Hurd adopted the Loden coat for his Foreign Office missions, we've realised how warm and comfortable it is. And how stylish, even if English men stick to their Crombies. This company uses the original Loden cloth in traditional navy or green and gives it a Teflon coat against rain. It sells hats, skirts, breeches and jackets but, best of all, the swinging, back-pleated coat.

> **Born for Loden**, The White House, Appleby in Westmorland, Cumbria CA16 6XF
>
> **Tel:** 01768 353118 **Fax:** 01768 353811
>
> **E-mail:** loden@seel.demon.co.uk
>
> **Website:** http://www.seel.demon.co.uk
>
> **Price range:** £29 to £350. Catalogue free.
>
> **Payment:** cheque, Mastercard, Visa.
>
> **Postage & packing:** £3.50 to £12 per order.
>
> **Delivery:** 24-hour courier service.
>
> **Refunds:** yes, return in original packaging.
>
> **Specials:** special sizes manufactured if required.

Brora Proof of the Scottish brilliance for outdoor, warm clothes for all the family in a single catalogue. Really stunning tweed jackets and bags, cashmere and woollen sweaters and Fair Isles for children, throws, tartan pyjamas, cashmere scarves, hats and gloves (perfect presents). With its shop in London's Kings Road, Brora has its finger on the fashionable pulse but all is classic in style.

> **Brora**, P O Box 16594, London SW6 2WP
>
> **Tel:** 0171 736 9944 **Fax:** 0171 736 7711
>
> **E-mail:** info@brora.co.uk
>
> **Website:** http://www.brora.co.uk
>
> **Price range:** £10 to £300. Catalogue free.

Payment: cheque, Access, Mastercard, Visa, Switch.
Postage & packing: £4 for orders under £150, £6 under £300, free thereafter.
Delivery: despatched within 1 week if in stock.
Refunds: yes, if returned within 14 days.

The Cashmere Company Given the cost of cashmere, it makes sense always to go for the classics, in colour as well as style. If you are buying for a relation or friend, make sure you know exactly what colours they regularly wear. This collection is well thought out, though I would take off gilt buttons in favour of plain mother of pearl.

The Cashmere Company, P O Box 694, Eversholt, Milton Keynes MK17 9GA
Tel: 01525 280888 **Fax:** 01525 280884
Price range: £99 to £795. Catalogue free.
Payment: cheque, postal order, major credit/debit cards.
Postage & packing: £4.95 in UK, £7.50 overseas.
Delivery: allow 28 days.
Refunds: yes, if returned unworn within 7 days.

CLOTHES AND ACCESSORIES 27

The Chelsea Collections It is always hard to choose catalogues of clothes for other people and I admit this is not for me for the outfits are both formal and colourful. They are, however, both stylish and glamorous and excellent for party clothes. There are hats, throws, furs and even a wedding dress. The designers, who I have not heard of, are individually named. This is their first mail order selection.

> **The Chelsea Collections,** 90 Fulham Road, London SW3 6HR
> **Tel/Fax:** 0171 584 1519
> **Price range:** £22 to £1,250. Catalogue £3.00.
> **Payment:** cheque, major credit/debit cards.
> **Postage & packing:** £10.
> **Delivery:** allow 28 days.
> **Refunds:** yes, if returned in perfect condition within 10 days.

Cleo The family business has been making clothes from Irish wool and linen for three generations and Sarah Joyce tells me that among its fans are Daniel Day-Lewis, John Hurt and Julia Roberts. Not surprising when the outfits are so wonderfully romantic. I can just see Day-Lewis in their poet's shirt or sultan's coat, both of linen and any beautiful girl wrapped in their soft wool throws.

> **Cleo Ireland Ltd,** 18 Kildare Street, Dublin 2, Ireland
> **Tel:** 00 353 1676 1421 **Fax:** 00 353 1676 7356
> **Price range:** £17 to £170. Catalogue £3 in Europe, £7 elsewhere.
> **Payment:** cheque, major credit cards.
> **Postage & packing:** varies according to weight of order.
> **Delivery:** normally within 14 days. Express delivery service available. Christmas orders by last posting delivery date.
> **Refunds:** yes, if returned immediately undamaged.

Cocoon Because the firm is based near Loch Lomond, it knows all about rainy weather and the catalogue is full of ways to beat it. The raincoats, jackets, capes and accessories are in the latest waterproof fabrics as lightweight, small and crease-resistant as possible. There is an excellent range of plain colours and you can also choose a snap-in tartan lining in Black Watch or Macdonald.

Cocoon, Lomond Industrial Estate, Alexandria, Dunbartonshire G83 0TL
Tel/Fax: 01389 755511
Price range: £10 to £240. Catalogue free.
Payment: cheque, major credit cards.
Postage & packing: £5 for coats and boots, £1 for accessories.
Delivery: normally within 20 days.
Refunds: yes, if returned unworn within 14 days.

CXD An offshoot of the TSE cashmere company which makes highly-desirable and generally minimalist fashion clothes to be seen in some top London stores. The mail order range tends to include their more classic lines.

CXD - Cashmere by Design, Bellside House, 4 Elthorne Road, London N19 4AG
Tel: 0171 263 3322 **Fax:** 0171 263 4303
E-mail: euro-hq@cxd.co.uk
Price range: £85 to £149. Catalogue free.
Payment: cheque, postal order, major credit cards.
Postage & packing: £3.50 in UK. £5 in Europe.

CLOTHES AND ACCESSORIES 29

Delivery: within 7 days.
Refunds: yes.

Cyrillus

This firm was started by a Frenchwoman who couldn't find the clothes she wanted for her children and so decided to create her own collection for all the family – and very stylish it is.

> **Cyrillus**, Wilberforce House, Station Road, London NW4 4QE
> **Tel:** 0171 734 6660 **Fax:** 0171 734 6661
> **Website:** http://www.cyrillus.com
> **Price range:** £3 to £158. Catalogue free.
> **Payment:** cheque, major credit/debit cards.
> **Postage & packing:** included.
> **Delivery:** allow 28 days, but normally sooner.
> **Refunds:** yes, if returned within 14 days.
> **Specials:** gift-wrapping £3 per parcel.

Denner Cashmere

The best thing you can do with cashmere is to keep it simple. Firms find it hard because it seems wildly expensive without any little gold buttons etc. But Denner's plain shades, from dark olive to honey and their sweaters manage it. I particularly like the ribbed polo, which could be worn over or under a shirt and a scoop-neck sweater which adapts to jeans or silk.

> **Denner Cashmere Ltd**, P O Box 8551, London SW11 1DY
> **Tel:** 0171 223 7754 **Fax:** 0171 787 0417
> **E-mail:** dennercashmere@bizonline.co.uk
> **Website:** http://www.bizonline.net/dennercashmere
> **Price range:** £49.90 to £279.90. Catalogue free.
> **Payment:** cheque, postal order, major credit/debit cards.
> **Postage & packing:** £3.50 in UK. Orders over £200 free. Next-day delivery add £3. Overseas £8.
> **Delivery:** allow 7 days. Last Christmas orders by 19 December for UK and 8 December for USA.
> **Refunds:** yes, if returned within 7 days, otherwise a credit note will be issued.

Denny Andrews

Fashion has caught up with this catalogue. Its strange mixture of Welsh and Oriental styles in natural fabrics features long loose salwar kameez shirts and trousers (as worn by Jemima Khan), mandarin jackets and lots of drawstring trousers. Real, cheery people model the clothes in verdant Welsh surroundings.

Denny Andrews, Clock House Workshop, Coleshill, near Swindon, Wiltshire SN6 7PT
Tel: 01793 762476 **Fax:** 01793 861615
Price range: £7.50 to £120. Send 3 second class stamps for catalogue.
Payment: cheque, major credit cards.
Postage & packing: see catalogue.
Delivery: allow 14 days. Last Christmas orders by 18 December.
Refunds: yes, if returned in good condition.

Di Gilpin Di Gilpin has been designing and hand-knitting her colourful jerseys, jackets and waistcoats since the early 80s, using a mixture of hand-woven wools, locally dyed or natural, chenille, tweed and silk. Some patterns are wild and colourful, others rely on knitting techniques to create pattern and texture. They can be bought either ready hand-knitted or, much more cheaply, as kits. The price list indicates if the knitter must be highly experienced.

Di Gilpin, The Old Mission Hall, Struan, Isle of Skye IV56 8FE
Tel: 01470 572284
Price range: yarn pack £29.75 to £80, handknits £85 to £225. Catalogue free.
Payment: cheque, Mastercard, Access, Visa.
Postage & packing: £5, free for orders over £200.
Delivery: by arrangement.
Refunds: by arrangement.

Higginbotham Pure cotton nightwear is, to me, as comfortable and luxurious as silk but a great deal easier to care for. Higginbotham uses fine poplin in shirting stripes for men's and women's pyjamas, nightshirts, piped dressing gowns and loose kimonos. They are generously sized and extremely comfortable. Arriving tissue-wrapped in a good brown box they also make good presents.

CLOTHES AND ACCESSORIES

Higginbotham Traditional Nightwear, P O Box 121, Diss, Norfolk
IP21 4JZ
Tel: 01379 668833 **Fax:** 01379 668844
E-mail: contact@higginbotham.demon.co.uk
Website: http://www.higginbotham.demon.co.uk
Price range: £45 to £75. Catalogue free.
Payment: cheque, postal order, major credit/debit cards except
Amex & Diners.
Postage & packing: £3 in UK. Overnight at cost.
Delivery: first class by return if in stock. Express delivery available.
Refunds: yes, if returned in original packaging within 10 days.

Judith Glue Many islands have a long tradition of knitwear
for their fishermen and Judith uses the old designs and patterns
of Orkney to make hand-framed garments. Design inspiration
comes from a Fair Isle pattern of 1885, marks made by the
masons on St. Magnus Cathedral and Viking runes scratched on
Orkney's neolithic tombs by the raiders. Scottish wool is extensively used and one range uses the highly-fashionable felting
technique.

Judith Glue, 25 Broad Street, Kirkwall, Orkney Isles, KW15 1DH
Tel/Fax: 01856 874225/876263
Price range: £13.50 to £195. Catalogue £2, deducted from first
order.
Payment: cheque, major credit/debit cards.
Postage & packing: £1.95 for orders up to £30, £3.95 to £95, free
thereafter in UK. Overseas postage at cost plus £2 handling
charge.
Delivery: allow 28 days. Last Christmas orders 3 weeks before
last posting date.
Refunds: yes.
Specials: gift-wrapping free of charge.

Kingshill The firm that single-handedly proved that high fashion
could be mail-ordered and, rightly, a howling success. Designers
now include Paul Costelloe, Jean Muir, Mulberry, Tomasz
Starzewski, Cerruti, Georges Rech and Betty Barclay. Full accessory back-up of shoes, jewellery and handbags from Georgina von
Etzdorf, Joseph Azagury, Dinny Hall plus luxurious own label
cashmere, suede and leather. A must-have catalogue.

32   MAIL ORDER MADE EASY

The Kingshill Collection Ltd, The Office, Little Kingshill Grange, Great Missenden, Buckinghamshire HP16 0DZ
Tel: 01494 890555   **Fax:** 01494 866003
E-mail: fashion@kingshill.co.uk.
Website: http://www.kingshill.co.uk.
Price range: £40 to £800. Catalogue twice a year plus preview and supplements £3 in UK, £5 in Europe, £10 elsewhere.
Payment: cheque, major credit cards.
Postage & packing: included.
Delivery: within 48 hours. Special 24-hour rush service.
Refunds: yes, if returned within 7 days. Also goods on approval if paid for first.
Specials: gift vouchers in multiples of £50. Gift wrapping service.

Lands' End A huge range of cotton polo shirts, sweats, T-shirts and sports shirts to suit every possible casual day out. There are newly-fashionable cotton twin sets, chambray, seersucker and gingham too. For winter there are ranges of fleeces from Polartec, Gore-Tex waterproofing and brilliant inventions which don't let rain in but breathe.

Lands' End Direct Merchants UK Ltd, Freepost MID15304, Oakham, Rutland LE15 6ZW
Tel: 0800 220106/01572 724580
Fax: 0800 222106/01572 758011
Price range: £4.50 to £195. Catalogue free.
Payment: cheque, major credit cards.
Postage & packing: £2.95 for orders up to £150, free thereafter.
Delivery: 3-4 working days.
Refunds: yes.
Specials: monogramming, gift boxes.

Long Tall Sally Though there are over 2m women taller than 5 foot 8 in Britain, this is the only specialist fashion outlet for them. The clothes are designed to look right (not difficult, since most models come this height) but to be wearable on all occasions. The catalogue is updated four times a year and, if you want to try sizes before ordering, there are 25 stores to sample the clothes. The idea is to cover most times of the day from nightwear to training gear.

CLOTHES AND ACCESSORIES   33

Long Tall Sally, Unit 1, Peterwood Way, off Beddington Farm
Road, Croydon CR0 4UQ
Tel: 0181 649 9009 **Fax:** 0181 649 9449
Price range: £20 to £200. Catalogue free.
Payment: cheque, major credit/debit cards.
Postage & packing: £1.95 for orders under £30, £2.95 over £30.
Free for orders over £150.
Delivery: normally despatched within a week but allow 28 days.
Next day delivery at extra charge.
Refunds: yes, if returned unworn within 8 days.

Madeleine Trehearne & Harpal Brar The pashmina
shawl is the luxury that celebs collect. It is made from the finest
cashmere in the world and is both light, warm and soft. The
Kashmiris – say the owners – use them to hatch eggs. Each
measures one by two metres, packs down to the size of a napkin and comes with its own silk envelope. The other range is of
silk nightgowns and kimonos in the richest, most sumptuously
coloured silks from India. These too are treasures when travelling – for long-haul flights, dreary hotels or tropical holidays.

Madeleine Trehearne & Harpal Brar, 20 New End Square,
Hampstead, London NW3 1LN
Tel: 0171 435 6310 **Fax:** 0171 794 8816
E-mail: mtrehearne@easynet.co.uk
Price range: £85 to £1,500. Catalogue free.
Payment: cheque, major credit/debit cards.
Postage & packing: included. Courier service at cost.
Delivery: despatched within 24 hours.
Refunds: by arrangement.
Specials: gift-wrapping free of charge.

Millers This is a very English firm making hand-framed
clothes from Nottinghamshire. They have a shop in North
Yorkshire and make regular visits to county shows. The knits,
often with snaffle, leather and button details are in our favourite
shades of dark navy, forest green and donkey brown. The wool
is 100% Merino and each piece is made to order.

Millers, 133 Papplewick Lane, Hucknall, Nottinghamshire
NG15 8BG
Tel: 0115 963 5613 **Fax:** 0115 968 1204

34   MAIL ORDER MADE EASY

Price range: £75 to £220. Catalogue free.
Payment: cheque, major credit cards.
Postage & packing: £3.50 for orders under £80, £6 thereafter.
Delivery: 4-6 weeks. Last Christmas orders by early December.
Refunds: yes, if returned in perfect condition within 7 days.

Muchen Silk Mysteriously, the price of pure silk has recently become affordable and, in many cases, washable too. The range here includes crêpe de chine and sandwashed silk, both of which are soft and matt, chiffon for scarves and silk satin for camisoles, French knickers and pyjamas. For men there are boxer shorts of silk twill, shirts, waistcoats and ties including specials for golfers.

Muchen Silk, P O Box 3432, London SE5 9BR
Tel: 0171 274 3387 **Fax:** 0171 346 0088
E-mail: silkties@lineone.net
Price range: £6.95 to £46.95. Catalogue free.
Payment: cheque, major credit/debit cards.
Postage & packing: £1.95 for orders up to £20, £2.95 thereafter.
Delivery: normally despatched within 2 working days. Last Christmas orders by 19 December.
Refunds: yes.

Natural Knitwear The company specialises in clothes made of undyed wool from the Jacob sheep which has grazed in small flocks in British parklands for centuries. The wool comes in shades of brown, grey and natural white and this is both mixed and used in pure shades to create soft knits and tweeds. These neutral colours are extremely fashionable at the moment.

Natural Knitwear, The Granary, West End Farm, Station Road, Epworth, Doncaster DN9 1JZ
Tel/Fax: 01427 872968
Price range: £15 to £170. Catalogue free.
Payment: cheque, Mastercard, Visa.
Postage & packing: £2 to £5.
Delivery: allow 28 days.
Refunds: yes, if returned in perfect condition within 14 days.

CLOTHES AND ACCESSORIES

Oliver Brown A small but luscious collection of perfectly-tailored British classics for men and women based on their Sloane Street shop. There are hunting and tweed jackets, wild appliqué jeans, smoking jackets and plus-fours for women along with men's velvet frock coats, tweed jackets and cord trousers.

> **Oliver Brown**, 75 Lower Sloane Street, London SW1W 8DA
> **Tel:** 0171 259 9494 **Fax:** 0171 259 9444
> **Price range:** £3 to £550. Catalogue free.
> **Payment:** cheque, major credit cards.
> **Postage & packing:** £4.50.
> **Delivery:** by return if in stock. Same day delivery at extra cost. Last Christmas orders 23 December.
> **Refunds:** yes.
> **Specials:** gift-wrapping.

Orvis How do you categorise a company which sells a superb range of fishing rods, shooting jackets and waders along with a middle-of-the-road American style clothes collection? It began with the fishing bit and extended into classical outdoorsy clothes for weekends, walks, and holidays In addition there are items like rugs, mattresses and lights, shoe trees and dog beds.

> **Orvis Co Inc**, Vermont House, Unit 30a North Way, Andover, Hampshire SP10 5RW
> **Tel:** 01264 349500 **Fax:** 01264 349505
> **Website:** http://www.orvis.com
> **Price range:** clothing and gifts £15 to £200. Fishing 50p to £580. Catalogue free.
> **Payment:** cheque, postal order, major credit/debit cards.
> **Postage & packing:** £3.95. Overseas rates on application.
> **Delivery:** within 7 days. Last Christmas orders by 21 December.
> **Refunds:** yes.

Pedlars Remember that snap of Chris Evans in a pair of strange trousers of mixed tartans? Well, he found them in this catalogue which takes the simple idea of mixing strong patterns and colours in one garment and adds style. You can mix the tartans with leopard and flower prints or have two different tartans

MAIL ORDER MADE EASY

on each trouser leg. Most garments are of natural fibres and trousers have the fashionable elasticated waist. Lots of skirts, dresses, sweats and shirts in the same mode.

Pedlars Clothing Ltd, The Stables, Glen Dye, Strachan, Kincardineshire AB31 6LT
Tel: 01330 850400 **Fax:** 01330 850490
Price range: £17 to £65. Catalogue free.
Payment: cheque, major credit/debit cards.
Postage & packing: £3 in UK.
Delivery: normally within 4 working days. Next day delivery available. Christmas orders by last posting date.
Refunds: yes.
Specials: gift-wrapping.

Peruvian Connection

Everything here is made in Peru in Peruvian alpaca and pima cotton. It also helps the World Wildlife Fund conserve the area's cloud forest. Especially appealing are the simple dresses, tank tops and wrapover skirts in pima cotton which pack beautifully and adapt to all occasions from beach to banquet.

Peruvian Connection, 3 Manor Farm Barns, Nettlebed, Henley-on-Thames, Oxfordshire RG9 5DA
Tel: 0800 550000, or from overseas: 00 44 1491 642173
Fax: 01491 642174. Tollfree fax from Germany: 0011 0130 820 346, France: 0011 05 901 085
E-mail: peruconnuk@aol.com
Website: http://www.peruvianconnection.com
Price range: £26 to £600. Catalogue free.
Payment: cheque, postal order, major credit/debit cards.
Postage & packing: £4 per order in UK. Overseas £15 per order.
Delivery: normally within 28 days. Last Christmas orders by 28 November.
Refunds: yes.
Specials: gift-wrapping £3.50 per item. Gift vouchers.

Polo Neck Designs

On their brochure, the firm proudly announces that they have held the prices of their cotton polo necks for the last six years. The range is very simple: nine plain shades, checks and spots and some wilder patterns like leopard, ladybirds, horses and golfers.

CLOTHES AND ACCESSORIES

Polo Neck Designs, High Havens Stables, Hamilton Road, Newmarket, Suffolk CB8 0NQ
Tel: 01638 561114 **Fax:** 01638 667913
Price range: £10 to £21.50. Catalogue free.
Payment: cheque, Mastercard, Visa.
Postage & packing: £1.90 in UK.
Delivery: allow 14 days. Last Christmas orders 10 days in advance.
Refunds: yes.

PS Polos The Canadians know all about keeping warm and these Lycra-reinforced polo-neck sweaters are extra snug around the neck and wrists. For women and children, they can be worn under shirts for extra layering or, on warmer days, on their own. The range includes about 20 plains and various all-over prints. They also have dickies to wear under cardigans and shirts in neutral colours. A new venture is called Legless and offers brilliantly patterned tights in 40 denier nylon. Patterns so far are leopard and zebra, tartan, psychedelic, checks and stripes.

PS Polos, The Manor Farm House, Chavenage, Tetbury, Gloucestershire GL8 8XW
Tel: 01666 505720 **Fax:** 01666 504901
Price range: £8 to £24. Catalogue free.
Payment: cheque, major credit cards.
Postage & packing: £2.10 for 1 or 2. £4 for 3 and over.
Delivery: allow 10 days. Some items sell out at Christmas.
Refunds: yes, with return form within 7 days.
Specials: Christmas wrapping available at £1.40 per polo.

Racing Green Unisex working clothes in the American style including a neat range of sweatshirts in pale greens and dark blues, cotton polo shirts in rainbow shades, jeans and window-pane check shirts. There are classic knits too, panamas and bandannas for the summer and swimwear is available all year round. Both men's and women's ranges work well for teenagers and sizes go from 8 to 18.

Racing Green, P O Box 100, Morley, Leeds LS27 0XB
Tel: 0990 411111 **Fax:** 0113 238 2465

Website: http://www.racinggreen.co.uk
Price range: £3 to £120. Catalogue free.
Payment: cheque, major credit/debit cards.
Postage & packing: £3.50. Express delivery add £5.
Delivery: allow 7 working days. Express delivery within 72 hours.
Refunds: yes.
Specials: gift vouchers.

Rainforest Clothing Company

Waxed jackets go Victorian – using subfusc tartans, waxed cotton in navy, rust and olive lined in wools and silks. The company makes waterproofs in redingotes, wrap coats, dusters and fantails. They are very full, thus fitting easily over wide skirts, sweaters and chunky trousers and, with the bright linings, more formal than most waxed clothes.

Rainforest Clothing Company, Chapel Studio, Ruspidge Road, near Cinderford, Gloucestershire GL14 3YA
Tel: 01594 825865
Price range: £25 to £695. Catalogue free.
Payment: cheque, major credit cards.
Postage & packing: included in UK. Overseas rates on application.
Delivery: 8-10 weeks.
Refunds: yes.
Specials: clothes made to order and exclusive.

Shetland Knitwear Associates

The feather-light, woolly white shawls which this firm makes for babies make the most wonderful presents for christenings. Otherwise, their range of traditional knitwear is long-lasting, will never go out of fashion and comes from one of the great knitting centres of the world.

Shetland Knitwear Associates, 31 King Harald Street, Lerwick, Shetland ZE1 0EQ
Tel/Fax: 01595 692746
E-mail: shetland.knitwear@zetnet.co.uk
Website: http://www.zetnet.co.uk/ska
Price range: £9 to £325. Catalogue free.
Payment: cheque, major credit cards.
Postage & packing: £1.80 per garment, 90p per accessory.

CLOTHES AND ACCESSORIES

Delivery: allow 28 days. Hand-knitted at home so supplies could be limited. Last Christmas orders by last week November.
Refunds: yes, if returned within 14 days.

Shilasdair If you are lucky enough to visit the firm's croft at Waternish, you can see the sheep whose wool is used, visit the dyehouse where it is coloured with natural dyes and browse in the shop which sells the yarn, knit kits and heavy wool sweaters. Alternatively, you can do it all by mail and just imagine the moors from which they come. The yarns – greys, soft blues, heathers and lichens – will carry you there.

Shilasdair, Waternish, Isle of Skye IV55 8GL
Tel: 01470 592297
Price range: yarn from £4.50 per 100g, knit kits £26 to £105, hand-knitted garments £45 to £195. Catalogue £2, samples £1.
Payment: cheque, major credit cards.
Postage & packing: included.
Delivery: allow 3 weeks for yarn and kits, 6 weeks for hand-knitted garments.
Refunds: yes if returned in original condition within7 days.

Silken Robes Every one of these kimono robes is made to order and, says the firm, one of their best customers, a rich 6ft 2in, has 13 of them. Kimonos, they add, can be Geisha sexy with a nipped in waist or "in a silk kimono one could fight off a determined samurai without showing lace or flesh". They are also excellent on holiday, travelling, in the evening and, in the shorter length, even good over jeans. These ones are made in brilliant stripes, checks and tartan silks, self-patterned jacquards or in a big range of 18 plains from palest cream to jet black.

Silken Robes, 2a Bangalore Street. London SW15 1QE
Tel: 0181 788 1223 **Fax:** 0181 785 2668
Price range: £95 to £325. Send A4 40p sae for catalogue.
Payment: cheque with order, credit card with £5 surcharge.
Postage & packing: £5 in UK, £10 overseas.
Delivery: normally 2-4 weeks by recorded delivery. Christmas orders as early as possible.
Refunds: yes.

40 MAIL ORDER MADE EASY

> **Specials:** Robes are made to individual order and packed in a garment cover on a complimentary padded hanger. Although the packaging is already attractive special wrappings can be provided at extra cost.

Taillissime This French catalogue from the Redoute company is devoted to those who aren't the size the department stores think they should be. The women's range begins at 14 and goes to 29 and the menswear reaches to a 56 inch hip. Shoes fit sizes 3 to $8^{1}/_{2}$ for women and up to 14 for men. Though the range does have a tendency to drop into kaftans (the worst answer for big hips) many of the clothes are skilfully designed to minimise inches while colours and patterns are good and smart.

> **Taillissime**, La Redoute, P O Box 777, Wakefield, West Yorkshire WF2 8XZ
> **Tel:** 0500 777777
> **Website:** http://www.redoute.co.uk
> **Price range:** £9.99 to £115. Catalogue free.
> **Payment:** cheque, major credit/debit cards, or pay in instalments by opening a personal account.
> **Postage & packing:** £2.45.
> **Delivery:** allow 10 days.
> **Refunds:** yes.

The Thai Shop Thai silk, which is bright, shiny and slightly stiff is not the easiest fabric either to make up or wear. Many of the styles in this list solve the problem by severe tailoring, no collars and straight shapes. Best of all is the Oriental jacket which is, of course, how it was intended to be worn. Some of the wilder bombers, patchworks and ruffles are a bit OTT but the softer Korean silk makes nice tapered trousers.

> **The Thai Shop,** 104 High Street, Tenterden, Kent TN30 6HT
> **Tel:** 01580 763132 **Fax:** 01580 766977
> **Price range:** £1.99 to £159.50.Catalogue free.
> **Payment:** cheque, major credit/debit cards.
> **Postage & packing:** £2.50 in UK. Overseas £3.50.
> **Delivery:** within 7 days if in stock, otherwise within 5 weeks. Last Christmas orders by last posting date.
> **Refunds:** yes, if returned in original condition within 7 days.

CLOTHES AND ACCESSORIES 41

Toast The fashion success of the year, brilliantly-named Toast sells pyjamas for lounging, not bed. I lounge myself in their heavy linen and lust after their pintucked cotton pyjamas and silk kimonos. Most have drawstrings for comfort and many have pockets. The range is expanding as I write with drawstring trousers and bags, towels, throws, T-shirts, soft blankets and linen shifts planned. Think of comfort round the fire or on the beach, in lovely fabrics, and you have the message of this catalogue.

> **Toast**, Llanfynydd, Carmarthenshire SA32 7TT
> **Tel:** 01558 668800 **Fax:** 01558 668875
> **Price range:** £10 to £150. Catalogue free.
> **Payment:** cheque, major credit/debit cards.
> **Postage & packing:** £4 in UK. 24-hour delivery £4 extra. Overseas postage £14 to £39.
> **Delivery:** allow 7 working days.
> **Refunds:** yes, if returned in perfect condition by registered post.
> **Specials:** gift-wrapping.

Wealth of Nations Under new management but still trawling the world for classic clothes which are comfortable and versatile. There are traditional Chinese work clothes but in silk, plenty of white shirts for both sexes and the fashionable loose trousers. If anything, the change of owner has meant more attention is paid to evening wear and the fabrics are a bit more glittery.

> **Wealth of Nations**, Cedars House, Farnborough Common, Orpington, Kent BR6 7BT
> **Tel:** 01689 816600 **Fax:** 01689 607676
> **Price range:** £25 to £155. Catalogue free.
> **Payment:** cheque, postal order, major credit/debit cards.
> **Postage & packing:** £3.50 in UK, express delivery add £7.50. Europe £10 (2 items), elsewhere £15 (2 items).
> **Delivery:** within 7 days if in stock.
> **Refunds:** yes, if returned carefully packed in original condition within 14 days.

The Woolshed Felt and knitwear is made for this range from the company's own North Ronaldshay sheep grazing around their croft. This is a rare breed with rich natural wool in ranges of brown to white. Felts are handmade and cut into bags, purses, hangings and throws, one with a Pictish symbol of a star. Handspun wool, in natural shades, is knitted into chunky sweaters and there's also a Fair Isle range.

The Woolshed, Benlaw, Costa, Evie, Orkney KW17 2NN
Tel/Fax: 01856 751305
Price range: £3 to £175. Send sae for leaflet.
Payment: cheque, postal order.
Postage & packing: included for orders over £300.
Delivery: allow 28 days.
Refunds: yes, if returned unworn and undamaged within 14 days.
Specials: commissions welcome.

See also: Aero Clothing, Bobbins, Boden, Cordings, Cath Kidson, Damask, Denewear, Holland & Holland, Little Treasures, L.L. Bean, Loch Ruray House, Minh Mang, Peta Flint, The Pyjama Box, Rachel Riley, The Real Pyjamas Company, Rosie Nieper, Spencers Trousers, T. M. Lewin, Word Out.

MEN'S CLOTHES

Men's clothes are ideal for mail order. Men, anyway, are generally allergic to shopping which brings on headaches, pained expressions and terminal boredom and their clothes tend to the uniform. Thus, once they have discovered the ideal shirt, not too narrow at the shoulders or long in the sleeves, or the perfect chino trousers, all they need is to go back to the same firm again and again, reordering when clothes begin to fall apart. The whole business can even be delegated to wife, partner, secretary or anyone who is passing.

CLOTHES AND ACCESSORIES 43

Dress your man kit

MEN'S CLOTHES - LISTINGS

Aero Clothing Co American fashions, especially leather jackets, from the 30s to the 50s. These include USAAF pilots' jackets, bikers' jackets in moody black and black leather jeans for men and women. In fact, though these are very masculine clothes, they are classical enough to be fine on women.

> **Aero Clothing Co**, Transatlantic Clothing Company, Greenbank Woollen Mill, Huddersfield Street, Galashiels TD1 3AY
> **Tel:** 01896 755353 **Fax:** 01896 755366
> **E-Mail:** aeroleather@virgin.net
> **Price range:** £250 to £550. Catalogue free.
> **Payment:** cheque, major credit cards.
> **Postage & packing:** included.
> **Delivery:** allow 14 days. Last Christmas orders preferably by 1 December.
> **Refunds:** yes.

Aviation Leathercraft Real cult stuff for fliers (and would-be Biggleses) with the catalogue foreword by Air Chief Marshall Sir Roger Palin. The star of the show is the Irvin jacket, designed by the American Leslie Irvin and made in Britain from 1926. You'll spot it in those old WWII films, zippered, fleeced and undeniably comfortable. Also jackets designed for Tornado and Red Arrow pilots, flight suits, leather helmets and – of course – glass goggles.

Aviation Leathercraft, Thruxton Airport, Andover, Hampshire SP11 8PW

Tel: 01264 772811 **Fax:** 01264 773102

Price range: £25.85 to £358.57. Send first class stamp for catalogue.

Payment: cheque, major credit/debit cards.

Postage & packing: £2.50 helmets and goggles, £8 flying jackets in UK. Overseas see catalogue.

Delivery: allow 28 days. Last Christmas orders by mid November.

Refunds: yes.

Boden

Very much the smart catalogue for Cotswold folk, the clothes are just what that set wears for play and just a bit of work. Lots of wool, cashmere, cotton, cords and silk; outfits colourful but not brash, clothes stylish but comfortable, such as soft natural suede jackets and linen shirts. For men and women of all ages.

Boden, Midland Terrace, Victoria Road, London NW10 6DB

Tel: 0181 453 1535 **Fax:** 0181 453 1536

Price range: £16 to £280. Catalogue free.

Payment: cheque, major credit/debit cards.

Postage & packing: £4. Faster delivery at extra cost.

Delivery: 4-5 working days by second class post.

Refunds: yes.

Cordings

Established in 1839, the firm has long been known for its English country clothes. The mail order catalogue is a distillation of this: tweeds, corduroys, brogues, Shetland sweaters and cashmere scarves and tattersall shirts. The quilted jackets, windowpane tweeds, shooting stockings and blazers have reached worldwide. Italians on the streets of Milan and Californians in San Francisco wear these classics which are just as good for women as men.

CLOTHES AND ACCESSORIES

Cordings Ltd, 19 Piccadilly, London W1V 0PE
Tel: 0171 734 0830 **Fax:** 0171 494 2349
Price range: £10 to £425. Catalogue free.
Payment: cheque, major credit cards.
Postage & packing: £6 in UK. Next-day delivery add £5.
Delivery: normally within 7 days.
Refunds: yes.

Denewear Dene is Mike and Rusty Dene, co-owners, and Denewear is tough outdoor clothing from around the world. There's Swanndri from New Zealand, tweed from Scotland and R.M. Williams from Australia. Other cult clothes are Flying Dodo sweats and fleeces, Akubra bushmen's hats and Sog's Power Plier, America's answer to the Swiss Army knife.

Denewear, Manor Farm, Higher Wraxall, Dorchester, Dorset DT2 0HR
Tel: 01935 83638 **Fax:** 01935 83762
E-Mail: mikedene@denewear.demon.co.uk
Price range: £3.90 to £180. Catalogue free.
Payment: cheque, postal order, Mastercard, Access, Visa, Switch.
Postage & packing: £3.95 for orders under £150, free thereafter. Overseas at cost.
Delivery: allow 28 days. Extra fast delivery service available.
Refunds: yes.

Holland & Holland A small but sumptuous catalogue of English traditional clothes for all seasons, There is a selection of bush jackets and cotton jackets for the tropics and unseasonal holidays, panamas and checked woollen sweaters. For women there are sassy sueded jodhpurs, bucket bags and tweed jackets along with driving and tropical hats. Virtually everything seems to match.

Holland & Holland, 31-32 Bruton Street, London W1
Tel: 0171 499 4411 **Fax:** 0171 499 4544
Price range: £15 to £4,985. Catalogue free.
Payment: cheque, major credit cards.
Postage & packing: £6 in UK.

Delivery: allow 28 days.
Refunds: by arrangement.

Loch Ruray House
Larissa Watson Regan is a young designer working in Northern Ireland who makes full use of the province's fine linen to create a range of ties, some bright and contemporary in design, others with the soft feel of the Irish landscape. I've never heard or seen of a linen tie before, but this is the fabric of the moment. Though it creases like mad, it takes colours as beautifully as silk and washes well too. She also makes wall hangings and scarves.

Loch Ruray House, 8 Main Street, Dundrum, Co. Down BT33 0LU
Tel: 01396 751544..**Fax:** 01396 751601
Price range: £35 to £200. Catalogue free.
Payment: cheque, Visa.
Postage & packing: at cost.
Delivery: by return if in stock, otherwise 2-3 weeks.
Refunds: by arrangement.
Specials: commissioning service.

The Pajama Box
This catalogue sells men's and women's nightwear – T-shirt and boxer styles, long-sleeved tops and long johns for men and pyjamas or nightdresses for women – packed in a PVC cube. A child's version is new for this year. There are also Pilar Peris's easy bathrobes in the softest luxury fleece, in bright colours blanket-stitched in contrast. This is a new company full of interesting ideas.

The Pajama Box, Harrington Corporation Ltd, 24 Jane Street, Edinburgh EH6 5HD
Tel: 0131 555 2448 **Fax:** 0131 554 6758
E-Mail: 106314.1400@compuserve.com
Price range: £19.95 to £85. Catalogue free.
Payment: cheque.
Postage & packing: £3 in UK, £7 elsewhere.
Delivery: 1 week. Last Christmas orders 18 December.
Refunds: by arrangement.
Specials: boxes can be sent wrapped with blue ribbon free of charge and a personalised message can be enclosed.

CLOTHES AND ACCESSORIES 47

Peta Flint 'Has recaptured the art of fine sock making' says her brochure, and these are truly wondrous socks in three styles. Long, medium and short, they have cable knitting where it counts and are knitted to size in wool in five soft moorland shades. Once you've worn them you won't want nylon ever again.

> **Peta Flint**, 246 Basford Road, Old Basford, Nottingham NG6 0HY
> **Tel:** 0115 978 2471 **Fax:** 0115 978 4205
> **Price range:** £10 to £28. Catalogue free.
> **Payment:** cheque, major credit cards.
> **Postage & packing:** included.
> **Delivery:** allow 14 days. Last Christmas orders by 1 December.
> **Refunds:** yes.

The Real Pyjamas Company "You spend a third of your life in bed," says the brochure, recommending that you wear their garments and enjoy it. These are pyjamas with old-fashioned cords and natural shell buttons in Swiss cotton. You can mix and match sizes, long or short bottoms, tops or bottoms only (how many people have to buy both to use only one) or nightshirts for men and women.

> **The Real Pyjamas Company**, Walnut House, Berry's Lane, Honingham, Norwich NR9 5AX
> **Tel/Fax:** 01603 880887
> **Price range:** £19.50 to £57.50. Catalogue free.
> **Payment:** cheque, major credit/debit cards.
> **Postage & packing:** £3 for second class recorded delivery, first class at extra cost.
> **Delivery:** normally by return. Last Christmas orders by last second class posting date.
> **Refunds:** yes, if returned in perfect condition.

The Shirt Press "All the shirts are made from non-iron cotton which sounds incredible. And it is," says the brochure. The designs are simple, the patterns classic. Anyone who has to iron shirts should immediately give several to their

MAIL ORDER MADE EASY

men. Men without unpaid ironers and business travellers should buy for themselves. But when can women have some too?

The Shirt Press, 65 Kingsway, London WC2B 6TD
Tel: 0171 430 1433 **Fax:** 0171 430 1436
Price range: £25.99 to £70. Catalogue free.
Payment: cheque, major credit/debit cards.
Postage & packing: £4 in UK. Overseas rates on application.
Delivery: normally despatched the following day by registered post. Extra fast delivery available. Last Christmas orders by last posting date.
Refunds: yes.
Specials: gift-wrapping, made to measure service, sleeve alterations.

Spencers Trousers From the rugged Pennines, Spencers have been making rugged trousers since 1922 and their current catalogue shows the original pattern drawing, halfway between a Da Vinci sketch and an engineering blueprint. The range consists of breeches, plus twos (less wide than plus fours) and regular trousers. They are handcut and made to measure and can have button flies or braces' buttons for no extra cost.

Spencers Trousers, Friendly Works, Burnley Road, Sowerby Bridge, West Yorkshire HX6 2TN
Tel: 01422 833020..**Fax:** 01422 839777
Price range: £60 to £85. Catalogue and swatches free.
Payment: cheque, major credit cards.
Postage & packing: included.
Delivery: allow 7 days.
Refunds: yes.

T. M. Lewin The classic Jermyn Street shirtmaker has been in business for a century but they're absolutely not slouches when it comes to fashion. The new brochure reinterprets formal shirts in brilliant plain colours – raspberry, emerald, sky – with bright, near plain ties. Reminds me of modern book design and works just as well. There are Friday shirts, weekend cord shirts and, for women, semi-fitted shirts designed to be worn outside

CLOTHES AND ACCESSORIES 49

the skirt. Not in the catalogue but for sale are boxers in a bag, socks, scarves and leather accessories.

T. M. Lewin, 106 Jermyn Street, London SW1Y 6EQ
Tel: 0171 930 4291, mail order freephone: 0800 376 1664
Fax: 0171 930 1855 **E-Mail:** headoffice@tmlewin.co.uk
Website: http://www.tmlewin.co.uk
Price range: £29.50 to £137.50. Catalogue free.
Payment: cheque, major credit/debit cards.
Postage & packing: UK £4, courier £7.50; Europe £10, express £20; elsewhere £15, express £25.
Delivery: guaranteed special delivery available at extra cost. Last Christmas orders by 17 December in UK, 7 December in Europe, 1 December elsewhere.
Refunds: by arrangement.
Specials: gift-wrapping, gift card messages can be enclosed, gift vouchers.

See also: The Alpaca Collection, Barnsbury Designs by Bicinc, The Bathrobe Company of Covent Garden, Birkenstock, Born for Loden, Brora, Calange, Carpet Bags Plus, The Cashmere Company, Cleo, Cocoon, Cyrillus, Higginbotham, J. P. Promos, Judith Glue, L.L. Bean, Lands' End, Madeleine Trehearne & Harpal Brar, Muchen Silk, Oliver Brown, The Original Celtic Sheepskin Co, Orvis, Pedlars, Racing Green, Shetland Knitwear Associates, Silken Robes, Simon Charles, Up Front Designs, Wealth of Nations, The Woolshed and entries under General Catalogues.

CHILDREN'S CLOTHES

There's a new realism in children's clothes, led, I suspect, by the children themselves. While it would be nice, no doubt, to have children in dinky little smocked dresses or grey flannels and a blazer, there is absolutely no chance of achieving it. Think, instead, of an acceptable version of fashionable street clothes – jeans, sweats, pumps (trainers are on the way out, it seems), denim shirts and sweaters and all kinds jokey clothes. Most are in sensible cotton, worn loose or elasticated for ease, and washable.

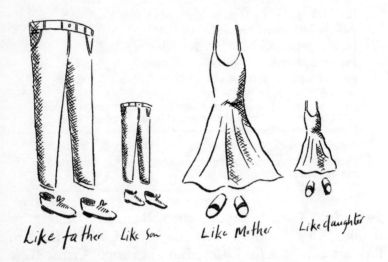

Like father   Like son   Like Mother   Like daughter

CHILDREN'S CLOTHES - LISTINGS

Bear Essentials The days when children wore pink or pale blue are long gone. Jane Hervè's range of cotton clothes for children up to 12 is brilliantly coloured in plains, stripes and dazzling geometrics. Sensibly, too, they are designed to mix and match so bits can be interchanged as the children get older.

Bear Essentials, Penselwood, Wincanton, Somerset BA9 8NF
Tel: 01747 821300
Price range: from £4.99. Catalogue free.
Payment: cheque, major credit cards.
Postage & packing: £1.50 for orders under £10, £3.50 thereafter.
Delivery: allow 28 days. Last Christmas orders 17 December by express post at extra cost.
Refunds: yes.
Specials: gift-wrapping.

CLOTHES AND ACCESSORIES 51

Calange Two separate ranges here but both dedicated to outdoor walkers and travellers. The Calange range uses many new fabrics and yarns for weather protection such as Karisma and Retro fleece and Pertex 5 Aquabloc. Other garments are brightly coloured for high-visibility in bad weather. The Bushbaby range is both to dress young children against the weather and to provide stout buggies and childcarriers "for families with a sense of adventure."

Calange Ltd, P O Box 61, Stockport, Cheshire SK3 0AP
Tel: 0161 474 7097 **Fax:** 0161 476 2647
Price range: £8.95 to £300. Catalogue free.
Payment: cheque, major credit/debit cards.
Postage & packing: included in UK. Next day delivery £3.
Delivery: normally within 4 days, but occasionally up to 28 days. Last Christmas orders 21 December.
Refunds: yes, if unused. Free home trial of Baby Carrier and All Terrain Pushchair.

Cotton Comfort The range is intended to make life more comfortable to those with eczema, sensitive skin or skin allergies by using chemical-free pure cotton. Mrs Dorothy Clark, who has worked in this field for 20 years, sells day gloves, nightwear, shirts, tights, underwear and school clothing.

Cotton Comfort, P O Box 2406, Bath BA1 5ZD
Tel: 01225 336559 **Fax:** 01225 336549
Price range: £4 to £35. Catalogue free.
Payment: cheque, postal order.
Postage & packing: 50p per item up to a maximum of £3.
Delivery: allow 14 days.
Refunds: yes, if returned in perfect condition within 10 days.

Cotton Moon Everything in this catalogue of children's clothes is made of cotton and is washable. The range goes from tiny babies' clothes from America up to those for eight year olds. Most are colourful and in small patterns without being garish. As well as clothes there are matching hairbands, sensible sun hats and "America's best-selling nightwear" printed with dinosaurs, ballerinas and the like.

52 MAIL ORDER MADE EASY

Cotton Moon, P O Box 280, London SE3 8DZ
Tel: 0181 305 0012 **Fax:** 0181 305 0011
Price range: £2.25 to £26. Catalogue free.
Payment: cheque, postal order, major credit/debit cards.
Postage & packing: £2 to £3, free on orders over £75 in UK. Overseas rates on application.
Delivery: orders sent promptly if in stock. Last Christmas orders by 16 December. Supplies can be limited.
Refunds: yes, if returned unworn within 14 days.

Dromedary Trading
Amynta Warde-Aldam taught at St. Martins, fashion's hotspot, until she moved to Northumberland. Now she designs this range of children's clothes which are made locally. They are intended to be smart but not copied from adult's wear. There are combat suits, sweatshirt dresses and moleskin jeans. The general feeling is loose-fitting and unstructured in mixed bright shades or, much to my taste, olive, navy and khaki which are excellent for children. Ages from 18 months to 12 years (more's the pity). Partner Anna Peile creates highly-desirable modern tapestry kits ideal for Christmas. They won't, she says, take a year to do.

Dromedary Trading, Estate Office, Healey Hall, Riding Mill, Northumberland NE44 6BH
Tel/Fax: 01434 673961
Price range: £10 to £40. Catalogue free.
Payment: cheque, major credit cards.
Postage & packing: approx £2.50.
Delivery: 7 days. Last Christmas orders by first week of December.
Refunds: yes, if returned unworn within 10 days.

Hansel & Gretel
One advantage of using small mail order firms is that you avoid the chainstore look. Caroline Trotter designs and has her children's clothes made in Fife. They are mostly in tartan, light or double cotton, corduroy and brushed cotton. She can make the designs using your choice of fabric from her range and will sew on a nametape too.

CLOTHES AND ACCESSORIES

Hansel & Gretel, Buckthorns, Upper Largo, Fife KY8 6EA
Tel: 01333 360219 **Fax:** 01333 360427
Price range: £3.50 to £35. Catalogue and swatches free.
Payment: cheque, postal order, Mastercard, Visa.
Postage & packing: £2 in UK, £3.50 elsewhere. Free for orders over £100.
Delivery: by return if in stock, otherwise allow 28 days.
Refunds: yes, if returned within 14 days, or after Christmas in case of gifts.
Specials: garments can be made to order in different fabrics, sizes or lengths at additional charge of £3.

Happy Flannelies

Flannel, that is, as in washcloth. The range is full of bathrobes, ponchos, washing gloves and bags but often the robe turns into a frog or the flannel into a dinosaur. The range is for toddlers and children up to five.

Happy Flannelies, The Crystal Garden Company, The White House, Dancers Hill Road, Bentley Heath, Barnet, Hertfordshire EN5 4RY
Tel: 0181 449 0443 **Fax:** 0181 441 6201
Price range: £3 to £32. Catalogue free.
Payment: cheque, postal order, Mastercard, Visa, Switch.
Postage & packing: £2.50 in mainland UK.
Delivery: allow 28 days.
Refunds: by arrangement.

Katie Mawson

A new mail order catalogue by Katie, who makes children's knitwear. She uses soft lambswool for sweaters with animal motifs, for jester's felted hats and caps with flaps plus a cotton range knitted with stars, fish or elephants.

Katie Mawson, Clockwork Studios, 38a Southwell Road, London SE5 9PG
Tel: 0171 326 1880 **Fax:** 0171 738 3743
Price range: £10 to £54. Catalogue free.
Payment: cheque, postal order, Mastercard, Access, Visa.
Postage & packing: £3 in UK. Overseas rates on application.
Delivery: allow 28 days, but normally earlier.
Refunds: yes, if returned unworn within 10 days.

MAIL ORDER MADE EASY

Kids' Stuff A very simple range of clothes for children up to 12 based on colourful cotton jersey. Yet the patterns of stripes, flowers, boats, frogs and the like are all skilfully scaled and coloured to match each other. The girls' outfits are pretty and modern and the boys, not too extreme. They don't shout and they're not twee.

> **Kids' Stuff Mail Order Ltd**, 10 Hensmans Hill, Bristol BS8 4PE
> **Tel:** 0117 970 6095
> **Price range:** £1.30 to £19.50. Catalogue free.
> **Payment:** cheque, postal order, Mastercard, Visa, Switch.
> **Postage & packing:** included.
> **Delivery:** normally by return, but allow 21 days.
> **Refunds:** yes, if returned promptly.

Little Badger Handmade children's clothes come with a strong fashion interest. Traditional hand-framed knits, for instance, are made in indigo-dyed cotton like jeans and with patterns like hearts, stars and skull and crossbones in contrasting colours. For babies there are leggings with attached feet, coat dresses and bootees (all in denim). Other bootees come in sheep or mouse styles in black wool with traditional white cashmere for the luxury kid. Cot blankets in cotton are more like American quilts.

> **Little Badger**, 6 Macaulay Road, London SW4 0QX
> **Tel:** 0171 498 6696/4707 **Fax:** 0171 498 4707
> **Price range:** £8 to £75. Catalogue free.
> **Payment:** cheque, major credit/debit cards.
> **Postage & packing:** £3 in UK, overseas rates on application.
> **Delivery:** by return if in stock, otherwise allow 28 days.
> Last Christmas orders by 31 November for items not in stock.
> **Refunds:** yes, if returned unworn within 10 days.
> **Specials:** gift-wrapping with embossed box £4.

Little Treasures Do you sigh for the days when little girls dressed in tartan smocks, Alice bands and frilled ankle socks and little boys in knickerbockers and cord waistcoats? This is your catalogue, especially if you sigh for twinsets and

CLOTHES AND ACCESSORIES 55

Viyella yourself. A comeback for classic English clothes is already on the way.

Little Treasures, 10 Braemar Crescent, Leigh-on-Sea, Essex SS9 3RL
Tel: 01702 559005 **Fax:** 01702 558988
Price range: £3 to £75. Catalogue free.
Payment: cheque, major credit/debit cards.
Postage & packing: UK £3, special delivery £3 extra; Europe by registered airmail £9; elsewhere by registered airmail £13.
Delivery: items in stock despatched within 3 days. For garments made to order allow 28 days. Last Christmas orders 1 December for non-stock garments, 20 December for stock items.
Refunds: yes, except sale goods.

Mini Boden Fresh from their success with adult styles, this fashionable mail order group now launches its range for children. Like the grown-up list, it features real children, identified by name, age, occupation. The clothes are practical, stylish and fashionable enough to pass muster with the children. There are baseball and legionnaire hats, lots of cotton sweats and sweaters, denim in bales plus pyjamas, shoes and bathrobes.

Mini Boden, Midland Terrace, Victoria Road, London NW10 6DB
Tel: 0181 453 1535 **Fax:** 0181 453 1536
Price range: £7 to £42. Catalogue free.
Payment: cheque, major credit/debit cards.
Postage & packing: £3 for standard service. 48-hour delivery £6.
Delivery: 4-5 working days. Same day delivery in London area at extra cost.
Refunds: yes.

Motley Crew Now that pirates have turned out to be really nice guys, you can wear one of this firm's dog and crossbones T-shirts as well as those featuring Pirate Percy on the chest. Val Gibbons has decided now not to send out a full catalogue but to work direct with mail order customers who, she says, seem to like the one-to-one way of business. Children's clothes are also available through Cotton Moon (qv) and adults' clothes direct.

Motley Crew, Freepost LON 6534, London E9 6BR
Tel/Fax: 0181 985 5472
Price range: £9.50 to £39.75. Leaflet free.
Payment: cheque, major credit cards.
Postage & packing: £1.50 for one item, £2.50 for more. Overseas at cost.
Delivery: allow 14 days. Last Christmas orders by 14 December.
Refunds: yes, if returned unworn within 14 days.

Rachel Riley Rachel lives in idyllic surroundings on the Loire with three pretty children who wear the pretty and traditional clothes she makes. Such is the success of her mail order business from France that she has now opened a London shop where the clothes can be seen and felt. She loves old-fashioned Viyellas, florals, smocking, button-strap slippers and twin-sets. There are a few clothes for adults and these are strongly reminiscent of the 1950s while being wildly chic, plus a traditional range for babies. Parcels come beautifully wrapped and thus make excellent presents.

Rachel Riley, La Roche Froissard, 49350 Gennes, France
Tel: 00 332 41 38 04 93 **Fax:** 00 332 41 38 02 20
Price range: £5.50 to £158. Catalogue free (in English with prices in pounds).
Payment: cheque, major credit cards.
Postage & packing: £4 to £10, hand-made box extra.
Delivery: allow 3 weeks. Express delivery available.
Refunds: yes, if returned in perfect condition within 14 days.
Specials: special orders, including bridesmaid and page boy outfits in own fabrics.

Sasti Would you like your children dressed up as wild cats or dragons? This is a lovely catalogue of wild clothes from 'three young women who have a love for children but a funky outlook on life', they say. Everything is hand-made to order so you can pick from the wild colour chart and mix the motifs. The cat suit is in fake leopard with ears and tail; dragons have tails and scaly hoods.

CLOTHES AND ACCESSORIES

Sasti, 23 Portobello Green Arcade, 281 Portobello Road, London W10 5TY
Tel: 0181 960 1125
Price range: £7 to £35. Catalogue free (possible charge of £1 in future, refundable against order).
Payment: cheque, major credit/debit cards.
Postage & packing: from £2.99 depending on weight.
Delivery: normally 2 weeks, but allow 28 days for certain items.
Refunds: yes.

Secret People

Secret People A new mail order company from Somerset devised by two young mothers with five children between them. The clothes are cheerful and somewhat traditional in style. The name of the company refers to "tiny woodland friends" – little toys – which are found in some of the clothes' pockets and bags.

Secret People, Pithers Yard, High Street, Castle Cary, Somerset BA7 7AN
Tel/Fax: 01963 351592
Price range: £7 to £39. 5% discount on orders over £100. Catalogue free.
Payment: cheque.
Postage & packing: £3.
Delivery: allow 28 days.
Refunds: yes, if returned unworn and undamaged within 7 days.

See also: Birkenstock, Blooming Marvellous, Bobbins, Born for Loden, Brora, Calange, Cyrillus, Damask, JoJo Maman Bébé, L.L. Bean, The Original Celtic Sheepskin Co, Pedlars Clothing, Polo Neck Designs, Pyjama Box, Up Front Designs.

ACCESSORIES

Life can be made so much simpler if you buy accessories and necessities through the post. I'm always concerned about the weight of shopping when I sally out into the centre of London. It adds up and there's nowhere to leave parcels so that I find I have to go out little and often – an immense waste of time when it can take an hour simply to get to the West End. So, why buy regulars like tights or underwear or gloves in the shops when you can find your favourites in the catalogues? Once you've sorted out the sizing of any particular make, it's simple to stick with it. Strangely, even a parcel of knickers arriving at the door can give me a treat. It's something about opening parcels, I suppose.

ACCESSORIES - LISTINGS

The A J Trading Company This range of luggage is in the new canvas and leather style, durable, good-looking and not too wildly expensive. There are sensible grips, like the Pusser's (or purser's), suit carriers, polo stick bags, a field office for mobile phone, laptop and change of clothes. Other accessories are braces, belts, flasks, keyrings and wallets. As you can guess, designed by a chap for other chaps.

> **The A J Trading Company**, 9 Town Farm Estate, Sixpenny Handley, Salisbury, Wiltshire SP5 5PA
> **Tel:** 01725 552800 **Fax:** 01725 552900
> **E-mail:** paj@ajtrade.co.uk
> **Website:** http://www.ajtrade.co.uk
> **Price range:** £12.50 to £225. Catalogue free.
> **Payment:** cheque, Mastercard, Visa, Switch, Connect.
> **Postage & packing:** £6 in UK.
> **Delivery:** despatched within 24 hours if in stock. 24-hour delivery at extra cost. Last Christmas orders by 18 December.
> **Refunds:** yes, if returned within 14 days.

Agent Provocateur Sexy underwear as in Soho stripper but with a sense of humour. You have to be very sure of your girl to give her this as a present because she may want Marks and Spencer's finest. There are bras which don't cover the nipples and brief-and-suspender sets which cover virtually nothing. There are outfits in ocelot and pink leopard and pink and red

CLOTHES AND ACCESSORIES 59

bustiers which need firm lacing. The range is shown with masks, whips, nurses' outfits and many a pouting lip.

Agent Provocateur, JEM House, Littlemead, Cranleigh, Surrey GU6 8ND
Tel: 01483 204469 **Fax:** 01483 268889
Price range: £8 to £95. Catalogue £5.
Payment: cheque, postal order, Mastercard, Visa.
Postage & packing: £3.50. Overseas at cost.
Delivery: allow 10 days.
Refunds: yes, return by recorded delivery within 7 working days.

The Barnsbury Collection Classic hand-stitched leather bags in sensible classic styles which won't date are supplied with good, heavy catches and checked linings. However, classic designs have a way of becoming fashionable and this collection includes rucksacks, shooting bags and duffel bags. There's even a version of the classic Kelly and a whole set of matching luggage. Other leather pieces are picnic and shooting gear, stud boxes and desk accessories.

Barnsbury Designs by Bicinc, 35 Britannia Row, London N1 8QH .
Tel: 0171 226 3377 **Fax:** 0171 359 1454
Price range: £15 to £95. Catalogue free.
Payment: cheque, major credit cards.
Postage & packing: £5, free for orders over £100. Overseas rates on application.
Delivery: allow 28 days. Last Christmas orders as early as possible to ensure stocks are available.
Refunds: yes.

Bates Gentlemen's Hatter It's hard to believe there are so many traditional hats for chaps. This firm offers old-fashioned bowlers, toppers and Homburgs, wonderful soft felt fedoras for the Mafia look and tweed hats for country folk. Summer hats look American, Australian, Cuban, teaplanter, big game hunter, racing man and fishmonger.

Bates Gentlemen's Hatter, 21a Jermyn Street, St. James's, London SW1Y 6HP
Tel: 0171 734 2722

Price range: £38 to £295. Catalogue free.
Payment: cheque, major credit cards.
Postage & packing: hats £5.50, caps, £3.
Delivery: by return.
Refunds: yes, if faulty, otherwise exchange or credit note.

Birkenstock

Birkenstock These healthy German shoes are often so ugly that they have become a cult like Doc Martens. The mail order catalogue pictures cool types from London's hot restaurants and design studios wearing them, also apprentices in a Royal Opera Wagner production in costume and Birkenstock flatties. There is a huge range for men, women and children, all designed to be extra comfortable and some ideal for vegetarians and vegans who won't wear leather.

Birkenstock, The Boot Tree Ltd, 1 Addison Bridge Place, London W14 8XP
Tel: 0800 132194/0171 602 2866 **Fax:** 0171 602 2085
E-mail: birkenstock@boottree.prestel.co.uk
Price range: £12.95 to £110. Catalogue free,
Payment: cheque, postal order, major credit/debit cards.
Postage & packing: £3.95. Express delivery £3.50 extra.
Delivery: usually 1 week. Last Christmas orders 18 December.
Refunds: yes.

Carpet Bags Plus

Carpet Bags Plus A variety of oriental, tapestry and Aztec traditional patterns are used to make into a thick, heavy fabric which the firm converts not only into carpet bags for travellers which are strong and foldaway but also a range of shoulder and duffel bags, hip bags and datacases. There's even a short jacket, if you want to match your luggage.

Carpet Bags Plus, 2000 St. John's Street, Bury St. Edmunds, Suffolk IP33 1SP
Tel: 01284 700170 **Fax:** 01284 700270
E-mail: info@carpetbags.co.uk
Website: http://www.carpetbags.co.uk
Price range: £8 to £175. Catalogue free.
Payment: cheque, postal order, major credit/debit cards.
Postage & packing: from £1.50 to £10 in UK. Overseas delivery

CLOTHES AND ACCESSORIES 61

£5 for orders under £25 and 20% for orders over £25.

Delivery: by first class post or next day carrier service. Last Christmas orders preferably by first week of December.

Refunds: yes.

Celestial Buttons
A shop, near me, which has the most stupendous selection of buttons. There are mother of pearl ones in lots of sizes and colours (they dye them) along with jokey designs like fluffy fur or metal animals. I especially like those using different shells, which are just as hard-wearing as mother of pearl. They have spots, stripes and tortoiseshell patterns, all of which really lift an outfit. Another trick I've learned from a top designer is to sew pearl buttons on back to front. Try it.

Celestial Buttons, 54 Cross Street, Islington, London N1 2BA

Tel/Fax: 0171 226 4766

Price range: approx.10p to £15. No catalogue, but they will send samples and match fabric swatches.

Payment: cheque, postal order.

Postage & packing: quoted with order.

Delivery: normally by return.

Refunds: by arrangement.

Connolly
This firm, which traditionally makes Rolls Royce upholstery, upgraded and relaunched itself a few years ago with the most desirable selection of accessories. There are briefcases, leather driving helmets, studded driving shoes, cashmere scarves and socks. The cashmere car rug with suede trim is a wonderful luxury as is the leather toolkit. The rubberised driving mac – highly chic, highly coloured – really keeps out the rain. The firm can be commissioned to work anything in leather, from a floor to a Lear jet.

Connolly Ltd, 32 Grosvenor Crescent Mews, London SW1X 7EX

Tel: 0171 235 3883 **Fax:** 0171 235 3838

Price range: £45 to £2,800 and beyond. 'The sky's the limit,' they say. Catalogue free.

Payment: cheque, major credit/debit cards.

Postage & packing: £10 to £30 for recorded delivery in UK. International courier service from £15.

Delivery: allow 3 working days. Some items are limited.

Refunds: yes, if faulty, otherwise exchange or credit note.

Specials: special orders undertaken. Will retrim yachts and private jets, wrap orders in leather.

Flavell and Flavell

A selection of solid, beautifully-crafted leather bags of pure classical style. They range from small 7-inch high versions designed for the orderly to gigantic holdalls for people, like me, who travel heavy. The range sells well in France and is priced in francs as well as pounds.

Flavell & Flavell, 3 Church Street, Kirkby Malzeard, North Yorkshire HG4 3RT

Tel/Fax: 01765 658502

Price range: £49.50 to £135. Catalogue free.

Payment: cheque.

Postage & packing: £2.50 per bag.

Delivery: by arrangement. Last Christmas orders preferably by end October, although later may be possible.

Refunds: yes, if unused.

Franchetti Bond

From Italy, home of the best leather, comes a range of classical accessories. Go for the simple loafers in nubuck or mock croc (or calf for men), bright lime or orange clutch bags or tortoiseshell buckled belts. There's even a mock tortoiseshell tote and clutch which, being brown and black, will team with almost anything.

Franchetti Bond Mail Order Ltd, Bemco Building, Jews Row, Wandsworth Bridge South, London SW18 1TN

Tel: 0181 874 1122 **Fax:** 0181 874 0234

Price range: £15 to £250. Catalogue free.

Payment: cheque, major credit/debit cards.

Postage & packing: £3.95 in UK. Overseas at cost.

Delivery: within 3 days if in stock, otherwise allow 28 days. Last Christmas orders by 21 December.

Refunds: yes, return within 14 days (leeway given at Christmas).

Specials: the company will bend over backwards for special requests, i.e. delivery, packaging, cards etc.

CLOTHES AND ACCESSORIES

Gilly Forge I am dedicated to her smart, sensible and wearable hats. In winter there are wide-brimmed pull-ons of waxed cotton which stylishly keep the rain out along with townie fake furs and soft velvets; in summer she uses cotton, linen, denim and panama straw in clever combinations such as black and cream or white and pale grey. Most fold up, pull on and rarely date.

> **Gilly Forge**, 14 Addison Avenue, Holland Park, London W11 4QR
> **Tel:** 0171 603 3833 **Fax:** 0171 603 2032
> **Price range:** £50 to £130. Catalogue free.
> **Payment:** cheque, Switch, major credit cards except Amex.
> **Postage & packing:** £3.50.
> **Delivery:** 10-28 days.
> **Refunds:** yes.

Green River Panamas One advantage of mail order (among many) is that if you want to holiday somewhere warm in the winter, you can buy suitable clothes when there's nothing in the shops. This selection of panamas varies from the classic gent's smart summer hat to some beautiful wide-brimmed hats for women which arrive with a silk rose for added chic. There's also a 1920s style with short brim at the front. Most will fold for travel and come with a lightweight balsawood box.

> **The Green River Trading Company**, 39 Erskine Hill, London NW11 6EY
> **Tel:** 0181 458 0047 **Fax:** 0181 209 0110
> **E-mail:** postbox@greenriver.demon.co.uk
> **Price range:** approx. £30 to £70. Catalogue free.
> **Payment:** cheque, major credit/debit cards.
> **Postage & packing:** usually £1.50. Special delivery at cost.
> **Delivery:** by return.
> **Refunds:** yes.
> **Specials:** personalised message can be enclosed.

J. P. Promos This company's product comes in useful if you indulge in over-sauced pasta, aromatic crispy duck or any of the other dangerously messy meals around today. The BibKlip can be whisked out in the restaurant or barbecue party and used neatly to attach the napkin you are given. As they say, it'll pay for itself in no time avoiding those dry-cleaning bills.

J. P. Promos, P O Box HH26, Leeds LS8 1TA
Tel: 0113 293 1518 **Fax:** 0113 269 6546
Price: £9.95.
Payment: cheque.
Postage & packing: included.
Delivery: allow 10 days. Last Christmas orders by 3rd week of December.
Refunds: yes.
Specials: supplied in gift box.

James Smith & Sons The firm's shop remains a shrine to Victoriana and so does its merchandise. There's a whole brochure for mail order shooting sticks, umbrellas for the city (subfusc with hickory, malacca, ash and cherry handles among others) or the country (big and tartan). Women get elegant parasols with fancy handles. Then there are "town, dress and presentation sticks and canes, a blackthorn shillelagh, thumb sticks and shepherd's crooks and plenty of folding sticks or umbrellas.

James Smith & Sons (Umbrellas) Ltd, Hazelwood House, 53 New Oxford Street, London WC1A 1BL
Tel: 0171 836 4731
Price range: £30 to £495. Catalogue free.
Payment: cheque, Mastercard, Visa.
Postage & packing: £2.75 for folding umbrellas and sticks, £7.95 for full-size umbrellas and walking sticks.
Delivery: despatched within 14 days.
Refunds: by arrangement.
Specials: umbrellas, sticks etc made to order and engraved.

CLOTHES AND ACCESSORIES 65

Janet Reger Famous for its naughty undies, the firm is now run by Janet Reger's daughter. Now that bosoms, cleavage and curves are back in fashion, so is glamorous underwear. Indeed, some of these styles are so wonderful you could wear them for a party. Then you could give the catalogue to your chap for the pin-ups. There's a girl who has kicked over a standard lamp to light up her knickers and another doing serious damage to her pearls.

Janet Reger Ltd, 2 Beauchamp Place, London SW3 1NG
Tel: 0171 584 9368 **Fax:** 0171 581 7946
Price range: £25 to £620.
Payment: cheque, postal order, major credit cards.
Postage & packing: £5 in UK.
Delivery: allow 28 days.
Refunds: yes, return in original packaging by registered post.
Specials: gift vouchers from £25.

Jeremy Law Jeremy Law, a Yorkshireman transplanted to Scotland, uses soft and supple deerskin for a whole range of accessories. Most popular are the moccasins which I can vouch for. They are a dream for tired feet but smart enough to wear during the day. He also does brogues and chukka boots, gloves, purses. There are neat deerskin jackets, waistcoats and jerkins plus a thigh-length jerkin in nubuck. I'm sorry he's dropped the horn buttons but, apparently, few people other than me, really wanted them.

Jeremy Law of Scotland, City Hall, Dunkeld, Perthshire PH8 0AR
Tel: 01350 727569 **Fax:** 01350 728748
Price range: £5 to £375. Catalogue free.
Payment: cheque, postal order, major credit/debit cards.
Postage & packing: £3 for orders under £50, free thereafter.
Delivery: allow 28 days. Last Christmas orders by last posting date.
Refunds: goods sent on approval but full refund available.

John Halifax Hats These are hats for holidays from the Globetrotter genuine panama (made in Ecuador) which has cooling vents and will fold for travel and the men's classic tril-by panama to a crushable rain hat in waxed cotton or another, in bush hat style, for wetter days off.

John Halifax, 1 Park Rise, Harpenden, Hertfordshire AL5 3AH
Tel: 01582 713921 **Fax:** 01582 622129
Price range: approx £25 to £35. Leaflet free.
Payment: cheque, major credit cards.
Postage & packing: included in UK.
Delivery: usually 4-5 days, but allow 28. Christmas orders are normally despatched the following day.
Refunds: yes, if returned in perfect condition.

Ķarrimor A most surprising cult. Once these were the ruck-sacks for bearded anoraks; now they are cool Britannia. More to the point, the backpacks, from expedition to daysacs, are extremely tough and practical. The firm offers carriers for babies, boots for climbers, expedition tents and clothing for very hot and very cold climates.

Karrimor International, Petre Road, Clayton-le-Moors, Lancashire BB5 5JZ
Tel: 01254 893134
Price range: ring for current prices. Catalogue free.
Payment: Mastercard, Visa, Switch.
Postage & packing: £4.
Delivery: 24-hour service on most items.
Refunds: by arrangement.

Katharine Goodison Millinery Not only did Katharine study hatmaking at the London College of Fashion, she also worked as a corporate finance lawyer. Her stunning hats are, she says, inspired by Renaissance paintings and her travels in the East. 1998 is the first year she will mail order a distinctive range of broad-brimmed Barbour rain hats, faux fur hats, velvet cossacks and hair accessories. She can also be commissioned to make hats for special occasions.

Katharine Goodison Millinery, 93 Winchester Street, London SW1V 4NX

CLOTHES AND ACCESSORIES

Tel: 0171 828 6498
Price range: £35 to £95. Catalogue free.
Payment: cheque.
Postage & packing: included.
Delivery: allow 3 weeks.
Refunds: yes, if returned within 10 days.

Liz Cox Brilliantly coloured jacquard fabric for luggage rich in exotic camels, sunflowers or elephants so you'll never lose it on the airport carousel. There are cabin bags for cruises, rucksacks for the city and a safari bag for lightweight journeys. All are waterproof, with brass, cotton-webbing and saddle leather trimmings.

Liz Cox, No. 17, Margaret's Buildings, Bath BA1 2LP
Tel: 01225 445509 **Fax:** 01225 448880
Price range: £25 to £375. Mail order pack free.
Payment: cheque, major credit/debit cards.
Postage & packing: £4.95 in UK, £9.95 in Europe, £15.95 elsewhere.
Delivery: normally 3 days.
Refunds: yes, if returned unused within a reasonable period.

Margaret Anne Gloves When wearing gloves, it's best to stick to classics which keep the hands warm without attracting undue attention with fiddly bits. These gloves are all you could wish, leather or suede, lined with fleece or backed with string. There's a range for men with names like Damon and Henry, elegant ladies' gloves (Camille and Carla) plus mittens for all ages. All are British made and unusual gloves can be ordered.

Margaret Anne Gloves, 160 Bath Street, Ilkeston, Derbyshire DE7 8FH
Tel: 0115 930 1073
Price range: £5 to £55. Catalogue free.
Payment: cheque, major credit cards.
Postage & packing: included.
Delivery: allow 28 days. Last Christmas orders by 20 November.
Refunds: yes for wrong sizes.

MAIL ORDER MADE EASY

Office Office (and its little brother, Offspring) sell the latest smart shoes and sports shoes. They have no catalogue because, in the shoe world, fashions move too fast to be categorised. Instead, watch the papers and magazines for their latest styles and simply order by phone. They have everything from the newest trainers to espadrilles and platforms.

> **Office**, 26 Park Royal Road, London NW10 7JW
> **Tel:** 0181 838 4447 **Fax:** 0181 961 7289
> **Price range:** £30 to £60. No catalogue, look at the press or telephone.
> **Payment:** major credit cards except Amex and Diners.
> **Postage & packing:** £3 for orders up to £30, £5 thereafter.
> **Delivery:** 10 days.
> **Refunds:** yes.

The Original Celtic Sheepskin Co Cornish craftsmen hand sew sheepskin into a range of warm and comforting shoes, boots, gloves and hats. Celt boots (like ski boots) can be made in your choice of 24 bright mixed colours – purple, red and brown all in one boot – for children from size 5 to adult 14. Extraordinarily, they are washable.

> **The Original Celtic Sheepskin Co**, Unit 40, Wesley Yard, Newquay, Cornwall TR7 ILB
> **Tel:** 01637 871605 **Fax:** 01637 851989
> **E-mail:** nick@celtic-sheepskin.co.uk
> **Price range:** £15 to £64.50. Catalogue free.
> **Payment:** Mastercard, Visa, Switch and debit cards.
> **Postage & packing:** £2 to £6.75. Extra fast delivery add £2.
> **Delivery:** allow 8 days. Last Christmas orders 3 working days in advance.
> **Refunds:** yes.
> **Specials:** gift-wrapping £2.

Pickett Fine Leather Handbags have recently made a comeback and Pickett has reinvented the classical Kelly as carried by Grace. They come in pigskin, ostrich, lizard and crocodile. Also from here the wildly smart pashmina shawls, currently chic Chinese embroidered silk purses and bags, briefcases, doc-

CLOTHES AND ACCESSORIES

ument cases and wallets. This is real luxury stuff – look at the catalogue's last page for a pile up of leather and canvas luggage ideal for a movie star.

> **Pickett Fine Leather**, 41 Burlington Arcade, London W1V 9AE
> **Tel:** 0171 493 8939 **Fax:** 0171 629 3836
> **Price range:** £20 to approx £3,000. Catalogue free.
> **Payment:** major credit/debit cards.
> **Postage & packing:** at cost.
> **Delivery:** by post or courier. Last Christmas orders by last posting date.
> **Refunds:** no, an exchange or credit note is offered.
> **Specials:** free gift-wrapping service, monogramming from £20.

Prizma Rather than create a range of embroideries for cushions, bell-pulls etc, Prizma will make up small embroideries for wedding and party dresses, travel bags, Shaker boxes and shawls. Bags, shawls and dresses are therefore co-ordinated or, by using a unique mix of patterns, can be customised for your needs.

> **Prizma Embroidery**, Glan Medeni, Betws Ifan, Newcastle Emlyn, Ceredigion SA38 9QJ
> **Tel:** 01239 851852 **Fax:** 01239 851076
> **E-mail:** prizma@saqnet.co.uk
> **Website:** http://www.prizma.co.uk
> **Price range:** £4.50 to £150. Catalogue free.
> **Payment:** cheque with order.
> **Postage & packing:** see catalogue.
> **Delivery:** allow 28 days, but probably earlier.
> **Refunds:** yes, if returned unused.
> **Specials:** most items can be customised. Made-to-order service.

Silver Moon I have loved moccasins since the moment I saw a pair in American Vogue 20 years ago and had to beg friends to bring me them back. Now you can mail order direct from Maine for a wondrous selection. They are in moose or deerskin, with soft leather soles, nubs of strong synthetic for driving mocs or with full waterproof soles. Some have fringes (v fashionable) or metal inserts, others are espadrilles in leather.

Silver Moon Enterprises, P O Box 158, Brewer, Maine 04412, USA
Tel: 00 1 207 234 2644 **Fax:** 00 1 207 234 2867
E-mail: swebb@mint.net
Website: http://www.moccasins.com
Price range: $19.95 to $100. Catalogue free.
Payment: Mastercard, Visa, Amex.
Postage & packing: on request.
Delivery: allow 14 days.
Refunds: yes.

Simon Charles

There are specialist fashion firms who spend much of their time selling to country fairs and who have sorted out the great British climate. Simon Charles, who goes to such events as Burghley Horse Trials and Badminton, not only sells dressage essentials like classic hard-top hats and bowlers, tweed cheese-slicer hats and workboots but fake fur pull-on hats, warm tweed jackets for both men and women and, in case global warming continues, folding panama hats too.

Simon Charles, P O Box 49, Market Harborough, Leicestershire LE16 7ZX
Tel: 01858 433553 **Fax:** 01858 461156
E-mail: 113207.2470@compuserve.com
Price range: £25 to £325. Catalogue free.
Payment: cheque, major credit/debit cards.
Postage & packing: £2.95 in UK. Overseas at cost.
Delivery: 5 working days. 24- and 48-hour delivery available
Refunds: yes, if returned in perfect condition within 14 days.

Soled Out

The intention of these shoes, says Noel Hill, is to be foot-shaped. Not something people generally think about when making them. The catalogue tells you how to measure your feet, to mention any odd lumps and bumps or, if your feet are "really difficult", to call in person. The results are solid, flat shoes with crepe or Vibram soles (much better lasting than leather) but brilliantly coloured and in styles from mules to walking boots. While teetering high heels are fashionable so too are good solid shoes and anyone with foot problems should start here.

CLOTHES AND ACCESSORIES

Soled Out, Unit 8, Saltash Business Park, Forge Lane, Moorlands Industrial Estate, Saltash, Cornwall PL12 6LX
Tel: 01752 841080
Price range: £30 to £150. Send sae for leaflet.
Payment: cheque, postal order, Mastercard, Visa, Eurocard.
Postage & packing: included for children's sizes 5 to 13, £5 for adult sizes 1 to 13+.
Delivery: Children's sizes 3-4 weeks (growth taken into consideration), adult sizes 6-8 weeks. Last Christmas orders adults: 31 October, children: 30 November.
Refunds: yes, if notified of any problem within 10 days.
Specials: repair service, free stretching service for children's shoes.

Thiz Bag

Brilliantly-coloured fabrics strewn with fish, bears, cats and even animals driving trains are used to make a clever range of bags for children. One design is a large storage bag with a zip-off section which turns into a smart rucksack. The Alzo bag has a detachable shoulderbag and purse. Some are to be worn by children, others to take all the impedimenta mothers need on journeys. The range is always increasing and includes little painted stools, cot blankets, baby boots, quilts and cushions.

Thiz Bag, The Barn, Boyton End, near Thaxted, Essex CM6 2RB
Tel: 07000 780745 **Fax:** 01371 831304
Price range: £10 to £42. Catalogue free.
Payment: cheque, major credit/debit cards.
Postage & packing: £2.50.
Delivery: 3 days. Last Christmas orders 21 December.
Refunds: yes if returned within 14 days.

Up Front Designware

Take a simple idea – the bib – and then make endless jokes about it and you get the measure of this catalogue. Bibs are patterned with Santa jackets or dinner shirts while party disposable bibs have boobs and union jacks, highland outfits and hairy chests. Also bibs for babies, for make-up and for old people.

Up Front Designware, Feveralls Lodge, Roe End Lane, Markyate, Hertfordshire AL3 8AG

Tel: 01582 840797 **Fax:** 01582 842505

Price range: £3.50 to £12.95. 10% discount for orders of 8 or more. Catalogue free.

Payment: cheque, postal order.

Postage & packing: £2.50 in UK.

Delivery: normally within 1 week. Last Christmas orders 21 December.

Refunds: yes.

Specials: bibs can be personalised with print or embroidery.

Wolford When anyone tests the tights and stockings on the market, Wolford's always come out top. I know why because I wear them myself: they are strong and rarely snag or ladder; the fibres used give absolute cling with no knee or ankle wrinkles; they are at the forefront of fashion and the colours are excellent. The deniers range from sheer to opaque and glossy to matt. There are wools and cottons, bodies and leotards, swimsuits and bikinis plus high fashion ranges which change regularly. Good news, too, for people needing warm or cool tights out of season.

Wolford Boutique, Unit 2, 28a Kensington Church Street, London W8 4EP

Tel: 0171 937 2995 **Fax:** 0171 937 5443

Price range: £7 to £200. Catalogue free.

Payment: cheque, major credit/debit cards.

Postage & packing: at cost.

Delivery: by return if in stock, otherwise allow 10 days.

Refunds: yes, if returned in perfect condition with original packaging intact within 7 days. Hosiery items should not be opened.

Specials: gift boxes and gift vouchers available. Expert advice from trained consultants.

See also: Hitchcocks' by Post, L.L. Bean, Prickly Pear Trading, Simon Charles, Smythson by Post, Tyrrell Katz.

CLOTHES AND ACCESSORIES

JEWELLERY

Britain has an enviable reputation for craft jewellers and these are the people who you can commission direct and order through the post. Galleries, both national and commercial, will have regular exhibitions where you can suss out whose style suits you and you can then get in touch with the jeweller direct and talk things through. Good jewellery does not need to be expensive – silver is not a costly metal – and there are also lots of young designers working in plastic, paper, base metals and even glass. Other jewellery companies mail idiosyncratic pieces which would get lost in the shops. Cuff-links, rings, pins and brooches also make excellent presents.

JEWELLERY - LISTINGS

Andrew Ransford The British end of Commonwealth Imports of Virginia, which specialises in sterling silver jewellery using the silver and craftsmen of Mexico. The jewellery tends to be simple and is just occasionally set with semi-precious stones like turquoise and agate. The designs are charming – shoals of fish, watering cans with garden implements, bees and insects and many varieties of links. The catalogue is helpful, showing pieces lifesize.

> **Andrew Ransford**, East Wing, Forde Abbey, Chard, Somerset
> TA20 4LU
> **Tel/Fax:** 01460 220147
> **E-mail:** andyran@aol.com
> **Price range:** £5 to £270. Catalogue free.
> **Payment:** cheque, major credit/debit cards.

Postage & packing: included.
Delivery: normally within 10 days, or 28 if out of stock. Order as early as possible for Christmas.
Refunds: yes.

Brett Payne
Using gold and silver only, Brett Payne makes bracelets and necklaces of complex link patterns. Some are near-abstract swans or fishes looped to each other, others are links held by little clasped hands or leaf shapes, balls, bobbles and snaffles. Classic and timeless, they are still very modern in feeling.

Brett Payne, Sydney Works, 111 Matilda Street, Sheffield S1 4QF
Tel: 0114 270 1088
Price range: £300 to £5,000. No catalogue, but information and photos on request.
Payment: cheque, Visa.
Postage & packing: included, sent by registered post, or delivered by hand for orders over £3,500.
Delivery: by return if in stock, otherwise allow 1 month. Last Christmas orders by 30 October, unless you want to take pot luck.
Refunds: yes.

Brigade Designs
Jewellery which is gold and silver plated need not be wildly expensive or dull. Brigade creates sharp, geometric pieces using hearts and stars, Greek columns, fish and arrow patterns for earrings, necklaces and pendants, bracelets and cufflinks. A pair of earrings is as little as £18.

Brigade Designs, Unit 21, Dock Street Workshops, 30/38 Dock Street, Leeds LS10 1JF
Tel: 0113 242 3957
Price range: £18 to £100. Send A4 sae (31p) for catalogue.
Payment: cheque.
Postage & packing: £3 for orders up to £40, £4.60 thereafter.
Delivery: 2-3 weeks. Next day delivery at extra cost. Last Christmas orders by 5 December.
Refunds: if defective or does not fit, otherwise replacement.
Specials: gift-wrapping.

CLOTHES AND ACCESSORIES

Carol Mather A craft jeweller whose best-selling range is of silver models of dogs. They come as pendants, brooches with leads, bracelets of doggy medallions, even earrings. The designs include dalmatians, bull terriers, dachshunds and indeterminate shaggy jobs. They are very modern, witty and distinctive, and bound to be much admired.

> **Carol Mather**, 10a Iliffe Yard, London SE17 3QA
> **Tel/Fax:** 0171 252 7524
> **Price range:** £24 to £156. Brochure with drawings free.
> **Payment:** cheque, Visa.
> **Postage & packing:** £3.50 to £4.
> **Delivery:** by registered post. Last Christmas orders by beginning of December.
> **Refunds:** yes.

Christopher Simpson Cufflinks for the whizz kid, top gun and City slicker. Simpson has ranges of shotgun cartridge cufflinks in shocking pink, orange, bright lemon and scarlet; plus sporting cufflinks of little jockey caps, tennis racquets and boxing gloves. There are piggy, elephant and rhino cufflinks and some patterned like sweetcorn and grapes. You can have them plated in gold or silver or in hallmarked sterling silver. Some, especially the fruit and animal cufflinks, would be just as good on women's shirts.

> **Christopher Simpson**, Savernake, 61 Clapham Common Northside, London SW4 9SA
> **Tel:** 0171 350 1741 **Fax:** 0171 350 2334
> **Price range:** £4.25 to £90. Catalogue free.
> **Payment:** cheque, Access, Visa.
> **Postage & packing:** £1.50 except shotgun links when cost is included.

Delivery: allow 28 days.
Refunds: by arrangement.

Cobra & Bellamy

This jeweller's designs manage to be beautiful at surprisingly low cost. The range of watches, for example, are reminiscent of the thirties, chrome plated and with leather or mesh straps – yet cost as little as £59. They are famous for elegant faux pearl necklaces and earrings and also have silver and amber jewellery. They are exclusive to the firm.

Cobra & Bellamy, 149 Sloane Street, London SW1X 9BZ
Tel: 0171 730 9993 **Fax:** 0171 824 8996
Price range: £18 to £800. Leaflet free.
Payment: cheque, major credit cards.
Postage & packing: £7 per order, by registered post.
Delivery: within 28 days.
Refunds: yes, if notified within 7 days.

Hamilton & Inches

Edinburgh's famous jeweller (royal warrant from the Queen) sells a huge range of heavenly presents. There is modern jewellery by Georg Jensen and Wellendorff; pearls, diamonds and other fine stones set in rings, bracelets and pendants; watches, silver, porcelain and enamel. More especially, the firm makes its own silver in the Scottish tradition, often beaten and set with semi-precious stones. It will remake redundant pieces and design to commission.

Hamilton & Inches, 87 George Street, Edinburgh EH2 3EY
Tel: 0131 225 4898 **Fax:** 0131 220 6994
Price range: £15 to over £500. Catalogue free.
Payment: cheque, money order, bank transfer, major credit/debit cards.
Postage & packing: £5 for items less than 2kg in UK. Rates for heavier parcels, and overseas on application. Free delivery in Edinburgh area.
Delivery: by arrangement. Last Christmas orders: UK 15 December, Europe 8 December, elsewhere 1 December.
Refunds: yes, if goods are returned within 28 days.
Specials: gift-wrapping, personalisation, antique and second-hand acquisitions, gift vouchers, wedding lists, valuations.

CLOTHES AND ACCESSORIES 77

Jack Joseph Designs The range is all gold-plated and set with Austrian crystal, nearly as brilliant as diamonds themselves and, they say, safe on delicate or sensitive skins. The designs are generally based on 18th and 19th century antiques – drop earrings, floral brooches, pendants and clips inset with pearls.

Jack Joseph Designs, Hen Ys Gol, Llangynidr, Powys NP8 1LU
Tel/Fax: 01874 730124
Price range: £9 to £21. Catalogue free.
Payment: cheque.
Postage & packing: 50p per item.
Delivery: by return.
Refunds: yes, if returned within 7 days, except earrings for health reasons.

Latham & Neve Jewellery lately has been taking on a kind of superstitious significance where the shapes and stones are intended to bring serenity or calm, to energise, steady or encourage – like feng shui – good luck to the bearer. This range has rings shaped like hearts and flowers, plus charm necklaces impressed with stars, hearts and the word 'love'. Anna Latham and Helen Neve also cast men's and women's torsos from hand-made wax models. The jewellery is sterling silver.

Latham & Neve, 14 Gloucester Road, London E10 7HT
Tel/Fax: 0181 518 7028
Price range: £41 to £160. Catalogue free.
Payment: cheque, postal order, international money order.
Postage & packing: £4.95. Overseas rates on application.
Delivery: by registered post normally within 10 working days, but allow 28. Last Christmas orders by 16 December.
Refunds: yes, if returned in perfect condition within 7 days.
Specials: commissions undertaken.

Mercator Cufflinks are about the only acceptable male jewellery (for most men at any rate) and this range makes the most of it. How about the Chinese character links which say "Hello Gorgeous" either to men or women? Or horn links from

Nepalese water buffalo carved into fish, turtles or elephants? There are silver pine cones and pen nibs, quotation marks and golf tees and a nice line in the seven deadly sins captured in enamel. Do you give your chap the one for gluttony or sloth, rage or pride? Or the lust devil which comes with a naked breast as the other link?

Mercator, 8 The Charterhouse, Eltringham Street, London SW18 1TD

Tel: 0181 870 3938 **Fax:** 0181 874 8732

Price range: £25 to £80 (prices for 18 carat gold on request). Catalogue free.

Payment: cheque, Mastercard, Visa.

Postage & packing: £2 recorded delivery in UK, £5 overseas..

Delivery: allow 14 days. Last Christmas orders 16 December.

Refunds: yes.

Specials: engraving, bespoke designs from £250.

Noël Productions

Everybody, says *Vogue*, is wearing one of Noël's necklaces and no wonder. They combine crystal cut as stars, rings, crosses, hearts and fishes strung apart on fine linen or silk thread. There are chakras to give calm and therapy through the coloured crystals, bear and fish fetishes offering wisdom and love and wild flowers within crystal. The concept, which combines jewellery with Eastern religions and crystal therapies is very nineties.

Noël Productions, 75A Falcon Road, London SW11 2PF

Tel: 0171 228 2061 **Fax:** 0171 730 3104

Price range: £8 to £180. Price of catalogue included in postage of order.

Payment: cheque. Additional charge of £7 for US$ cheques.

Postage & packing: average £2.

Delivery: 5-10 days. Last Christmas orders 16 December

Refunds: yes.

Specials: gift-wrapping in cellophane with flower petals £2.

Sarah Parker-Eaton

Inspiration for this craft jeweller comes from deep-sea animals, their fins and tentacles, segmented bodies and pop eyes. Sarah doesn't make botanical

CLOTHES AND ACCESSORIES

copies but creates weird beasts which are both jokey and sinister. She uses gold and silver, oxidising the silver for shade and contrast.

> **Sarah Parker-Eaton**, 33 Honeygate, Luton, Bedfordshire LU2 7EP
> **Tel:** 01582 431185
> **Price range:** £50 to £500. Catalogue £1.
> **Payment:** cheque.
> **Postage & packing:** included.
> **Delivery:** allow 28 days.
> **Refunds:** by arrangement.
> **Specials:** all made to order. Discuss with Sarah.

Seriously Smart A range of well-priced costume jewellery of traditional design. Because jewellery doesn't display well in catalogues, you need to scour the pages carefully for what you want. I like the mixed long "pearl" necklaces and the enamelled butterfly and bee brooches. Because the designs are uncontroversial, this is a good place to find jewels for people whose taste you are unsure of.

> **Seriously Smart**, P O Box 3020, Wokingham, Berkshire RG40 3TU
> **Tel/Fax:** 01252 860671
> **Price range:** £4.50 to £46. Catalogue free.
> **Payment:** cheque, postal order, major credit cards.
> **Postage & packing:** £1.
> **Delivery:** normally 48 hours. Christmas orders allow 3 working days.
> **Refunds:** by arrangement.
> **Specials:** free gift-wrapping service.

See also: Bond & Gibbins, Chelsea Collections, Claire Sowden, Clivedon Collection, First Impressions, Fortum & Mason, Harrods, Hitchcocks' by Post, Johnny Loves Rosie, Sarah Broadhead-Riall.

Chapter Three

HOUSE AND GARDEN

ART AND REPLICAS

It is quite possible today to buy an old master through the post, though more likely a print, watercolour or drawing rather than a full-scale oil. There is, too, a company which sells artifacts thousands of years old from the stone-age to the Roman Empire. Several stately homes have teamed together to create interesting replicas and there are one-off catalogues for reproductions of naive art, iron antiques and furniture.

ART AND REPLICAS- LISTINGS

Abbott and Holder For 50 years, the firm has stocked affordable pictures, often by famous artists, and they are whizzes at attribution (a refund and box of chocs if they get it wrong). You can see pictures on approval (well, you have to really) or can reserve from their helpful and readable lists. Artists are mostly British, mostly from the 19th century to the present and mostly sketches, prints and watercolours. I warn you, buying here is seriously addictive.

Abbott and Holder,
30 Museum Street,
London WC1A 1LH
Tel: 0171 637 3981
Fax: 0171 631 0575

HOUSE AND GARDEN

81

Website: http://www.artefact.co.uk/aah
Price range: £25 to £5,000. Free lists of new stock sent every 7 weeks.
Payment: major credit cards except Amex.
Postage & packing: at cost.
Delivery: by arrangement.
Refunds: yes, if returned in 2 days, p&p paid both ways.
Specials: framing service, conservation department.

Ancestral Collections Some of Britain's greatest houses have clubbed together and picked interesting, beautiful and useful objects from their rooms to reproduce for this list. Some new arrivals include a 'fly' brooch from Burghley based on a 1690 design or a silver 'walnut key' like a sharp arrow to crack a walnut shell. From Blair Castle there is a cut glass vase cum ice bucket with gilded Chinoiserie figures and from Alnwick Castle a set of table mats inspired by pietra dura panels. A delightful new arrival is a pair of 19th century pewter figures of Paris street vendors with large baskets to hold salt, sweets or small flower arrangements.

Ancestral Collections Ltd, The Old Corn Store, Burghley House, Stamford, Lincolnshire PE9 3JY
Tel: 01780 482522 **Fax:** 01780 765305
Price range: £20 to £1,175. Catalogue free.
Payment: cheque, banker's draft, major credit/debit cards.
Postage & packing: £4 to £10 depending on weight.
Delivery: allow 28 days.
Refunds: yes, if returned by recorded delivery within 10 days with original packing.

Ancient Art A wonderful catalogue filled with objects I would love to have. It is organised by date, from the prehistoric of 160m years ago (fossils, dinosaur eggs, amber) through Mesopotamian (beads, arrow heads, cuneiform tablets), Egyptian, Greek and Roman. It's salutary to realise that, 2,400 years ago in Apulia, they were serving salt in dishes much the same as we use today and that you can buy Byzantine crosses for as little as £30. At the top end of the range, there are

Chinese terracotta warriors from the Han dynasty, red figure kraters from the Hellenic world and wonderful Tang dynasty horses.

Ancient Art, 85 The Vale, Southgate, London N14 6AT
Tel: 0181 882 1509 **Fax:** 0181 886 5235
E-mail: ancient.art@btinternet.com
Website: http://www.antiquities-on-line/publications
Price range: £4.95 to £2,500. Catalogue free.
Payment: cheque, major credit/debit cards.
Postage & packing: £3 for orders under £100, free thereafter.
Delivery: despatched within 10 days. Last Christmas orders by 21 December.
Refunds: yes, if returned in original condition within a week.
Specials: items are guaranteed authentic and are supplied with a certificate of authenticity.

The Archival Fine Art Print Collection

This is based on the 200-year-old archive from the Minton china factory, which became so famous that couturiers, top interior designers and fabric makers took inspiration from it. The prints are from drawings of Minton pieces over the centuries, of careful drafts made to be painted on the china and prints of animals, fruits and flowers from various sources. There are also prints of classical buildings which are very decorative.

The Archival Fine Art Print Collection, 78 Walcot Street, Bath BA1 5BG
Tel: 01225 422909 **Fax:** 01225 422910
Price range: £10 to £226. Catalogue £5.
Payment: cheque, major credit cards.
Postage & packing: at cost.
Delivery: allow 28 days.
Refunds: no.

Art Room

Part of the Past Times stable of mail order companies, this one specialises in objects inspired by great artists. These vary from straight reproductions of prints, drawings and paintings, like Charles Rennie Mackintosh's stylised watercolours and Seurat's Lighthouse at Honfleur, to umbrellas,

HOUSE AND GARDEN

shopping bags and Melamine trays printed with Monet's water lilies. There are also books, scarves, ties and hangings. You should find presents here for any adult.

Art Room, Witney, Oxfordshire OX8 6BH
Tel: 01993 770444 **Fax:** 01993 770477
Price range: £3.95 to £600. Catalogue free.
Payment: cheque, postal order, major credit/debit cards.
Postage & packing: £2.95. Next day delivery add £4.95. Overseas rates on application.
Delivery: allow 7 days.
Refunds: yes.

Ashfield Traditional I read that when people give each other presents, the gifts are more often for the house and garden than for themselves personally. Old houses and gardens would love these hand-forged curtain poles with decorative dragons' tails or scrolls, iron doorpulls and latches, bolts, hinges, window catches and lovely rosehead nails which look medieval.

Ashfield Traditional, Forward Green, Stowmarket, Suffolk IP14 5HP
Tel: 01449 711273 **Fax:** 01449 711133
Price range: £8 to £125. Catalogue free.
Payment: cheque, major credit/debit cards.
Postage & packing: £5, curtain poles £10.
Delivery: allow 28 days. Last Christmas orders by 16 December.
Refunds: yes, if notified within 3 days, and returned in perfect condition.

Bow Art This selection of print reproductions of 20th century works of art is a joy. I love and lust after them all, from Eric Ravilious's garden and interior at Furlongs, Winifred Nicholson's window paintings and Christopher Wood's China Dogs in a St. Ives Window. The works have been carefully picked to work as prints. New prints come out each year.

Bow Art, 145 High Street, Marshfield, Chippenham, Wiltshire SN14 8LU
Tel/Fax: 01225 892009
Price range: £34.50 to £65. Information pack free.

84 MAIL ORDER MADE EASY

Payment: cheque, postal order.

Postage & packing: UK £2.50, Europe £6, elsewhere £9.

Delivery: within 10 days. Express delivery available. Last Christmas orders by 20 December.

Refunds: yes, goods should be returned by post in the tube provided.

British Museum Company A selection of the most popular replicas from the British Museum shop. Egyptian pieces are, deservedly, top sellers. There are tiny figures of jerboas, hippos and cats in the typical blue earthenware and copies of bronze cats (the thirteen-inch high Gayer-Anderson cat at over £350 is quite stunning). The 12th-century Lewis chess set from the Hebrides is world famous. There are replicas of classical sculpture and casts which include bits of Michelangelo's David. The quality is superb and many make outstanding decorative pieces.

British Museum Company Ltd, Mail Order, Unit A, Chettisham Business Park, Ely, Cambridgeshire CB6 1RY

Tel: 01353 668400

Price range: £6.95 to £550. Catalogue free.

Payment: cheque, major credit/debit cards.

Postage & packing: £2.95 to £5.95 in UK. Overseas rates on application.

Delivery: normally within 14 days, but allow 28. Express delivery available. Last Christmas orders by 12 December.

Refunds: yes, if returned within 28 days.

CCA Galleries Prints, etchings, lithographs and silk screens are the firm's stock in trade. The chosen artists are modern but acceptably so (ie not fountains of chocolate and mud footprints). There are English landscapes by artists inspired by John Piper, Annora Spence's naive men and animals, and prints evoking summer holidays on the beach, island and Mediterranean along with still lifes and abstracts. There are also one-off paintings and sculptures.

CCA Galleries, 517-523 Fulham Road, London SW6 1HD

Tel: 0171 386 4900 **Fax:** 0171 386 4919

HOUSE AND GARDEN

Price range: £45 to £4,000. Catalogue free.

Payment: cheque, Visa, Access, standing order for purchases over £250.

Postage & packing: £9 unframed, £16 framed.

Delivery: framed allow 3 weeks. Last Christmas orders by last posting date for unframed, 3 weeks in advance for framed.

Refunds: everything sent on 45 days approval. Return within that time.

Specials: gift vouchers.

Contemporary Artworks A new company selling prints by living artists. The first selection is by David Case, a clever graphic designer whose brilliantly-coloured prints are clearly inspired by Picasso. Each is in three sizes but the large size (36in x 49.5in) is ideal for the modern loft look.

Contemporary Artworks Ltd, Freepost (SCE5889), Edgware, Middlesex HA8 5BR

Tel: 0800 068 1805 **Fax:** 0181 200 6101

E-mail: artworks@dircon.co.uk

Price range: £66.95 to £230. Catalogue free.

Payment: cheque, Mastercard, Visa, Switch, Delta.

Postage & packing: £3.70.

Delivery: allow 28 days.

Refunds: yes.

Halcyon Days The firm has four royal warrants for its objets d'art won since it began to revive the art of English enamelling in 1970. These are not just 18th century versions but include enamels of Britannia, a Seurat painting and another by Peter Blake. The dome of St Paul's makes a fine enamel musical box while Chelsea porcelain on an enamel base makes charming bonbonnieres. There's a dalmatian and an elephant modelled on Echo, a famous Kenyan matriarch. A range of scented candles in porcelain vases is based on antique designs in country houses. Despite their quality and elegance, these little pieces are not hugely expensive.

Halcyon Days, 14 Brook Street, London W1Y 1AA

Tel: 0171 629 8811. Free 24-hour credit card hotline: 0800 515925.

24-hour toll-free number from USA: 1800 445 8058
Fax: 0171 409 7901

Website: http://www.halcyon-days.co.uk

Price range: £30 to £660. Christmas catalogue £3, smaller brochures free.

Payment: cheque, major credit/debit cards.

Postage & packing: up to £3.50 in UK. Guaranteed next day delivery £5. Overseas rates on application.

Delivery: allow at least 3 weeks. Last Christmas orders up to 21 December if items are in stock.

Refunds: yes.

Specials: free gift-wrapping service, special inscriptions from £25.

Imperial War Museum

The museum's collections provide a fine resource for the catalogue. Many of these are familiar posters such as the one with Lord Kitchener saying your country needs you and these come as posters themselves, as key rings, mugs, playing cards or chocolates. There are also evocative photographs from the wars. The museum is constantly changing and upgrading its wares, so ask for an up-to-date list.

Imperial War Museum, Mail Order, Duxford Airfield, Cambridgeshire CB2 4QR

Tel: 01223 835000 ext. 245 **Fax:** 01223 837267

Price range: £1.80 to £100. Catalogue free.

Payment: cheque, postal order, Mastercard, Access, Visa.

Postage & packing: £1.50 for orders up to £7.50, 20% of order value thereafter. Overseas rates on application.

Delivery: normally within 10 days, but allow 28. Last Christmas orders by 10 December.

Refunds: yes, if returned unused in original packaging with documents within 7 days.

Loon Cartoons

The artist reverses the roles of humans and animals to show pheasants cheeking gundogs, pigs snuffling in the boardroom and drunken stags having a wild night out. You can buy them as limited edition prints, postcards and greetings cards.

Loon Cartoons, Greenhill House, Redcastle, Muir of Ord, Ross-shire IV6 7SG

Tel: 01463 871029 **Tel/Fax:** 01463 870423

Price range: 50p to £94. Catalogue free.

Payment: cheque, Mastercard, Visa, Eurocard.

Postage & packing: £1 for orders under £10, £2 under £18, £3 under £30, £5 thereafter. Overseas at cost.

Delivery: 7-10 days. Last Christmas orders 2 weeks in advance.

Refunds: yes, if returned undamaged.

Specials: author will sign books.

Lovers "Our customers," says Olwyn Butler, "buy old and antique china by post. It sounds incredible, but it works. We have customers in 25 countries and never a piece broken!" Most is the highly-collectable and highly-decorative blue and white Staffordshire dating from the 19th century onwards.

Lovers of Blue & White, Steeple Morden, Royston, Hertfordshire SG8 0RN

Tel: 01763 853800 **Fax:** 01763 853700

E-mail: china@blueandwhite.com

Website: http://www.blueandwhite.com

Price range: £3 to over £300. Catalogue £2.50 refundable against first order.

Payment: cheque, Mastercard, Visa.

Postage & packing: £5 for orders up to £100, £10 up to £200, £15 thereafter. Overseas rates on application.

Delivery: normally next day. Overseas by airmail. Last Christmas orders by 22 December.

Refunds: yes.

Specials: gift-wrapping, free "no obligation" search service.

The National Trust for Scotland There's lots of tartan, clootie dumplings, thistle motifs and the like but few replicas. Also featured are objects inspired by Charles Rennie Mackintosh and gifts for children, gardeners and fishermen.

The National Trust for Scotland Trading Company Ltd, 5 Charlotte Square, Edinburgh EH2 4DU

Tel: 0131 243 9393 **Fax:** 0131 243 9397

Price range: £1.20 to £350. Catalogue free.

Payment: cheque, Visa, Mastercard, Amex, Switch.

Postage & packing: £3.75.
Delivery: allow 28 days.
Refunds: by arrangement.

The Obelisk Collection Taking inspiration from the well-stocked historic houses of Ireland, this range is enormously stylish. I love the bookends inspired by Sir William Chambers's Casino building, the Castletown bowl which is black and yellow with a golden border and the charming faux ivory hair brush which can be decorated with special initials.

The Obelisk Collection, 41 Kensington Square, London W8 5HP
Tel: 0171 938 2628 **Fax:** 0171 938 4360
Price range: 70p to £1349.99. Catalogue free.
Payment: Mastercard, Visa, Amex.
Postage & packing: ring to check.
Delivery: allow 28 days.
Refunds: yes, if damaged.

Past Times This is the original mail order repro service, a very slick marketing operation which has good ideas if you pick carefully. The goods are set out by period, from Roman, Viking and Medieval to 20th century Art Deco. Some objects are naff but the Giverny blue wrought iron table and chairs, inspired by Monet's farmhouse, are simple and elegant and there is a varied selection of gifts from soaps and jewellery to a brass sundial and Victorian glass bell cloches.

Past Times, Witney, Oxfordshire OX8 6BH
Tel: 01993 770400 **Fax:** 01993 770477
Price range: £5 to £600. Catalogue free.
Payment: cheque, major credit/debit cards.
Postage & packing: £2.95. Express delivery add £4.95.
Delivery: allow 7 days. Last Christmas orders by mid December.
Refunds: yes.
Specials: gift-wrapping.

HOUSE AND GARDEN

Rowan Prints Cynthia Rowan is an artist inspired as much by Japanese prints as by naive painters. Her prints have just started to be published by her daughter, Tiddy, who, until recently, worked in London and Hong Kong as a commercial film producer. Her work is realistic but formal in design and uses images from the countryside, garden and farmyard.

> **Rowan Prints**, Wern, Llanfairfechan, County Conway, North Wales LL33 0HR
> **Tel/Fax:** 01248 680765
> **Price range:** £5 to £25. Catalogue free.
> **Payment:** cheque with order.
> **Postage & packing:** at cost.
> **Delivery:** usually 7 days but allow 21.
> **Refunds:** by arrangement.
> **Specials:** gift-wrapping.

The Singing Tree Dolls' houses and miniatures of all kinds quite definitely not intended for childish fingers. Since the 17th century, adults have been playing fantasy house with such tiny porcelain plates, silver, copper kettles and furniture as this catalogue offers. From it you can build up entire interiors – Georgian, Victorian and earlier – and people them. You can have a minute garden with statues and wheelbarrows and a nursery with toys. Quite addictive.

> **The Singing Tree**, 69 New Kings Road, London SW6 4SQ
> **Tel:** 0171 736 4527 **Fax:** 0171 736 0336
> **Price range:** £1 to £5,000. Catalogue £5 in UK, £5.50 by airmail to Europe, £7.50 by airmail elsewhere.
> **Payment:** cheque, major credit/debit cards.
> **Postage & packing:** £1.75 for orders up to £10, £2.75 up to £25, £3.75 up to £80, £4.50 over £80. Overseas rates on application.
> **Delivery:** varies as items are hand-made. Last Christmas orders as early as possible as goods can be in limited supply.
> **Refunds:** yes.

Soo San Susanna Murray makes regular forays into China to collect old furniture and objects. As she says, most of the furniture is 19th century but other pieces come from Burma and

90 MAIL ORDER MADE EASY

there is porcelain which is much older. Though these must be one-offs, she has regular supplies of leather trunks, lacquer rice buckets, ginger jars and so on. She will send photos and information when she finds out what you are looking for. It's very chic but, better still, beautiful.

Soo San, 239a Fulham Road, London SW3 6HY
Tel: 0171 352 8980 **Fax:** 0171 352 9880
Price range: approx £50 to £6,000. Photographs and information free.
Payment: cheque, Mastercard, Visa, Switch.
Postage & packing: normally around £40 in UK and Europe. Elsewhere rates on application, typically £60-£75 per sq. metre.
Delivery: next day in London area, 2-3 days elsewhere in UK.
Refunds: yes, if returned undamaged within 7 days.

Waddesdon Manor The Rothschild Collection: though Waddesdon Manor in Buckinghamshire is part of the National Trust, the shop at the vast house has a huge input from the Rothschild family not least the Rothschild wines (though not currently including Mouton Rothschild). There are, too, chocolates decorated in white chocolate with the family's famous five arrow crest, tablemats adapted from the Sèvres porcelain collection there and extremely pretty toile de Jouy cushions. Much is exclusive to Waddesdon.

Waddesdon Manor, near Aylesbury, Buckinghamshire HP18 0JH
Tel: 01296 651282 **Fax:** 01296 651293
Price range: £1.95 to over £500. Catalogue free.
Payment: cheque, Access, Visa, Switch.
Postage & packing: £3.95 in mainland UK.
Delivery: normally by return. Next day delivery at cost.
Refunds: yes.
Specials: gift-wrapping £1.95 per item.

Wiseman Originals You don't have to pay a fortune for modern art as Caroline and Garth Wiseman have proved. They use their Lambeth house in London to show what prints can do, selling works by Picasso, Matisse, Braque, Frink, Piper and

HOUSE AND GARDEN

Hockney. Though, of course, it's best to see the works in situ, prints, unlike paintings, can be easily photographed or described and the firm is very happy to advise.

Wiseman Originals Ltd, 34 West Square, Lambeth, London SE11 4SP.
Tel: 0171 587 0747 **Fax:** 0171 793 8817
Price range: £100 to £10,000. Catalogue free.
Payment: cheque, major credit cards.
Postage & packing: included.
Delivery: delivered personally or by courier.
Refunds: exchange.

See also: Annie Sloan Ltd, Classic Car Art, The National Trust (Enterprises) Ltd, The Old Stile Press, Sophie Allport Cards.

HOME

A perfect subject for mail order, even though companies like Habitat seem to have drawn back from the full service. Virtually anything for the house comes into the category of un-carryable, including duvets and pillows (try taking them on the bus), lampshades (I once tried to take one as hand-luggage on a plane – never again), furniture of all kinds and breakables like tumblers or plates. This explains why there is such a huge choice of firms in the field. Some import direct from Europe, Russia, China, Vietnam and America, others design over here and have their objects made overseas, others just put together catalogues using their own choice of goods. What is certain is that these firms are in the forefront of design and their cata-logues will be an inspiration.

HOME - LISTINGS

After Noah Matthew Crawford describes what he sells in his shops in Islington and King's Road as "an exciting, eclectic mix of useful, decorative and sometimes bizarre items". I can vouch for that – and also that he manages to stay just ahead of the designer pack. Generally, the firm has a good line in iron beds, Anglepoise and other lamps, old telephones and 20th century furniture. They produce a small brochure but you can order by mail anything you see in their shops or anything in the frequent press mentions.

> **After Noah**, 121 Upper Street, London N1 1QP
> **Tel:** 0171 359 4281
> **E-mail:** mailorder@afternoah.demon.co.uk
> **Price range:** £2.50 to £945. Catalogue free.
> **Payment:** cheque, major credit cards.
> **Postage & packing:** from £3.95.
> **Delivery:** allow 28 days, or up to 8 weeks for beds. Last Christmas orders by last posting date.
> **Refunds:** by arrangement.

Air de Provence Britain has a love affair with French fabrics – perhaps they remind us of sunny picnics on holiday. This firm has a range which does just that. They are made into tablecloths, some spongeable, bags filled with Provençal lavender, some of the most scented available, sponge bags and lavender cushions. I am always on the look-out for good value presents which would suit any age or person and these come close.

> **Air de Provence**, Redhouse Farm, Eynsham Road, Botley, Oxford OX2 9NH
> **Tel/Fax:** 01865 862442
> **Price range:** £2 to £39.50. Catalogue free.
> **Payment:** cheque, major credit cards.
> **Postage & packing:** prices on application.
> **Delivery:** orders are sent by return.
> **Refunds:** yes, if returned within a reasonable period.

HOUSE AND GARDEN

Andrew Martin A big noise in the interior decorating world which reports on current trends. The new bed and bath collection offers 60% linen sheets in crisp white, white cotton piqué and the black contrast trim of the Astaire range. Also sensuous cashmere throws, bathrobes and towels. All come packed in a classy box.

Andrew Martin Direct, P O Box 99, Sudbury, Suffolk CO10 6SN

Tel: 0800 328 1346 **Fax:** 01623 759045

Price range: £12.50 to £169. Catalogue free.

Payment: cheque, postal order, major credit cards except Amex.

Postage & packing: included in UK. Overseas at cost.

Delivery: allow 10 days.

Refunds: yes, if returned within 14 days. Free return post label included.

Annie Cole Traditional Hand Knitting Remember those chunky, bumpy bedspreads hand-knitted for cottage beds? Annie Cole now recreates them in hand-knitted cotton on fine needles. The technique is called white work and mixes textures and lacy stitches so the pattern is in the knitting, not the colour. All are monochrome and generally white or écru. You can buy the spreads, shawls, cushion and cot covers in kit form or ready-made. Patterns have lovely names like the architectural Acanthus, lacy Canterbury Bells and heavily textured Garden Plot.

Annie Cole Traditional Hand Knitting, 18 Holmesdale Avenue, Sheen, London SW14 7BQ

Tel: 0181 878 9686

Price range: kits from £17.60 for a cushion to £117.50 for a double bedspread. Send 4 first class stamps for catalogue.

Payment: cheque, postal order, Access, Visa. Deposit on ready-mades.

Postage & packing: included for kits.

Delivery: normally within a week for kits but allow 28 days. Ready-mades up to 3 months.

Refunds: yes, if kit unopened.

MAIL ORDER MADE EASY

Annie Sloan Annie was one of the first designers to produce ranges to satisfy our current lust for historic and artistic paints and the varnishes, scumbles and so on needed for paint techniques. Her mail order catalogue has both a traditional range of colours to evoke, she says, "the feel of antique painted furniture, classic interiors and old textiles" and an Impressionist range especially suited to modern, country and southern interiors. She also offers sets of papers for découpage and kits of glue, sponges, brushes, scissors etc to get going with. Her seven books on paint and antique effects are also in her catalogue.

> **Annie Sloan Ltd**, Knutsford House, Park Street, Bladon, Oxford OX20 1RW
> **Tel:** 0870 602 0082 **Fax:** 01993 813710
> **E-mail:** paint@anniesloan.com
> **Website:** www.anniesloan.com
> **Price range:** £2.75 to £25. Catalogue free.
> **Payment:** cheque, Mastercard, Visa.
> **Postage & packing:** £3.95.
> **Delivery:** 3 working days in UK.
> **Refunds:** yes. Opened tins of paint cannot be refunded.

Anta Way north of Inverness, Anta makes its own ranges of original stoneware tartan-painted Ballone crockery, named after the owner's castle, and a collection of softly coloured throws using their cleverly recoloured tartan sets. I use their Ballone ware myself – it goes from Aga or oven to the table without problems and the shapes mould to the hand.

> **Anta**, Fearn, Tain, Ross-shire IV20 1XW
> **Tel:** 01862 832477 **Fax:** 01862 832616
> **Price range:** £8.95 to approx. £75. Catalogue free.
> **Payment:** cheque, major credit/debit cards.
> **Postage & packing:** £7.
> **Delivery:** allow 28 days.
> **Refunds:** by arrangement.

The Art Guild A range of limited edition floor rugs are grouped under four headings – Romanticism, Minimalism,

HOUSE AND GARDEN 95

Modernism and Expressionism. Many are wildly coloured and patterned and need careful siting to look good – but the brochure shows how. I especially like the plainer Chinese style ones like Peking and those with a border but no central motif, like Chequers and Broadway.

The Art Guild, Freepost NEA3904, Dearne Mills, Darton, South Yorkshire S75 5WZ
Tel: 0800 783 8159
Price range: £95 to £245. Catalogue free.
Payment: cheque, postal order, major credit/debit cards.
Postage & packing: included.
Delivery: normally within 14 days.
Refunds: yes, if returned within 21 days.

Artifex Using traditional English cottage furniture designs, Artifex hand-paints pieces to order in a variety of finishes such as crackle-glaze, distressed and stencilled. They will also, for a small extra charge, paint pieces in your own colours. Painted furniture, which, of course, can be repainted, will stand out or retreat into the walls depending on your choice of shade. The firm also sells the sort of accessories – cushions, pots, photo frames – that fit in with their style.

Artifex, 3 Vale Road, Tunbridge Wells, Kent TN1 1BS
Tel: 01892 511110 **Fax:** 01892 536709
Price range: accessories from under £10. Painted furniture from £100 approx. Catalogue free.
Payment: cheque, major credit cards.
Postage & packing: accessories £3.50 per order, furniture delivery charges quoted on request.
Delivery: accessories allow 28 days, painted furniture 6 weeks.
Refunds: by arrangement.
Specials: all furniture hand-painted to suit customers' requirements. Goods sent abroad by arrangement.

Artisan The firm is dedicated to curtain perfection. Forget those horrid plastic rails and hooks and look what can be achieved with curly wrought iron rails, holdbacks and hooks, others with brilliantly coloured finials or what they call "curtain jewellery". These are hooks decorated with shells, pebbles or washed glass from which to hang lightweight or sheer curtains. There are also rich fabric tassels and tiebacks.

> **Artisan**, 4a Union Court, 20 Union Road, London SW4 6JP
> **Tel:** 0171 498 6974 **Fax:** 0171 498 2989
> **Price range:** £3.50 to £280. Catalogue free.
> **Payment:** cheque, Mastercard, Visa.
> **Postage & packing:** on request.
> **Delivery:** despatched within 7 days if in stock.
> **Refunds:** by arrangement.

Baileys

Baileys The firm started as architectural salvage but has metamorphosed into selling reproduction iron urns for the house and garden, decorative metal brackets, door stops and shoe scrapers and a charming range of naive art – gigantic cows and pigs, sailing ships and fruit.

> **Baileys Architectural Antiques,** The Engine Shed, Station Approach, Ross-on-Wye, Herefordshire HR9 7BW
> **Tel:** 01989 563015 **Fax:** 01989 768172
> **Price range:** £33 to £176. Catalogue free.
> **Payment:** cheque, Mastercard, Access, Visa, Switch.
> **Postage & packing:** £8.
> **Delivery:** allow 28 days, overnight delivery at extra cost.
> **Refunds:** yes.

Beardmore

Beardmore Half the doors in London seem to sport Beardmore's fierce lion knocker but the firm, established in 1860, sells a huge variety of brass and iron fittings. There are curtain tie backs, rope handles, espagnolettes for French windows and a huge array of handles for antique furniture. Their grilles are excellent for radiator covers and for kitchen cupboards where you need to hide the gubbins. All are sturdy and high quality as you'd expect.

> **J D Beardmore & Co Ltd**, 3/4 Percy Street, London W1P 0EJ
> **Tel:** 0171 637 7041 **Fax:** 0171 436 9222
> **Price range:** 25p to £500. Catalogue £5, refundable against first purchase of £5 or over.

HOUSE AND GARDEN

Payment: cheque, Mastercard, Visa.
Postage & packing: quoted with order.
Delivery: many items by return, special orders can take 12 weeks.
Refunds: by arrangement.

Bel Frames

Belinda Oppenheimer is a single framer who works to order making patterned and gilded photo frames. Many are ornate and would suit pictures of people who mean a lot to you. She also makes multiple mounts to take photos of an entire family or group of friends. Frames can be sent with or without glass.

Bel Frames, 56 Longfield Avenue, Mill Hill, London NW7 2EG
Tel: 0181 203 7477 **Fax:** 0181 202 7855
Price range: £3 to £20. No catalogue.
Payment: cheque.
Postage & packing: varies according to size of frame.
Delivery: allow 7 days. Last Christmas orders by 20 December.
Refunds: by arrangement.

Bennett & Green

Wallshelves are both useful and decorative and this firm sells attractive two or three shelf units, gothic, chinoiserie, scalloped or latticed, along with brackets, corner shelves and bedside tables. They can be painted in a choice of six greeny, bluey or creamy shades or, for an extra £20, in any of the Farrow and Ball National Trust range. If, like me, you swear by these paint colours, you can make sure your shelves and cupboards complement the walls.

Bennett & Green, Rock Lane, Offwell, Honiton, Devon EX14 9SW
Tel/Fax: 01404 831403
Price range: £16 to £120. Catalogue free.
Payment: cheque.
Postage & packing: £4.95 for orders up to £10, free thereafter in mainland UK except Highlands.
Delivery: allow 28 days.
Refunds: by arrangement.
Specials: furniture can be modified in accordance with special requirements.

Black Dog of Wells Using natural terracotta, Black Dog makes complicated tiles in relief (though you can stand hot dishes on them). The original designs come from antique carvings and tapestries and are given suitable messages. A William Morris design is interwoven with a quote from him, "Love is Enough"; Dr. Johnson's comment "Here lives a very fine cat indeed" is married with a contented puss. Some would suit lovers, others thank-you presents.

> **Black Dog of Wells**, 18 Tor Street, Wells, Somerset BA5 2US
> **Tel/Fax:** 01749 672548
> **Price:** £11. 10% discount for orders of 4 or more items to the same address.
> **Payment:** cheque, major credit cards.
> **Postage & packing:** included in UK. Overseas by airmail £1.50.
> **Delivery:** within 7 days. Last Christmas orders by last posting date.
> **Refunds:** yes.

Bobbins Jackie Bastable's company sells delicious cushions with co-ordinated throws, tablecloths, bedspreads and towels along with huckaback towels (once used for visitors) which are making a comeback. There are also charming nighties for women and children so you don't let your duvet cover down.

> **Bobbins**, 24 Bridge Road, Chertsey, Surrey KT16 8JN
> **Tel/Fax:** 01932 560479
> **Price range:** £1 to £300. Catalogue free.
> **Payment:** cheque, major credit cards.
> **Postage & packing:** £1-£10 depending on weight.
> **Delivery:** usually within a week.
> **Refunds:** yes, if returned unused and quickly.

Bombay Duck A good general household and present catalogue featuring a lot of metal from aluminium bins, photo frames and albums to a separate list of hand-forged iron. The curvy chairs, coffee and occasional tables, French bakers' stands and accessories are ideal for outdoor eating, conservatories and normal interiors.

HOUSE AND GARDEN

Bombay Duck, 231 The Vale, London W3 7QS
Tel: 0181 749 7000 **Fax:** 0181 749 9000
E-mail: info@bombayduck.co.uk
Website: http://www.bombayduck.co.uk
Price range: £1 to £1,500. Catalogue free.
Payment: cheque, postal order, major credit/debit cards.
Postage & packing: £3.50 in UK, free for orders over £100.
Overseas rates on application.
Delivery: within 7 days, next day delivery available. Last
Christmas orders by 17 December, or 22 December for next day
delivery.
Refunds: yes, if returned within 7 days with original packaging
intact.

Bond & Gibbins Using mild steel, aluminium, brass and
nickel silver, the designers make a variety of hanging basket
brackets, brooches, bookends and pencil holders based on animal silhouettes. They also use their brooch designs to create
attractive handmade greetings cards.

Bond & Gibbins, Unit 11, Dukes Close, West Way, Andover,
Hampshire SP10 5AP
Tel: 01264 337878 **Fax:** 01264 337880
Price range: £1.95 to £22.50. Catalogue free.
Payment: cheque, postal order, major credit/debit cards.
Postage & packing: 60p for orders up to £10, £3.50 thereafter.
Overseas rates on application.
Delivery: allow 28 days. Last Christmas orders by 9 December.
Refunds: yes, if returned within 30 days.

Bouchon Just in case you have difficulty in finishing your
bottle of champagne, Bouchon have a range of stoppers, drop-
pers and bungs to stop the bottle – there's a difference but I
can't tell you exactly what. All have decorative finials from
minimalist to Michelin man and all are silver plated. The smart
catalogue also has corkscrews in matching patterns and a silver
plated salt and pepper set.

Bouchon Ltd, 309 Metrostore, 5-10 Eastman Road, London
W3 7YG
Tel: 0181 740 9744 **Fax:** 0181 749 7566

Price range: £21.50 to £49.95. Catalogue free.
Payment: cheque.
Postage & packing: included in UK.
Delivery: 5 working days. Last Christmas orders 5 days in advance.
Refunds: yes, if returned in perfect condition within 14 days.

Carden Cunietti At the cutting edge of home design, like many whose products move fast, this firm prefers to respond to mail order enquires only when their products are shown in the press. They have no catalogue and their range goes from simple pots to full-scale furniture. There are even antiques which, of course, tend to be one offs. Alternatively, they can be visited at their shop in Westbourne Park Road and contacted by mail thereafter.

Carden Cunietti, 83 Westbourne Park Road, London W2 5QH
Tel: 0171 229 8559 **Fax:** 0171 229 8799
E-mail: @cc-id.demon.co.uk
Price range: £5 to £5,000. No catalogue.
Payment: cheque, Mastercard, Visa, Switch.
Postage & packing: varies depending on weight.
Delivery: subject to availability.
Refunds: exchange or credit note.

Cargo The firm has its own block printing workshop in India where they can use their own colours and designs to create some delicious fabrics in pure cotton. The patterns are traditionally Indian but 300-years ago these made their way to Europe to turn up in Provençal chintzes and in English country house fabrics. There are also checks, stripes and plains. Cargo does not sell fabric by the yard but offers a big range of bedlinen, throws, table cloths and napkins, cushion covers and handkerchiefs. The cards, which come in a neat envelope, give an excellent idea of the range.

Cargo Furnishing Company, 23 Market Place, Cirencester, Gloucestershire GL7 2NX
Tel: 01285 652175 **Fax:** 01285 644827

HOUSE AND GARDEN

Price range: £1.75 to £85. Catalogue free.

Payment: cheque, postal order, major credit cards.

Postage & packing: £2.50 for orders up to £30, £4.75 up to £100, free thereafter.

Delivery: by post or overnight carrier. Last Christmas orders by 13 December.

Refunds: yes, if returned within 14 days.

Specials: gift service and vouchers. Swatches available.

The Carrier Co Tina Guillory designs and has made in Norfolk a series of carriers and pockets perfect for working at home or in the garden. The carrier itself is jute trimmed in dark green and is big enough to tote awkward parcels and objects as well as weeds or plants. Her Pockets are belts with two sets of pockets for tools, seeds, dusters or mobile phones. There's also a boot pull and a fire blower. This year sees a carry sack, a toast rack and a jute apron.

The Carrier Co, Church Farmhouse, Wighton, Norfolk NR23 1AL

Tel/Fax: 01328 820699

Price range: £12 to £33. Catalogue free.

Payment: cheque.

Postage & packing: included in UK. Overseas rates on application.

Delivery: within 14 days. Immediate despatch available on request. Last Christmas orders by 7 December.

Refunds: yes, if returned in perfect condition within 14 days.

Cath Kidston Cath has made her name – and a cult – from reworking gentle 1950s type designs into modern fabrics. Last year she was way ahead of the craze for roses with everything and she caught on to old-fashioned bath-time fabrics even before that. The patterns turn up on robes, spongebags, towels, aprons, bedlinen, lampshades and are constantly evolving. Fashionable London flocks to her shop, but you can buy over the phone.

Cath Kidston Ltd, 8 Clarendon Cross, London W11 4AP

Tel: 0171 221 4000 **Fax:** 0171 229 1992

Price range: £4.50 to £125. Catalogue free.

Payment: cheque, postal order, Access, Visa, Switch.
Postage & packing: £4 for orders up to £20, £6 thereafter.
Delivery: within 7 days, if later, they will phone.
Refunds: yes, if notified within 3 days.

China Beasts
A range of tableware that has the bright brashness of British Airways tailfins – but placed more appropriately. The black and white Tribal design, for instance, consists of African-inspired snakes and creepy-crawlies circling mugs and plates, Multi-Fish has shoals of black, yellow, green and blue fish swimming along on multi-backgrounds. Also look out for bright Poppies, farmyard and jungle animals and other fishy designs.

China Beasts, Gannetts Cottage, Todber, Sturminster Newton, Dorset DT10 1HS
Tel/Fax: 01258 820868
Price range: £4.50 to £50. Send A5 sae with first class stamp for catalogue.
Payment: cheque.
Postage & packing: 10% of total order.
Delivery: allow 28 days or 6 weeks for large orders. Extra fast delivery available if items are in stock. Last Christmas orders 15 December.
Refunds: yes.
Specials: monogramming, gift boxes.

Ciel Decor
Think of Provence and all the good things it has produced (Souleiado and Les Olivades) and you get the measure of this catalogue. Brilliant fabrics, very loosely based on Indian chintz designs, by the metre and made into all sorts of bags, tablecloths, napkins; scented soaps and others based on natural oils; pot pourri from the heavily scented herbs which grow on the hills plus some food.

Ciel Decor, 187 New King's Road, London SW6 4SW
Tel: 0171 731 0444 **Fax:** 0171 731 0788
Price range: £17.99 to £77 per metre. No catalogue, but swatches can be sent.
Payment: cheque, major credit/debit cards.

Postage & packing: £8.
Delivery: allow 28 days. Last Christmas orders by 11 December, or 18 December if in stock.
Refunds: no.

Claire Sowden Claire is a designer whose machine embroideries in silk dupion, organza and chiffon are layered to create frames for clocks or mirrors, intricate jewellery and tiny, jewel-like boxes. By layering the transparent and semi-opaque fabrics she manages to create soft shimmering colours. Her styles, though influenced by Eastern designs and, I would say, stumpwork needlework, are very much of the moment and sport hearts, fish and geometrics.

Claire Sowden, 7 Hartford Terrace, Hartley Wintney, Hampshire RG27 8PL
Tel: 01252 843182 **Fax:** 01252 845745
Price range: £14 to £110. Catalogue free.
Payment: cheque or postal order.
Postage & packing: recorded delivery charged at cost.
Delivery: allow 28 days.
Refunds: yes if damaged, return within 4 working days.

Cloakrooms As it suggests, this is a company with a mission to tidy what the Americans sensibly call mud rooms because you will find lots of mud in them but very few cloaks. There are special pegs for organising the unorganisable – fishing waders, tennis racquets, rubber gloves and wellies. There are also shoe cleaning boxes, roller towel rails (and hardwearing roller towels) and holders for wine, kitchen paper and loo rolls.

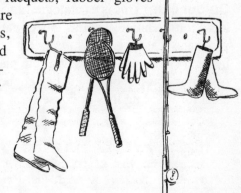

Cloakrooms,
Dodbrooke House,
Kingsbridge, Devon
TQ7 1NW

Tel/Fax: 01548 853583
Price range: £3.95 to £110. Catalogue free.
Payment: cheque, Mastercard, Visa.
Postage & packing: £1 to £3.50.
Delivery: allow 28 days.
Refunds: yes, if returned in original packaging within 7 days.
Specials: Designs can be modified to suit customer requirements. Prices on application.

Cologne & Cotton

I try very hard to keep all my household linen white, it makes washing and bedmaking so much easier. C&C have an excellent range but their colours are also extremely tempting: blue and white striped flannelette (due for a comeback) with woollen throws, for instance, and a fine range of Indian cotton in red, yellow and blue. The colognes are exclusive, spicy and floral and just as tempting.

Cologne & Cotton Ltd, 74 Regent Street, Leamington Spa, Warwickshire CV32 4NS
Tel: 01926 332573 **Fax:** 01926 332575
Price range: £1.75 to £200. Catalogue £2.50 refundable on first order.
Payment: cheque, major credit cards.
Postage & packing: £2.50 for orders up to £30, £4.50 up to £150, free thereafter.
Delivery: by 48-hour Parcel Force.
Refunds: yes.
Specials: awkward sizes to order.

Colour Blue

This is a catalogue absolutely stuffed with smart ideas for the home. There's lots of galvanised metalware from vases and watering cans to milk churns and trays; candles and lighting are a major element as are pieces of country furniture from iron fourposters to kitchen cupboards. It is very chic and ideal for wedding lists or housewarmings, too.

Colour Blue, Beckhaven House, 9 Gilbert Road, Kennington, London SE11 4LN
Tel: 0171 820 7700 **Fax:** 0171 793 0537
Price range: 89p to £1,000. Catalogue £2.50.
Payment: cheque, postal order, major credit cards.

HOUSE AND GARDEN

Postage & packing: from £2.95. Rush service at extra cost.

Delivery: allow 28 days for stock items, 8 weeks for furniture and special orders. Last Christmas orders 5 working days beforehand. Rush service available until 23 December if stocks allow.

Refunds: yes, if faulty and company is notified in writing within 3 working days of delivery.

Specials: Wedding list and gift service.

Country Traditionals

Marianne Ford and Suzanne Hillen (proud to have nine children between them) started to mail order the original Bunzlau ceramics from Poland last year and were surprised at the enthusiastic response. They shouldn't have been: these stoneware pieces, from teapots to lasagne dishes are patterned with tiny bright spots like a guinea fowl's feathers but in blue and white. They mix and match, are delightfully pretty and are tough and oven-proof.

Country Traditionals, Bramblehurst House, Wall Hill Road, Ashurst Wood, West Sussex RH19 3TQ

Tel: 01342 822622 **Fax:** 01342 826827/826550

E-mail: 101333.442@compuserve.com

Price range: £3.80 to £242. Catalogue free.

Payment: cheque, major credit/debit cards.

Postage & packing: £6.00 per shipment irrespective of size.

Delivery: normally within 2 working days. Next day delivery on request. Last Christmas orders by mid-December.

Refunds: yes, for genuine complaint if notified within 4 days.

Specials: gift-wrapping.

Crucial Trading

The king of the natural floor covering, CT virtually singlehandedly covered the smartest floors in seagrass and then went on to make boring old coir fashionable once again. Keep watching their lists, for they are ever inventive of new materials, weaves, colours and patterns. One of the more recent is paper as a floor covering – it turns out to be both versatile and hard-wearing.

Crucial Trading, P O Box 11, Duke Place, Kidderminster, Worcestershire DY10 2JR

Tel: 01562 825200 **Fax:** 01562 825177

E-mail: crucial@dial.pipex.com

Price range: from £10 per sq. metre. Catalogue and individual samples free. Sample index box available at small charge.

Payment: cheque with order.

Postage & packing: from £15 for orders up to 12 sq. metres to £70 for over 100 sq. metres.

Delivery: allow 28 days.

Refunds: by arrangement.

Damask Like many firms in this book, Damask has its own shop where you can feel the goods before you buy (in New King's Road, London SW6). It sells beautiful bedding, quilts in white and traditional patterns like Provençal. Also, new for them, simple, stylish nightwear, amazingly sexy though in white cotton. I personally love their scented organdie bags full of petals and leaves. Put one in your lingerie drawer and come up smelling of roses.

Damask Furnishings & Finery Ltd, 7 Sulivan Enterprise Centre, Sulivan Road, London SW6 3DJ

Tel: 0171 731 3470 **Fax:** 0171 384 2358

Price range: £1.95 to £410. Catalogue £2.50, refundable on orders over £25.

Payment: cheque, major credit cards.

Postage & packing: £3 for orders under £100, £6 over £100. Overseas rates on application.

Delivery: usually within a week, but allow 28 days. Last Christmas orders 5 days in advance.

Refunds: yes, if returned within 7 days.

Specials: goods can be wrapped in tissue paper with ribbon.

David Mellor David Mellor is a top designer and silversmith and, even if some of the goods are not designed by him, they all reflect his sense of style and practicality. The knives, pans, chopping boards, even the measuring jugs, sieves and rolling pins, are as beautiful as they are useful. Most are traditional shapes but often in modern stainless steel with non-stick inners. Ranges of kitchen knives and cutlery are designed by him. The catalogue is simple and beautiful too.

David Mellor, 4 Sloane Square, London SW1W 8EE

Tel: 0171 730 4259 **Fax:** 0171 730 7240

Price range: 90p to £1,000. Catalogue £1.
Payment: cheque, major credit cards except Amex and Diners.
Postage & packing: from £3.50.
Delivery: allow 28 days. Last Christmas orders by 20 December.
Refunds: yes, if faulty or at manager's discretion.

Direct Import
Jolly Mediterranean pottery ideal for country cottages – plates of Italian animals and fruit, frosted carafes and wine jugs. Also, a series of French trays featuring wedding days, topiary and "La Main Verte" for gardeners.

Direct Import, Chipping Campden, Gloucestershire GL55 6PP
Tel: 01386 841923 **Fax:** 01386 841937
E-mail: blomefield@aol.com
Price range: £1.80 to £95. Send £1 in stamps for catalogue, refunded on first order.
Payment: cheque, major credit/debit cards.
Postage & packing: £3.95.
Delivery: usually within a week.
Refunds: yes, if returned within 30 days.

Divertimenti
No one interested in cooking could fail to find necessities and luxuries in this catalogue, a honed-down version of the lovely French-orientated London shop. It ranges from the sensible potato peeler which swivels for left-handers like me to classic American blenders and stylish Irish linen teatowels. Divertimenti was a pioneer in creating butcher's block tables for the ordinary kitchen and importing tough peasant crockery from the Mediterranean. Their green leaf dishes are made to a traditional French design while a set of plates, each with a pear progressively being eaten from whole to core, is unusual and jokey.

Divertimenti (Mail Order) Ltd, P O Box 6611, London SW15 2WG
Tel: 0181 246 4300 **Fax:** 0181 246 4330
Price range: £3.95 to £399.95. Catalogue free.
Payment: cheque, postal order, major credit cards.
Postage & packing: £3.95.
Delivery: allow 21 days.
Refunds: yes, if returned within 28 days.

MAIL ORDER MADE EASY

Dream Team Design Like many designers and makers, Annabella Adams ("with plenty of input from husband and children") began to create furniture for children because she couldn't find what she wanted in the shops. Her cupboards, benches, mirrors, beds and chairs deliberately have friendly faces and curves. There's a jolly snail whose shell is a shelf tidy, a dragon made into a book or video rack and a circus elephant painted on a closed cupboard plus a range of mirrors featuring fairies, soldiers or dalmatians. You can choose paint colours from a range of primaries and pastels. The furniture is perfect, too, for christening presents.

> **Dream Team Design**, Hunts Green House, Hunts Green, near Newbury, Berkshire RG20 8BY
> **Tel:** 01488 608807 **Fax:** 01488 608827
> **E-mail:** dreamteamdesign@btinternet.com
> **Website:** http://www.thecountrytimes.com
> **Price range:** £125 to £165. Catalogue free.
> **Payment:** cheque.
> **Postage & packing:** from £10.
> **Delivery:** allow 6 weeks.
> **Refunds:** yes, if damaged or faulty: notify the company within 3 days.
> **Specials:** designs can be personalised or painted to order.

Elizabeth Bradley Needlework is the perfect antidote to stress and is genuinely practised by tycoons, sewing away on Concorde, and a journalist colleague of mine who took out her canvas when others were holding the front page. Elizabeth Bradley's designs are inspired by the Victorians, when needlework was in its heyday, and use lots of charming nosegay flowers and favourite animals.

> **Elizabeth Bradley Designs Ltd**, 1 West End, Beaumaris, Anglesey, North Wales LL58 8BD
> **Tel:** 01248 811055 **Fax:** 01248 811118
> **E-mail:** ebd@elizabethbradley.co.uk
> **Price range:** £18 to £66. Catalogue £2 refundable with order.
> **Payment:** cheque, major credit/debit cards.
> **Postage & packing:** included.

HOUSE AND GARDEN

Delivery: allow 28 days. Last Christmas orders by 19 December.
Refunds: yes, if returned unused, in good condition, within 14 days.

England at Home

England at Home The firm started as a shop in Brighton and was deluged with requests for a mail order catalogue. This is the first, offering a small range of cult household objects from the Dualit toaster and blender to Sharkey clothes pegs and Guzzini's funky juicers and vacuums. Shop here for movers and shakers.

England at Home, 32 Ship Street, Brighton, East Sussex BN1 1AD
Tel: 01273 738270 **Fax:** 01273 723109
Price range: £3.50 to £350. Catalogue free
Payment: cheque, postal order, credit/debit cards.
Postage & packing: £3.95 per order.
Delivery: allow 28 days, however most items sent by return.
Refunds: yes.
Specials: gift-wrapping £1.50 per item. Customised wedding lists.

English Picnic Basket Company

English Picnic Basket Company Do you long for those blissful summer days when you can spread out a travelling rug on a hill or deserted sand-dune and get out the smart picnic box? This firm doesn't descend to cheapo fittings but uses china, crystal glasses and willow trays to recall the days when Toad was on the road. The six versions of picnic basket are for two or four people and there is a choice of four different china patterns. An ideal wedding present, too.

English Picnic Basket Company, Willow Bank, 11 Beech Road, Upwey, Weymouth, Dorset DT3 5NP
Tel/Fax: 01305 813450
Price range: £135 to £485. Catalogue free.
Payment: cheque, major credit/debit cards.
Postage & packing: £7 standard 3-day delivery, £10.99 next day delivery.
Delivery: allow 3 weeks. Last Christmas orders 7 December.
Refunds: yes, by arrangement.

MAIL ORDER MADE EASY

The English Stamp Company A large and jolly range of stamps which can be inked and used on paper, fabric, walls, furniture or any flat surface which will take the ink. The firm sells 30 differently coloured ink pads, from shocking pink to gold, 16 different colours of Mulberry paper imported from Thailand and made from the bark of the saa tree. Large size sheets make excellent wrapping paper. Stamps include animals, heraldic motifs, leaves and flowers plus a special range for Christmas.

> **The English Stamp Company**, Worth Matravers, Dorset BH19 3JP
> **Tel:** 01929 439117 **Fax:** 01929 439150
> **E-mail:** sales@englishstamp.com
> **Website:** http://www.englishstamp.com
> **Price range:** £1.75 to £50. Catalogue free.
> **Payment:** cheque, major credit/debit cards.
> **Postage & packing:** included in UK. Overseas rates on application.
> **Delivery:** generally within a few days.
> **Refunds:** yes, when faulty.
> **Specials:** custom-made stamps.

Eurolounge Behind this curious name hides a range of designs by top designer, Tom Dixon. Best known is his Jack light, shaped like the metal throwing jacks but in plastic, it is a floor light, stacking light, even a chair or table base. Other designs, like the Star light, can be hung or stood on tables or floors. All are bright coloured and some are luminous in the dark. Expect more from this catalogue soon.

> **Eurolounge**, 28 All Saints Road, London W11 1HG
> **Tel:** 0171 792 5499 **Fax:** 0171 792 5488
> **E-mail:** t-dixon@dircon.co.uk
> **Website:** http://www.british-design.com/tomdixon
> **Price range:** £90 to £200. Catalogue free.
> **Payment:** cheque, Switch, Mastercard, Visa, Amex.
> **Postage & packing:** £10 in UK.
> **Delivery:** allow 28 days. Last Christmas orders 6 weeks before required delivery date.

HOUSE AND GARDEN

Refunds: by arrangement.
Specials: express delivery service at additional cost.

Farmer John Quilts
In Wales, teased wool rather than feathers is traditionally used for quilts and duvets. It is just as light, good for asthmatics and cheaper to produce. Sally Judd makes everything by hand on her farm using hand-washed wool. There are cot duvets for babies and chair duvets for the old, covered in cotton prints or, by arrangement, in your own fabric.

Farmer John Quilts, Gaer Farm, Cwmyoy, Abergavenny, Monmouthshire NP7 7NE
Tel: 01873 890345
Price range: £47 to £148. Catalogue free.
Payment: cheque.
Postage & packing: £3 for small, £6.50 for large.
Delivery: allow 2-3 weeks. Last Christmas orders by 5 December as supply is limited.
Refunds: yes, if returned unused within 10 days.

A Feast of Frames
In general, the firms sells frames for photographs, rather than works of art. Most are quite small and range from the traditional, in enamel and gilt to bevelled glass or wood with little sports motifs attached (football, riding boots, tennis racquet etc). The advantage of buying from them, however, is that you can pick your favourite frame and buy a range of sizes so that the collection of favourite snaps on the windowsill, desk or piano will all match.

A Feast of Frames, P O Box 691, Stalham, Norwich NR12 9FG
Tel/Fax: 01692 650220
Price range: £4.50 to £99. Catalogue free.
Payment: cheque, Mastercard, Access, Visa.
Postage & packing: £2 for orders up to £19.99, £3.50 to £95, free thereafter. Overseas at cost.
Delivery: allow 28 days, but phone in an emergency and they'll try to help.
Refunds: yes, if returned within 10 days.
Specials: gift-wrapping £1.50 per parcel.

Fired Earth This catalogue will give your floors a real treat – anything from Roman mosaics to brilliant tribal rugs. But they specialise particularly in floors of slate, limestone, French and Italian terracottas and painted wall tiles. The company is now extending into fabrics – mostly traditional country ones to suit the floors – and has joined up with the Victoria & Albert Museum to create a wildly fashionable range of historic paints. As well as the usual stones, beiges and Pompeian reds, this range has a bright section of colours taken from Pugin and William Morris. I love the shocking Bengal Rose and Mediterranean Periwinkle blue along with Morris's Half Indigo and rusty Madder Red.

Fired Earth plc, Twyford Mill, Oxford Road, Adderbury, Oxfordshire OX17 3HP

Tel: 01295 812088. for catalogue ring: 01295 814300. Export line: 44 1295 814316 **Fax:** 01295 810832

E-mail: enquiries@firedearth.com

Export E-mail: export@firedearth.com

Price range: from £6.50 for a side plate to £1299 for a rug. Tiles from £18.94 + VAT per sq. metre. Catalogue free.

Payment: cheque, major credit cards.

Packing and delivery charges: from £2.50 to £76 in most parts of UK.

Delivery: allow 10 working days. 48-hour delivery quoted on request.

Refunds: by arrangement.

Friars Goose The firm sources its own individual pieces from Spain and Portugal and has recently added a range of sundials to the frost-proof house number tiles it has specialised in. The dials are made up of a generously-sized ceramic tiles painted with a cheerful sun face and, variously, crowing cocks, hot-air balloons or rural scenes. They come with a brass pointer and full instructions for mounting.

Friars Goose Ltd, Unit 3, Pound Barton, Sutton Veny, Warminster, Wiltshire BA12 7BT

Tel: 01985 840024 **Fax:** 01985 840991

Price range: £1.95 to £15.95. Catalogue free.

Payment: cheque.

HOUSE AND GARDEN

Postage & packing: included.
Delivery: allow 28 days. Last Christmas orders by 15 December.
Refunds: yes.

Glazebrook & Co

Glazebrook has made its mission the recreation of 17th and 18th century cutlery patterns. These are invariably comfortable to handle and simple to eat with, unlike modern designs which seem to delight in forks with short teeth and spoons with no bowls. The firm sells the early rat-tail pattern in a matt pewter-like finish along with old English patterns in a more usual mirror finish. There are pistol-grip knives and faux ivory handled knives with both square and rounded ends.

Glazebrook & Co, P O Box 1563, London SW6 3XD
Tel: 0171 731 7135 **Fax:** 0171 371 5434
Price range: £3.25 to £8.80. Catalogue free.
Payment: cheque, Mastercard, Access, Visa.
Postage & packing: included.
Delivery: 2-3 weeks. Last Christmas orders 3 weeks in advance.
Refunds: yes.
Specials: free sample service, wedding lists, engraving.

Glorafilia

Tapestry making is extremely popular with both men (who find it relief from stress) and women to whom it comes naturally. This company regularly produces kits which have a fashionable edge – toile de Jouy, bright designs from oriental rugs, lots of animal prints and pictures. It's surprising how such a traditional technique, transferred to leopard or giraffe skins, will look good in the most modern interior.

Glorafilia, The Old Mill House, The Ridgeway, Mill Hill Village, London NW7 4EB
Tel: 0181 906 0212 **Fax:** 0181 959 6253
E-mail: mail@glorafilia.com
Price range: £6.50 to £295. Catalogue £2.
Payment: cheque, postal order, Mastercard, Visa, Amex.
Postage & packing: £2.50 for orders up to £75, £5 to £100, free thereafter. See catalogue for overseas rates.
Delivery: allow 28 days. Hand-painted specials may take longer.

Refunds: yes, if returned unused within 7 days, except special designs.
Specials: special commissions – many needlepoint designs can be adapted.

Glover & Smith
A new pair of handles can make a huge difference to a rundown chest of drawers and these handles are wild: pewter knotty twigs, oak leaves hand-gilded and a seashore range of shells, ammonites and seahorses. Similar natural forms are used for hooks and tie backs and corkscrews. Don't, however, be tempted to change the handles on antiques. It's a crime.

Glover & Smith, Makers' Cottage, 14 London Road, Overton, near Basingstoke, Hampshire RG25 3NP
Tel/Fax: 01256 773012
Price range: £9.99 to £49.99. Catalogue free.
Payment: cheque, major credit cards.
Postage & packing: £1.50 to £3 in UK.
Delivery: allow 28 days. Last Christmas orders by 14 December, 7 December for hand-gilded work.
Refunds: yes, if returned within 28 days.

Grenadier Firelighters
Say goodbye to miserable smouldering fires, bad-tempered Agas which refuse to light or bonfires which sulk. The Grenadier is an electric gadget which directs a blast of hot air at the kindling and then, when it's alight, can be turned simply to fan the flames. Bad tempers reduced all round.

Grenadier Firelighters Ltd, Unit 3c, Barrowmore Enterprise Estate, Village Road, Great Barrow, Chester CH3 7JS
Tel: 01829 741649. **Fax:** 01829 741659
Price: £89.95. Leaflet free.
Payment: cheque, postal order, Mastercard, Visa, Eurocard, Switch, Delta.
Postage & packing: £9.00.
Delivery: within 14 days.
Refunds: by arrangement.

HOUSE AND GARDEN

The Handmade Wooden Tray Company Butler's trays are useful to ordinary mortals too, the idea being that the hefty wooden tray can be set on its own legs to make a table. The company makes tables at coffee height and, more useful, at full height, as well as a laptop tray with its own cushion – very useful indeed.

> **The Handmade Wooden Tray Company**, Teignbridge Business Centre, Cavalier Road, Heathfield, Newton Abbot, Devon TQ12 6TZ
>
> **Tel:** 01364 621229 **Fax:** 01364 621370
>
> **Price range:** £24.99 to £325. Catalogue free.
>
> **Payment:** cheque, major credit cards.
>
> **Postage & packing:** included.
>
> **Delivery:** allow 28 days.
>
> **Refunds:** yes.

The Holding Company Dawna Walter started the firm when she found it impossible to buy the storage tidies that were commonplace in America. She found such a niche in the market that she plans to expand all over Britain. Her best ideas are all in the mail order catalogue from the Kenyan sisal baskets in four sizes and 14 colours to drawer and shoe tidies, filing boxes and systems for using the space you never knew you had. She's passionate about it – and practises what she preaches.

> **The Holding Company Mail Order**, Burlington House, 184 New Kings Road, London SW6 4NF
>
> **Tel:** 0171 610 9160 **Fax:** 0171 610 9166
>
> **Website:** http://www.theholdingcompany.co.uk
>
> **Price range:** £1.75 to £341.95. Catalogue free.
>
> **Payment:** cheque, postal order, major credit/debit cards.
>
> **Postage & packing:** £3.50 for orders up to £250, free thereafter in UK. Overseas rates on application.
>
> **Delivery:** allow 5 working days. Last Christmas orders by 16 December, but 24-hour service available for extra charge.
>
> **Refunds:** yes, if returned within 14 days with original packaging intact.

House I once had the luck to watch the Suffield family, which runs this catalogue and a marvellous shop in Dorset,

116 MAIL ORDER MADE EASY

prepare for Christmas. It was as though the stylish glossies had come to life. Their Moroccan teaglasses regularly sell out and their various baskets walk off the page. The point is that the extended family, from grandparents to tiny children, use themselves what they sell. If you want to share in their cleverness and eye for design, House offers a range for Christmas and all the year.

House, 42 Salisbury Street, Blandford, Dorset DT11 7PR
Tel: 01258 454884 **Fax:** 01258 454225
Price range: £1.95 to £95. Catalogue free.
Payment: cheque, Mastercard, Visa.
Postage & packing: £3.50.
Delivery: allow 28 days. Fast delivery service available. Last Christmas orders 16 December.
Refunds: yes.
Specials: gift-wrapping.

The House Nameplate Company

While I'm not too keen on the flowery ceramic name plates that they offer and absolutely hate the butterflies intended to be stuck on outdoor walls, the company's restrained slate nameplates are engraved with clear, classical type and the range of steel continental letterboxes are extremely useful in the country. They all come with a pair of keys and will save endless hassle with postie.

The House Nameplate Company, Unit 16, Vauxhall Industrial Estate, Ruabon, Wrexham, Clwyd LL14 6ES
Tel: 01978 822772 **Fax:** 01978 810201
Price range: £14 to £99. Catalogue free.
Payment: cheque, major credit cards.
Postage & packing: included in UK.
Delivery: allow 28 days. Last Christmas orders beginning December.
Refunds: yes.

If Only...

I have picked this firm out, from a weirdly mixed catalogue (parasols, sculpture, porcelain figures, teddy bears in pinstripes) for its huge range of glass flowers in vases which,

HOUSE AND GARDEN

though they don't photograph well, are not far off Fabergé pieces. Go for the less gaudy ones like lily of the valley, wood garlic and celandine.

If Only... Ltd, Glanrafon, Rhoshirwaun, Pwllheli, Gwynedd LL53 8LF
Tel: 01758 760600 **Fax:** 07070 600760
Website: http://www.caernarfon.co.uk/ifonly
Price range: £17.95 to £400. Catalogue free.
Payment: cheque, major credit/debit cards.
Postage & packing: £3.95 for orders up to £50, £6.95 for orders up to £100, free for orders over £100.
Delivery: most items despatched within 5 working days, otherwise as stated in the catalogue. Last Christmas orders by 14 December.
Refunds: yes.

The India Shop Indian design first came to Britain in the 17th century and the popularity of its paisleys and chintzes has endured. This company sells cushions with typical tree of life, paisley and mughal animal patterns, woven check throws and geometric wool rugs. There is also hand-made sheesham wood furniture and a few presents like puppets, writing paper with incorporated flower petals, bags and scarves.

The India Shop, 5 Hilliers Yard, Marlborough, Wiltshire SN8 1NB
Tel: 01672 851155 **Fax:** 01380 728118
Price range: £2.95 to £305. Catalogue free.
Payment: cheque, Mastercard, Visa.
Postage & packing: included.
Delivery: normally despatched within 5 working days. Next day delivery by courier available at cost. Last Christmas orders by 19 December.
Refunds: yes, if returned within 7 days.

Inthebag Really organised people have matching bags to suit everything in their wardrobes and suitcases. You, too, can get tidy with this firm which makes bags for any outfit from an evening dress to a gent's suit along with bags for shoes, washing equipment and "occasional" bags for odds and ends. Also they have jewellery rolls, pads for shoes and padded hangers. The bags are in eight cotton furnishing fabrics such as Florentine and red and yellow checked Surat. There's also a wedding set of bags in gold or cream fabric.

Inthebag, 3 Lydgate Road, Shepley, Huddersfield, West Yorkshire HD8 8DZ
Tel/Fax: 01484 603641
Price range: £8.50 to £99. Leaflet free.
Payment: cheque, major credit cards.
Postage & packing: £2.50 for orders up to £25, £3.75 for orders up to £50, £5.75 thereafter.
Delivery: allow 28 days.
Refunds: yes, if returned within 14 days.

The Iron Bed Company The idea of buying beds through the post was such a success that the company has added some funky modern ones ("the last word in industrial chic"), a classic Shaker style and a chrome and suede modernist version to the traditional iron beds. There are also mattresses, a small range of bed linen and a few accessories.

The Iron Bed Company, Terminus Road, Chichester, West Sussex PO19 2ZZ
Tel: 01243 778999 **Fax:** 01243 778123

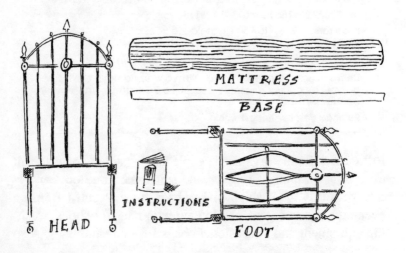

HOUSE AND GARDEN

E-mail: info@ironbed.co.uk
Website: http://www.ironbed.co.uk
Price range: headboards/bedsteads £99 to £699, accessories from £7.49.
Payment: cheque, major credit/debit cards.
Postage & packing: £25 in mainland UK, timed delivery £65. Accessories £3.95.
Delivery: within 28 days. Accessories allow 3 working days.
Refunds: yes.

Joanna's Good range of easily packed presents (so important if you've wrestled with lampshades in the post). There are fine leather-covered albums and address books, gingham notice-boards and keyboards, walnut photo frames and little scented candles and soapdishes.

Joanna's, 20 Upper Wimpole Street, London W1M 7TA
Tel/Fax: 0171 289 1149
Price range: £5 to £80. Catalogue free.
Payment: cheque.
Postage & packing: £3.50 to £5.50.
Delivery: by post or Parcel Force. Allow 28 days. Last Christmas orders by about 15 December.
Refunds: yes, if returned in perfect condition within 7 days.
Specials: gift-wrapping, gold embossing and engraving on certain items. Prices on application.

Kantara Francis Suttill is a furniture designer who took to making children's furniture because he thought he could do better. He does a very nice set of wall-mounted shelves designed like a Palladian house along with a neat set based on bi- and tri-planes. New this time round is a ship shelf unit with either a steam funnel or mast.

Kantara, Bishopswood Leigh, Ross-on-Wye, Hereford HR9 5QX
Tel/Fax: 01594 860328
Price range: £24 to £99. Leaflet free.
Payment: cheque with order.
Postage & packing: £4 to £8 – see leaflet for details.
Delivery: normally within 10 days.
Refunds: no, but goods replaced if damaged in transit.

MAIL ORDER MADE EASY

Katie Eastaugh Ceramics This potter produces work in a subtle range of colours far removed from many of today's gaudy pots. She uses slip clay, coloured by oxides, to produce her free-flowing patterns, which are generally of flowers in the Chinese manner. The slip clay gives these patterns a translucency and depth which transfer or painted work cannot copy. She works to commission and needs several weeks to fulfil an order, so be warned.

Katie Eastaugh Ceramics, Willow Cottage, Kingsland, Leominster, Herefordshire HR6 9RU
Tel/Fax: 01568 708173
Price range: £16 to £170. No catalogue, price list on application.
Payment: cheque.
Postage & packing: varies according to size of order.
Delivery: allow 6 weeks.
Refunds: no.
Specials: gift-wrapping, dating of work.

Kirker Greer Like many interesting mail order firms, this one started at the kitchen table but now sells candles and their accessories, room scents and decorations from a custom-built factory. The emphasis is on elegance and quality and everything is beautifully packaged. Even bees are brought into the business – the brochure claims that the insects fly the equivalent of three times round the world to collect half a kilo of honey and that it takes 10 kilos of honey to produce one of beeswax. And then we burn it!

Kirker Greer, Belvedere Road, Burnham-on-Crouch, Essex CM0 8AJ
Tel: 01621 784647 **Fax:** 01621 785546
Price range: £1 to £50. Catalogue free.
Payment: cheque, Access, Visa.
Postage & packing: £2.95.
Delivery: 2-3 weeks. Last Christmas orders by beginning December.
Refunds: by arrangement.
Specials: gift-wrapping.

HOUSE AND GARDEN

Kynes Feather Bed Company If you've ever slept on a feather mattress (not a duvet but feathers under you) you'll know how amazingly soft and comfortable it can be. Bridgette Kynes-Hughes makes feather mattresses of duck feather in cotton cambric along with pillows and bolsters in a softer feather. She makes to order and has been commissioned to create mattresses for circular beds and "coffin-shaped" beds on yachts. Because of this, delivery times vary greatly and it's best to arrange a date with her.

Kynes Feather Bed Company, Gresham House, 63 Streetsbrook Road, Solihull, West Midlands B90 3PD

Tel/Fax: 0121 680 7366 or ring 07000 ALL BEDDING

Price range: £24.39 to £639.24. Catalogue free.

Payment: cheque.

Postage & packing: from £4.50 for a pillow to £16.15 for a 6 ft mattress. Free delivery to the same address on one mattress for an order of two and on two mattresses for an order of three

Delivery: allow 28 days. Christmas orders should be placed in September or October if possible.

Refunds: by arrangement.

Specials: Monogrammed sheets and pillow cases in generous sizes should also be available soon.

Lakeland This is a no-nonsense kitchen supply company which started out selling plastic storage boxes and now offers an excellent and comprehensive range of kitchenware and appliances. They also put out a special Christmas catalogue which includes tablecloths, candles, foods such as marzipan fruits from France and marrons glacés plus lots of pretty wrapping papers and ribbons. The service is notably friendly.

Lakeland, Alexandra Buildings, Windermere, Cumbria LA23 1BQ

Tel: 01539 488100 **Fax:** 01539 488300

Price range: £3 to £100. Catalogue free.

Payment: cheque, postal order, major credit/debit cards.

Postage & packing: £2.95 for orders up to £35, free thereafter. Next day delivery add £5.

Delivery: see catalogue. Last Christmas orders by mid December.

Refunds: yes.

Louise Bradley

Louise Bradley A mail order range based on this designer's Walton Street shop which is very ritzy. How about a pair of silver plated mussel shells, with gold interiors for eating the molluscs or a life-size pewter lobster? You can buy caviar bowls and boards, salt and peppers in the shape of grouse, fruit or fish.

Louise Bradley, 15 Walton Street, London SW3 2HX

Tel: 0171 589 1442 **Fax:** 0171 589 2009

E-mail: enquiries@louise-bradley.demon.co.uk

Price range: £10 to £1,285. Catalogue free.

Payment: major credit/debit cards.

Postage & packing: on application.

Delivery: different services available in UK depending on urgency. Overseas delivery by express courier. Last Christmas orders 2 weeks in advance, but they will do their best to accommodate last minute orders.

Refunds: by arrangement. They will do everything possible to satisfy customers.

Specials: free gift-wrapping service. Personalised engraving available.

Marks & Spencer

Marks & Spencer The empire continues to grow. The home catalogue is the biggest ever and will probably completely furnish your house. The style is middle of the road but sensible and, of course, good quality. There's a wedding list service (though you don't have to marry to buy) along with year-round direct delivery for flowers and wine. The flowers are beautifully chosen for all celebrations and there are hampers and trees in the Christmas run-up.

Marks & Spencer Home Delivery Service, Freepost, P O Box 288, Warrington, Cheshire WA1 2BR

Tel: 0345 902902 **Fax:** 0345 904904

Price range: £3 to £1899 Catalogue £3.

Payment: cheque, M&S Chargecard, Delta, Switch. Two years interest free credit on orders of £399 or more.

Postage & packing: £3.50 per order. Free for orders of £200 or more.

Delivery: 4 days, excluding furniture and made-to-measure items.

Refunds: yes.

Specials: gift-wrapping £3, free swatches, wedding list service.

HOUSE AND GARDEN

McCord Though the catalogue falls out of every magazine and is printed on poor paper, don't imagine that it's commonplace. The goods are up-to-the-minute household stars, lots of wickerwork, baskets, woven chairs; there's good-looking iron work, multi-drawered and painted storage chests and I love the transparent bathroom scales. From them you can get smart toasters, vacuum cleaners and butchers' block trolleys.

McCord, Blagrove, Swindon, Wiltshire SN38 4NN
Tel: 0990 535455 **Fax:** 01793 487002
Website: http://www.mccord.uk.com
Price range: £3.99 to £899. Catalogue free.
Payment: cheque, postal order, major credit/debit cards.
Postage & packing: £2.95, free for orders over £75.
Delivery: normally despatched within 10 days, but allow 28.
Refunds: yes, except for made-to-order furniture unless faulty.
Specials: free fabric swatch service.

Melin Tregwynt In an idyllic valley in one of the prettiest parts of Wales, the Griffiths family produce magical blankets, rugs and throws from an old stone mill. Their range is ever-growing but you can find woollens in subtle greys and navys to contrast with others of brilliant scarlet and orange. There are, also, soft pink and blue versions ideal for children and the traditional Welsh blankets in tapestry patterns.

Melin Tregwynt, Tregwynt Mill, Castle Morris, Haverfordwest, Pembrokeshire, Dyfed SA62 5UX
Tel: 01348 891644 **Fax:** 01348 891694
Price range: £17 to £150. Catalogue free.
Payment: cheque, Access, Visa, Amex.
Postage & packing: £2.75 for orders up to £30, £3.50 to £55, £6 thereafter.
Delivery: normally despatched within 7 days, but allow 28. Last Christmas orders by 16 December, or later with £6.50 supplement.
Refunds: yes.

Minh Mang East meets West fashion is very much in the air and this firm, delighted by the fabrics it saw in Vietnam and

Cambodia, has made some delicious, brilliant-coloured notebooks, folders, frames covered in patterned silk. There are, too, silk bags in a choice of 24 colours and ikat patterns. New this year are embroidered bags with bright lacquered handles, ones in knitted silk and purses and keyrings to match existing lines. Perfect for anything from stocking fillers to thank-you presents for all generations.

Minh Mang Ltd, 182 Battersea Park Road, London SW11 4ND
Tel: 0171 498 3233 **Fax:** 0171 498 3353
Price range: £5 to £126. Catalogue free
Payment: cheque.
Postage & packing: included in UK.
Delivery: allow 14 days unless out of stock. Last Christmas posting 19 December.
Refunds: yes if faulty, otherwise goods can be exchanged: notify the company within 3 days.

Morgan Bellows Why is it so hard to find bellows when they are so useful? These are the Rolls Royce of bellows with brass nozzles so thin that a powerful blast makes smouldering logs glow white hot. They're just as good with recalcitrant coal. Short or long handled, they come plain with green, brown or burgundy leather and brass studs, or painted navy, dark green or black with a foliage border. They can be painted with initials or a crest. There are also candlesticks, wine coasters, bookends and cachepots – all ideal for personalising.

Morgan Bellows, Knockhill, Lockerbie, Dumfriesshire DG11 1AW
Tel: 01576 300232 **Fax:** 01576 300818
Price range: £16 to £80. Leaflet free.
Payment: cheque, major credit cards.
Postage & packing: £3 to £6, free for orders over £200.
Delivery: allow 28 days. Ring if urgent.
Refunds: yes, if returned within 21 days.
Specials: gift-wrapping £1.50 per item. Personalisation.

Mulberry Hall In a half-timbered building dating from 1434 in one of York's most beautiful streets, the firm has 14 separate

HOUSE AND GARDEN

showrooms to display the best porcelain and glass they can find in Europe. Names like Herend, Meissen, Lalique, Royal Copenhagen, Wedgwood, Spode and Ginori are on their books. The mail order catalogue is comprehensive, perfect for wedding presents, christenings or anniversaries while the Halcyon Days enamels make charming thank-you presents. A new venture is the Dining Room Warehouse, with names like Alessi, Emma Bridgwater and Designers Guild (among many others) and these, too, can be sent by post.

Mulberry Hall, Stonegate, York YO1 8ZW
Tel: 01904 620736 **Fax:** 01904 620251
E-mail: mailorder@mulberryhall.co.uk
Website: http://www.mulberryhall.co.uk
Price range: £5.95 to £1,995. Catalogue free.
Payment: cheque, major credit/debit cards.
Postage & packing: 10% of order value to a maximum of £7.50 for orders under £250, free thereafter.
Delivery: despatched within 48 hours, 24-hour delivery in mainland UK and international delivery by Fastrack.
Refunds: replacement if notified immediately about loss or breakage.
Specials: gift-wrapping free of charge, gift vouchers.

The Natural Fabric Company A lovely range of classic fabrics for curtains, cushions, upholstery and tablecloths (you could probably make them into clothes, too). There are plain damasks and chintzes (over 50 plain colours), checked denim, gingham and chambray, striped ticking, pretty toiles and natural linens and sheers. The firm will send swatches.

The Natural Fabric Company, Wessex Place, 127 High Street, Hungerford, Berkshire RG17 0DL
Tel: 01488 684002 **Fax:** 01488 686455
Price range: £1.99 to £15 per metre. Catalogue £3.
Payment: cheque, Visa, Switch.
Postage & packing: £3 orders up to £15, £6 orders over £15.
Delivery: allow 14 days. Last Christmas orders 1 December.
Refunds: by arrangement.

The Nether Wallop Trading Company

The Nether Wallop Trading Company Jane Vere-Hodge designs many of the objects in her catalogue and has them made locally. So here are ideas to be found nowhere else. There's a gadget to make plant pots from old newspaper, wooden door stops, trivets and dibblers and beech chopping boards. Her latest idea, the Card Curve, is a curved piece of wood which holds cards, invitations, recipes, memos upright in your home or office.

The Nether Wallop Trading Company, Maltings, Nether Wallop, Hampshire SO20 8EW

Tel/Fax: 01264 781734

Price range: £3 to £30. Catalogue free.

Payment: cheque, postal order, major credit cards.

Postage & packing: £1.50 for orders under £10, £3 for orders £10-£20, £4 thereafter.

Delivery: allow 28 days. Last Christmas orders by 20 December.

Refunds: yes.

Newell Glass

Newell Glass Glass blowing has recently had a revival and smart modern shapes are highly sought after. Newell's bowls, jugs and vases are all handmade and come in a range of bright clear or sandblasted glass. Their small juglets, for instance, are in 10 colours, from rose pink to pewter grey while the Spirit vases, softly angled on round bases, look just like friendly phantoms. There are palely coloured plates, winged candle holders and tall clear vases just waiting for a big bunch of tulips. They will do commissions, too.

Newell Glass Glassworks (London) Ltd, 12 Victoria Terrace, London N4 4DA

Tel: 0171 272 9341 **Fax:** 0171 281 9252

Price range: approx £10 to £100. Catalogue free.

Payment: cheque.

Postage & packing: calculated for each order.

Delivery: allow 3 weeks.

Refunds: yes if damaged.

Specials: goods can be monogrammed or personalised.

HOUSE AND GARDEN

Nice Irma's Since the heady days of the 60s, Nice Irma's has been selling the relaxed life style. Moving with the times, there are now lots of soft throws, bright kilim rugs, ironwork handles and colourful pottery. The bright door handles and glass pulls are particularly luscious.

> **Nice Irma's by Post**, Unit 2, Finchley Industrial Centre, 879 High Road, London N12 8QA
> **Tel:** 0800 328 1867/0181 343 9766 **Fax:** 0181 343 9590
> **Price range:** £1.50 to £127.30. Catalogue free.
> **Payment:** cheque, postal order, major credit cards.
> **Postage & packing:** £3.95. Overseas rates on application.
> **Delivery:** normally within 14 days, but allow 28.
> **Refunds:** yes, if returned unused within 14 days.

Nisbets Chefs Choice I can't open this catalogue without wanting something to bits but then I love cooking and cookware. Not necessarily pieces which make life easier but machines which extend what I can do. I really want the huge Magimix which chips, juliennes, presses oranges and lemons; or the giant Waring blender which whips soups to smoothness. I've almost convinced myself that I would enjoy a chef's white cotton jacket and checky trousers, so cool and relaxed over the stove, and I've always wanted to try those Japanese knives in funny shapes.

> **Nisbets Chefs Choice**, 1110b Aztec West, Bristol BS12 4HR
> **Tel:** 01454 855655 **Fax:** 01454 855565
> **E-mail:** nisbets@dial.pipex.com
> **Price range:** £1 to £250. Catalogue free.
> **Payment:** cheque, postal order, major credit/debit cards.
> **Postage & packing:** £2.95 for orders up to £30, free thereafter.
> **Delivery:** within 2 or 3 working days. Last Christmas orders by 23 December.
> **Refunds:** yes, if returned within 30 days.

Nordic Design This company is so new that I can only guess what it will be selling. There will be, says Nikki Bakewell (who decided to set up the company after finding she was constantly travelling to Denmark for her presents) wooden and nursery toys, decorations, mobiles and objects for the home. She also plans a special Christmas supplement with baubles for the tree and your home.

Nordic Design Ltd, Birchwood House, Cowesfield Green, Whiteparish, Wiltshire SP5 2QS

Tel: 01794 884294 **Fax:** 01794 884267

Price range: £2 to £25. Catalogue free.

Payment: cheque, postal order, major credit/debit cards.

Postage & packing: £2.50 to £3.50, free for orders over £50.

Delivery: allow 28 days, but probably less. Last Christmas orders by end November.

Refunds: yes, if returned within 10 days.

Nordic Style The simple furniture, fabric and accessories from homes all over Scandinavia is still very much in vogue as it has been for a decade. Probably, like English 18th century ware, it is here to stay. The firm, run by Scandinavians, imports delightful pieces from the north.

Nordic Style, 109 Lots Road, London SW10 0RN

Tel: 0171 581 8674 **Fax:** 0171 937 6033

Price range: £4.75 to £3,900. Send large sae for brochure.

Payment: cheque, major credit cards.

Postage & packing: quoted with order.

Delivery: 3-6 weeks.

Refunds: credit note only.

Ocean There was a point last Christmas when virtually every list of present ideas included one from the Ocean catalogue. I can see why – it's stuffed with sensible ideas which are brilliantly designed. There's a coffee set in tiger and giraffe skin patterns, vases hollowed from large stones or wall-mounted test-tubes; plant pots turn up in coloured glass or aluminium and boxes and bins in re-cycled leather. There's even a loo-brush like a cactus. Everything here screams designer chic.

Ocean Home Shopping Ltd, 5 Pensbury Street, London SW8 4TL

Tel: 0171 501 2500 **Fax:** 0171 498 8898

HOUSE AND GARDEN

Website: http://www.oceancatalogue.co.uk
Price range: £2.95 to £495. Catalogue free.
Payment: cheque, postal order, major credit/debit cards.
Postage & packing: £3.95, free for orders over £100. Overseas charges vary according to weight and distance.
Delivery: by return. Last Christmas orders 23 December.
Refunds: yes, if returned within 14 days.
Specials: gift-wrapping £3.95, wedding list service.

Papers and Paints

Patrick Baty was selling historically-based paints long before the fad hit the high street. He believes he has the largest selection of paint colours in Europe and will also match colours you send him.

Papers and Paints, 4 Park Walk, London SW10 0AD
Tel: 0171 352 8626 **Fax:** 0171 352 1017
Price range: 15p to £135. Catalogue hand painted: Historical Colour Range £9.40, Traditional Colour Range £7.52, Off White Colour Range £3.
Payment: cheque, banker's draft, Mastercard, Visa, Switch.
Postage & packing: depends on weight.
Delivery: by Amtrak normally by return.
Refunds: yes, if returned in original condition within 7 days, except for mixed paints.

Penkridge Ceramics

Lorraine Taylor and Nicky Smart make the most extraordinarily life-like fruit and vegetables in semi-porcelain. If they didn't feel harder and heavier than the real thing, people would be constantly and painfully biting into their Cox's apples and Conference pears. Their gourds and pumpkins are wonderfully knobbly and their conkers perfection.

Penkridge Ceramics. Argent Works, Bott Lane, Walsall, West Midlands WS1 2JJ
Tel: 01922 625181 **Fax:** 01922 722449
Price range: £8.50 to £250. Price list and postcards free.
Payment: cheque.
Postage & packing: from £3.50, included for orders over £100.
Delivery: 4 to 8 weeks.
Refunds: no, unless damaged in transit.

Specials: overnight delivery subject to availability, plus surcharge.

The Period House Group

A firm which makes beautiful traditional nails, hinges and hasps in black iron, designed for traditional country cottages. They have lovely names: cranked strap hinge, pintle hinge, fish-tail bolt and monkey tail window catch. Even the nails are called rosehead!

The Period House Group, Fold Court, Buttercrambe, York YO4 1AU
Tel/Fax: 01653 658554. Mobile 0585 878383
Price range: from £2.75.
Payment: cheque, postal order, major credit cards.
Postage & packing: £4.75 for orders under £50, £6 thereafter. Guaranteed next day delivery £12.
Delivery: by return if in stock.
Refunds: yes, if notified within 48 hours, except bespoke items.

Pier Direct

With 15 shops all over Britain and more on the way, the firm sells furniture, textiles, pots and accessories for the home at the cutting edge of design. If you want to copy the glossy mags, this is one catalogue for you. It's not a bad idea, if you are after large pieces, to browse in the shop and then buy from the catalogue.

Pier Direct, 91-95 King's Road, Chelsea, London SW3
Tel: 0171 814 5004
Price range: £1.50 to £695. Catalogue free.
Payment: major credit cards.
Postage & packing: call handlers will quote for individual items.
Delivery: within 14 days.
Refunds: yes, if returned in perfect condition within 28 days.

Plainfeather

Don't ask me how Fiona Goble and Samantha Stas arrived at this name, since they sell a range of wall-hangings, cot covers, cushions, bags and totes for young children. They decorate them all with cheerful motifs of fishes, bugs, daisies and birds. The whole has a slightly Shaker, American pioneer feeling.

HOUSE AND GARDEN

Plainfeather, 16 Park Lane, Harefield, Middlesex UB9 6BJ
Tel/Fax: 01923 721424
Price range: £19 to £225. Catalogue free.
Payment: cheque, Mastercard, Visa, Delta, Switch.
Postage & packing: £3 in UK, £4.50 in Europe, elsewhere on application.
Delivery: allow 21 days.
Refunds: yes, if returned within 14 days.
Specials: throws can be personalised with names and dates from £6.

Prickly Pear French to its fingertips, this range has charming ideas in Provençal fabrics – wash and laundry bags, totes and baskets, wonderful espadrilles, aprons and oven gloves. There's bright painted furniture and a folding stool with a rush seat.

Prickly Pear Trading, Suite C, Cliffe Business Centre, Rusbridge Lane, Lewes, East Sussex BN7 2XX
Tel: 01273 472728 **Fax:** 01273 472729
Price range: £3.50 to £225. Catalogue free.
Payment: cheque, Mastercard, Visa.
Postage & packing: £2.50.
Delivery: 7-21 days.
Refunds: yes.

Robert Smith Fine Hand-Made Pepper Mills If you've had the annoyance of using a duff peppermill which produces nothing but fine dust you'll appreciate, as I do, Robert Smith's range of beautiful mills in veined or stained wood and all with the brilliant Peugeot mill mechanism (yes, they also make cars but that's more recently). Robert also has mills for salt, nutmeg and chillies. Better still, his mills have an indefinite guarantee and he will repair anything that goes wrong without charge.

Robert Smith, 1 Homeleigh, Whempstead, near Ware, Hertfordshire SG12 0PL
Tel/Fax: 01920 830478
Price range: £15 to £150. Leaflet free.
Payment: cheque.
Postage & packing: approx. £2.50.

Delivery: special delivery at extra cost. Last Christmas orders up to last first class posting date.

Refunds: yes

Robert Welch

The silversmith has been creating beautiful modern cutlery, table ware and other metal pieces for 40 years and is still coming up with new designs. Recently there has been cutlery with ammonite ends to the handles and Seadrift, a traditional range with a twist. There are table settings in this (going down a storm, says his daughter, Alice) and some wavy, organic candlesticks. The range includes iron standard lamps, nut crackers, corkscrews and some wicked-looking poultry shears.

Robert Welch Studio, Lower High Street, Chipping Campden, Gloucestershire GL55 6DY

Tel: 01386 840522 **Fax:** 01386 841111

E-mail: welch@robertwelch.demon.co.uk

Website: http://www.welch.co.uk

Price range: £1.50 to £600. Catalogue free.

Payment: cheque, major credit cards.

Postage & packing: £1.50 for small items, £3.95 large.

Delivery: normally despatched within 48 hours. Last Christmas orders by 18 December.

Refunds: yes.

Sarah Broadhead-Riall

Sarah's glass pieces are worked in two stages to laminate and trap colours between layers of glass. The results are individually numbered objects like bowls, coasters, clocks and vases which are coloured with shifting and abstract forms. The coasters are treated so they don't transfer heat and are patterned with seahorses, dolphins, Chinese calligraphy and, for Christmas, holly and candles.

Sarah Broadhead-Riall, 36 Complins, Holybourne, Alton, Hampshire GU34 4EJ

Tel: 01420 85083

Price range: £7 to £350. Send sae for catalogue.

Payment: cheque, Mastercard, Visa.

Postage & packing: quote will be given at time of order.

HOUSE AND GARDEN

Delivery: allow one month, depending on quantity. Next day delivery available at extra cost. Last Christmas orders by end November.

Refunds: by arrangement.

Sarah Hamilton

Using images of animals, birds, fish and plants pared down to their basics, Sarah makes colourful mirrors and furniture such as cupboards and boxes for kitchens, bedrooms and bathrooms. There are, too, silk-screen prints in limited editions and a really splendid blanket box. She will also make to commission.

Sarah Hamilton, 8 Doverfield Road, Brixton Hill, London SW2 5NB
Tel/Fax: 0181 674 5625
Price range: £1.50 to £450. Catalogue free.
Payment: cheque.
Postage & packing: at cost.
Delivery: allow 28 days.
Refunds: by arrangement.
Specials: gift-wrapping.

The Shaded Candle Company

An excellent range of shades for real candles, from the classical ones with Greek key and wreath patterns to brightly coloured and twinkling versions perfect for Christmas. There are also tartan shades (much beloved by decorator Nina Campbell) and metallics. There is, too, a "constant candle" with a wax insert to burn for 10 hours.

The Shaded Candle Company, Spaldings Hall, Long Lane, Burston, Norfolk IP22 3UQ
Tel: 01379 677710 **Fax:** 01379 77228
Price range: £4.50 to £28. Catalogue free.
Payment: cheque, Access, Mastercard, Visa.
Postage & packing: £4.95, smaller items at cost.
Delivery: within 14 days.
Refunds: yes.
Specials: gift-boxed packaging, bespoke service using clients' own materials.

134 MAIL ORDER MADE EASY

Shaker Desperately fashionable – and pricey – American products based on designs produced by a simple Christian sect. The styles are exceptional and manage to cross the country/town barrier. There are plain wooden chairs which hang from wooden rails, simple tables and curved wooden boxes.

> **Shaker**, 27 Harcourt Street, London W1H 1DT.
> **Tel:** 0171 724 7672 **Fax:** 0171 724 6640
> **Price range:** £5 to £5,000. Catalogue free.
> **Payment:** cheque, major credit cards.
> **Postage & packing:** on request.
> **Delivery:** 7 days. Last Christmas orders by 20 December.
> **Refunds:** yes.
> **Specials:** gift-wrapping, gift vouchers.

Silver Direct The firm's notepaper comes with a marvellous crest involving lions and spears and Peregrine Pole-Carew will put your crest (or initials) onto the silver he sells for an added fee. Silver is surprisingly cheap for all its aristocratic connections and this range goes from cufflinks to toastracks. Good for presents at all times.

> **Silver Direct**, P O Box 925, Shaftesbury, Dorset SP7 9RA
> **Tel:** 01747 855844 **Fax:** 01747 854700
> **Price range:** £5 to £300. Catalogue free.
> **Payment:** cheque, postal order, major credit/debit cards.
> **Postage & packing:** included.
> **Delivery:** allow 14 days. Last Christmas orders 3 working days in advance.
> **Refunds:** yes, if notified within 24 hours (excluding engraved pieces).
> **Specials:** gift-wrapping.

Silver Editions Everything you can think of in silver, or silver plate from clocks and calendars to pens, paper knives, chopsticks and spaghetti spoons. Silver, which is not as expensive as most people think, makes excellent gifts for special occasions.

HOUSE AND GARDEN

Silver Editions, P O Box 16, Chalfont St. Giles, Buckinghamshire HP8 4AU
Tel: 01753 888810 **Fax:** 01753 888830
E-mail: sales@silver-editions.demon.co.uk
Price range: £4.95 to £3,399. Catalogue free.
Payment: cheque, Mastercard, Visa, Switch.
Postage & packing: £2.95 in UK. Europe and USA £12. Free on orders over £250.
Delivery: allow 28 days.
Refunds: yes, if notified within 24 hours.
Specials: free gift-wrapping service, engraving, wedding lists.

Sitting Pretty Jane Elliott's range is highly personal and small. She makes a good-looking cheese board based on a wooden wine crate plus some chunky woollen rugs and throws in a loose tweed. Similar fabrics are used for shoulder bags and grips.

Sitting Pretty, Oakhampton Park, Wiveliscombe, Taunton, Somerset TA4 2RW
Tel: 01984 624950 **Fax:** 01984 624949
Price range: £13 to £32. Catalogue free.
Payment: cheque.
Postage & packing: included.
Delivery: by arrangement.
Refunds: by arrangement.

Space Appeal You need to pick and choose from this catalogue. Some of their metal and glass pieces are so fashionable that they will date; others are wildly clever and unlikely to survive. But the simpler pieces of brilliant yellow, scarlet and orange glass and the simple metal shapes of their large table bowls are strong enough to stand alone in an empty room. I also have a weakness for their Cosmos collection of bright steel office cabinets and chests of drawers.

Space Appeal Ltd, Unit 1, Paslow Hall Farm, King Street, High Ongar, Essex CM5 9QZ
Tel: 01277 366610 **Fax:** 01277 366620
Price range: approx £10 to £100. Catalogue free.
Payment: cheque.

Postage & packing: prices on application.
Delivery: allow 28 days.
Refunds: by arrangement.

Stuart Buglass Interior Design Ironwork

Iron furniture suddenly went indoors about a decade ago and we have come to appreciate how very good it looks. Stuart updates traditional designs from French shop fittings like brackets and shelves, kitchen favourites like pan stands and a whole range of iron light fittings. Interior iron seems to suit the current minimalist style as well as gothic or country.

Stuart Buglass Interior Design Ironwork, Clifford Mill House Workshop, Little Houghton, Northampton NN7 1AL

Tel: 01604 890366 **Fax:** 01604 890372

Price range: £5 to £20,000. Catalogue free.

Payment: cheque, major credit cards.

Postage & packing: £4.50 for smaller items, price for larger items quoted at time of order.

Delivery: curtain poles and small items 10 days, larger items/commissions advised at time of order.

Refunds: by arrangement.

Susan Lethbridge Designs

A stylish range of tapestry kits which look to me, a tyro, simple to work. Her children's designs of spotty dogs and horses, cats, apes and farmyard animals are charming and I love the Jack Russell terrier design and the stylised wild flowers on striped backgrounds. She sells smart sewing bags and hampers and a small range of children's furniture.

Susan Lethbridge Designs, Honeymead, Simonsbath, Minehead, Somerset TA24 7JX

Tel: 01643 831348. **Fax:** 01643 831647

Price range: £6 to £59.95. Send A5 sae for catalogue.

Payment: cheque, money order, Mastercard, Access, Visa.

Postage & packing: £3.50 for orders up to £50, included in UK for orders over £50.

Delivery: times vary according to demand, goods sent by return if possible.

Refunds: yes, or exchange according to complaint.

HOUSE AND GARDEN

Specials: gift-wrapping, personalised tapestry kits, colours can be changed to customer's requirements

Susie Thomson

It's surprising how many rural industries flourish in London. Susie Thomson, for instance, not only makes modern baskets in Battersea – she also grows her own willow on her South London allotment. This means that she can grow traditional willows like Black Maul plus six others she has found work well after experiments. Other varieties come from commercial growers in Somerset and Holland. Currently, there are six willow patterns to order from a traditional German basket made for brides to a laundry basket or her exclusive Strawberry basket, shaped like the fruit.

Susie Thomson, 15 Ursula Street, London SW11 3DW
Tel/Fax: 0171 223 4806
Price range: £30 to £180. Information sheet and postcards free.
Payment: cheque.
Postage & packing: £5 to £12.
Delivery: allow 12 to 16 weeks.
Refunds: yes.

Sussex House and The English Home Collection

Sussex House sells a sumptuous range of cushions inspired by early tapestries and needlework along with table runners, throws and quilts in soft old colours typical of the English country house style. There are, too, some very fanciable tassels, tiebacks and fringes in restrained shades of cream, stone and beige. English Home Collection is a new company selling cushions sourced from early textiles and documents discovered in museums and private houses. Currently, cushions will be of crushed and embroidered velvet and hand-woven raw silk.

Sussex House/The English Home Collection, 92 Wandsworth Bridge Road, London SW6 2TF
Tel: 0171 371 5455 **Fax:** 0171 371 7590
E-mail: Sussex House: sales@cushion.demon.co.uk
The English Home Collection: sales@englishhome.co.uk
Website: Sussex House: http://www.cushion.co.uk
The English Home Collection: http://www.englishhome.com

Price range: £29 to £175. Catalogue approx. £2.

Payment: major credit cards.

Postage & packing: £3.50 for 1 item, £6.50 for 2 or more, free for orders over £400. Express delivery £12.

Delivery: 10-14 days in UK, 14-21 days elsewhere. Handmade velvet products can take 3-6 weeks if out of stock. Last Christmas orders by 5 December.

Refunds: by arrangement.

Thomas Goode

The grandest tableware company in London, Thomas Goode was established in 1827, has three royal warrants and, since 1994, has its own china works in Staffordshire. The styles vary from the opulent and traditional to re-workings of classics in brilliant colour combinations. The crystal glasses, decanters, champagne jugs and centrepieces are superbly designed and cut and there are ranges of Limoges boxes, scented candles, soap and dried flower arrangements ideal for presents. Wedding lists have their own department and dinner services can be custom-made.

Thomas Goode & Co Ltd, 19 South Audley Street, London W1Y 6BN

Tel: 0171 499 2823 **Fax:** 0171 629 4230

Website: www/thomasgoode.co.uk

Price range: £20 to £48,000. Catalogue free.

Payment: major credit cards.

Postage & packing: free within W1 area, otherwise according to weight and destination.

Delivery: allow 28 days. Last Christmas orders one week ahead.

Refunds: Credit note or exchange.

Specials: Gift-wrapping, bespoke china, bridal registry.

Tobias and the Angel

The list evolved from the antique shop of the same name and one well known for its fine country furniture and objects. The mail order list now includes some wonderful painted furniture based on 18th century English and Swedish designs including a sensational dresser, a big farm-house table and pretty cots and chairs; the special Christmas range has beautiful decorations made from old fabrics. They are not especially seasonal – little brocade hearts, gilded wal-

HOUSE AND GARDEN

nuts and silk and sequin fish and would therefore make year-round presents (Valentines, Christenings).

Tobias and the Angel, 68 White Hart Lane, Barnes, London SW13 0PZ
Tel: 0181 296 0058 **Tel/Fax:** 0181 878 8902
Price range: £1.25 to £2,225 and over. Catalogue free.
Payment: cheque, major credit/debit cards.
Postage & packing: at cost.
Delivery: allow 15 working days. Some items are limited.
Refunds: yes.

Touch Design   Like many small, personally-run businesses, Touch and its customers help each other. Erica Wolfe-Murray's catalogue is constantly changing and she will custom-make objects when she can. Her ideas are simple and stylish – a copy of a Georgian glass wine funnel, sandblasted glass trays and wall-mounted glass flower vases are classics. There are beech and wicker baskets, shelves for the bathroom and natural cushions in anything from organza to linen.

Touch Design Ltd, 51 High Street, Sixpenny Handley, Salisbury, Wiltshire SP5 5ND
Tel: 01725 552888 **Fax:** 01725 552605
Price range: £1.55 to £499. Catalogue free.
Payment: cheque, major credit/debit cards.
Postage & packing: £3.50 for orders up to £25, £5.50 to £65, £6.50 thereafter.
Delivery: allow 28 days. Express delivery available at extra cost. Last Christmas orders one week ahead.
Refunds: yes, if returned unused in perfect condition.
Specials: gift-wrapping and bespoke service.

Volga Linen Company   Did you know that 90% of the world's flax is grown in Russia and the Baltic? No, nor did I. But clever Theresa Tollemache and Yelenz Doletskia have used the factories on the banks of the Volga to create their own linen collection of luxurious sheet and duvet sets, towels, tablecloths and napkins in 100% linen. There are plain whites with pulled threadwork and a sumptuous range

140 MAIL ORDER MADE EASY

of brown and white checks as well as damasks in gothic and geometric patterns. Highly luxurious.

Volga Linen Company, P O Box 16, Saxmundham, Suffolk IP17 1LZ
Tel: 01728 604434 **Fax:** 01728 604435
E-mail: volgalinen@aol.com
Price range: £15 to £300. Catalogue free.
Payment: cheque, Visa.
Postage & packing: £4 for orders under £150, £6 for orders from £150 to £350, free for orders over £350.
Delivery: allow 28 days.
Refunds: yes, if returned within 14 days.

W. R. Outhwaite & Son

I once visited this rope works in the Yorkshire dales and was amazed to see how easy it seems to twist a rope but how difficult it was in practice. I still have the evil bundle I produced as a dog lead. But Outhwaite will sell you perfect banister ropes, ideal for steep and narrow stairs or those in a confined space. You can choose from a variety of bright and natural flax yarns, fixing brackets and mounts. I suppose you could also buy bannister rope by the length for all sorts of other uses.

W. R. Outhwaite & Son, Town Foot, Hawes, North Yorkshire DL8 3NT
Tel: 01969 667487 **Fax:** 01969 667576
Price range: £6 to £8 per metre. Catalogue free.
Payment: cheque, major credit/debit cards.
Postage & packing: £7.
Delivery: normally despatched 2 weeks from receipt of order.
Refunds: by arrangement.

Walcot Reclamation

One of the first firms to realise the potential in architectural salvage, Walcot now has a catalogue which can be used for mail order in consultation with the staff. From them you can buy Victorian and Georgian grates, old wooden floors and panelling, antique roll top baths, thunderboxes and old iron gates (I seem to give my husband a gate a

HOUSE AND GARDEN

year). There is a repro list too including lighting, hooks, sundials and lead cisterns. But be warned, architectural salvage can become an obsession.

Walcot Reclamation. 108 Walcot Street, Bath BA1 5BG
Tel: 01225 444404 **Fax:** 01225 448163
Price range: £1 to £2500. Catalogue £1.25. Information sheets sent free on request.
Payment: major credit/debit cards.
Postage & packing: ask for quotation.
Delivery: times vary as some items are bespoke.
Refunds: by arrangement.

The White Company

Everything from towelling bathrobes to giftpacks of sheets and towels in this range along with a selection of style books, designer soaps and bathroom accessories plus a range for babies.

The White Company (UK) Ltd, 298-300 Munster Road, London SW6 6BH
Tel: 0171 385 7988 **Fax:** 0171 385 2685
Price range: £2.99 to £178.99. Catalogue free.
Payment: cheque, major credit/debit cards.
Postage & packing: £3.95 for orders under £50, £4.95 thereafter.
Delivery: normally within 3 days. Last Christmas orders around 18 December, china orders must be placed by 15 December.
Refunds: yes, postage reimbursed if goods are faulty.
Specials: monogramming at £8 per letter.

Woollons Brothers

I remember this firm when it was an old-fashioned hardware store in the city of York – though not as far back as 1901, when it opened. Woollons now sells a comprehensive range of kitchenware which combines the useful, the good-looking and the novelty. You can order the latest Magimix or breadmaker, traditional pottery mixing bowls along with olive oil drizzlers, woks and whistling kettles.

Woollons Brothers Ltd, 49 Wheelgate, Malton, North Yorkshire YO17 0HT
Tel: 01653 697095 **Fax:** 01653 600225
Price range: £2.25 to £450. Catalogue free.

Payment: major credit/debit cards.
Postage & packing: £3.95, free for orders over £50.
Delivery: normally within 7 days. 24-hour delivery at extra cost. Last Christmas orders 20 December.
Refunds: yes.
Specials: gift-wrapping.

Yeoward William Yeoward is an extremely talented designer in traditional mode. He works in two areas – simple furniture which is essentially modern but with nods in the direction of Georgian and Art Deco and cut glasses, mostly after 18th century designs. Like many firms, he doesn't mail order formally but has various brochures and photographs which can be sent to you and the goods later despatched. Furniture comes from The Old Imperial Laundry and glass from King's Road.

Yeoward South (Furniture), Space 'S', The Old Imperial Laundry, 71 Warriner Gardens, London SW11 4XW.
Tel: 0171 498 4811 **Fax:** 0171 498 9611
William Yeoward Crystal, 336 Kings Road, London SW3 5UR
Tel: 0171 351 5454 **Fax:** 0171 351 9469
Price range: furniture approx £300 to £2,500.
Payment: cheque, major credit cards.
Postage & packing: at cost.
Delivery: within a week if in stock, otherwise 6-8 weeks.
Refunds: only if faulty.

See also: Ashfield Traditional, The Barometer Shop, Candlesby Herbs, Czech & Speake Direct, The Heveningham Collection, Jane Hogben Terracotta, Karin Hessenberg, L.L. Bean, Les Senteurs, The Perfumers Guild, Prizma Embroidery, Sheridan & Hunter, The Truggery.

GARDEN

Gardening is currently the smartest occupation around. Forget interiors – it's exteriors which are occupying our best designers, from Conran to Lagerfeld. We've suddenly realised that gardens, especially small ones, are simply exterior rooms. They can be decorated using painted furniture to match the flowers, tubs, buckets and planters. Galvanised iron has become immensely fashionable as have growing willow seats, woven hurdles and old tools. Gardening catalogues have risen to meet the challenge. I've included the most interesting ones along with nursery catalogues for plants, plugs and seeds and the essential, large-scale equipment which can also be bought through the post, like greenhouses, cold frames, compost and watering systems. The catalogues have the latest technology and help keep us up to date with what is going on.

GARDEN - LISTINGS

Andrew Crace Increasingly, people give each other presents for the garden and this firm is all about garden hardware from teak plant labels to ensure you remember which variety you've dug in to full-scale gazebos and covered seats. If you want a Chinoiserie octagonal pagoda, this is where you'll find it along with furniture conceived by Lutyens and the designers of gardens as far apart as Edo-period Japan and Versailles. Crace also has numerous bronze statues, stone Japanese lanterns and wire frames for topiary animals.

Andrew Crace Designs, Bourne Lane, Much Hadham, Hertfordshire SG10 6ER
Tel: 01279 842685 **Fax:** 01279 843646
Price range: £10 to £9,000. Catalogue free.
Payment: cheque, major credit cards.
Postage & packing: at cost, minimum £2.25.
Delivery: by return for most items.
Refunds: yes.

Architectural Plants This nursery is run by a clever designer, with all plants chosen for their architectural quality. Many are evergreen with few flowers. Lots of rare house and conservatory plants and exotics collected from the wild are included. The plant quality is excellent – my house plants have survived even me. Good for bamboo, yucca, eucalyptus, palms and large-scale trees. All come with provenance and tips for upkeep.

Architectural Plants, Cooks Farm, Nuthurst, Horsham, West Sussex RH13 6LH

Tel: 01403 891772 **Fax:** 01403 891056

Website: http://members.aol.com/gshaw29868/archpltn.htm

Price range: Plants £6.50 to £82.50. Larger plants individually priced. Catalogue free.

Payment: cheque, major credit/debit cards.

Postage & packing: from £17.30 for up to 10 kg then 36p + VAT per kg in mainland UK. Elsewhere on application.

Delivery: following day by Interlink.

Refunds: by arrangement.

Arne Herbs

It's extraordinary to think herbs had gone so out of fashion in the 19th century that there was not a single herb garden known in Britain in 1900. Today, they're a top priority for anyone with a small plot. This nursery grows one of the biggest ranges of herbs in the world from Acacia karroo (the sweet thorn) to Withania somniferum (ashwaganda). Each listed plant has its common name which is a great help. The nursery will send out gift vouchers or deliver plants when conditions are suitable.

Arne Herbs, Limeburn Nurseries, Limeburn Hill, Chew Magna, Avon BS18 8QW

Tel/Fax: 01275 333399

Price range: £1.30 to £40. Catalogue £2 refundable on first order.

Payment: cheque, overseas by bank transfer.

Postage & packing: via 24-hour courier £15.

Delivery: vouchers sent by return, plants as soon as the whole order is ready, usually between March and the end of May.

Refunds: yes, if notified within 24 hours.

HOUSE AND GARDEN 145

Avon Bulbs Bulbs from this nursery, a regular gold medal winner at Chelsea, are divided into sections for spring, late summer and autumn despatch. They range from delicate winter flowering narcissi to such heralds of summer as showy agapanthus or brilliant crocosmia. Avon also has recently produced a gardener's five-year diary based on one they used at the nursery. "We realised that our well-thumbed diary, which had become a priceless record of activities on the nursery with weather details, flowers notes... had limited space left. We looked everywhere to replace it." They couldn't so they now publish their own. It has a page for each day, divided into five, a list of monthly jobs and likely flowers in bloom. Essential, I'd say.

> **Avon Bulbs**, Burnt House Farm, Mid Lambrook, South Petherton, Somerset TA13 5HE
>
> **Tel/Fax:** 01460 242177
>
> **Price range:** bulbs from £1.50 for 15. Catalogue sent in return for 4 x second class stamps or US$5 cash or equivalent in postal coupons. Diaries £14, leaflet free.
>
> **Payment:** cheque, Mastercard, Access, Visa (surcharge for credit card payments).
>
> **Postage & packing:** from £3.40, included for diaries in UK.
>
> **Delivery:** bulbs despatched in season, diaries normally by return. Last Christmas orders 3 working days ahead.
>
> **Refunds:** by arrangement.
>
> **Specials:** gift vouchers.

Blooming Things These plants are organically grown and are mostly herbs or vegetables. The list is comprehensive, especially for vegetables, with cardoons, celeriac, Tigerella striped tomatoes and eight varieties of lettuce. Obviously, most plants will be sent when the weather is good – but think of the anticipation.

> **Blooming Things**, Y Bwthyn, Cymerau, Glandyfi, Machynlleth, Powys SY20 8SS
>
> **Tel:** 01654 781256
>
> **Price range:** plants from 17p. Catalogue free, A5 sae appreciated.
>
> **Payment:** cheque, postal order.

Postage & packing: varies according to size of order, e.g. 10 plants £1.51.
Delivery: varies according to item ordered. see catalogue.
Refunds: yes.
Specials: plants can be grown to order.

Classic Garden

If you inherit a patch of weed-filled dust, a field or a patio and want quick effects, go for trellises, planters and obelisks. This catalogue offers them all. Then plant quick growing herbs, climbers or mature boxes and bay trees and you will have instant height and variety. It's a good tip to have the hardware painted by the firm in a colour which will suit your house.

Classic Garden, Lower Puncheston, Pembrokeshire SA62 5TG
Tel/Fax: 01348 881451
Price range: £35 to £520, 5% discount on orders of 2 or more items. Leaflet free.
Payment: major credit cards.
Postage & packing: included in England, Wales and south, central and eastern Scotland. Elsewhere prices on application.
Delivery: allow 28 days.
Refunds: yes, if notified within 7 days in case of damage or defect. Items other than those made to order may be returned for refund within 14 days.

Cottage Garden Roses

John and Teresa Scarman are fanatically interested in the old varieties of roses from the near wild ones grown for their petals and used to make rose water in the middle East to old shrub and climbing roses with evocative names like Gloire de Dijon and Great Maiden's Blush. They also sell their own book, *Gardening with Old Roses* (£16.99 plus p&p), and pure Persian rosewater brought back by them from the East in hand-blown glass bottles. The nursery will also send out vouchers and a catalogue as a present.

Cottage Garden Roses, Woodlands House, Stretton, near Stafford ST19 9LG
Tel: 01785 840217 **Fax:** 01902 850193
Price range: roses £7 each. Catalogue £2.
Payment: cheque with order.

HOUSE AND GARDEN

Postage & packing: £4 for 5 plants, £5 for 6 to 10, £6 for 10 or more.
Delivery: allow 28 days.
Refunds: yes.
Specials: gift vouchers.

David Austen Roses

The family firm produces a huge list of old fashioned and species roses, selected modern varieties and new introductions of its own. The nursery's catalogue is superb: it tells you each plant's history, behaviour, looks and foibles. I use it all the time as a reference book on roses.

David Austen Roses Ltd, Bowling Green Lane, Albrighton, Wolverhampton WV7 3HB
Tel: 01902 376300, orders 01902 376377 **Fax:** 01902 372142
Price range: roses from 4.75 to £21.50. Catalogue free.
Payment: cheque, postal order, Access, Visa.
Postage & packing: £4.25 for up to 3 roses, £5.25 for 4 or more. Add £4.25 for standards. 24-hour delivery £10.
Delivery: orders received by mid December delivered before Christmas. Spring despatch from mid February depending on weather conditions.
Refunds: replacement if plant fails to grow during first year through fault of David Austen Roses.
Specials: gift vouchers.

English Garden

A useful catalogue of all those large and awkward pieces of garden furniture, tools and terracotta that are so much better sent by mail. Though some of the stuff is a bit garden-centre, you can get the excellent Felco secateurs, specialised spades with narrow blades or sharp ends and there are aerating forks, scotch hoes and cultivators. There are a few books, some fancy plants and pleasant baskets and pots to decorate your outdoor rooms.

English Garden Collection, Cowley Bridge Road, Exeter EX4 5HQ
Tel: 0870 606 0304 **Fax:** 01392 431025
Price range: £1.75 to £810. Catalogue free.
Payment: cheque, major credit/debit cards.
Postage & packing: £3.50, free for orders over £100. Large item supplement £9.50, flower supplement £2.50.

148 MAIL ORDER MADE EASY

Delivery: allow 21 days.
Refunds: yes.

English Hurdle

English Hurdle This company has its own withy beds of over 100 acres on the Somerset levels where willows are grown especially for their range of hurdles, plant climbers, arbours and baskets. The craft of willow weaving dates back to the Bronze age and hurdle fences have been used ever since. Arbours came in with medieval gardens. Another range is of living willow which can be planted around the new year in rich, wet soil and will sprout into a growing hedge, seat or display plant.

English Hurdle, Curload, Stoke St. Gregory, Taunton, Somerset TA3 6JD
Tel: 01823 698418 **Fax:** 01823 698859
E-mail: hurdle@enterprise.net
Website: http://www.hurdle.co.uk
Price range: £14 to £440. Catalogue free.
Payment: cheque, major credit/debit cards.
Postage & packing: from £7.
Delivery: allow 28 days.
Refunds: by arrangement.

Flower Plots

Flower Plots "Don't send flowers, send a garden" says this catalogue. True to their words, you can get twig obelisks, armilliary spheres, wall fountains and topiary animals. Other ideas are Sussex trugs, a fashionable windowsill box of herbs and gardeners' tool bags. The intention is that these should be gifts (a great idea) but you can always treat yourself.

Flower Plots, Garden Art & Design, 97 Queens Road, Weybridge, Surrey KT13 9UQ
Tel: 01932 855050 **Fax:** 01932 847405
E-mail: fionas@netcomuk.co.uk
Price range: £5 to £260. Catalogue free.
Payment: cheque, major credit/debit cards.
Postage & packing: included.
Delivery: next day for orders before 1 pm. Last Christmas orders by 22 December.

HOUSE AND GARDEN 149

Refunds: yes, if returned within 2 weeks.
Specials: gift-wrapping included, sundials can be engraved at cost.

Future Foods

The nursery describes its produce as "weird and wonderful things for the edible garden" and I first came across them through a magazine offer of seeds like purslane, rocket and chopsuey greens. From them you can get seeds for all those recipes which assume you live next to an oriental market or drop in monthly to Mexico. With greenhouse and enthusiasm tackle tropical African eggplants or achoccha Fat Baby (a lost crop of the Incas, they claim).

Future Foods, P O Box 1564, Wedmore, Somerset BS28 4DP
E-mail: ff@seeds.cix.co.uk
Website: www: http://www.futurefoods.com
Price range: £1.25 to £30. Minimum order £5. Send A5 sae or 4 first class stamps to receive both spring and autumn catalogues.
Payment: cheque, major credit cards.
Postage & packing: included in UK.
Delivery: allow 2 weeks, some items available only at certain times of the year and many are scarce.
Refunds: complaints are heard sympathetically and return not always necessary.

The Garden Factory

A comprehensive list of ornamental and practical equipment for the garden. It's fairly varied in its taste (the frightful picnic table which requires athletic contortions to leave, for instance) but there's plenty of good stuff alongside.

The Garden Factory, Cannock Gates Ltd, Freepost (MID 15056), Cannock, Staffordshire WS11 1BR
Tel: 01543 462500 **Fax:** 01543 506237
Price range: £2.45 to £999. Catalogue free.
Payment: cheque, postal order, major credit/debit cards.
Postage & packing: £1.95 for orders up to £10, £3.95 to £30, £9.95 to £100, free thereafter.
Delivery: usually 7-14 days.
Refunds: yes, if returned within 14 days.

Garden Systems I've been using the leaky pipe system for a few years now and it is the answer to hot dry summers. A porous rubber hose is easily dug into the beds (I promise it's easy) and can be turned on at source to provide a slow, economical drip of water to seep around the plants. The firm also has a system for watering plants in hanging baskets and troughs and a good range of equipment for greenhouses.

Garden Systems, White House Farm, Grundisburgh, Woodbridge, Suffolk IP13 6RR

Tel: 01473 738280 **Fax:** 01473 735101

Price range: £24.99 to £380. Catalogue free.

Payment: cheque, postal order, major credit/debit cards.

Postage & packing: included in UK. Overnight delivery from £10. Overseas rates on application.

Delivery: 7-10 days. Last Christmas orders by 18 December.

Refunds: by arrangement.

The Heveningham Collection Ironwork furniture is very much in fashion, both indoors and out, but these pieces, designed by Annie Eadie, are notable for their simple style. There is a luxurious chaise longue with back wheels to move it about easily and a plain black iron-framed deckchair with a natural canvas sling. There are matching chairs, stools and tables, shown in the catalogue in conservatories, gardens and beside the pool. There are even standard candelabra for elegant outdoor meals. New designs include a chrome dining chair and a children's collection of iron painted furniture. She has not made one design error.

The Heveningham Collection by Annie Eadie, East Stoke Farmhouse, Stoke Charity, Winchester, Hampshire SO21 3PL

Tel: 01962 761777 **Fax:** 01962 761888

Price range: £220 to £860. Catalogue £2.50 refundable against order.

Payment: cheque, Mastercard, Visa.

Postage & packing: prices on application.

Delivery: 4-6 weeks.

Refunds: no.

HOUSE AND GARDEN

Highfield Nurseries From this nursery you can create an entire orchard including some old varieties of fruit tree like the apple, D'Arcy Spice, Williams pear and the marvellously-named Coe's Golden Drop greengage. You can also order delicious summer fruits like figs, mulberries, grapes and quinces plus general shrubs and perennials.

Highfield Nurseries, School Lane, Whitminster, Gloucestershire GL2 7PL

Tel: 01452 740266/741309 **Fax:** 01452 740750

Price range: £1.49 to £39.95. Catalogue free (stamp appreciated).

Payment: cheque, major credit/debit cards.

Postage & packing: £7.95 per order.

Delivery: plants sent out at correct planting times throughout the year. 24-hour delivery service on request.

Refunds: free replacement of plants which fail within 12 months provided the plant has not been neglected.

Specials: gift vouchers.

Hopleys The nursery will only mail order plants during October and November but that's the best time to have them anyway. Theirs is a good, general list with plants which you cannot easily find in garden centres. There are, for instance, four different foxgloves, five pulmonarias and 30 good salvias. The catalogue is helpful and well laid out.

Hopleys Plants, High Street, Much Hadham, Hertfordshire SG10 6BU

Tel: 01279 842509 **Fax:** 01279 843784

E-mail: hopleys@compuserve.com

Price range: 90p to £20. Catalogue £1.30.

Payment: cheque, postal order, Access, Visa, Switch.

Postage & packing: from £5.80 to £13 depending on order value.

Delivery: sent by parcel post during October and November.

Refunds: yes, if notified in writing within 14 days.

Hortus Ornamenti Damian Grounds's wonderful gardening tools make weeding a pleasure. I am a firm fan of his Jekyll weeding fork (used by Gertrude) and have used it faithfully for

152 MAIL ORDER MADE EASY

at least three years. Now there is a fern trowel, hand hoe and daisy grubber (though I like daisies). None are cheap but they are beautifully made and really do last. More products, each as seductive as the last, keep appearing.

Hortus Ornamenti, Saltham Barns, Saltham Lane, Runcton, Chichester, West Sussex PO20 6PU

Tel: 01243 782467 **Fax:** 01243 785844

Price range: £2.95 to £250. Catalogue free.

Payment: cheque, Mastercard, Visa.

Postage & packing: £1.95 to £7.95. Express delivery add £3.50.

Delivery: express delivery available. Last Christmas orders by 20 December.

Refunds: yes.

Specials: gift-wrapping £3.50.

Howels of Sheffield

These English-made thermometers can be ordered either with a plain white dial or illustrated with poppies, butterflies or birds. I find thermometers very necessary when gardening – if only to marvel at the ferocity of the cold or the blinding heat in which I have been working. The illustrations will not fade.

Howels of Sheffield, P O Box 383, Sheffield S8 0AT

Tel: 0114 255 0172 **Fax:** 0114 255 6024

Price range: £20 to £25. Catalogue free.

Payment: cheque, postal order, major credit cards.

Postage & packing: £2.

Delivery: within 7 working days. Same day despatch on credit card orders if requested. Last Christmas orders by 14 December.

Refunds: yes.

Specials: gift card can be enclosed.

Indian Ocean

One of the largest ranges of teak furniture available but, they say, sourced from well managed forests. Teak is by far the best wood for outdoor furniture being almost impervious to rain while going an attractive grey colour in a few seasons. I refuse to oil my teak furniture and it hasn't suffered at all. There is a huge choice of chairs, loungers, tables of all sizes to seat between two and 14, even teak garden lights.

HOUSE AND GARDEN

There are two London showrooms and another near Chester if you want to see the pieces first.

Indian Ocean Trading Co, 155-163 Balham Hill, London SW12 9DJ
Tel: 0181 675 4808 **Fax:** 0181 675 4652
E-mail: sales@indian-ocean.co.uk
Website: http://www.indian-ocean.co.uk
Price range: £15 to £1,450. Catalogue free.
Payment: cheque, major credit/debit cards.
Postage & packing: £20 in mainland UK.
Delivery: by carrier.
Refunds: by arrangement.

J.G.S. Metalwork This company specialises in weathervanes made of steel then coated with powdered polyester which is baked on hard to stop rust. There are many shapes from the traditional, boastful cock, running fox and leaping horse (and these are the ones I prefer) to bears fishing for salmon, witches on broomsticks and traction engines. Most are simple black silhouettes but there is a splendid golden cockerel. All come with fixing brackets and instructions.

J.G.S. Metalwork, Broomstick Estate, High Street, Edlesborough, near Dunstable, Bedfordshire LU6 2HS
Tel: 01525 220360 **Fax:** 01525 222786
Website: http://www.web-marketing.co.uk/jgs
Price range: £15 to £215. Send sae for catalogue.
Payment: cheque, major credit cards.
Postage & packing: £2 to £10.
Delivery: allow 4 weeks, earlier if in stock.
Refunds: by arrangement.

Jane Hogben Terracotta Even people with the smallest balconies or roof gardens have realised that it's possible to garden with pots. Jane Hogben makes a wide variety of shapes and sizes and I specially like the simple square pots and those with scalloped edges. To my taste, pots should be subordinate to the plants in them. She also makes more decorative affairs which might suit kitchen herbs or houseplants.

> **Jane Hogben Terracotta**, Grove House, East Common, Gerrards Cross, Buckinghamshire SL9 7AF
> **Tel:** 01753 882364 **Fax:** 01753 892283
> **Price range:** £6.50 to £150. Catalogue free.
> **Payment:** cheque.
> **Postage & packing:** 10% of order value.
> **Delivery:** allow 28 days.
> **Refunds:** by arrangement.

Karin Hessenberg

A fellow of the Craft Potters Association, Karin's pots are big and bold and made of frost-proof stoneware, which requires higher firing than earthenware. She was inspired to create her planters and birdbaths by visits to India and Nepal. The pressed and decorated slabs are glazed with blue ash or green slip and are striking enough to be used for vistas or focal points in the garden.

> **Karin Hessenberg**, 72 Broomgrove Road, Sheffield, South Yorkshire S10 2NA
> **Tel:** 0114 266 1610
> **Price range:** £10 to £320. Catalogue free.
> **Payment:** cheque.
> **Postage & packing:** included in UK.
> **Delivery:** allow at least 8 weeks.
> **Refunds:** yes if damaged or faulty and notified within 7 days.

Keith Metcalf's Garden Heritage

The Japanese work wonders in small gardens so it's no surprise that their style is catching on in English cities. Keith Metcalf specialises in Japanese garden accessories like bamboo palisades and water spouts and small, heavy granite jars for water features. He has recently added carved marble and granite in Italian and English styles but I haven't yet seen them.

> **Keith Metcalf's Garden Heritage**, The Studio, Braxton Courtyard, Lymore Lane, Milford-on-Sea, Hampshire SO41 0TX
> **Tel:** 01590 644888 **Fax:** 01590 645825
> **Price range:** £39 to £350. Zen-Japanese information pack £5.
> **Payment:** cheque.
> **Postage & packing:** subject to weight.

Delivery: by carrier.
Refunds: yes.

Kootensaw Dovecotes

Free standing and wall-mounted dovecotes in a choice of fifty-seven National Trust colours which are draught-and weather-proofed to be cosy enough to keep the doves happy. You can buy the doves too – "delightful little creatures... very easy to look after", say the owners. They also sell various dove accessories like homing nets, feeders, food and leg rings.

Kootensaw Dovecotes, Moorcott, Diptford, Totnes, Devon TQ9 7NX
Tel/Fax: 01548 821415.
E-mail: info@dovecotes.co.uk
Website: http://www.dovecotes.co.uk
Price range: Dovecotes £195 to £620. Doves £45 for 1 pair, £65 for 2 pairs. Surcharge of £10 for doves only customers. Catalogue free.
Payment: cheque, major credit/debit cards.
Postage & packing: included for doves. Other items £1 for orders up to £2.75, £7.50 up to £30, £15 up to £185, £25 up to £500, £38 up to £800, orders over £800 - prices on application.
Delivery: generally 2-3 weeks.
Refunds: 14 day money back guarantee on dovecotes.

Mills Farm Plants

Pinks are the speciality here. The nursery offers modern pinks, which flower non-stop from May to autumn, old-fashioned pinks as found in old cottage gardens which bloom for six weeks in the summer and rare collectors' pinks like Nonsuch and Queen of Sheba which were grown in Britain in the 17th century. There are collections of 10 different varieties chosen for their scent or history.

Mills Farm Plants and Gardens, Norwich Road, Mendlesham, Suffolk IP14 5NQ
Tel/Fax: 01449 766425
Price range: from £1.40 – average cost of special collection of 10 plants £14. Send 5 x second class stamps for catalogue.
Payment: cheque, postal order, major credit cards.
Postage & packing: from £5.95 for up to 15 plants to £8.95 for over 50.

156 MAIL ORDER MADE EASY

Delivery: February to May and October to December.
Refunds: yes.

Neptune Classics

Neptune Classics While most catalogues in this area keep your nose to the soil with hoes and secateurs, Neptune want gardeners to relax occasionally. They have a great range of rocking deck chairs for all the family, parasols for gentle shade, and, better still, canvas hammocks. These can be either slung between trees or, if your trees are too small or inconvenient, you can buy a free-standing hammock. There are dining tables and chairs in Courbaril, an abundant South American hardwood plus a gas-fired garden heater for chilly evenings.

Neptune Classics, The Garden Shop, Freepost, Chippenham, Wiltshire SN15 3GZ
Tel: 01249 656467 **Fax:** 01249 657200
Price range: £16.95 to £649.95. Catalogue free.
Payment: cheque, postal order, Mastercard, Visa, Delta, Switch.
Postage & packing: £5.95 up to 30 kg.
Delivery: allow 14 days.
Refunds: yes, if returned within 14 days.

Norfolk Lavender

Norfolk Lavender Half the catalogue is devoted to soaps, scents, candles and accessories for the enjoyment of the scent of lavender. The other half is about the plants themselves. There are some charming lavenders available, from the quirky and tender French lavender which has flowers like wings to white, pink and deep blue lavenders. They will grow in the smallest garden, pot or windowbox, can be clipped into topiary and kept in drawer sachets. The firm also has a Vivaldi selection, scented plants for all seasons from the winter-flowering Viburnum (smells of Gripfix) to honeysuckle, lilac and philadelphus. A nice idea.

Norfolk Lavender, Caley Mill, Heacham, Norfolk PE31 7JE
Tel: 01507 466466 **Fax:** 01485 571176
Price range: 75p to £37. Catalogue free.
Payment: cheque, postal order, major credit/debit cards.
Postage & packing: £1.95 for up to 2 items, £3.45 for 3 or more.

HOUSE AND GARDEN

Delivery: allow 21 days.
Refunds: replacement if notified within 3 days.
Specials: gift-wrapping, gift vouchers.

The Organic Gardening Catalogue

The Henry Doubleday Research Association, from which this catalogue comes, is dedicated to promoting organic gardening and offers a huge list of vegetables, herbs, wild flowers and organically grown fruit trees which are sent direct from the growers. Just as useful are the organic manures, insect repellents, mousetraps which don't kill and books on the subject.

The Organic Gardening Catalogue, River Dene Estate, Molesey Road, Hersham, Surrey KT12 4RG
Tel: 01932 253666 **Fax:** 01932 252707
Price range: from 71p. Catalogue free.
Payment: cheque, postal order, major credit/debit cards.
Postage & packing: 80p handling charge for orders under £14, free for orders over £14. Express delivery £3.70. Overseas rates see catalogue.
Delivery: normally despatched within 5 days.
Refunds: by arrangement.
Specials: special offers for orders over £7.

Planta Vera

Violas are most satisfactory plants. They are strongly scented, perennial, the flowers are held high above the leaves and they are hardy. They are also most charming and come in colours from pure white to pretty near black (I love black plants). Planta Vera hold the world's largest collection (which are not to be confused with violets or violettas). They tend to be named after girls, from Clodagh to Myfawnny, so you may be able to find the plant to suit a friend.

Planta Vera, Lyne Hill Nursery, Lyne Crossing Road, Chertsey, Surrey KT16 0AT
Tel/Fax: 01932 563011
Price range: £2 each with a minimum order of 12. Send £1 in stamps for catalogue.
Payment: cheque.
Postage & packing: £9 for up to 24 plants, then free in UK.

Delivery: plants are sent out in April.
Refunds: yes, if not received in good condition.

Sarah Raven's Cutting Garden

The first thing you notice is that the catalogue cover is made with a delightful paper including real flower petals and grasses. The inside is equally elegant, with a range of seeds grown specifically for cutting. "It is highly selective and subjective," says Sarah, who has made a name for herself as the modern flower arranger par excellence. "based on experience from the hundred of varieties that have been trialed in the cutting gardens at Perch Hill Farm. These are the elite of cut flowers." They include nigella, corn poppy, clary sage and zinnias along with biennials like wallflowers, Iceland poppies and foxgloves.

Sarah Raven's Cutting Garden, Perch Hill Farm, Brightling, East Sussex TN32 5HP

Tel: 01424 838181 **Fax:** 01424 838571

Price range: Seeds £1.50. Gardening and flower arranging courses £125 to £300. Catalogue free.

Payment: cheque.

Postage & packing: £1.50 for orders up to £20, free thereafter.

Delivery: orders despatched as soon as possible.

Refunds: yes.

Sheridan & Hunter

If these metal seats and tables were genuine antiques, you might have to pay thousands for them. But, as skilful repros, the prices are sensible and it's hard to tell the difference anyway. The seats, from single to triple benches, are based on simple Regency designs, so much more elegant than the heavy Victorian designs. The table, based on a French cafe design, works as well indoors as out. Martha Stewart, the American household queen, suggests that a huge basket of cushions should be kept handy for iron seats.

Sheridan & Hunter, 64 Kingsdown Parade, Kingsdown, Bristol BS6 5UQ

Tel/Fax: 0117 908 1949

Price range: £110 to £355. Catalogue free.

HOUSE AND GARDEN

159

Payment: cheque.
Postage & packing: £15 for orders up to £200, £25 thereafter.
Delivery: allow 29 days. Last Christmas orders by 21 November.
Refunds: by arrangement.

Suffolk Gardens Now that French and Italian gardens are fashionable, we have come to realise how useful garden furniture can be – especially in small, dull or immature gardens. An obelisk, planted with a climber, gives instant height and trellises combined with planters make movable shields or suit areas with no soil. Suffolk Gardens has a small but neat collection of such pieces made of meranti hardwood which combines toughness with lightness.

Suffolk Gardens, Box Tree Farm, Kettlebaston, Suffolk IP7 7PZ
Tel: 01449 740195 **Fax:** 01449 741318
Price range: £39.50 to £94.50. Catalogue free.
Payment: cheque, major credit cards.
Postage & packing: included in UK.
Delivery: normally within one week. Express delivery service on request. Last Christmas orders 15 December.
Refunds: yes, if returned unused within 14 days.

Suffolk Herbs This claims to be Europe's number one organic seed catalogue and it's certainly enormous. It seems to have every herb known to man, including smart leaves from the far East, along with cottage garden flowers, drying flowers and vegetables. If you haven't discovered the pleasures (and profits) of growing from seed, this is the place to start.

Suffolk Herbs, Monks Farm, Pantlings Lane, Coggeshall Road, Kelvedon, Essex CO5 9PG
Tel: 01376 572456 **Fax:** 01376 571189
Price range: 60p to £197.50. Catalogue £1.
Payment: cheque, postal order, Access, Visa.
Postage & packing: included.
Delivery: normally despatched within 1 week.
Refunds: by arrangement.
Specials: gift vouchers.

The Tank Exchange This eco-friendly family business specialises in recycled plastic rain tanks which started life as containers for fruit juice, anchovies or resin binder. There are also oak whisky barrels and half barrels, solar powered lamps and fountains, plus their award-winning solar powered pebble pool which was featured on Gardeners' World.

The Tank Exchange, Lewden House, Barnsley Road, Dodworth, Barnsley S75 3JU

Tel: 01226 206157, brochureline 01226 203852 **Fax:** 01226 299424

Price range: £6 to £180, Catalogue free.

Payment: cheque, postal order, Mastercard, Visa, Delta, Switch.

Postage & packing: included.

Delivery: by carrier for most items. Allow 28 days.

Refunds: by arrangement.

Terrace & Garden Where other firms offer neat willow hurdles and planters, this one has them wild with unclipped tops, wiry extensions to frames and screens that might have come through a hedge backwards. They make little Christmas trees from black twigs and plain glass baubles, discs and spirals which are really for terraces and conservatories but would make sensational indoor decorations. In addition, there are pots and urns, lanterns, sundials and nesting boxes.

Terrace & Garden Ltd, Orchard House, Patmore End, Ugley, Bishop's Stortford, Hertfordshire CM22 6JA

Tel: 01799 543289 **Fax:** 01799 543586

Price range: £1.50 to £510. Catalogue free.

Payment: cheque, Access, Visa.

Postage & packing: £2 for orders up to £20, £4 to £75, free thereafter, excluding certain items.

Delivery: by arrangement.

Refunds: by arrangement.

Thompson & Morgan This claims to be the world's largest illustrated seed catalogue at over 225 pages with lots of helpful, if too perfect, blooms on show. You have to know what you

HOUSE AND GARDEN

want, as browsing is too overwhelming, but the catalogue is helpfully divided into sections like flowers for fragrance, for baskets and for cutting. There's also a big vegetable seed section where you will find smart foods like radicchio, striped tomatoes and red spring onions.

Thompson & Morgan (UK) Ltd, Poplar Lane, Ipswich, Suffolk IP8 3BU
Tel: 01473 688821 **Fax:** 01473 680199
Price range: about £1 to £5. Catalogue free.
Payment: cheque, Access, Visa, Switch.
Postage & packing: 75p per order.
Delivery: seeds at once, plants and bulbs in correct season.
Refunds: yes.
Specials: gift vouchers

The Traditional Garden Supply Company Is it the brilliant summers which we have had so regularly, or a renewed fascination with the outdoors as an extra room which have made garden catalogues so popular? This one has all the hardware you need for the conservatory or the summer room on the patio or back garden. There's a good range of outdoor furniture, equipment for watering pots and hanging baskets, tools, cloches and coldframes.

The Traditional Garden Supply Company, Corinium Centre, Love Lane, Cirencester, Gloucestershire, GL7 1FE
Tel: 0870 600 3366 **Fax:** 0990 449800
E-mail: www.sales@scottsofstow.demon.co.uk
Website: http://www.scottsofstow.co.uk
Price range: £3.95 to £699. Catalogue free.
Payment: cheque, postal order, major credit cards.
Postage & packing: £2.95 for orders up to £29.99, £3.95 thereafter. Additional charge for heavy items.
Delivery: allow 14-28 days.
Refunds: yes, if returned within 90 days.

The Truggery I am living proof that you cannot have too many trugs. I use them for weeding, for gathering flowers and, indoors, for my vegetables and even make-up basket. A tiny trug goes with me for picking herbs. When I get hens, I'll use one for eggs too. The curved English trug is native to Sussex where you can see them being made at the roadside. The Truggery now mail orders a wide variety from small eight-inch ovals to 30-inch baskets which hold a full bushel. Others are long (for cucumbers), round and square or come with a useful walking stick. They are made of cricket-bat willow with chestnut rims and handles and will last for years (as I have proved).

The Truggery, Coopers Croft, Herstmonceux, Hailsham, East Sussex BN27 1QL

Tel/Fax: 01323 832314

Price range: £12.50 to £45. Send sae for leaflet.

Payment: cheque.

Postage & packing: from £3.50.

Delivery: allow 28 days. Last Christmas orders by first week of December.

Refunds: by arrangement.

Specials: trugs can be personalised with pokerwork.

Two Wests & Elliott

A terrifically useful catalogue – everything you could possibly need for the greenhouse plus greenhouses themselves. There are propagators, hoses and attachments, staging of various heights, pots, seed trays and plugs, air blowers and misters. This is an area where new materials and techniques are constantly appearing and this is the catalogue which will keep you up to date. Elliott, by the way, is the family dog.

Two Wests & Elliott Ltd, Unit 4, Carrwood Road, Sheepbridge Industrial Estate, Chesterfield, Derbyshire S41 9RH

Tel: 01246 451077 **Fax:** 01246 260115

Price range: £1 to £2,500. Catalogue free.

Payment: cheque, postal order, major credit/debit cards.

Postage & packing: £5 or free in UK depending on item. Overseas rates on application.

Delivery: 5-7 days. 24-hour delivery at extra cost. Last Christmas orders by 21 December.

Refunds: yes.

HOUSE AND GARDEN

Vigo Vineyard Supplies With global warming it's not too fanciful to imagine Britain as a serious wine producing area expanding beyond the few brave growers who cope with our frosts. If you feel like planting acres of grapes, Vigo can provide the necessary presses and crushers. They can also be used for apples and other fruit juices. The firm sells its own sparkling cider by mail order.

Vigo Vineyard Supplies, Station Road, Hemyock, Devon
EX15 3SE
Tel: 01823 680230, catalogue request line: 01823 680844
Fax: 01823 680807
E-mail: jo@vigovs.demon.co.uk
Price range: from £60. Catalogue free.
Payment: cheque, postal order, Access, Visa, Switch.
Postage & packing: from £4.50 for up to 3kg to £15 for 40kg.
Delivery: normally within 5 working days. Last Christmas orders 7 working days in advance.
Refunds: yes, if returned in good condition within 1 month.

W. Robinson If you have an urge to grow bigger vegetables than anyone else or win prizes at the village fête, get these seeds. The family-owned firm has been honing its seeds for size since 1860 and can offer the largest red onion in cultivation (it reaches twenty-two inches in circumference), 1lb beefsteak tomatoes and thirty-inch runner beans. There's also Big Max, the giant pumpkin, big enough for Cinderella.

W. Robinson & Sons Ltd, Sunny Bank, Forton, near Preston, Lancashire PR3 0BN
Tel: 01524 791210 **Fax:** 01524 791933
Price range: £1 to £2.50. Catalogue free.
Payment: cheque, major credit/debit cards.
Postage & packing: included.
Delivery: by first class post. Last Christmas orders by 15 December.
Refunds: no.

The Wadham Trading Company Topiary is a current garden craze and this firm supplies the iron frames needed to control the shape. There are rabbits and giraffes, a cuddly sheep shape and more traditional urns which look almost as good without planting. Other accessories are iron rose supports, jardinières and ornamental spheres to put each side of the front door. There are also convincing lead-effect cherubs and cisterns, actually made of marble resin.

The Wadham Trading Company, Wadham House, Southrop, near Lechlade, Gloucestershire GL7 3PB
Tel/Fax: 01367 850499
Price range: £13 to £1,000. Catalogue free.
Payment: cheque, Mastercard, Access, Visa.
Postage & packing: on request.
Delivery: normally 7-10 days, but allow 21 subject to availability.
Refunds: yes, if returned within 7 days.

Wells & Winter

A small catalogue full of fun for gardeners. There's a black metal cat's face with green glass eyes to scare the birds, miniature garden hurdles of Kentish chestnut which I find invaluable for deterring dogs from plants or keeping sprawling ones in order, bright yellow painted labels and a gardener's apron with integral padded knees. A new venture is Pears, the first book on pears grown in Great Britain since 1920.

Wells & Winter, Mere House Barn. 34 The Street, Mereworth, Maidstone, Kent ME18 5NB
Tel: 01622 813627
Price range: 20p to £30. Catalogue free.
Payment: cheque.
Postage & packing: £2 for orders up to £8, £3 for orders over £8.
Delivery: normally by return. Last Christmas orders by 12 December.
Refunds: yes, if damaged or faulty.

Wheelie Bin Cover Company

Garden enthusiasts, especially those with small plots, despair about intrusive rubbish bins – in particular those giant, if useful, wheelie bins. This firm can make them disappear by covering them with self-adhesive sheets printed with flowering clematis, a beech hedge, variegated ivy or, horror, Cupressus leylandii.

Wheelie Bin Cover Company Ltd, Leigh Road, Worsley, Manchester M28 1JY

Tel: 0800 783 4767 **Fax:** 0800 783 4768

E-mail: wheelie@aspull.com

Price range: £14.95. Leaflet free.

Payment: cheque, postal order, Mastercard, Visa, Delta, Switch.

Postage & packing: included in UK.

Delivery: allow 28 days.

Refunds: by arrangement.

Whichford Pottery

Because these hefty and traditional flower pots and urns are made from blended local clays, hand-thrown and finished, they have a 10-year guarantee against frost. Over 20 people now work in this smart pottery, which uses more than five tons of clay each week. The biggest pots are huge and can take six weeks to create. Styles vary from plain terracotta to swagged and garlanded urns.

Whichford Pottery, Whichford, near Shipston-on-Stour, Warwickshire CV36 5PG

Tel: 01608 684416 **Fax:** 01608 684833

Price range: £3.50 to £1,595. Send 6 first class stamps for catalogue.

Payment: cheque.

Postage & packing: £15.50 per order in mainland UK except Scotland and Cornwall which are £20.

Delivery: allow 30 days, longer for large pots. Supplies can be limited.

Refunds: yes, if returned undamaged within 14 days.

Specials: set of charming postcards for £3.95 including p&p.

Wiggly Wigglers

When you order the brochure, it comes entitled *A Home Guide to Worms at Work* which explains that there are 28 different species of earthworm in Britain but you will get a deep burrowing common earthworm plus two composting worms, Reds and Dendras. You can buy composting kits, a wormery and up to 2,000 worms to go with it plus feeding treats for your worms. They repay the effort by turning household rubbish into nutritious compost.

Wiggly Wigglers Ltd, Lower Blakemere Farm, Blakemere, Herefordshire HR2 9PX
Tel: 01981 500391
Fax: 01981 500108
Price range: £3.99 to £84.90. Catalogue free.
Payment: cheque, postal order, Mastercard, Visa, Switch, Eurocard.
Postage & packing: £2.95. Express delivery add £3. Saturday delivery add £5.
Delivery: normally despatched by carrier within 3 days.
Refunds: yes.
Specials: gift tokens.

Wild Seeds It's curiously difficult to get bluebells in the sort of quantity you need for a bluebell wood without going bankrupt. But Mike Thorne can send you 10,000 bluebell seeds for £40 or 1,000 five-year-old bulbs for £100. Also wild daffodils, snowdrops, wild garlic and primroses in quantity.

Wild Seeds, Branas, Llandderfel, Gwynedd LL23 7RF
Price range: £7 to £500. Catalogue free.
Payment: cheque.
Postage & packing: 10% of order.
Delivery: 24-hour delivery available at extra cost.
Refunds: yes.

Windrush Mill A good general mail order catalogue for gardeners. It doesn't bother too much with plants but concentrates on accessories. These may be foldaway wheelbarrows or hefty log splitters at the practical end to statues and sundials at the ornamental end. There is even a wooden tool store, five foot high, which will tuck into a corner and solve storage problems in small gardens.

HOUSE AND GARDEN

Windrush Mill, Witney, Oxfordshire OX8 6BH
Tel: 01993 770456 **Fax:** 01993 770477
Price range: £5 to £600. Catalogue free.
Payment: cheque, postal order, major credit/debit cards.
Postage & packing: £2.50 for orders under £30, £3.50 thereafter. Next day delivery add £4.95. Overseas rates on application.
Delivery: allow 7 days.
Refunds: yes.

See also: Baileys Architectural Antiques, The Barometer Shop, Black Dog of Wells, Bond & Gibbins, The Carrier Co, Colour Blue, The English Picnic Basket Company, Friars Goose Ltd, G.R.B.S. (Enterprises), Garden Books by Post, The Gluttonous Gardener, Grenadier Firelighters, Halzephron Herb Farm, If Only..., Periwinkle Productions, R.H.S. Enterprises, Touch Design, Walcot Reclamation, Woollons Brothers.

Chapter Four

FOOD AND DRINK

GENERAL

When you consider the amount of food, drink and other essentials a small family uses a week, you will understand why most of us feel the need to do A Big Shop at the local supermarket. But why not leave the whole business to someone who will deliver it to your door? Most supermarket shopping does not need a trained eye or a discriminating palate, you simply plough your way along the rows of baked beans and kitchen paper. Firms who deliver will generally arrange to drop packages off in basements, outhouses or with neighbours.

GENERAL FOOD CATALOGUES - LISTINGS

Bon Goût Luxury foods are becoming ever more acceptable for presents as recipes require arcane ingredients. David and Cynthia Edwards lived in the Lot region of France and now import the delicacies they discovered there. Try their virgin oils from walnuts, hazelnuts and almonds as well as fashionable truffle oil; also nuts in cocoa and, new this year, Perigord prunes in dark chocolate. The firm also makes up hampers.

> **Bon Goût Ltd**, Folieu View, Maughold, Isle of Man IM7 1BN
> **Tel/Fax:** 01624 815810
> **Price range:** £3.35 to £77.25. Catalogue free.
> **Payment:** cheque, major credit cards.
> **Postage & packing:** at cost.
> **Delivery:** by return. Last Christmas orders by 20 December.
> **Refunds:** by arrangement.

FOOD AND DRINK

Carluccio's The Italian shop run by this well-known cook and mushroom enthusiast is a delight and the mail order catalogue mirrors his enthusiasms. There are hampers like the Piccolo Gourmet to introduce you to Italian cooking at its best which includes pasta, polenta, sundried tomatoes and special olive oil from Liguria, a box of groceries from Southern Italy with chillies, char-grilled artichokes, biscuits made with wild fennel and salted baby peaches. You can get a large chunk of parmesan with its own knife and board; a special mushroom knife with a brush at the end; a box of Vin Santo and almond biscuits, panforte, oil, balsamic vinegar or, simpler still, Carluccio's inspiring cookery books or a gift voucher. Antonio and Priscilla (she's Terence Conran's sister) say the range is ideal for presents of all kinds – weddings, moving house, birthdays and celebrations along with corporate gifts. Everything is beautifully packed.

> **Carluccio's**, 28a Neal Street, London WC2H 9PS
> **Tel:** 0171 240 1487 **Fax:** 0171 497 1361
> **E-mail:** carluccios@cix.compulink.co.uk
> **Price range:** 98p to £260. Catalogue free.
> **Payment:** cheque, postal order, major credit cards.
> **Postage & packing:** £5 for orders up to £60, £7.50 to £150, £10 to £499, free thereafter in mainland UK.
> **Delivery:** by courier. Last Christmas orders by 19 December.
> **Refunds:** no.
> **Specials:** bespoke gift service.

Chatsworth Farm Shop The shop has won numerous awards for its goods – recently the BBC Good Food award for the Best Specialist Shop – and I have enormous admiration for the Duchess of Devonshire, who is behind it. Like everything she touches, it is imaginative, tops in quality and extremely efficient. Using local produce and the huge Chatsworth estate, the range includes a good all-round meat selection, the Duchess of Devonshire's range of cakes, preserves, puddings and biscuits, cordial from the Belvoir fruit farms and cheese from the Chewton dairy farms. The Cavendish ham, a combined effort of Chatsworth and Mooreland Foods, a Cheshire smokehouse, is new on the market. From Cheshire pigs, it is marinaded in molasses, honey, spices and juniper berries from an 18th century recipe, and hung for four months to mature. There are no additives, injected water or artificial colourings – in fact, this is a ham which could easily have been eaten by the Duke's ancestors 250 years ago.

Chatsworth Farm Shop, Stud Farm, Pilsley, Bakewell, Derbyshire DE45 1UF

Tel: 01246 583392 **Fax:** 01246 582514

E-mail: farmshop@chatsworth-house.co.uk

Website: http://www.chatsworth-house.co.uk

Price range: £1 to £350. Catalogue free.

Payment: cheque, postal order, major credit/debit cards.

Postage & packing: £9.50 or less for smaller orders.

Delivery: next day. Timed deliveries at extra cost. Last Christmas orders by 14 December.

Refunds: in the case of fresh foods phone for instructions, otherwise return by post

Specials: presentation boxes for hampers/gifts.

The Clark Trading Company

A small general catalogue of food, mostly Mediterranean. The idea is to stock your store cupboard with pâtés, cassoulets, confits and various luxury game stews from France along with the best ingredients such as Carnaroli rice, saffron, good pasta, the ubiquitous but still delectable olive oils and balsamic vinegars from Italy. Their specials include caviar, foie gras, smoked sturgeon, jamon serrano, the best paprika and sweet quince cheese. The catalogue is a good source for special meals which need no preparation.

The Clark Trading Company, 17 Southbrook Road, Lee, London SE12 8LH

Tel: 0181 297 9937/0800 731 6430 **Fax:** 0181 297 9993

Price range: 95p to £61.50. Catalogue free.

Payment: cheque, Mastercard, Visa, Delta, Switch.

Postage & packing: £3.95 for orders up to £75, free thereafter. Possible premium for Highlands and Islands.

Delivery: usually same day despatch for overnight delivery by courier, possibly longer at busy times. Timed delivery at cost.

FOOD AND DRINK

Last Christmas orders by 17 December.
Refunds: yes.
Specials: gift-wrapping, hampers, gift vouchers.

Felicitous One of a new breed of shops which sells exciting foods sourced from all over the world but will also mail order on request. British food includes breads from De Gustibus, cheese from Neal's Yard, wild flower honey from Colonsay and there are cookies from Florida, aromatic vinegars from Corsica and pasta from Tuscany. With notice the company can produce an entire dinner party for you, and make a children's party go with a whizz. There are presents, hampers, wines and special Christmas goodies. Currently Felicity Osborne is developing her own range of sauces, marinades and dressings which will be available soon.

Felicitous, 19 Kensington Park Road, London W11 2EU
Tel: 0171 243 4050 **Fax:** 0171 243 4052
Price range: from 55p. No catalogue at present but staff are happy to discuss orders on the telephone.
Payment: cheque, major credit/debit cards.
Postage & packing: at cost.
Delivery: delivery arranged within Central London, elsewhere by post. Express delivery available.
Refunds: yes, if goods are returned unopened.
Specials: gift-wrapping.

Fine Food Club For an annual membership fee, currently £12.50, but free membership offers occasionally available, you get access to specialist food producers who normally won't sell direct or to major stores. The list includes bacon and ham from Dorset, Chewton Mendip cheddar, chutneys, smoked foods and English wines. There's an enthusiastic newsletter. Orders are sent off monthly on a fixed date.

Fine Food Club, Unit 43, Vanalloys Business Park, Busgrove Lane, Stoke Row, Oxfordshire RG9 5QB
Tel: 01491 682311 **Fax:** 01491 682425
E-mail: finefood@aol.com
Price range: £1.25 to £70. Catalogue free.

Payment: cheque, major credit/debit cards.
Postage & packing: £6.95 up to 25 kg.
Delivery: next day carrier service.
Refunds: credit note.
Specials: gift parcels custom made. Seasonal specials.

The Food Ferry Only for Londoners, I'm afraid, because this is a brilliant idea – a home delivery supermarket which is not tied to the big chains. For a small fee, the company will deliver the equivalent of your big weekly shop – food, drink, kitchen towels, kettle de-scalers, stamps, shampoos and organic and ready-made foods. But, not only is it easier than the superstore, you get a better and more sophisticated choice. People in big cities everywhere should rise up and demand their own.

The Food Ferry Company,
Telephone, fax, e-mail, and internet only.
Tel: 0171 498 0827 **Fax:** 0171 498 8009
E-mail: sales@foodferry.co.uk
Website: http://www.foodferry.co.uk
Price range: normal grocery prices. Catalogue free.
Payment: cash, cheque, major credit/debit cards. Corporate accounts negotiable.
Postage & packing: no charge for first order, £3-£4 + VAT for each subsequent delivery.
Delivery: each area has specified delivery day. Last Christmas orders by 23 December.
Refunds: yes, if still resaleable and returned in 48 hours.

The Fresh Food Company Thoby Young has been delivering fresh fish direct from Cornwall to Londoners for eight years. Now he's expanded to include organic fruit and vegetables, bread, meat, wines and other drinks and spring water from the National Trust. There are also free range eggs, chicken, steak and pork pies, cheese, untreated milk, cream and butter. Fish boxes include "catch of the day", "prime catch", boxes for barbecuing and of shellfish, live crabs and white fish fillets. In season, you can buy oysters too.

FOOD AND DRINK 173

The Fresh Food Company, 326 Portobello Road, London W10 5RU
Tel: 0181 969 0351 **Fax:** 0181 964 8050
E-mail: organic@freshfood.co.uk
Website: http://www.freshfood.co.uk
Price range: 95p to £59.95. Catalogue free.
Payment: major credit/debit cards.
Postage & packing: included for most items, £5 for meat orders under £75.
Delivery: weekly or fortnightly.
Refunds: by arrangement.
Specials: weekly newsletters and recipes.

James & John Graham The firm has been in Penrith, a market town near the borders, since 1793 and their shop has an 18th century air about it. The labels they put on their teas, preserves and other products date from then and show a fine horse and carriage. This means that their hampers are extremely decorative and their range of Cumberland foods – mustard, cheese, fudge and smoked Cumberland sausage – beautifully packaged. You can even get a teatowel to match.

J & J Graham Ltd, Market Square, Penrith, Cumbria CA11 7BS
Tel: 01768 862281 **Fax:** 01768 867941
E-mail: grahams@cumbria.com
Website: http://www.cumbria.com/grahams/
Price range: £28 to £370. Catalogue free.
Payment: cheque, major credit cards.
Postage & packing: £7.95 to £15 in mainland UK. Overseas rates on application.
Delivery: by overnight carrier, despatched within 24 hours by arrangement. Last Christmas orders by 14 December. After this date by arrangement.
Refunds: by arrangement. Damaged goods will be replaced within 48 hours.
Specials: hampers can be tailor-made to requirements.

Made in America Suffering Americans away from home use this catalogue to remind them of Stateside tastes but the majority of customers are British. Since we discovered that

American food was not just Chicken Maryland and waffles, we've been mad about Tex Mex hot sauces from hell, hot dog relishes and chowder soups. There are lots of snacks and mixes to make life easy (including Margherita and Pina Colada for drinks) along with cooking accessories like Bagel slicers, which no expat can be without.

Made in America Ltd, Unit 5B, Hathaway Retail Park, Foundry Lane, Chippenham, Wiltshire SN15 1JG

Tel: 01249 447558 **Fax:** 01249 446142

Price range: about £1 to £7 for most items. Catalogue free.

Payment: major credit cards.

Postage & packing: £5.99 for orders under £25, £3.99 for orders under £50, £1.99 for orders over £50. EU by individual quotation.

Delivery: normally within 2 weeks. Last Christmas orders by 17 December.

Refunds: yes.

Monte's

This is an Italian food shop a few hundred yards from my door. It has a splendid array of oils, cheeses, salamis and pasta along with traditional Italian presents like silvered almonds, biscuits, salt and herbs in decorative layered bottles. Though not officially a mail order company, they will send by mail anything they can. I can thoroughly recommend them.

Monte's, 23 Canonbury Lane, Islington, London N1 2AS

Tel: 0171 354 4335

Price range: from around £1. No catalogue.

Payment: cheque, major credit cards.

Postage & packing: according to weight.

Delivery: normally 48 hours.

Refunds: by arrangement.

Morel Bros, Cobbett & Son

Excellent general list of packed foods including pastes such as Patum Peperium and anchoiade, relishes, mustards (both English and French), truffles and caviar. Especially good on peppercorns and salts including fleur de sel, salt with seaweed and large grain sea salt, black, pink, green pepper and allspice. Also tea and coffee, jams and chocolates.

FOOD AND DRINK

Morel Bros, Cobbett & Son Ltd, Unit 7, 129 Coldharbour Lane, London SE5 9NY
Tel: 0171 346 0046 **Fax:** 0171 346 0033
E-mail: info@morel.co.uk
Website: http://www.morel.co.uk
Price range: £1.45 to £150. Catalogue free in UK.
Payment: cheque, major credit/debit cards.
Postage & packing: £3.95. Perishable food delivery £7.95 in mainland UK. Overseas at cost.
Delivery: usually within 10 days.
Refunds: if faulty and returned within 10 days.
Specials: gift-wrapping £3.50.

Organics Direct More for the vegetarian, this firm delivers organic fruit and vegetables, cheese, milk and eggs direct to the door. Equally interesting for those with allergies or strong views, they do organic bread like rye, spiced buns and onion or rosemary bread, organic olive and sunflower oil, sprouted seeds, cakes and herbs. There are baby foods for four-month-olds and infant cereals plus wine and beer for older people.

Organics Direct, 1-7 Willow Street, London EC2A 4BH
Tel: 0171 729 2828 **Fax:** 0171 729 0534
Website: www.organicsdirect.com
Price range: 55p to £325. Catalogue free.
Payment: cheque, major credit/debit cards.
Postage & packing: included in mainland UK if a vegetable box is part of the order, otherwise £5 up to 25 kgs.
Delivery: 48 hours for orders received before 2.30 pm Monday to Wednesday, orders received Thursday/Friday delivered following Tuesday.
Refunds: yes, if notified immediately.

Quintessentials Europe French foods from the Comtesse du Barry range are available either as packed gifts such as a box of duck and goose foie gras, six pâtés and rillettes, or even as a presentation dinner for two (for instance, duck bordelais with ceps, pear soufflé with pear brandy and two half bottles of wine chosen to suit). There is a large range of other French delicacies to order, including cassoulet, salted pork with Puy lentils and lots of terrines and pâtés. Hampers are sent out in pretty wicker baskets.

Quintessentials Europe Ltd, 5a, 77 Anson Road. London N7 0AX
Tel: 0171 580 5068 **Fax:** 0171 637 8683
Price range: from £1.20. Catalogue free.
Payment: cheque, major credit cards.
Postage & packing: £2.50 or free for orders over £50.
Delivery: allow 12 working days. Last Christmas orders by 7 December.
Refunds: yes.

See also: Meat Matters.

BREADS, CAKES AND PUDDINGS.

While I occasionally make bread, I am completely useless at both cakes and puddings so, instead of struggling, I buy from the professionals. All these foods are very easily transported and, with the exception of bread, do not need to be eaten within a day or so. There is a huge range available which includes traditional British puddings and cakes – it's getting smart to provide British meals for guests at the moment – while firms offer breads for those who have allergic reactions to flour or yeast or to diabetics.

BREADS, CAKES AND PUDDINGS - LISTINGS

Betty's and Taylors of Harrogate Everything you need for afternoon tea from this typically English café which has become world-famous. From the Betty's department there are fruit cakes in tins (Old Peculier made with Yorkshire's own ale and Earl Grey flavoured with the tea), biscuits and shortbread, as well as German and Swiss biscuits to commemorate the

FOOD AND DRINK

café's Swiss founder. There are also charming hand-made chocolates and special coffees and teas which they have been blending since 1886.

Betty's and Taylors of Harrogate Ltd, 1 Parliament Street, Harrogate, North Yorkshire HG1 2QU
Tel: 01423 886055 **Fax:** 01423 881083
Price range: 68p to £150. Catalogue free.
Payment: cheque, major credit/debit cards.
Postage & packing: £5.90.
Delivery: allow 14 days.
Refunds: by arrangement.
Specials: gift-wrapping, special date delivery.

Bryson's of Keswick

This is an old-fashioned bakery, established in the 1940s, in the heart of the Lake District. The mail order list includes the shop's most popular lines and those which last longest, for virtually no additives are used. The list is typically British, with rich, orangey Dundee cake, simnel cake with almond paste baked for Easter and Bryson's Finest Fruit Cake made, they say, with the finest ingredients money can buy. Also there are selections to bring a tear to the expat's eye – high tea with cherry and madeira slab cakes, the Fellside selection including ginger cake and almond fancies and the Lakeland selection of rum butter, Borrowdale tea bread and ginger cake, among others. There's also a Christmas pudding. What's more, they come in old-fashioned cake tins.

John Bryson Ltd, 42 Main Street, Keswick, Cumbria CA12 5JD
Tel: 01768 771222 **Fax:** 01768 775456
Price range: £9.75 to £29.95. Leaflet free.
Payment: cheque, major credit cards.
Postage & packing: included in UK, Europe £4 extra per item, elsewhere £11 extra per item.
Delivery: 7 days. 3-day delivery at extra cost. Last Christmas orders by last posting date.
Refunds: at company's discretion.
Specials: special requests if possible.

MAIL ORDER MADE EASY

Cartmel Village Shop Based near the Lake District, the shop sells a single product – their own sticky toffee pudding. It's home made and more like a beautifully rich, but not over-sweet, old-fashioned treacle pud. We loved it and intend to get more. Also the sticky toffee sauce, which the firm suggests should be poured over ice-cream. Both can be stored in the freezer.

Cartmel Village Shop, The Square, Cartmel, Grange-over-Sands, Cumbria LA11 6QB
Tel/Fax: 01539 536201
Price range: pudding £2.15 for 250g, sauce £1.50 for 170g.
Payment: cheque.
Postage & packing: at cost to a maximum of £6.50 for orders under £35, free over £35.
Delivery: by first class post. Last Christmas orders by 16 December.
Refunds: yes.

Collin Street Bakery If you want a cake with a difference, get in touch with this bakery in Texas. The baker makes 80,000 lbs of cake a day and sends them all over the world including 75,000 to Britain. The cake has quantities of pecan nuts in the recipe plus cherries and pineapple from its own plantation. It arrives in a tin illustrated with an old-fashioned house under snow.

Collin Street Bakery, 401 W 7th Avenue, Corsicana, Texas 75110, USA
Tel: 001 903 872 8111 **Fax:** 001 903 872 6879
E-mail: collin@airmail.net
Price range: $16.15 to $38.95. Catalogue free.
Payment: major credit cards.
Postage & packing: $6.45, $6.95 and $7.45 for small, medium and large cakes respectively.
Delivery: Last Christmas orders by 5 November.
Refunds: yes.

Dickinson & Morris The firm has been making the Original Melton Hunt Cake since 1854, when it was served to the hunt together with a stiff drink in a stirrup cup. Designed to give

FOOD AND DRINK

179

energy, it is stuffed with good quality dried fruit, almonds and butter with an added measure of rum . Almonds and glacé cherries stud its top, and each cake comes packed in a special carton. This is a firm favourite round the world, especially among ex-pats who find it a taste of home.

Dickinson & Morris Ltd, Ye Olde Pork Pie Shoppe and The Sausage Shop, 8-10 Nottingham Street, Melton Mowbray, Leicestershire LE13 1NW
Tel/Fax: 01664 562341
Price range: £7.20 a cake. Catalogue free.
Payment: cheque, postal order, major credit cards.
Postage & packing: £3.90 in UK.
Delivery: allow 14 days.
Refunds: no.
Specials: hampers, gift service.

Doves Farm Foods This farm has been producing organic foods since 1978, specialising in different grains. Some of these make interesting breads and cakes; others are for those with allergies to gluten. The ordinary wheat flour includes wholemeal, white, bleached and unbleached, and self-raising. Stoneground rye flour makes North European speciality breads while 'spelt' was a discovery of early man. There is gram flour for Indian dishes and brown rice flour for baby food and gluten-free bread. There are also organic cornflakes and digestive biscuits.

Doves Farm Foods Ltd, Salisbury Road, Hungerford, Berkshire RG17 0RF
Tel: 01488 684880 **Fax:** 01488 685235
Price range: £14.50 to £28.70. Send A4 sae for catalogue.
Payment: cheque, postal order.
Postage & packing: included.
Delivery: usually 7 days, but allow 21.
Refunds: by arrangement.

Hobbs House Bakery A really exciting bakery which is slightly half-hearted about mail order: they generally sell to caterers of upmarket events and those who already know their produce. Obviously, the best way to sample their breads, cakes, quiches and buns is to try them direct and then order by mail but I think it's probably worth a try without that. They have a huge list of overnight breads, white breads, wholemeal and malted brown breads along with some interesting specialities: bread made of flour and ground sunflower seeds, soda bread, sourdough rye and the popular Italians like ciabatta, foccacia, Pugliese and bread flavoured with olives or sun-dried tomatoes.

Hobbs House Bakery, Unit 6, Chipping Edge Estate, Hatters Lane, Chipping Sodbury, Bristol BS37 6AA
Tel: 01454 321629 **Fax:** 01454 329757
Price range: 14p to £9.79. Minimum order 10kg. Price list free.
Payment: cheque.
Postage & packing: £13.69 for 10kg.
Delivery: by Amtrak.
Refunds: by arrangement.

Jenkins & Hustwit Two experienced home economists got together to create the sort of cakes for which the north of England has always been known. There are rich fruit cakes to cut and keep, fruit loaves to slice and munch with butter and special fruity Christmas puddings. The list also includes low fat cakes and others ideal for diabetics.

Jenkins & Hustwit Ltd, Farmhouse Fruit Cakes, 3b Laurel Way, Bishop Auckland, County Durham DL14 7NF
Tel: 01388 605005 **Fax:** 01740 622359
Price range: £2 to £250. Catalogue free.
Payment: cheque.
Postage & packing: from £3.
Delivery: within 1 week. Last Christmas orders 7 December.
Refunds: by arrangement.
Specials: goods presented according to occasion.

John Pimblett The bakery, which has been in the family for three generations, has had the neat idea of mail ordering its goods for all celebrations. These range from Christmas,

FOOD AND DRINK

Twelfth Night and Valentine's Day in winter to a whole slew in summer. There are packages for all the British saints' days, May Day and Whitsun, April Fool's day (a cardboard cake perhaps?), Guy Fawkes and Hallowe'en. Besides this, the firm will make corporate gifts and those for your own special occasion.

John Pimblett & Sons Ltd, College Bakery, College Street, St Helens, Merseyside WA10 1TP

Tel: 01744 28644 **Fax:** 01744 454027

E-mail: john@pimbletts.demon.co.uk

Price range: £6.50 to £30. Catalogue free.

Payment: cheque, major credit/debit cards.

Postage & packing: £5.25 for up to 5kg. Overnight delivery £10.95. Overseas rates on application.

Delivery: 4-5 days by carrier. Overnight delivery available. Last Christmas orders by 15 December.

Refunds: by arrangement.

Specials: gift-wrapping, corporate gifts, individual attention.

The Little Red Barn To look at Adriana Rabinovich's brochure is to drool at the mouth. Then, when you try her double-chocolate brownies, you realise that the pictures don't tell you half. They and other delicious cookies and savouries come beautifully packed and make marvellous presents. You can have brownies for stocking fillers, trays gift wrapped and even sweetheart brownies. Once tried, you are hooked.

Little Red Barn Ltd, New Timber Lodge, Little London Road, Silchester, Berkshire RG7 2PN

Tel: 0118 971 4322 **Fax:** 0118 971 4515

E-mail: redbarn@dial.pipex.com

Price range: from £3.99. £12 minimum for mail order. Catalogue free.

Payment: cheque, major credit/debit cards except Amex.

Postage & packing: from £3.75 for parcels up to 1kg.

Delivery: allow 10 days. Next day delivery service £8.50. Last Christmas orders by 16 December for postal delivery or by 20 December for delivery by courier at additional cost.

Refunds: yes, if notified within 7 working days.

Specials: gift wrapping at £2.50. Customised gift service.

MacGregor's Galloway Oatcakes

MacGregor's Galloway Oatcakes MacGregor's have been baking oatcakes for over a century and they know how it is done. The current bakers are James and his daughter, April. The mail order business started because so many customers wanted the oatcakes sent to far corners of the world. The oatcakes are suitable for vegetarians.

MacGregor's Galloway Oatcakes, 22-24 Albert Street, Newton Stewart, Wigtownshire DG8 6EJ

Tel: 01671 402678

Price: £6.60 per box (12 packets). Special rates for 4 boxes or more.

Payment: cheque, postal order.

Postage & packing: £3.35. Overseas at cost.

Delivery: by Parcel Force, normally 3 working days. Last Christmas orders preferably 3 weeks in advance.

Refunds: by arrangement.

Meg Rivers Cakes and Gifts by Post

Meg Rivers Cakes and Gifts by Post Cakes for rowers and golfers, sailors and cricketers can be accompanied by a large Royal Worcester teacup appropriately decorated. Meg Rivers also ices cakes to order for children, birthdays or special occasions and there's a zodiac cake to suit your sign. She naturally has a Christmas special and there are even hampers, Christmas pudding and wheat-free cake for those allergic to flour.

Meg Rivers Cakes and Gifts by Post, Middle Tysoe, Warwickshire CV35 0SE

Tel: 01295 688101 **Fax:** 01295 680799

Price range: £2 to £55. Catalogue free.

Payment: cheque, major credit/debit cards.

Postage & packing: £2.95 for each address in mainland UK. Overseas rates on application.

Delivery: allow 4-5 days. Express delivery available. Last Christmas orders by 12 December (UK), 5 December (Europe), 28 November (elsewhere).

Refunds: by arrangement.

Specials: Cake club membership £96.50 – members receive six different delicious cakes during the year. Custom hampers.

FOOD AND DRINK

Mrs Gill's Country Cakes I sometimes get the feeling that everyone in the west country is busy making fruit cakes. Mrs Gill (in reality Jacqueline Gill) makes delicious Christmas cakes both for personal and corporate customers and a gigantic square fruit cake covered with walnuts, almonds and cherries for hotels (or your family at Christmas). There are, too, tiered cakes for weddings and others for christenings or birthdays. Or just for days when you fancy a slice.

Mrs Gill's Country Cakes, Link House, Leat Street, Tiverton, Devon EX16 5LG
Tel/Fax: 01884 242744
E-mail: mrs_gills_country_cakes@compuserve.com
Price range: £3.60 to £50. Catalogue free.
Payment: cheque.
Postage & packing: £3 to £6.75.
Delivery: allow 14 days. Overnight delivery at extra charge. Last Christmas orders 12 December.
Refunds: yes.
Specials: gift boxes available for some cakes.

Real Cakes Last year, when I was on GMTV for my previous book, we all had a mouthful of delicious cake from Anna and Hugh Evans's company. Most in the range are traditional fruit cakes with the addition of toddy, port, brandy and sherry. Anna says she has now been asked for a teetotal cake and has come up with Almond Surprise (a thin layer of almond paste runs through the cake and tests are encouraging). All the cakes use free-range eggs, Devon butter, organic flour and delicious dried fruits and come in presentation tins.

Real Cakes, Anne's Park, Cowley, Exeter, Devon EX5 5EN
Tel/Fax: 01392 211286
E-mail: anna.evans@ndirect.co.uk
Price range: £13.55 to £23. Catalogue free.
Payment: cheque, major credit cards.
Postage & packing: included.
Delivery: by first class post allow 14 days, usually less . Last Christmas orders by 10 December.
Refunds: yes for genuine complaint.

184 MAIL ORDER MADE EASY

Sarah Meade's Special Occasion Cakes Cooks have hardly begun to experiment with fusion food and exotic spices for cakes but Sarah Meade produces some original ideas (like Sticky Lemon and Whisky Ginger Cake) as well as Medieval Twelfth Night cakes, Victorian Plum Fruit Cake and even a limited edition Christmas pudding. All are carefully packaged and presented in checked or "wickerwork" card boxes. Other cakes celebrate Easter and birthdays.

> **Sarah Meade's Special Occasion Cakes**, 8 The Calvert Centre, Woodmancott, Winchester, Hampshire SO21 3BN
> **Tel:** 01256 397163 **Fax:** 01256 397874
> **Price range:** from £8.75 to £17.95. Leaflet free.
> **Payment:** cheque, major credit cards except Amex.
> **Postage & packing:** included in UK.
> **Delivery:** Last Christmas orders by 10 December.
> **Refunds:** by arrangement.

Squires Kitchen If you enjoy making elaborate cakes, this is the firm to talk to. Their catalogue is renowned among cake-makers everywhere. They sell equipment for baking cakes and for displaying them, as well as ingredients such as flavouring essences and icing colours. There are tools for complex icing and modelling, stencils (including a Christmas range) plus videos and books on the subject.

> **Squires Kitchen**, Squires House, 3 Waverley Lane, Farnham, Surrey GU9 8BB
> **Tel:** 01252 711749/734309 **Fax:** 01252 714714
> **Price range:** from 10p. Send £2 cheque or postal order for catalogue.
> **Payment:** cheque, major credit/debit cards.
> **Postage & packing:** from £1.50 for £5 order, free over £100.
> **Delivery:** within 2 weeks.
> **Refunds:** will replace within 10 days.
> **Specials:** gift vouchers.

Truffles This is the real thing, food cooked by the grand-child of a genuine country house cook. You can't get much more

FOOD AND DRINK

authentic than Barbara Bayfield's Victorian and Christmas puddings. New this year are fig and ginger pudding with cider brandy and apricot and pineapple with rum. Neither, she says, have any mixed peel or glacé cherries, they are made with vegetable suet and come in one or two pound sizes.

Truffles, 72 Belle Vue Road, Salisbury, Wiltshire SP1 3YD
Tel: 01722 331978
Price range: £3 to £14.75. Larger sizes available on request.
Payment: cheque, postal order.
Postage & packing: 90p to £4.
Delivery: allow 14 days. Last Christmas orders by 15 December.
Refunds: yes, if faulty.

The Village Bakery

Andrew Whitley has been making organic bread, puddings and cakes using traditional wood-fired ovens for twenty years. His range is small but good. Bread includes French and Russian rye and the smart breads with olives, tomato and wild mushroom mixed into the dough. There are gingerbreads and tea breads as well as Christmas cakes and mince pies, shortbread, parkin and flapjacks. Brandy butter, Cumberland rum butter and organic Christmas hampers are also available.

The Village Bakery Melmerby Ltd, Melmerby, Penrith, Cumbria CA10 1HE
Tel: 01768 881515 **Fax:** 01768 881848
Price range: 99p to £16. Catalogue free.
Payment: cheque, major credit cards.
Postage & packing: £6 for orders up to £20, £5 to £30, £3 to £60, over £60 free.
Delivery: within 7 days.
Refunds: yes.
Specials: organic gifts.

CHEESE

Though the list includes some stalwarts like Paxton and Whitfield, whose cheeses come from all over the world, many of those in my list are cheesemakers themselves or people who have access to small British cheesemakers.

There has recently been a great upsurge among dairy farmers creating their own cheese, from Cornish Yarg to Northumberland cheese. I do recommend that you try as many as you can to discover your own favourites.

I, personally, really enjoy the enormous variety of tastes in our traditional Cheddar, preferably eaten alone, without biscuits or butter.

CHEESE - LISTINGS

The Cheese Hamlet For 25 years, this firm has specialised in cheeses English and foreign and now sell about 250 varieties, some of which are seasonal. The list is mouthwatering from the Swiss Glarus Schabziger, flavoured with melilot which arrived in Europe from Asia in the 11th century to Cornish Yarg made by Mike Horrell and wrapped in nettle leaves. They will also make up special packs for presents.

> **The Cheese Hamlet**, 706 Wilmslow Road, Didsbury, Manchester M20 2DW
> **Tel:** 0161 434 4781 **Fax:** 0161 445 0451
> **E-mail:** cheese.hamlet@onyxnet.co.uk
> **Website:** http://www.webart.co.uk/clients/hamlet
> **Price range:** up to £150. Catalogue free.
> **Payment:** cheque, major credit/debit cards.
> **Postage & packing:** £5 to £10.

Delivery: times vary according to availability.
Refunds: yes, if faulty.
Specials: gift packs available.

The Fine Cheese Co

Cheese makes a splendid gift all year round, for vegetarians too The packs and hampers from this firm are beautifully wrapped in coloured card and scarlet ribbons. They include chutneys and chocolates along with an excellent selection of unpasturised cheese. "We are confident that the contents have the power to thrill", they say.

The Fine Cheese Co, 29 Walcot Street, Bath BA1 5BN
Tel/Fax: 01225 483407
Price range: £25 to £75. Catalogue free.
Payment: cheque, major credit/debit cards.
Postage & packing: £6.95 to a single address within UK mainland, by overnight carrier. £2 for every additional item to same address.
Delivery: 24-hour delivery service available. Last Christmas orders by 18 December.
Refunds: by arrangement.

Jeroboams

This is a small and select mail order catalogue from the shop which sells wine, charcuterie but especially good cheeses. There are boxes of speciality British cheeses like Appleby Cheshire, Bassett Stilton and the Irish Milleens, a Normandy box of Camembert, Livarot and Pont l'Evêque and jars of Stilton. Also cheese accessories such as a small cheese larder like a tiny meat safe or a raclette machine which melts cheeses at the table. The company offers hampers, hams and foie gras and a very nice glass ice bucket, as well as its normal cheese list.

Jeroboams, 96 Holland Park Avenue, London W11 3RB
Tel: 0171 727 9792 **Fax:** 0171 792 3672
E-mail: cheese@jeroboam.co.uk
Website: http://www.jeroboam.demon.co.uk
Price range: £12.50 to £150. Catalogue free.
Payment: cheque, major credit/debit cards.
Postage & packing: £3.95.

Delivery: by overnight carrier. Last Christmas orders by 15 December.

Refunds: yes.

Specials: gift selections for Christmas, gift subscriptions to Jeroboams Cheese Club, which will send four seasonal cheeses per month.

The Northumberland Cheese Co Whenever I have people for a meal, I try to give them something unusual which, preferably I don't need to slave over. Unusual cheeses are ideal. Northumberland cheese is smooth and creamy, mild at first but full-flavoured while the smoked version won a gold medal in 1996 at the London International Cheese Competition; Elsdon goat cheese has, says Mark Robertson, "a memorable asparagus, goaty tang," which sounds beastly but isn't. The Coquetdale Cheese is semi-hard and, say critics, "a triumph of independent thinking." Make Me Rich Boiles, named after his farm, are small squares preserved in oil – and he also does a selection for you to try. Many will freeze.

The Northumberland Cheese Company Ltd, Make Me Rich Farm, Blagdon, Seaton Burn, Northumberland NE13 6BZ

Tel: 01670 789798 **Fax:** 01670 789644

E-mail: enquiries @northumberland-cheese.co.uk

Price range: from £7.95 per lb. Make me Rich Boiles from £4.25. Discounts on orders over £30 to one address. Catalogue free.

Payment: cheque, Mastercard, Access, Visa.

Postage & packing: included.

Delivery: allow 15 days.

Refunds: yes.

Specials: gift boxes and baskets.

Paxton & Whitfield Now 201 years old, the venerable cheese shop filled with Jermyn Street pinstripes has a gigantic selection of cheeses which they will mail to you on request. They run a Cheese Society which, for £22.50 a month, delivers seasonal cheeses – December gets, perhaps, Epoisses, Cheshire, Pavé d'Affinois and Bleu d'Auvergne; June has Gouda with cumin seed, gratte paille, bleu de Bresse and Port Salut. Then

FOOD AND DRINK

there are traditional accompaniments like port, hampers, pickles, cured hams, foie gras and smoked salmon.

Paxton & Whitfield Ltd, 93 Jermyn Street, London SW1Y 6JE
Tel: 0171 930 0259 **Fax:** 0171 321 0621
Website: http://www.ioi.co.uk/food/paxton.htm
Price range: approx £20 to £200. Catalogue free in UK. Postage charge overseas.
Payment: cheque, major credit cards.
Postage & packing: see catalogue.
Delivery: within 14 days worldwide.
Refunds: each case treated on its merits.
Specials: personal service. All requests considered.

Quicke's Traditional

This firm makes one of the zingiest pure Cheddar cheeses you can buy and has won many awards for it. Don't, therefore, serve foreign cheeses all the time but get a really good home-produced one. Quicke's also makes excellent butter and sells other top quality British cheeses.

J. G. Quicke & Partners, Home Farm Office, Newton St. Cyres, Exeter, Devon EX5 5AY
Tel: 01392 851222/851425 **Fax:** 01392 851382
Price range: £16.95 to £18.95. Price list free.
Payment: cheque, postal order.
Postage & packing: included.
Delivery: Last Christmas orders by 8 December.
Refunds: by arrangement.
Specials: selection boxes and presentation baskets available.

The Teddington Cheese

A terrific catalogue of European cheeses with emphasis put upon British and Irish cheeses, which have been having a renaissance. The catalogue is divided by country and variety of milk – cow, ewe, goat – whether pasteurised or not and whether suitable to vegetarians or pregnant women. Many come from dedicated cheesemakers and have glorious names like Stinking Bishop, Flower Marie and the famous Lanark Blue. About 50 French cheeses appear, nine Italians plus a handful from

MAIL ORDER MADE EASY

Scandinavia, Germany, Holland, Switzerland and Spain. Also a few biscuits, butters, pickles and cider.

The Teddington Cheese, 42 Station Road, Teddington, Middlesex TW11 9AA

Tel: 0181 977 6868 **Fax:** 0181 977 2318

E-mail: doug&tony@teddingtoncheese.co.uk

Website: http://www.teddingtoncheese.co.uk

Price range: cheese orders to any value. Hampers and selections from £7.50 to £165. Catalogue free.

Payment: cheque, major credit/debit cards.

Postage & packing: £5.95 for next day delivery in UK. Same day delivery prices on request. Overseas by arrangement.

Delivery: by next day courier to most UK destinations. Last Christmas orders one week in advance, but preferably earlier.

Refunds: yes.

Specials: custom hampers and selections available. Greetings cards with personalised messages can be enclosed.

See also: Graig Farm, Sharpham Partnership.

CONFECTIONERY

The argument between continental chocolates and British ones continues to rage. Should more cocoa butter be added or subtracted, is extra milk a good thing, should chocolate be dark or light? I think it's all a matter of taste, of choosing what you like, when. Several firms will pander to your views or try to convert you with new sweetie tastes. Either way, chocolate and sweets in general are still luxury goods with an element of naughtiness about them.

CONFECTIONERY - LISTINGS

The Cavendish Chocolate Company These are rich, beautifully designed and wonderfully made luxury chocolates

FOOD AND DRINK   191

from a small list. Some arrive with a bouquet of flowers or in a willow basket with a bottle of champagne while the smallest box, the ballotin, holds just 16 chocolates and makes an excellent small gift.

The Cavendish Chocolate Company Ltd, 3 Field End, Long Crendon, Buckinghamshire HP18 9EJ
Tel: 01844 201690 **Fax:** 01844 201680
Price range: £7.95 to £61.35. Catalogue free.
Payment: cheque, Mastercard, Visa.
Postage & packing: included. Guaranteed next day delivery at small surcharge. Overseas rates on application.
Delivery: by first class post or Parcel Force. Flowers by courier.
Refunds: yes, if valid.

Charbonnel & Walker In the 1890s a Madame Charbonnel started making truffles by having fresh cream sent to Bond Street every day. Today the firm uses pasteurised cream but, other than that, the recipe stays the same. As well as truffles there are delicious bittermints, sugared almonds, peppermint creams and special boxes for the theatre, for celebrations (a heart-shaped one for Valentine's day), cooking chocolate and chocolate drink for soothing nightcaps.

Charbonnel et Walker, One The Royal Arcade, 28 Old Bond Street, London W1X 4BT
Tel: 0171 491 0939 **Fax:** 0171 495 6279
Price range: £1.90 to £199. Catalogue free.
Payment: major credit cards. Special arrangements for overseas.
Postage & packing: see order form.
Delivery: up to 4 days. Last Christmas orders by 14 December.
Refunds: no.

Choc Express Chocolate as you never imagined it. You can buy a kit to mould your own choccy fruits or a night-time kit for hot chocolate drinks for two. There are champagne truffles which come in their own chocolate chest, tiny bars of dark and milk chocs making up 648 squares (roughly two a day for a year), chocolate pasta and a surprise box for children which should keep them quiet and sated for hours. With two catalogues a year, there are always new ideas on the way.

Choc Express, Mint House, Newark Close, Royston, Hertfordshire SG8 5HL
Tel: 01763 257744 **Fax:** 01763 245460
Price range: £4.95 to £49.95. Catalogue free.
Payment: cheque, postal order, major credit/debit cards.
Postage & packing: included. Overseas by arrangement.
Delivery: allow 2 days. Delivery by courier next working day for certain items. Last Christmas orders 21 December.
Refunds: yes.

The Chocolate Club The club has Ackermann's Bittermints 'enrobed' in dark chocolate with 99% cocoa solids, chocolate coated nuts such as brazils, almonds and hazelnuts and Melchior's Swiss-made pralines, while France supplies chocolate-filled prunes and hand-made chocolates containing Muscadet grapes soaked in Cléray spirit. To round off the sugar feast, there's panforte and Ricciarelli's almond biscuits from Italy.

The Chocolate Club Ltd, Unit 9, St Pancras Commercial Centre, 63 Pratt Street, London NW1 0BY.
Tel: 0171 267 5375 **Fax:** 0171 267 5357
Price range: under £5 to £20. Catalogue free.
Payment: cheque, postal order, major credit/debit cards.
Postage & packing: £3.50, free for orders over £60. Overseas rates on application.
Delivery: within 14 days.
Refunds: yes.
Specials: gift-wrapping at small additional charge. Anniversary and birthday gift service.

The Chocolate Society The firm makes its own range using only Valrhona chocolate which is low on sugar and high on cocoa. Bars may have candied fruit or stem ginger, nuts come coated with chocolate and there's a kit for making hot chocolate (including a molinillo, a South American swizzle stick). The catalogue branches out into coffee, Russian tea, caddies and hampers.

FOOD AND DRINK

The Chocolate Society, Clay Pit Lane, Roecliffe, near
Boroughbridge, North Yorkshire YO5 9LS
Tel: 01423 322230 **Fax:** 01423 322253
Website: http://www.chocolate.co.uk
Price range: £2 to £50. Send A4 envelope with 31p stamp for
catalogue.
Payment: cheque, major credit/debit cards.
Postage & packing: £2.50 for under 1kg, £5.50 for over 1kg in UK.
Overseas rates on application.
Delivery: allow 14 days. Last Christmas orders 10 days in
advance.
Refunds: yes, if faulty or damaged and returned within 3 days.
Specials: gift-wrapping £2.50 with hand-written card.

Devon Fudge Direct Really truly hand-made fudge which
has been made in Devon for three decades. But the company
also makes fudge for vegetarians and vegans and those with
allergies to dairy produce (which the owner's wife and daughter suffer from). There are 23 varieties of loose fudge to try,
from clotted cream to Devon nutty and six non-dairy flavours,
including my favourites of vanilla and chocolate. Other fudges
come covered in Belgian chocolate (a bit much for my taste,
but then I don't have a sweet tooth) and in wrapped bars.

Devon Fudge Direct, Quarry House, Heath Road, Brixham,
Devon TQ5 9AU
Tel/Fax: 01803 852592
Price range: from £1.40. Order form free.
Payment: cheque, major credit cards.
Postage & packing: included. Overseas by arrangement.
Delivery: by post. Last Christmas orders 17 December.
Refunds: by arrangement.
Specials: gift-wrapping.

Humphreys Exclusive Confectionery Delicious chocolates are made by David Humphreys in a small shop in the
moorland town of Ilkley. He has travelled Europe to get ideas
and recipes and the results are rich and sensuous. The chocolate
ranges are traditional English with rose, violet and strawberry
creams; Belgique with pralines and marzipan and Swiss truffles

flavoured with liqueurs. At Christmas there are marzipan petits fours and 'Christmas puddings' filled with praline and caramel plus novelties such as two-foot high Santas. He also makes Easter eggs in a choice of milk, plain or white chocolate including one over a metre tall weighing 40 kg.

Humphreys Exclusive Confectionery, 16 Leeds Road, Ilkley, West Yorkshire LS29 8DJ
Tel: 01943 609477
Price range: £6 to £30.65. Leaflet free.
Payment: cheque with order.
Postage & packing: included.
Delivery: by first class post.
Refunds: by arrangement.

The Toffee Shop I was given a small pack of Mr. Boustead's toffee and it is quite delicious. He tells me that it is made to a secret family recipe which is about 90 years old and is, of course, made by hand. There are two varieties of toffee: butter and treacle, and three of fudge: butter, chocolate and mint. Go for it.

The Toffee Shop, 7 Brunswick Road, Penrith, Cumbria CA11 7LU
Tel: 01768 862008
Price range: £3.95 to £16.95. Price list free.
Payment: cheque.
Postage & packing: included.
Delivery: by return.
Refunds: no.

See also: Vintage Roots for organic chocolates.

FISH.

Fish, like vegetables, must be eaten fresh. Buy them straight from the fisherman if you can. The next best thing is to buy them from the supplier who goes direct to the quay, picks the best of the catch and mails them to you in a coolbox overnight. Unless you live by the sea or near a seafood market, this is the best way to pick your fish. Similarly, smoked fish are best bought from the producer. You can choose those who use oak chips, whisky-soaked barrels or hot smoking as you please. Even though fish have been smoked for centuries, new techniques are constantly being tried and these firms will tell you about them first.

FISH - LISTINGS

Abbotsbury Oysters Oysters have been farmed on the Fleet lagoon, a nature reserve, since the 18th century and oysters themselves were growing there long before. The area, says the firm, is especially rich in plankton and other nutrients which oysters enjoy. Without any chemicals or additives, they take three years to grow from "seed" to market size. These are Pacific oysters which can be delivered within 24 hours of ordering.

> **Abbotsbury Oysters 1994 Ltd**, Ferrybridge, Weymouth, Dorset DT4 9YU
> **Tel:** 01305 788867 **Fax:** 01305 760661
> **Price range:** £16 to £52. Leaflet free.
> **Payment:** cheque, postal order, major credit cards.
> **Postage & packing:** included.
> **Delivery:** Tuesday to Friday within 24 hours.
> **Refunds:** by arrangement.

Alba Smokehouse Based in the Highlands, Alba supplies restaurants with interesting smoked foods (their smoked queen scallops won an award in 1995 and they were voted Scottish food company of the year in 1995, 96 and 97). Their smoked salmon comes with a honey roast flavour or with Cajun spices (which got a gold medal and best new food product of the year award in 1997). They also smoke trout, king and queen scallops and mussels. A connoisseur's pack gives the chance to try out most of the range.

Alba Smokehouse, The Smokery, Lochgilphead, Argyll PA31 8RR
Tel/Fax: 01546 606400
Price range: £4.50 to £30. Catalogue free.
Payment: cheque, major credit cards.
Postage & packing: included.
Delivery: despatched within 2 days of order. Last Christmas orders preferably by 15 December.
Refunds: yes.
Specials: gift cards and messages can be enclosed. Products are vacuum packed and suitable for freezing.

Glendevon Smoked Salmon

Smoked salmon from Glendevon comes to you direct from the smokehouse where it is smoked in the traditional manner. The vacuum-packed fish (delivered in a scarlet box) comes in sizes which are ideal for presents.

Glendevon Smoked Salmon, Crook of Devon, Kinross KY13 7UL
Tel: 01577 840297 **Fax:** 01577 840626
Price range: from £10.50 for 277 gms.
Payment: cheque, major credit cards.
Postage & packing: included in UK, Europe £2, elsewhere £7-£12.
Delivery: by first class post, despatched within 48 hours of order.
Refunds: yes.
Specials: products are all gift-wrapped.

Hebridean Seafoods

Salmon, fished from around the Isle of Lewis, is cured with a mixture of salt and sugar and then gradually smoked over smouldering oak shavings. You can buy it cut thin and interleaved or in thicker slices (surprising the difference this makes to the taste) or in small, trimmed bits which

FOOD AND DRINK

are just as good when made into pâté or sandwiches. 90% of the firm's customers order every year.

Hebridean Seafoods Ltd, Mackenzie's Smokehouse, Scaliscro, Uig, Isle of Lewis HS2 9EL

Tel: 01851 672325 **Fax:** 01851 672393

Price range: from £7.25 for a 200g pack. Leaflet free.

Payment: cheque, postal order, major credit cards.

Postage & packing: included in UK. Overseas rates on application.

Delivery: normally within 48 hours. Last Christmas orders at least 2 weeks in advance.

Refunds: yes.

Specials: messages can be enclosed. Discount on larger orders.

Inverawe Smokehouses While many of the smokehouses specialise in sending presents, this one is more for the dedicated cook. It not only sells an interesting range of smoked fish from the family-owned netting rights on the Awe – eel, halibut, kippers and smoked Loch Etive trout – but also smoked meats like ham, venison and beef. It can supply virtually all the ingredients for a dinner party (eg smoked duck with pears and kiwi fruit, Loch Etive fresh trout fillets with dill sauce, mince pies and brandy butter, cheese and biscuits at a cost of around £55 if you take six portions). It also sells Aberdeen Angus beef, cheeses, bacon and Christmas hams, cake, preserves and puddings.

Inverawe Smokehouses, Taynuilt, Argyll PA35 1HU

Tel: 01866 822446 **Fax:** 01866 822274

E-mail: info@inverawe.co.uk

Price range: £7.95 to £120. Catalogue free. International catalogue also available.

Payment: cheque, major credit/debit cards.

Postage & packing: included, next day delivery £3.

Delivery: allow 4 days. Order before 2 pm for next day delivery (no despatch on Fridays). Last Christmas orders by 12 December.

Refunds: where applicable.

Specials: hampers, gift boxes, gift vouchers, new and innovative products.

James Baxter You can spend a whole afternoon shelling tiny Morecambe bay shrimps, then enshrining them in spicy butter. Or you can buy your potted shrimps from Baxter, sent within 24 hours of being made. If there's any difference, Baxter's are better. I used to believe in the martyrdom of shelling each tiny crustacean – now I just buy direct and enjoy the delicacy on hot toast for a quick lunch alone or to serve at posh dinner parties. They freeze perfectly and defrost quickly.

James Baxter & Son, Thornton Road, Morecambe, Lancashire LA4 5PB

Tel: 01524 410910 **Fax:** 01524 833363

Price range: from £30 for 10 x 2oz cartons. Minimum order £30.

Payment: cheque, major credit cards.

Postage & packing: included.

Delivery: despatched Monday to Thursday in insulated containers by first class post or overnight courier. Give a week's notice for guaranteed delivery.

Refunds: by arrangement.

James of Pershore A reader recommended this firm to me for its huge variety of frozen fish which is delivered the next day at trade prices. On offer are the British staples like cod, haddock, halibut and plaice, along with exotics like swordfish, tuna, shark and hoki. There are shellfish, smoked fish and fish to cook in ready-made sauces. The firm prides itself on no-nonsense selling but top class produce.

James of Pershore, Freepost, Evesham WR11 6QL

Tel: 01386 45131

E-mail: mrjames@dial.pipex.com

Price range: 74p to £4.99 per lb. Catalogue free.

Payment: cheque, major credit cards.

Postage & packing: £7.05 for orders up to 40lb £14.10 thereafter.

Delivery: next day before noon.

Refunds: by arrangement.

Kileravagh Despite its name, the company smokes food in leafy Kent and will mail order either separate packs of its foods or three different hampers with an excellent choice. Not only is there the traditional smoked salmon, gravadlax and trout on offer but smoked eels, chicken, turkey, duck breasts and venison. The firm also sells special mayonnaise for smoked salmon flavoured with tarragon and lime or the hot Portuguese sauce, Piri Piri, and dill sauce for gravadlax. Even pets are catered for with Posh Pussy and Posh Pooch offcuts.

Kileravagh Smoked Foods, Hedgend Estate, Birchington, Kent CT7 0NB
Tel: 01843 847086 **Fax:** 01843 848000
Price range: £3.75 to £75. Leaflet free.
Payment: cheque, Mastercard, Visa, Switch.
Postage & packing: included.
Delivery: generally 24-hour service. Last Christmas orders 5 working days in advance.
Refunds: yes.
Specials: gift service, flexible orders for hampers.

Loch Fyne Oysters

Actually, they sell more than the oysters grown in their own fishery on the shore of Ardkinglas, Loch Fyne. There are mussels, scallop meat and langoustines from the baited creels off West Argyll. Smoked salmon, of course – the classic smoked for seven and more hours over oak chips from whisky barrels and bradan orach and rost (golden and roasted in Gaelic) which are interesting versions, one longer smoked, the other flaky – plus smoked fillet and gravadlax. They smoke mussels, trout, cod roe, kippers and eel fillets, too. There are also various marinaded herrings.

Loch Fyne Oysters Ltd, Clachan Farm, Cairndow, Argyll PA26 8BL
Tel: 01499 600264 **Fax:** 01499 600234
E-mail: loch_fyne_oysters@compuserve.com
Price range: £1.90 to £32. Price list free.
Payment: cheque, major credit/debit cards.
Postage & packing: £5.95, free for orders over £50.
Delivery: next day on mainland.
Refunds: yes, if notified within 48 hours of receipt.
Specials: gift boxes.

Lochengower

Lochengower This smokehouse specialises not only in smoked salmon but also in the mild-flavoured, soft-textured sea trout plus rainbow trout and venison. These foods are also used in special hampers and gift packs with a Scottish flavour. The Lochengower hamper, for instance, includes smoked salmon, shortbread, oatcakes, Dundee cake, raspberry preserve with Drambuie, a clootie dumpling and lots more. These hampers are well selected.

Lochengower, Kempleton Mill, Kirkcudbright DG6 4NJ
Tel: 01557 330361 **Fax:** 01557 330385
E-mail: lochengow@aol.com
Price range: £8.95 to £50. Catalogue free.
Payment: cheque, major credit cards.
Postage & packing: included in UK.
Delivery: by first class post. Last Christmas orders by last posting date.
Refunds: yes.
Specials: gift packs available.

Mackenzies

Mackenzies The smoking method of this firm is secret but no preservatives are used. Along with smoked salmon, they also smoke haddock (uncoloured), Wensleydale, Cheddar and Northumberland cheeses, ham and prawns which are delicious. They will also smoke to order if you have some abstruse cooking wish.

Mackenzies Smoked Products, Unit 1, Wood Nook Farm, Hardesty Hill, Blubberhouses, North Yorkshire LS21 2PQ
Tel: 01943 880365. Mobile: 0802 213633.
Price range: £1.95 to £7.90 per lb. Catalogue free.
Payment: cheque, major credit cards.
Postage & packing: at cost.
Delivery: by arrangement. Last Christmas orders by 15 December.
Refunds: never been asked.

Salar

Salar Based in the Outer Hebrides, Salar has created a new kind of smoked salmon which was launched last November.

FOOD AND DRINK

Instead of being thin sliced like the traditional variety, Flaky Smoked Salmon comes in a large chunk which has been smoked over wood. It flakes easily into bite-size pieces and, say the makers, should be given a good squeeze of lime plus plenty of black pepper and brown bread and butter. Claire MacDonald, the fish cook, makes a salad of eating apples, horseradish and crème fraîche to add to the salmon. Any leftovers can be added to kedgeree or fish soup.

Salar Ltd, The Pier, Lochcarnan, South Uist, Outer Hebrides HS8 5PD

Tel: 01870 610324 **Fax:** 01870 610369

Price range: £9.90 to £30.75. Leaflet free.

Payment: cheque or postal order.

Postage & packing: included in UK. Overseas by arrangement.

Delivery: by first class post. Last Christmas orders the day before last first class posting date.

Refunds: yes.

The Weald Smokery Specialised brick kilns and open log fires are used to make this firm one of only a few still smoking the old way. Of course, they do smoked Scottish salmon and trout but you can also mail kippers, gravadlax, cold-smoked undyed haddock, eel and mussels among the fish plus smoked ham, chicken and duck breasts and bacon. Foreign cures include Bresaola beef, air-dried ham like Parma and smoked pork with juniper berries hot smoked over maple and oak. There are special hampers all year round.

The Weald Smokery, Mount Farm, Flimwell, East Sussex TN5 7QL

Tel: 01580 879601 **Fax:** 01580 879564

Price range: £2.60 to £277. Catalogue free.

Payment: cheque, postal order, major credit cards.

Postage & packing: from £2.95 to £6.95.

Delivery: by overnight courier or first class post. Last Christmas orders 12 December.

Refunds: yes.

Specials: gift boxes available.

See also: The Fresh Food Company, Graig Farm.

FRUIT AND VEGETABLES.

I am not satisfied with this area of shopping by post. When you consider that fruit and vegetables may be flown from Kenya or Chile to your local supermarket, there is no reason why they should not be brought direct to your door from Suffolk or Perthshire. Yet few people have yet to move into this area. Here are a couple who do. I can guarantee that, in the next few years, we will see English asparagus growers, salad-leaf experts and those with apple orchards at last realising what a huge market is available on their doorstep.

FRUIT AND VEGETABLES - LISTINGS

Charlton Orchards This company can provide you with boxes of the best English apples from Somerset. You can have a box of Cox's Orange Pippins (which will keep for several months) or a mixture of old varieties. Another box will include apples and apple juice from the same trees and there are cases of single variety apple juice as well. Apples are excellent fried in sugar and butter, serve them with cheese, mix with celery and walnuts for salad, or just plunge your teeth straight in.

> **Charlton Orchards**, Charlton Road, Creech St. Michael, Taunton, Somerset TA3 5PF
> **Tel:** 01823 412959/412979
> **Price range:** apples £11.95 to £20.75, juice £24.95 for 12 bottles. Leaflet free.
> **Payment:** cheque.
> **Postage & packing:** included in most of UK.
> **Delivery:** allow 14 days.
> **Refunds:** yes, without returning goods.
> **Specials:** gift packs.

Secretts Ideally asparagus should be eaten within a few hours of cutting but if you're not lucky enough to have your own bed (or live near Secretts, where you can pick your own) the best

FOOD AND DRINK

alternative to the limp spears languishing on the supermarket shelves is a box of freshly cut asparagus delivered to your door within 24 hours. Secretts, who also supply cut flowers and rustic flower-filled baskets by post, grow the green-stemmed Boonlym and Franklym varieties, which are packed in a presentation box containing 25 or 50 spears tied with raffia. In season a box would make an unusual and delicious gift.

Secretts, Hurst Farm, Chapel Lane, Milford, Surrey GU8 5HU
Tel: 0500 110711 **Fax:** 01483 861703
E-mail: mail@secretts.co.uk
Website: http://www.secretts.co.uk
Price range: £8.99 to £29.99. Catalogue free.
Payment: cheque, postal order, Mastercard, Access, Visa, Delta, Switch.
Postage & packing: included.
Delivery: usually within 24 hours. Asparagus normally available from end April to mid June but supplies may be limited by adverse weather.
Refunds: yes.
Specials: special orders accommodated.

See also: The Fresh Food Co, Meat Matters, Organics Direct.

HAMPERS.

Time was when the hamper would arrive as a thank-you present, only to be a huge disappointment. Jars of crab paste, maraschino cherries and other useless foods would emerge from the wrappings of what was clearly a very expensive gift. Today, hamper makers are far better. They don't exploit their customers by adding groceries that they can't sell but offer the latest, fashionable foods, local produce sourced nearby and collections suited to the occasion, whether Christmas, Thanksgiving, a Bar Mitzvah or Glyndebourne. Make sure, if you are giving such a present, that you know exactly what will be inside that smart, willow-woven box.

HAMPERS - LISTINGS

The Caribbean Hamper Company The special Christmas hamper has two bottles of Jamaican rum from the Appleton estate, the sought-after Jamaica Blue Mountain coffee along with cakes, biscuits, sauces and seasonings all made in the islands. This hamper will be ideal for the adventurous cook – and rum lover.

> **The Caribbean Hamper Company**, 40 Park Road, Bearwood, Warley, West Midlands B67 5HS
> **Tel/Fax:** 0121 434 5007
> **Price:** £75 per hamper.
> **Payment:** cheque.
> **Postage & packing:** £5 per hamper.
> **Delivery:** Last Christmas orders by 15 December.
> **Refunds:** by arrangement.

The Devon Hamper Company You can pick and mix your box or willow hamper from a choice of Devon foods selected by the company. There are very few counties in Britain which produce such a good range of foods as Devon – the land is fertile and the animal breeds interesting. Devon cream, plain and clotted, is much used as are fruits from the hedgerows. There are cheeses, biscuits, smoked meats, mustards and sauces. The extra virgin olive oil does not, I suspect, originate in Devon.

> **The Devon Hamper Company**, The Old Stables, Morganhayes, Southleigh, Colyton, Devon EX13 6RY
> **Tel:** 01297 553703 **Fax:** 01297 553702
> **Price range:** £30 to £100. Catalogue free.
> **Payment:** cheque.
> **Postage & packing:** included.
> **Delivery:** by Amtrak. Last Christmas orders by 14 December.
> **Refunds:** yes, notify the company as soon as possible.
> **Specials:** happy to accommodate customer's requirements from hamper contents to greetings cards.

FOOD AND DRINK

The Gluttonous Gardener The clever idea of combining a plant with an allied food has gone from strength to strength with regular press mentions. Ned Trier has kits for olive or tomato lovers, a gin drinker's companion (juniper bushes, gin, lemons and recipes for cocktails), a tea pack with tea bush suitable for growing in Britain and, now, an orchard collection of cherry, plum, pear and apple. When a baby is born, he suggests you send a gooseberry bush and bottle of champagne.

The Gluttonous Gardener, Vitis House, 50 Dickens Street, London SW8 3EQ

Tel: 0171 627 0800 **Fax:** 0171 627 8300

Price range: £5 to £65. Catalogue free.

Payment: cheque, major credit/debit cards.

Postage & packing: £6, 24-hour delivery £7.

Delivery: 48 hours.

Refunds: by arrangement.

Hay Hampers This company supplies goodies to corporate customers through its food service and also its sister company, The Vintners Selection, and is thus able to team up good (and interesting) food and drink. I like the idea of the sweet tooth's Christmas hamper of cream sherry, Christmas pudding and all the trimmings plus miniature brandy and fruit cake – a bit incorrect for wine purists but just the job at Christmas. There are also picnic hampers including almost everything you can think of (cold bag for a bottle, for instance). They come in proper hampers with good-looking cutlery and crockery.

Hay Hampers, The Barn, Church Street, Corby Glen, Grantham, Lincolnshire NG33 4NJ

Tel: 01476 550 420/476/548 **Fax:** 01476 550777

E-mail: hayhampers@aol.com

Price range: £10 to £270. Catalogue free.

Payment: cheque, major credit cards.

Postage & packing: 48-hour delivery £4.99, 24-hour delivery £7.99 in mainland UK.

Delivery: see above. Last Christmas orders by 7 December.

Refunds: yes.

Low Sizergh Barn Like many mail order companies, this firm is constantly on the move, changing its list to suit its customers. They currently do three hampers, mainly from local produce but warn that by Christmas there will be more choice – so phone for up-to-the-minute details. The produce they include in the hampers is their own apricot chutney, Village Bakery organic oatcakes, Cumberland farmhouse cheese, Westmorland honey, Cumberland rum butter, and home-made cakes and plum puddings. Very traditional, very English and locally sourced.

> **Low Sizergh Barn**, Low Sizergh Farm, Sizergh, Kendal, Cumbria LA8 8AE
>
> **Tel:** 01539 560426 **Fax:** 01539 561475
>
> **Price range:** hamper prices start at £25. Catalogue free.
>
> **Payment:** major credit/debit cards.
>
> **Postage & packing:** £8.85 for hampers.
>
> **Delivery:** normally 24 hours. Last Christmas orders by 22 December.
>
> **Refunds:** by arrangement – they haven't had any returns to date.

The Norfolk Provender Do you know someone who pines for Norfolk and its foods? If so, this is the firm for them. Their hampers include local Elmham wines and punch made to a medieval recipe, Norfolk ham, pickles, chutney and hot honey mustard (deliciously crunchy). There is mincemeat with brandy, brandy butter with stem ginger and wassail cup from Cartwright & Butler, plus local smoked salmon cured in demerara sugar and brandy. They all come in willow hampers or baskets.

> **The Norfolk Provender**, Drove Farm Place, Breckles, Attleborough, Norfolk NR17 1ER
>
> **Tel/Fax:** 01953 498639.
>
> **Price range:** £15 to £100. Catalogue free.
>
> **Payment:** cheque, postal order, major credit cards.
>
> **Postage & packing:** included.
>
> **Delivery:** by courier, allow 4 working days for order processing. 24-hour delivery at extra charge. Last Christmas orders by 14 December.

FOOD AND DRINK 207

Refunds: by arrangement.
Specials: hampers can be created to individual requirements.

The Original Orkney Hamper Co The islands have a tradition as much Scandinavian as Scottish and their foods are an interesting mix of the two cultures. The hampers, therefore, are as interesting to foodies as they are nostalgic to Orcadians. Find here flavoured oatcakes, fudge, shellfish harvested around the coast and Island Park whisky all in the Scottish tradition along with marinated herring, smoked mussels and beers with Viking names like Skullsplitter and Dragon Head in the Scandinavian mode. This is a really unusual present.

The Original Orkney Hamper Co, 21 Graham Place, Stromness, Orkney KW16 3BY
Tel/Fax: 01856 850551
E-mail: orkhamp@aol.com
Price range: £20 to £100. Catalogue free.
Payment: major credit/debit cards.
Postage & packing: £5.85 up to 2kg, £13.50 up to 10 kg.
Delivery: 24 hours within UK. Last Christmas orders 21 December.
Refunds: yes.
Specials: gift-wrapping, messages or cards can be enclosed.

Panzer's "More and more", says Stephanie Vogl of Panzer's, "we are asked for themed or corporate hampers throughout the year. We can make Italian, Japanese, American, Spanish etc baskets. At Christmas we specialise in 'the smartest food of the moment' and we also do Jewish New Year hampers." They will make up trugs as well as traditional hampers and baskets and positively enjoy a challenge.

Panzer's, 13-19 Circus Road, St John's Wood, London NW8 6PB
Tel: 0171 435 0165/0171 722 8596 **Fax:** 0171 586 0209
Price range: from £35. Catalogue free.
Payment: cheque, Access, Visa.
Postage & packing: London £5.50, mainland UK £10.
Delivery: 24 hours in UK. Last Christmas orders by 23 December, if not a Sunday.

Refunds: by arrangement.
Specials: custom-made hampers.

Scotland's Larder A choice of three hampers from the firm which runs a restaurant on the Firth of Forth combined with an exhibition of Scottish food, cookery demonstrations and tastings. Hampers include traditional Scottish food like whisky, black bun and haggis but also chocolates or coffee from top Scottish makers.

> **Scotland's Larder**, Upper Largo, Leven, Fife KY8 6EA
> **Tel:** 01333 360414 **Fax:** 01333 360427
> **Price range:** £30 to £80.
> **Payment:** cheque, major credit cards.
> **Postage & packing:** £7.35 for 3-day delivery, £9.25 overnight.
> **Delivery:** 3 days, overnight at extra cost.
> **Refunds:** by arrangement.

See also: Bon Goût, The Clark Trading Company, Fortnum and Mason, Fresh Olives Direct, J & J Graham, Harrods, H.L. Barnett, Lochengower, Morel Bros, Cobbett & Son, Quintessentials, Ramsay of Carluke, Valvona & Crolla, Vintage Roots, Waitrose Direct, The Weald Smokery.

MEAT, GAME AND POULTRY.

This is a hugely growing area for mail order. The various food scares, from salmonella and e-coli to BSE, have made us want to know where our meat comes from; a concern for the well-being of animals makes us want to ensure that, at least, the beasts have had a happy, free-range existence before they are slaughtered while we also realise that happy animals fed properly make much tastier meat. I use a recipe by Nigel Slater which consists simply of a free-range chicken and good potatoes. It is simplicity itself to cook but, unless the ingredients are superb, it is pointless. One strand of modern cooking, tak-

FOOD AND DRINK 209

ing inspiration from Italy, insists that cooking should be simple, straightforward and plain. The secret is in the sourcing, not the sauce.

MEAT, GAME AND POULTRY- LISTINGS

Barrow Boar In radio and TV interviews about mail order, I have endless fun talking about this firm whose list is wildly exotic (and may be wielded to make unwelcome guests depart). There are, for example, packs of ten African desert locusts, frozen crocodile tail (bone in or filleted), oven-ready peacocks, fresh ostrich and emu along with ordinary foods like guinea fowl, pheasant and venison. There is also a range of wild boar and interesting sausages. Christmas boxes might include wild boar, bison, kid, ostrich, sausage and, to be traditional, a sachet of dried cranberries.

> **Barrow Boar**, Foster's Farm, South Barrow, Yeovil, Somerset BA22 7LN
>
> **Tel:** 01963 440315 **Fax:** 01963 440901
>
> **Price range:** £1.75 to £19.29 for 500kg. Catalogue free, sae welcome.
>
> **Payment:** cheque, Mastercard, Visa, Eurocard, Delta.
>
> **Postage & packing:** generally £8.50.
>
> **Delivery:** in insulated boxes by next day courier before 1 pm. Last Christmas orders 2 weeks in advance.
>
> **Refunds:** by arrangement.
>
> **Specials:** gift card service.

Brillbury Hall Farm Food Company Meat from Brillbury – a 130-acre traditional grassland farm – has used no chemicals or "artificial inputs" for six years and is certified organic. Not only that, the farm tries to protect the landscape and wildlife as best it can. The animals are also well cared for. The result is that if you buy from here you will get delicious meat – beef, pork, lamb and bacon – and will help encourage good farming.

210   MAIL ORDER MADE EASY

Brillbury Hall Farm Food Co, Brill, Buckinghamshire HP18 9TN
Tel: 01844 238407/0831 601621   **Fax:** 01844 238151
Price range: £5 to £23.75 per kg. Price list free.
Payment: cheque.
Postage & packing: £5 for up to 10kg weekdays, weekend deliveries at extra cost.
Delivery: in insulated boxes with ice packs, by next day courier.
Refunds: by arrangement.

The Country Victualler This small company specialises in a narrow range of hams, pâtés and terrines, smoked food and Christmas pudding, and it's none the worse for that. The Alderton ham, invented by an old colonel, is cured to a secret formula and glazed with marmalade; the Victuallers Ham is cooked with honey and Guinness and glazed with marmalade. Pâtés are of coarse pork or wild boar, either en croûte or with juniper berries; smoked foods include chicken, turkey and duck. The Christmas pud is from a 19th-century Yorkshire recipe including fresh lemon, apple and breadcrumbs as well as normal dried fruits. All are delicious.

The Country Victualler, Winkburn Hall, Newark, Nottinghamshire NG22 8PQ
Tel: 01636 636465   **Fax:** 01636 636717
Price range: from £30. Catalogue free.
Payment: cheque, major credit cards.
Postage & packing: £10 for orders under £50, otherwise free except where post office surcharges.
Delivery: 24-hour carrier service.
Refunds: yes.

Donald Russell From 1974, Donald Russell supplied the top hotels and restaurants in the world with their beef from Scotland. Then came the ban on British beef. The firm smartly changed tack and decided to sell its luxury cuts of Aberdeen Angus meat to the public by mail order. The joints are a combination of English cuts and continental: defatted rump, tafelspitz, rib eye roll and chateaubriand. There are fillet, rump, rib and sirloin steaks. They are proud that the cattle are aged

FOOD AND DRINK

between 16 and 22 months, can be traced back to the farm of origin and are free from additives, hormones and recycled protein. As well as beef, they will send lamb cuts including legs, short saddles, loin and racks along with smoked back and streaky bacon and smoked salmon.

Donald Russell Direct, Harlaw Road, Inverurie, Aberdeenshire AB51 4FR

Tel: 01467 629666 **Fax:** 01467 624200

Price range: from £2.95 to £11.57 per lb. Catalogue free.

Payment: cheque, major credit/debit cards.

Postage & packing: £9 for orders under £100, free thereafter.

Delivery: by overnight courier on Tuesdays and Wednesdays – allow 3 days. Last Christmas orders by 22 December.

Refunds: yes.

Dukeshill Ham As traditional butchers are put out of business by the supermarkets, it becomes gradually more difficult to find regional hams, cured in the proper way. This company specialises in England's different ham recipes. There is Wiltshire ham, the most popular, which is smoked or cured in brown sugar and is mild in flavour. York hams are both drier and saltier, cured in the way country houses once used, and matured for over ten weeks. Shropshire black starts off like York ham but is then infused with a delicious mix of molasses, herbs and juniper. It is the sweetest of the three and sold only at Christmas. The firm also does an air-dried Parma-type ham to eat raw with fruit. The English hams can be ordered on the bone for drama and York and Wiltshire cures in smaller quantities and sliced.

Dukeshill Ham Co Ltd, Deuxhill, Bridgnorth, Shropshire WV16 6AF

Tel: 01746 789519 **Fax:** 01746 789533

Price range: £7 to £77. Catalogue free.

Payment: cheque, major credit cards.

Postage & packing: included in UK.

Delivery: 24-hour despatch in UK. Last Christmas orders by 22 December, but order as early as possible for York Hams and Shropshire Black Hams to avoid disappointment.

Refunds: yes.

Eastbrook Farms Organic Meat

Eastbrook Farms Organic Meat Over 1,000 acres of land – owned by the Church of England – have been managed by the Browning family for forty years. They have been farming organically since 1986 and the Eastbrook range includes their own smoked Wiltshire ham and bacon, lamb grazed on wild-flower meadows and free-range poultry. The list also includes sausages, organic cheeses, humanely treated veal and well-hung beef.

> **Eastbrook Farms Organic Meat**, Bishopstone, Swindon, Wiltshire SN6 8PW
>
> **Tel:** 01793 791460 **Fax:** 01793 791239
>
> **Price range:** £5.97 to £39.25 per kg. Catalogue free, sae appreciated.
>
> **Payment:** cheque, major credit/debit cards.
>
> **Postage & packing:** £10 for orders up to £35, £8 up to £75, £4 up to £150, free thereafter.
>
> **Delivery:** by courier, vacuum packed, in insulated boxes with ice packs. Last Christmas orders by 30 November.
>
> **Refunds:** by arrangement.
>
> **Specials:** farm visits are encouraged.

Fletchers of Auchtermuchty

Fletchers of Auchtermuchty Venison is growing in popularity, both fresh and smoked. The secret is to get it tender and that means farmed rather than wild. John Fletcher is a vet who farms his herd organically in paddocks on an upland farm. The products vary from delicious hot and cold smoked venison to a selection of joints, casseroles, game pie mix, venison haggis and sausages. The smoked venison is perfect treated like bresaola, drizzled with olive oil and topped with shavings of parmesan – or teamed with left-over cranberry sauce or jelly. The meat is vacuum packed, giving a shelf life of one to two weeks, and the smoked meats last longer. Venison is unusual enough for a special occasion and the smoked varieties and casseroles need no preparation.

> **Fletchers of Auchtermuchty**, Reediehill Farm, Auchtermuchty, Fife KY14 7HS
>
> **Tel:** 01337 828369 or 07000 VENISON **Fax:** 01337 827001
>
> **E-mail:** fletchers.scotland@virgin.net

FOOD AND DRINK

Price range: no minimum order. Catalogue free.

Payment: cheque, major credit/debit cards.

Postage & packing: £9.95, orders over £95 free. Small orders by post at £2 plus postage.

Delivery: overnight before noon, subject to availability. Last Christmas orders 3 weeks in advance to allow for hanging time.

Refunds: yes. Carriage refunded if delivery is late, full refund if food perished.

Goodman's Geese

Judy Goodman started to raise geese as a hobby in 1982 and her flock has now grown to over 3,000. She added 750 bronze turkeys in 1991 and now rears over 2,000. She has won numerous awards for her poultry and her business. The birds are free range and sold oven-ready. She includes goose recipes – necessary as no two cookbooks agree on times.

Goodman's Geese, Walsgrove Farm, Great Witley, Worcester WR6 6JJ

Tel: 01299 896272 **Fax:** 01299 896889

Price range: geese £6.45 per kg, turkeys £5 per kg. Catalogue free.

Payment: cheque with order.

Postage & packing: £10 for one bird, £15 for two, £17 for three.

Delivery: by overnight carrier. Last Christmas orders by 25 November.

Refunds: yes, if genuine.

Graig Farm

If you are worried about how your meat is reared and slaughtered, buy from this farm. The animals are not given drugs, growth promoters or animal offal, they are fed organically and humanely slaughtered. The meat also tastes better. The farm sells chicken like it used to taste, free-range bronze or white turkey, duck, wood pigeon and guinea fowl. Meats include wild venison, rabbit, goat and wild boar along with more usual meats and mutton. Also sold are local cheeses, dolphin-friendly trawled fish from St. Helena, organic Christmas cakes, wines, beers, ciders and baby food as well as local wild honey. A recipe book on how to cook the rarer foods is available.

214 MAIL ORDER MADE EASY

Graig Farm, Dolau, Llandrindod Wells, Powys LD1 5TL
Tel: 01597 851655 or 07000 ORGANIC **Fax:** 01597 851991
E-mail: sales @graigfarm.co.uk
Website: http://www.graigfarm.co.uk
Price range: 56p to £32. Catalogue free.
Payment: cheque, Mastercard, Visa, Eurocard.
Postage & packing: at cost, free for orders over £40.
Delivery: normally despatched within 10 days in insulated boxes by overnight courier. Last Christmas orders by late November. Supplies, especially organic turkeys, may be limited.
Refunds: yes, if reasonable.

Heal Farm Meats

Old-fashioned breeds are used for superb fresh and cured meat and poultry. Gloucester Old Spots, Tamworths and British Lops are among the pigs; beef is from North Devon cattle; Shetland, Ryeland and Southdown produce the lamb. Rouen cross ducks, bronze turkey and guinea fowl are on offer, as are special joints, ready-to-cook stews and curries and home-cured West Country hams and bacons. Rearing and killing is humane and additive-free by the farm.

Heal Farm, Kings Nympton, Umberleigh, Devon, EX37 9TB
Tel: 01769 574341 **Fax:** 01769 572839
Price range: from 67p for lard to £37.89 per kg for fillet steak. Catalogue free.
Payment: cheque, postal order, major credit/debit cards.
Postage & packing: normally £8.75, but special offers often include delivery.
Delivery: Tuesday to Friday by overnight courier in insulated boxes with ice packs.
Refunds: yes, in case of genuine complaint.
Specials: trial packs available.

Hereford Duck Company

These are dedicated duck breeders, using the Rouen as the base of a bird bred specially for flavour and raised in apple orchards. The ducks are not fed any antibiotics, hormones, enzymes or animal protein and are killed humanely, too. Because the Trelough ducks are not fatty, the skin should not be pricked and owner Barry Clark recommends a glaze of clear honey and water left on the skin

FOOD AND DRINK

overnight. Other recipes come with the package. The Trelough duck was voted the best in Britain by Albert Roux after a tasting competition. More recently, Mr. Clark has started to rear chickens and the Devereux is a typical French farmyard bird, reared free range and again without harmful additives. The firm also sells duck eggs, giblets, confit and smoked duck breast.

Hereford Duck Company, Trelough House, Wormbridge, Hereford HR2 9DH

Tel: 01981 570767 **Fax:** 01981 570577

Price range: ducks £2.50 per lb, chickens £2.10. Catalogue free.

Payment: cheque, postal order, major credit/debit cards.

Postage & packing: £10 for orders up to £25, £6 up to £49.99, £4 up to £99.99, free thereafter.

Delivery: by overnight carrier.

Refunds: only for genuine complaint.

Hughes Butchers This traditional butcher's shop in the charming seaport of Fishguard has just started to mail order and now offers delicious Welsh lamb from the flowery pastures nearby. They also cure their own bacon and make their own special sausages, including the bicentenary, named after the French invasion of the town in 1797. It mingles pork and venison and is extremely tasty. You can order specials, too, like cushion of Welsh lamb stuffed with apricots and brandy.

Hughes Butchers & Son, Anchor House, 4 High Street, Fishguard, Pembrokeshire SA65 9AR

Tel: 01348 872394

Price range: £1.18 to £9.09 per lb. Minimum order £50. Catalogue free.

Payment: cheque, major credit/debit cards.

Postage & packing: £5.90.

Delivery: 24 hours.

Refunds: by arrangement.

Jack Scaife Bacon cured the proper way by Chris Battle of Jack Scaife butchers is despatched regularly to the House of Lords, Fortnum's, British embassies worldwide and Annabel's nightclub. Chris had been curing his own bacon for breakfast for thirty years and experience shows. The bacon, which comes from Berkshire cross large white pigs which are slaughtered late in life, is slightly sweet and crisps up well. It is matured in a space designed to feel like a Yorkshire farmhouse cellar and hung for up to nine days. This firm also mail orders oak-smoked and unsmoked hams, home-made sausage such as Cumberland and honey roast pork, old-fashioned black pudding and dry-cured ox tongue.

Jack Scaife Butcher Ltd, The Factory, Mill Lane, Oakworth, Keighley, West Yorkshire BD22 7QH

Tel: 01535 647772 **Fax:** 01535 646305

E-mail: sales @jackscaife.co.uk

Website: http://www.classicengland.co.uk/scaife.html

Price range: £1.90 to £3.15 per lb. Leaflet free.

Payment: cheque with order, Mastercard, Visa.

Postage & packing: from £3.20 for up to 2lb to £5.70 for up to 60lb. Overseas rates on application.

Delivery: allow 7 days.

Refunds: no.

Kelly Turkey Farms
This company is famous for its KellyBronze turkey, the bronze-feathered bird that is the original American native. The firm won the award for Best Speciality Food from Food From Britain and was an overall winner when Anton Edelman did a turkey tasting in 1995. Delia Smith has also endorsed the bird. Kelly turkeys are additive free, and grown to maturity on fresh straw with access to open woodland. Their diet has no growth promoter.

Kelly Turkey Farms, Springate Farm, Bicknacre Road, Danbury, Essex CM3 4EP

Tel: 01245 223581 **Fax:** 01245 226124

E-mail: info@kelly-turkeys.com

Website: http://www.kelly-turkeys.com

Price range: £5 to £7 per lb for collection. For mail order see price list. Catalogue free.

Payment: cheque, major credit cards.

Postage & packing: see price list.

Delivery: overnight. Last Christmas orders by 18 December.

Refunds: yes.

FOOD AND DRINK

Specials: free booklet of tips and recipes, £1 voucher and set of place cards with each order.

Macsween This Edinburgh firm has been noted for its haggises for over forty years and is now on the third generation of experts. Haggises, which come from cocktail size to ceremonial chieftain, are vacuum packed and will keep up to four weeks in a fridge or a year in a freezer. There is also a vegetarian haggis, which I don't think Rabbie Burns would like, and some Scottish specialities such as clapshot pie, Lorne sausage and fruit pudding.

Macsween of Edinburgh, Dryden Road, Bilston Glen, Loanhead, Edinburgh EH20 9LZ

Tel: 0131 440 2555 **Fax:** 0131 440 2674

Price range: from £9.50. Catalogue free

Payment: cheque, major credit/debit cards except Amex.

Postage & packing: from £5.60 by next-day courier.

Delivery: usually next day by noon. Last orders for Burns night by 14 January.

Specials: beef-free haggis available. Gift packaging.

Manx Loaghtan Produce The Manx Loaghtan is a primitive mountain sheep which has lived on the Isle of Man since prehistoric times like the Soay and Boreray sheep in Scotland. Though primarily known for its brown wool, the animal's meat is darker and stronger than traditional lamb. The sheep graze on the island's mountains until they are over 15 months old. The firm sells legs, shoulders and sides of the animal and suggests cooking them with a garlic and tomato sauce.

The Manx Loaghtan Produce Co, Croit Vane, Corlea Road, Ballasalla, Isle of Man IM9 3BA

Tel/Fax: 01624 822578

Price range: £4.25 to £5 per lb. Catalogue free.

Payment: cheque, Visa.

Postage & packing: £5 per item. Overseas by arrangement.

Delivery: normally within 24 hours. Last Christmas orders 48 hours in advance.

Refunds: yes.

Specials: special offers throughout the year, eg leg and shoulder (approx 10lb) £40 including postage & packing.

Meat Matters Basically, as its name suggests, the firm sells a huge range of organic meats, poultry, game and sausages but they also offer organic fruit and vegetables (very rare to get vegetables by mail order) from a bag of spuds to a fruit basket. Also groceries like organic butter and cheese, organic cornflakes, pasta, tea and even organic ready meals like beef olives. For Christmas they excel themselves with turkey, geese, wild boar, duck or chicken and trimmings, cold cuts and wild smoked salmon, spiced apples and mulling spice – all organic. Then they'll bring you fresh holly and ivy wreaths, garlands and table decorations. If you're lucky enough to live in London or South Oxfordshire delivery is free on specific days. Rest of the country has an overnight, paid-for service.

Meat Matters, 2 Blandy's Farm Cottages, Letcombe Regis, Wantage, Oxfordshire OX12 9LJ

Tel: 01235 762461 **Fax:** 01235 772526

Price range: meat from £2.25 to £13.50 per lb. Groceries from 99p.

Payment: cheque, major credit cards or cash when delivering in their own van.

Postage & packing: £2.50 per kg outside normal delivery areas.

Delivery: free delivery by refrigerated van to most London post-codes, and south Oxfordshire from Wednesday to Friday. Overnight delivery service elsewhere in UK on Thursdays and Fridays. Meat is packed in insulated boxes with ice packs. Last Christmas orders by mid-December.

Refunds: yes.

R & J Lodge Selling in West Yorkshire where they don't tolerate anything less than the best, this firm is noted for its outstanding pies and bacon. The pies are hand-raised and include pork, turkey and ham and game (hare, mallard, venison and pheasant cooked in red wine). There's dry-cured bacon from pigs reared humanely in the Derbyshire Dales and cheese from specialist farms around the area.

FOOD AND DRINK

R & J Lodge, Greens End Road, Meltham, Huddersfield HD7 3NW
Tel: 01484 850571
Website: http://www.gbdirect.co.uk/food/r&jlodge
Price range: £11.25 to £16.75. Catalogue free.
Payment: cheque.
Postage & packing: £7 for one item, £12 for more.
Delivery: allow 4 working days.
Refunds: no.

Ramsay of Carluke

The family has been curing bacon since 1857 and offers an Ayrshire cure with no added water or artificial polyphosphates. You can buy rashers, gammon joints and steaks and whole smoked hams up to 19lb in weight. Also in the range is Perthshire pork, Scotch beef, sausages and black pudding and cooked meats. For gifts you can send a breakfast box with bacon, sausage and black pudding among other goodies or a full hamper with these and more.

Ramsay of Carluke Ltd, Wellriggs, 22 Mount Stewart Street,
Carluke, Lanarkshire ML8 5ED
Tel: 01555 772277 **Fax:** 01555 750686
E-mail: ramsay@wellriggs.demon.co.uk
Price range: 94p to £68. Catalogue free.
Payment: cheque, postal order, major credit cards.
Postage & packing: £7.70 for next day delivery.
Delivery: within 7 days. Last Christmas orders by mid-December.
Refunds: yes.
Specials: greetings card with message can be enclosed.

Rannoch Smokery

Wild red deer, which need to be culled periodically, are used to make the most delicious smoked venison which should be eaten with just a touch of lemon juice or with scrambled eggs. It also make excellent nibbles at parties and the firm suggests ideas. Each carcass is checked by a vet and the best cuts brined and smoked with oak chips from whisky barrels. There is also a smoked venison pâté, smoked chicken, duck and pheasant and fresh venison steaks.

Rannoch Smokery, Kinloch Rannoch, Pitlochry, Perthshire
PH16 5QD

Tel: 01882 632344/632715 **Fax:** 01882 632441

Price range: £1.30 to £14. Catalogue free.

Payment: cheque with order, Mastercard, Visa.

Postage & packing: £1.80 per 250g. Overnight delivery from £6.99.

Delivery: by first class post. Overnight delivery is recommended for chicken and steaks. Last Christmas orders by first week December.

Refunds: by arrangement.

The Real Meat Company Animals reared for this company are subject to independent checks on their welfare and conditions by student vets from Bristol. Once the animals are humanely slaughtered, they are hung for the correct time; ham and bacon is cured in the old-fashioned way and sausages are made from proper cuts of meat. Along with normal cuts of beef, pork and lamb, there is Wiltshire bacon and ham, sausages and burgers. At Christmas, the firm sells turkeys, large chickens, ducks and geese and special packs. The Festive Pack contains a goose, leg of lamb, gammon joint, bacon, sausage, Stilton and Cheddar. All you need for the holiday at £98.

The Real Meat Company, Warminster, Wiltshire, BA12 9AZ

Tel: 0345 626017 **Fax:** 01985 218950

Price range: £2.29 to £98. Catalogue free.

Payment: cheque, major credit/debit cards.

Postage & packing: £3.95 per order.

Delivery: within 24 hours.

Refunds: by arrangement.

Specials: special offers. Ring for details.

Stroff's Speciality Sausages I can't remember when I first noticed that the traditional British banger had gone exotic but now it's hard to choose between the fancy flavours on offer. Stroffs are one of the most interesting with a mail order selection of sausages from different areas – Cumberland, Oxford, Cambridge, Smithfield and Suffolk to name a few; a range of organic meat sausages, vegetarian bangers and those with flavours like Cajun Smokey, Sicilian and Thai Pork. An

FOOD AND DRINK 221

"Epicurean Selection" includes pheasant boudin or wild boar and there are Christmas and cocktail specials: try the vodka, dill and lime ones or gin, juniper and lemon.

Stroff's Speciality Sausages, 96 The Market, Oxford OX1 3DY
Tel: 01865 200922 **Fax:** 01865 514888
Price range: sausages £2.35 to £4.95 per lb. Minimum order 6lbs. Leaflet free.
Payment: Mastercard, Access, Visa.
Postage & packing: £4.95.
Delivery: allow 5 days.
Refunds: by arrangement.

Swaddles Green Farm A good selection of organic foods, especially meat, including ham and offal, poultry, sausages and burgers plus specials like ketchup burgers for children. There is also a charcuterie section ranging from oak-smoked Frankfurters to pâté and onion marmalade, a good range of pies plus dinner party meals of starters, main courses and rich puddings. Everyday meals include Bolognese sauce, stews and curry. The firm sells organic soup, marinades, vegetarian dishes and free range eggs. There's a free delivery service to London.

Swaddles Green Farm, Hare Lane, Buckland St. Mary, Chard, Somerset TA20 3JR
Tel: 01460 234387 **Fax:** 01460 234591
E-mail: organic@swaddles.co.uk
Price range: £4.85 to £34.50 per kg. Seasonal specials such as a three-bird roast (to serve 40) at £152.50.
Payment: cheque, major credit/debit cards except Amex and Diners.
Postage & packing: £10 for orders up to £40, £5 up to £80, free thereafter. Free delivery to much of London, Surrey and Middlesex. Saturday delivery £15 extra.
Delivery: by overnight carrier in insulated boxes Tuesday to Friday. Saturday at surcharge. Christmas orders as early as possible since supplies are limited.
Refunds: only if unsatisfactory.
Specials: gift cards and messages can be included with orders.

Tombuie The firm is a smokehouse but its unique feature is Tombuie smoked lamb which, it says, produces a unique flavour but does not destroy the meat's tenderness. They send a recipe with it, cooking the lamb in a mint and breadcrumb crust with a sauce of meat juices, crème fraîche and redcurrant jelly. Otherwise, there are smoked cheeses like Weem, Aberfeldy and Strathtay, and smoked duck, guinea fowl, chicken and quail.

Tombuie Smokehouse, Aberfeldy, Perthshire PH15 2JS

Tel: 01887 820127 **Fax:** 01887 829625

Price range: £1.45 to £28. Catalogue free.

Payment: major credit cards.

Postage & packing: £1.75 up to 500g, £3 up to 1kg, £7.50 up to 20kg, free for orders over £50 in Fife, Angus & Perth and over £125 elsewhere in UK. Overseas rates on application.

Delivery: next day by courier for orders over 1kg, smaller orders by first class post. Christmas orders as early as possible.

Refunds: by arrangement.

Traditional Farmfresh Turkeys This organisation will advise on which of their members will mail order to your door.

Traditional Farmfresh Turkeys, 5 Beacon Drive, Seaford, East Sussex BN25 2JX

Tel: 01323 899802 **Fax:** 01323 899583

OILS, SAUCES, HERBS AND SPICES

Now that we're hot on fusion food, we need herbs and spices that cannot be grown but which can be flown in fresh from countries as diverse as Thailand and Mexico. Salsas and curries demand the real thing as much as goulash and gravadlax did before. The best companies, listed here, offer a huge range of hundreds of tastes as well as herbs for relaxation, sleep, cosmetics or medicine. Others come up with the seeds to grow in greenhouses or the soil or with packets of fresh herbs, newly cut. Over the last three decades, the change has been extraordinary. In the 70s,

FOOD AND DRINK

curly parsley, mint and dried sage were the only standbys. Now we have a choice of over a dozen chillies alone.

OILS, SAUCES, HERBS AND SPICES - LISTINGS

Candlesby Herbs Husband and wife team, John and Jane Stafford Allen, put together their joint knowledge of farming, cookery and herbal medicine to produce a list of cooking mixtures, tisanes (try rosehip and morning bright), pot pourri from tea rose to Lincolnshire Mist (bracing), along with insect repellents, sleep pillows and bath oils with names like Suggestive or Submissive.

> **Candlesby Herbs**, Cross Keys Cottage, Candlesby, Spilsby, Lincolnshire PE23 5SF
> **Tel/Fax:** 01754 890211
> **E-mail:** candherbs@aol.com
> **Price range:** up to £10. Send A5 sae for catalogue.
> **Payment:** cheque.
> **Postage & packing:** from 85p for orders under £1 to £4.50 for orders over £50.
> **Delivery:** normally by return. Christmas orders by last posting date.
> **Refunds:** yes.

Claudio Vanelli Claudio is an Italian student working in London. To increase his grant, he decided to sell single-estate olive oil from his home village of Batignano, deep in the Tuscan Maremma region. What you get is the most direct chain between the olive grower, with his own trees on the salty hillsides and your own cooking with Claudio, a charming ambassador for everything Tuscan, as the only link. The oil comes in 5-litre cans with the simplest of labelling.

> **Claudio Vanelli**, 22 Chalcot Square, London NW1 8YA
> **Tel:** 0171 586 2184 **Fax:** 0171 813 1907
> **Price range:** around £10.50 per litre. Minimum order 5 litres. No catalogue.

Payment: cheque, postal order, Mastercard, Access, Visa, Delta, Switch.

Postage & packing: at cost. Free delivery in London area.

Delivery: normally despatched following day.

Refunds: by arrangement.

Cool Chile Co

Once you discover what a chile can do to your cooking, you'll never be without. They come in a huge variety of heats and flavours, some sweet and mild and some terrifying. The leaflet from the firm explains them all, from choricero (1 out of 10 for heat) to habanero (10). They can be bought dried and whole, powdered or in decorative wreaths. There are also two starter packs, mild and hot. If it comes too hot, the firm says the best cure is dairy products – so drink milk.

Cool Chile Co, P O Box 5702, London W11 2SG

Tel: 0870 9021145

E-mail: dodie@coolchile.demon.co.uk

Price range: £1.70 to £34.90. Leaflet free.

Payment: cheque, postal order, Eurocheque. Major credit/debit cards (£20 minimum order).

Postage & packing: £1.60 for orders of 1-3 products, included for orders or 4 or more. European delivery 30p extra per 100g.

Delivery: allow 7 days. Last Christmas orders by last first class posting date. European orders by early December.

Refunds: yes.

The Curry Sauce Co

What a boon. The company makes three fresh, authentic curry sauces, mild korma, spicy tikka masala and hot Madras in 475 ml pots which will keep several weeks in the fridge. Each is made with fresh ingredients – no colourings, preservers or thickeners and it shows. Add quick fried chicken or prawns (or, at Christmas, the dreaded cold turkey) to the sauce, garnish with cream, flaked almonds and coriander and you have an easy meal. Extra vegetables like carrot and courgette can be added along with fruits like pineapple and banana to the korma. I've tried them and they're delicious. This year another three have joined the list: balti, rogan josh and jalfrezzi.

FOOD AND DRINK

The Curry Sauce Co Ltd, The Old Bakery, The Green, Chiddingfold, Surrey GU8 4TU
Tel: 01428 685440 **Fax:** 01428 685510
E-mail: debbie@currysauce.com
Website: http://www.currysauce.com
Price range: all sauces £22.20 for 6 pots, £37.36 for 12. Leaflet free.
Payment: cheque, major credit/debit cards.
Postage & packing: included.
Delivery: next day except Friday. Overseas by arrangement.
Refunds: by arrangement.

Gordon's Condiments

Charles and Jo Gordon have been making unusual mustards for over 20 years, specialising in coarse-ground mustard seeds – a technique used since the middle ages. Gradually the business expanded from the first mustard, England Vineyard Mustard, flavoured with white wine from Denbies Wine Estate in southern England. Now there are mustards flavoured with beer, whisky and cajun spices and smooth mustards with garlic, honey and tarragon. Some are ideal for fish, others for cheese or barbecues. As mustards can be kept for ages, they make an ideal present or an addition to the good cook's battery. The firm has added chutneys, including apricot, plum and wild blueberry, sauces for savouries such as mint, horseradish and redcurrant plus brandy butter to its range.

Charles Gordon Associates Ltd, Gordon House, Littlemead Industrial Estate, Cranleigh, Surrey GU6 8ND
Tel: 01483 267707 **Fax:** 01483 267783
E-mail: gordonsspot@aol.com
Website: http://www.gordons-condiments.co.uk
Price range: £1.35 to £2.35. Catalogue free.
Payment: cheque, major credit cards.
Postage & packing: £3.40 for 4 jars, £5.15 for 8, £5.80 for 12. in UK.
Delivery: 14 to 20 days. Last Christmas orders 2 weeks in advance.
Refunds: exchange if valid problem.

Halzephron Herb Farm

Herbs are grown free from pesticides and growing agents on this Cornish farm and then used to create a whole selection of marinades, dressings, oils and vinegars along with dried herbs, recipes and honey made by bees from the herbs. Where herbs are not locally grown – tropical lime or ginger for instance – proper fresh ingredients are used. This year, Halzephron will also mail herb plants, so ask for latest details. New this year too is a Hungarian marinade with red wine, paprika and chilli, herb dips including Provençal and Thai and a Cornish herb mustard with fresh mixed herbs.

Halzephron Herb Farm, Gunwalloe, Helston, Cornwall TR12 7QD

Tel: 01326 240652 **Fax:** 01326 241125

Price range: from under £2 to £10. Catalogue free.

Payment: cheque, major credit cards.

Postage & packing: from £1.50 to £5.

Delivery: within 5 working days. Last Christmas orders 18 December.

Refunds: yes.

Specials: can be sent with gift tags and personal messages.

Hambleden Herbs

A big list of organic herbs, teas, herb infusions along with organic rose and lavender water, macerates in oil and tinctures, certified by the Soil Association as being free from additives and preservatives. The herb list itself runs from agar-agar to Yucca and includes all those herbs and spices used in a good kitchen – lemon grass, caraway seed, poppy seed – and there's helpful advice on their uses and storage. They recommend old Marmite jars to keep the herbs in the dark. There is also a good collection of herbal teas and tea bags as well as dyeing herbs, beeswax sheets for candle-making, plus books and posters.

Hambleden Herbs, Court Farm, Milverton, Somerset TA4 1NF

Tel: 01823 401205 **Fax:** 01823 400276

Price range: 70p to £35. Catalogue free.

Payment: cheque, major credit/debit cards.

Postage & packing: £3.50 for orders under £30, free thereafter.

FOOD AND DRINK

Delivery: allow 7 working days. Last Christmas orders 10 days in advance.
Refunds: yes, if returned within 28 days.

Kari Mix Micky Bausola is the daughter of a Sri Lankan diplomat father and a Chinese film-star mother born in Malaysia, so she's in a fine position to understand various oriental spice mixtures. Her list includes dry spice mixes for Indian Madras or Korma curry, Malaysian Beef Rendang and Sri Lankan yellow rice along with pickles, relishes and chutneys of tamarind, shrimp, aubergine and chilli. Her leaflet also includes recipes.

Kari Mix Ltd, Limuru, Cowgate Lane, Hawkinge, Folkestone, Kent CT18 7AR
Tel/Fax: 01303 892134
Price: £1.99 each. Send sae for catalogue.
Payment: cheque.
Postage & packing: £3.50 for up to 4 jars, £4.95 for 4 jars and over.
Delivery: 21 days. Last Christmas orders by first week December.
Refunds: no.
Specials: gift packs available.

Mamble Foods A real food innovation comes from Mamble – four African sauces imported exclusively. There is Zulu Fire Sauce, Xhosa, Malawi Gold and Swazi – all made in Cape Town and extremely decoratively packed with strings of beads. Because few will have tried them before, labels suggest how to use them. All are free of artificial colourings or preservatives.

Mamble Foods, Upper Moor End, Mamble, Worcestershire DY14 9JD
Tel: 01299 832995 **Fax:** 01299 832077
E-mail: mamble.foods@virgin.net
Price: £5. Leaflet free.
Payment: cheque.
Postage & packing: £3.45 to £6.40.
Delivery: allow 14 days.
Refunds: yes, if returned within 14 days.

The Oil Merchant

The Oil Merchant Eighteen pages of oils, vinegars, olives and accessories for the dedicated taster or salad maker. These oils are treated like wines – we are told about the estates, the aroma, the olive variety and, sometimes, the grower too. Olive oils come from the Mediterranean, California and South Africa (a new venture by an Italian immigrant); there are nut and seed oils, oils flavoured with anything from pimento to mandarins and an array of balsamic vinegars, including one which costs over £70 for 15 cl. Not surprisingly, you can also buy a dispenser for it. Also, books on olives and oils.

> **The Oil Merchant**, 47 Ashchurch Grove, London W12 9BU
> **Tel:** 0181 740 1335 **Fax:** 0181 740 1319
> **E-mail:** the_oil_merchant@compuserve.com
> **Price range:** from £2.50 to £78. Catalogue free.
> **Payment:** cheque.
> **Postage & packing:** £3 for orders under £25, otherwise included.
> **Delivery:** normally 1 week, but allow 28 days.
> **Refunds:** by arrangement, replacement if damaged.

Peppers by Post

Peppers by Post Lots of us want to use unusual varieties of chile, whether we are cooking Eastern or Western or Tex-Mex. This new firm grows the hot little devils from all around the world: they have Habanero, the chile from hell and reputedly the hottest there is, along with Jalapeno, used in America to season corn bread and salsa, Hungarian hot wax, for goulash or hot pepper salads and the Thai hot which competes for strength with Habanero. Peppers are supplied fresh and there are also tomatillos, like green tomatoes in appearance, which are related to Chinese lanterns.

> **Peppers by Post**, Sea Spring Farm, West Bexington, Dorchester, Dorset DT2 9DD
> **Tel:** 01308 897892 **Fax:** 01308 897735
> **Price range:** £1.50 per packet.
> **Payment:** cheque with order.
> **Postage & packing:** from £1.95 for up to 5 packets to £5 for over 20.
> **Delivery:** despatched twice a week from July to November. Out of season orders held until chiles are available.

Refunds: replacement.
Specials: gift packages with personal card.

The Spice Shop The range of 850 different spices is rather daunting. I found that I had made out a list to order but just couldn't make up my mind what to add or cross out. There are, for instance, 26 different kinds of chiles and chilli powders from the mild-ish ancho to the blazing African devils and 12 versions of paprika. There are spices I've never heard of like Zedoary and echinacea root. The whole is complicated by the fact that the owner is German and her spelling slightly erratic. But who's complaining? This is a terrific list of every spice known to woman along with essential oils, graters and grinders and spice blends. Even as you read this, she's probably added another 10 flavours to the list.

The Spice Shop, 1 Blenheim Crescent, London W11 2EE
Tel: 0171 229 1591
Price range: 55p to £2.99. Send A5 or A4 sae for catalogue.
Payment: major credit/debit cards.
Postage & packing: normally £2.65, more for extra large or heavy orders.
Delivery: within 8 days. Last Christmas orders by 12 December.
Refunds: by arrangement.
Specials: gift baskets decorated with chillies and cinnamon quills at no extra cost.

Tracklements I came across this firm more than 20 years ago when they were one of the first to produce unusual mustard. Though speciality mustards and sauces can now be found in every supermarket, these still take some beating. There are Urchfont chilli and English herb or beer, spiced honey, black and tarragon mustard and strong English mustard, which has been almost overwhelmed recently by fancier varieties. They have savoury jellies for meat dishes, traditional English sauces like horseradish and Cumberland, seven different chutneys and, on the sweet side, mincemeat and flavoured butters. These make excellent presents, especially for people living abroad where a jar of horseradish is worth its weight in gold.

Tracklements, The Dairy Farm, Pinkney Park, Sherston, Malmesbury, Wiltshire SN16 0NX
Tel: 01666 840851 **Fax:** 01666 840022
Price range: £1.75 to £2.75 per jar. Leaflet free.
Payment: cheque, Visa.
Postage & packing: £2 for a minimum order of 6 jars.
Delivery: 3-5 days. Last Christmas orders 2 weeks in advance.
Refunds: yes on breakages.

Welsh Mountain Garden

Using the Welsh countryside and based at the Welsh Country House Hotel at Maes-y-Neuadd, the firm sells preserves and dressings made in small batches. No additives are used, but they will last for up to two years. The produce comes from the hotel kitchen garden and the hedgerows. There are products like onion and thyme, leek and apple, rosemary and apple jelly and ginger marmalade plus herb oils and vinegars, dressings like carrot and cardamom. New products include stir-fry oil, chocolate sauce and gravlax marinade. Very useful standbys for holidays and, in hamper form, marvellous presents.

Welsh Mountain Garden, Hotel Maes-y-Neuadd, Talsarnau, near Harlech, Gwynedd LL47 6YA
Tel: 01766 780319 **Fax:** 01766 780211
E-mail: wmg@marketsite.co.uk
Website: http://www.marketsite.co.uk/wmg
Price range: £2.80 to £25. Catalogue free.
Payment: cheque, major credit cards.
Postage & packing: £3 plus insurance. Orders over £25 free plus 75p insurance.
Delivery: by post, normally within 3 days. Last Christmas orders 10 working days in advance.
Refunds: yes.
Specials: hampers, gift-wrapping.

See also: Conservas Rainha Santa for piri piri, The Clark Trading Company and Valvona & Crolla for olive oil.

FOOD AND DRINK

MISCELLANEOUS

While sounding very dull, miscellaneous food in fact includes some of the pleasures of life. Not only is olive oil now sold by vintage and variety – so are olives from small coquilles to giant kalamata. All have different characteristics and make interesting tastings. You could say the same for honey flavoured with pollen from acacia trees to heather. As we get more and more foodie, specialist firms are springing up to indulge our rarified tastes.

MISCELLANEOUS - LISTINGS

Conservas Rainha Santa A specialist list of Portuguese food from Estremoz, Alentejo and Douro which includes honey, olives, olive oil, marmalade and Elvas plums. Try piri piri, a hot, hot chilli sauce, or the marinades with lemon, pimento and garlic flavourings. Their descriptions are nectarial – " local bee keepers place their hives under the greengage trees in the orchards which produce fruit for our famous Elvas plums". Who can resist?

> **Conservas Rainha Santa**, Clements E Companhia Ltd, Old Spitalfields Market, 49 Brushfield Street, London E1 6AA
> **Tel/Fax:** 0171 247 2802
> **Price range:** £1.95 to £10.75. Catalogue free.
> **Payment:** cheque, Mastercard, Visa, Switch.
> **Postage & packing:** £3.95.
> **Delivery:** allow 28 days.
> **Refunds:** yes.

Fresh Olives Direct Very tempting, this. With an office in France, this firm imports the best olives from the midi. There are tiny, delicious coquilles from the mountains behind Nice, giant green Lucques Royales from around Carcasonne and black olives mixed with Provençal herbs.

Also "cracked" green olives scented with garlic, lemon or basil and various olive oils, pastes and the inevitable balsamic vinegar. Buy a selection of six or so and have an olive tasting before dinner.

Fresh Olives Direct, Unit 1, Hanover West Industrial Estate, Acton Lane, London NW10 7NB
Tel: 0181 453 1918 **Fax:** 0181 838 1913
Price range: £3.50 to £50. Catalogue free.
Payment: cheque, postal order. Credit cards soon.
Postage & packing: from £1.80 to £4.50.
Delivery: 4 days. Last Christmas orders a week ahead.
Refunds: yes.
Specials: hampers and gifts sent direct.

New Quay Honey Farm Strangely, few apiaries sell by mail order, though honey is easier than many foods to transport. This farm, the largest honey farm in Wales with 500 hives and 50,000 bees, is sited in unspoilt countryside with wooded valleys and coastal vegetation which results in delicious honey. There are pure wildflower and heather honeys (from bees working the moors of mid Wales) along with walnuts and ginger in honey and honey fudge. Also beeswax polishes and candles, which can be dipped to order.

New Quay Honey Farm, Cross Inn, New Quay, Ceredigion SA44 6NN
Tel: 01545 560822
Price range: from £2.50. Catalogue free.
Payment: cheque.
Postage & packing: £2.60 for orders of fewer than 10 jars, otherwise free.
Delivery: allow 7 days. Christmas orders by last posting date.
Refunds: by arrangement.

Olives Et Al Giles and Annie Henschel took a year off to travel around the Mediterranean and came back to import the foods and flavours that they missed in Britain. The foods are imported but prepared here. These include olives marinated in the

FOOD AND DRINK

Sicilian and Moroccan style, stuffed with garlic and anchovies or sourced from Greece, Spain and France. There are oils from around the area, olive paste and balsamic vinegar which, mixed, make excellent gift packs.

Olives Et Al, Unit D2, Quarry Fields, Mere, Wiltshire BA12 6LA
Tel: 01747 861446 **Fax:** 01747 861448
Price range: £4.95 to £110. Catalogue free.
Payment: cheque, major credit cards for orders over £10.
Postage & packing: £4.95 for orders under £50, free for orders over £50.
Delivery: 48 hours. Last Christmas orders 21 December.
Refunds: yes.
Specials: personal messages or cards can be enclosed.

Rosebud Preserves An 1830s barn on a North Yorkshire farm was specially converted into a kitchen and pantry for this family firm to make all its preserves, adapted from home recipes. You can visit them there to try the produce but they also mail order. Try their Old Yorkshire chutney, rich and of mixed fruits or the Spiced Plum chutney to go with cheese or cold meats. There are, too, pickles of cucumber and bitter lemon, relishes and traditional chutneys like Bengal and Malay. There is, too, a wild crabapple jelly (wild foods are very smart at present), garlic jelly for stir fries and all the usual jams and preserves.

Rosebud Preserves, Rosebud Farm, Healey, Ripon, North Yorkshire HG4 4LH
Tel/Fax: 01765 689174
Price range: £1.95 to £2. Catalogue free.
Payment: cheque.
Postage & packing: £5 per address.
Delivery: allow 14 days. Faster delivery available. Last Christmas orders by 10 December.
Refunds: replacement.
Specials: gift-wrapping.

Wendy Brandon Most of us no longer have the time or the equipment to make traditional preserves but Wendy Brandon has. Her preserves are divided into four varieties; the green label covers chutneys and fruit sauces, made without added salt or sugar and including delicious and unusual varieties such as apricot, Kashmiri apple with a spicy Indian flavour and a Jamaican style mango chutney; the orange label is for coarse cut marmalades made from all varieties of citrus fruit from lemon to kumquat; the red label is for jams, jellies, spiced vinegars and pickles; and the blue is the international range of pickles and chutneys from Europe, India and even Australia (hot piccalilli). You can choose a mixture of preserves (up to eight jars) to pack in a willow tray for a present.

Wendy Brandon, Felin Wen, Boncath, Pembrokeshire SA37 0JR
Tel: 01239 841568 **Fax:** 01239 841746
Price range: £1.50 to £5.45. Catalogue free.
Payment: cheque, Mastercard, Access, Visa.
Postage & packing: £5.75 per address.
Delivery: some preserves in limited supply. Last Christmas orders by 15 December.
Refunds: by arrangement.

DRINK

It's fascinating to look at wine lists today. Only a decade ago, 90% would be French wines, mostly claret, burgundy and a few grand whites with a rather apologetic postscript for Germany, Italy and Spain. Now, wine lists travel the world. French wine is taking a back seat, except for the real greats, having been outclassed by the old colonies. Australia, New Zealand and South Africa, along with the Americas, are the places where it happens now. They are the innovators while the French plough the same furrow. Italy has at last got its denominazione act together, while exciting wines are emerging from Eastern Europe. Even England and Canada are producing interesting varieties. At the same time, drinks of anything from cider apples to elderflowers are blooming, while coffee is hugely popular and tea enjoying a great revival. Naturally, the dedicated mail order firms are at the front of this revolution and it is in their catalogues that you will find the innovations.

DRINK - LISTINGS

The Australian Wine Club A couple of decades ago, no one would own to Australian wine. Now it's one of the major growth areas, as this club shows. As you might expect, the wine descriptions are far from pseudy (one is described as a blinder) and another innovation is to list some whites by the degree of oaking. Useful since some are allergic to oak. Also, sparkling and fortified Aussies and even an Oz olive oil from the south.

> **The Australian Wine Club**, Freepost WC5500, Slough, Berkshire SL3 9BH
> **Tel:** 0800 856 2004 **Fax:** 01753 591369
> **E-mail:** austwine.demon.co.uk
> **Website:** www.australian-wine.co.uk
> **Price range:** £4.99 to £19.99 per bottle (minimum order 12 bottles). Catalogue free.
> **Payment:** cheque, major credit cards.
> **Postage & packing:** included in mainland UK inc Northern Ireland.
> **Delivery:** allow 10 days. Last Christmas orders by 13 December.
> **Refunds:** yes.

The Beer Cellar A collection of over 170 classic beers from more than forty countries which can be ordered in single cases, mixed cases and special selection cases of twelve or twenty-four bottles. There's a millennium ale and a beer from France called Sans Culottes; from Germany there's Schloss Hell and there are also beers from Thailand and Tahiti, Israel and Peru, Sri Lanka and Cyprus. Special collections include fruit beers, a selection brewed by Belgian monks and, for Christmas, a case of Santa's favourites plus an ales and cheese basket.

The Beer Cellar, 31 Norwich Road, Strumpshaw, Norwich, Norfolk NR13 4AG
Tel: 01603 714884 **Fax:** 01603 714624
E-mail: cellar@paston.co.uk
Price range: £6.99 to £52.50. Catalogue free.
Payment: cheque, postal order, major credit cards.
Postage & packing: £3.95 per case up to £9.75 for 4 cases.
Delivery: allow 14 days.
Refunds: yes, if damaged or not delivered.
Specials: gift baskets.

Champagne Select

This company imports champagne from the small house, Veuve Cheurlin, in Celles-sur-Ource which is near Troyes and in the south of the champagne area of France. The two qualities on offer are reserve and prestige, which is top of the range. They will send out gift bottles with a personal message as well as cases of six or a dozen. For an extra charge, these can be delivered the next day.

Champagne Select, P O Box 265, Billingham, TS23 3FF
Tel/Fax: 01642 560536
Price range: £20 to £25. Catalogue free.
Payment: cheque, major credit cards.
Postage & packing: included in mainland UK.
Delivery: 3-5 days. Next-day delivery available. Last Christmas orders by 17 December.
Refunds: by arrangement.

Espresso Warehouse

Coffee has been around for some time so why has it suddenly taken over from wine and olive oil as the foodie focus? Every second shop in London has turned into a bean-ridden café and now, along with the traditional mail order coffee firms, we have this professional catalogue dedi-

FOOD AND DRINK

cated to coffee beans and "equipment for the entire coffee experience". There is a full range of replacement parts for cafetières, as well as Italian crockery, flavoured syrups, sugar sticks and coffee quality timers. In addition there are teas, from Earl Grey to Steep Teas, which are apparently favoured by American rock stars.

> **Espresso Warehouse**, 8-10 Lawmoor Road, Glasgow G5 0UL
> **Tel:** 0141 420 2422 **Fax:** 0141 420 2399
> **Price range:** £1.35 to £130. Catalogue free.
> **Payment:** cheque, Mastercard, Visa.
> **Postage & packing:** from £1.50 for orders up to £5 to £4.50 for orders over £70 in UK. Overseas rates on application.
> **Delivery:** allow 14 days.
> **Refunds:** by arrangement.

The Exclusive Brandy Club You do have to pay £15 membership fee to join for which you get a quarterly newsletter but you also get the chance to buy bottles not just of cognac but also armagnac, calvados and marcs from France. There are, too, a couple of Spanish brandies and three Pineau des Charentes. No one says they are cheap (up to £385 a bottle for an 80-year-old La Fontaine de la Pouyade) but they are often otherwise unobtainable.

> **The Exclusive Brandy Club**, Crooked Holme Farmhouse, Brampton, Cumbria CA8 2AT
> **Tel/Fax:** 01697 73744
> **Price range:** £10 to £500 and over for special vintages. List free.
> **Payment:** cheque, major credit cards.
> **Postage & packing:** £5 for orders under £50, free thereafter.
> **Delivery:** allow 2 weeks. Next day delivery at extra cost. Last Christmas orders 2 weeks ahead.
> **Refunds:** yes, if returned unopened and undamaged.
> **Specials:** vintages available for special anniversaries.

The Great Northern Wine Company Wine firms seem to be calling themselves after railways and this one, based in Leeds and Ripon in Yorkshire, keeps a good list of champagnes

238   MAIL ORDER MADE EASY

along with other wines. Also, they have good ranges of whisky, port and cognac – but are not too traditional to take orders over e-mail.

The Great Northern Wine Company, Granary Wharf, The Canal Basin, Leeds LS1 4BR

Tel: 0113 246 1200 **Fax:** 0113 246 1209

E-mail: gnw.leeds@onyxnet.co.uk

Price range: from £3.29. Catalogue free.

Payment: cheque, major credit/debit cards.

Postage & packing: free in and around the Leeds area, elsewhere £5 to £10.

Delivery: by courier. Last Christmas orders by 7 December.

Refunds: breakages will be replaced.

Specials: gift packs, personalised labels, free glass loan.

Great Western Wine

As well as mail ordering their own wines – most wine merchants deliver to the door and, thus, are mail order firms – this one puts together its own gift cases and hampers both for personal and corporate buyers. You can get a tour of French wines in a case, for instance, or one from around the world from Chile to Australia. Then there are boxes of chocolate truffles and port, champagne and truffles, port and stilton or chablis and salmon. The general list is now less than half French, with good selections from the rest of Europe, Australia, California, New Zealand and South Africa.

Great Western Wine Company, The Wine Warehouse, Wells Road, Bath BA2 3AP

Tel: 01225 446009 **Fax:** 01225 442139

E-mail: post@greatwesternwine.co.uk

Price range: mixed wine cases from £40, gift packs from £10. Catalogue free.

Payment: major credit/debit cards.

Postage & packing: £5 to £6.50.

Delivery: by 24-hour carrier. Last Christmas orders 7 days in advance.

Refunds: replacement.

Specials: gift boxes, personalised labels, greeting cards in cases.

FOOD AND DRINK

H.R. Higgins I have been buying my coffee mail order from Mr. Higgins for decades (I won't say how many). First, I began because it was impossible to get proper varieties and beans in the north where I lived. And I continue because, though coffee is making huge comeback, Mr. Higgins always seems one step ahead of the shops. For effect and taste try Maragogype ("mara-go-jeep") which is the biggest bean in the world or Huehuetenango ("way-way-ten-an-go") a Mexican smoothie or a newish introduction, Mark T.U.J. San Marcos de Tarrazu from the mountains of Costa Rica. I tend to like American and Caribbean coffee but if you prefer African, Indian or Indonesian, he has them too. Also an excellent tea list. These both make excellent thank-you presents.

H.R. Higgins (Coffee Man) Ltd, 10 Lea Road Industrial Park, Waltham Abbey, Essex EN9 1AS

Tel: 01992 768254 **Fax:** 01992 787523

Price range: coffee £13.28 to £66 per kg, tea £10.24 to £26.24 per kg. Discounts for orders of 3kg or more. Catalogue free.

Payment: cheque, Access, Visa, Switch.

Postage & packing: £3.20 for orders up to 1kg, £4.20 for 2.25kg, free for 2.5kg and over in mainland UK.

Delivery: by first class post for small orders, larger orders by parcel post. Last Christmas orders by first week December.

Refunds: yes.

Specials: gift packs, free 125g sample with orders of 2.5kg or more.

James Nicholson Wine Merchant Working from a remote area of Northern Ireland, but nominated Wine Merchant of the Year for the province five years running, James Nicholson introduced no fewer than 200 new wines to his list for the year and his neat, ringbound catalogue is full of descriptions of them, the estates from which they came and the growers. It's nice to know, for example, that your Portuguese Vila Santa is grown by a Richard Gere lookalike.

James Nicholson Wine Merchant, 27a Killyleagh Street, Crossgar, Co. Down, BT30 9DQ

Tel: 01396 830091 **Fax:** 01396 830028

Price range: £3.60 to £79.50. Catalogue free.

Payment: cheque, major credit/debit cards.

Postage & packing: free in Northern Ireland, elsewhere at cost.

Delivery: despatched within 48 hours by carrier. Last Christmas orders by 16 December.

Refunds: yes.

James White

You don't just get plain apple juice from this Suffolk farm but can pick varieties like fruity Cox's juice, dry Bramley or rich Russet. They make their own cider ("treat with respect") and apple juice mixed with elderflower, blackberry and cinnamon. Big Tom is created extra rich and spicy for mixing in Bloody Mary or just on its own in Virgin Mary. All very refreshing after an evening's indulgence or an excellent present all year round.

James White Apple Juices. Whites Fruit Farm, Ashbocking, Ipswich, Suffolk IP6 9JS

Tel: 01473 890111 **Fax:** 01473 890001

Price range: £24 to £28 per case. Leaflet free.

Payment: cheque, major credit cards.

Postage & packing: included.

Delivery: 10 days, UK only. Last Christmas orders 14 December.

Refunds: yes.

Specials: gift cards can be sent with order. Mixed cases.

Justerini & Brooks

The Queen's wine merchants, who have been going for 200 years, thus also serving George III, IV and VI, Victoria and Edward VII, who knew something about wines. Their house wines, from £3.95 per bottle, are excellent value, especially the house claret. These are safe to buy even for wine buffs. You can also buy a 1934 first growth Haut-Brion for £225 if you feel less secure. This is very much a traditional list, heavy on good port but with little from the new world. The house London Dry Gin stays at 40% proof while others have gone down to 37.5%. There is also a sloe gin.

Justerini & Brooks Ltd, 61 St James's Street, London SW1A 1LZ

Tel: 0171 493 8721 **Fax:** 0171 499 4653

FOOD AND DRINK 241

Price range: £3.50 to £2,990, discount for orders of 2 or more cases. Catalogue free.

Payment: cheque, major credit/debit cards.

Postage & packing: £9 for 1-23 bottles, free thereafter in mainland UK.

Delivery: same day delivery available within London and Edinburgh at extra cost. Last Christmas orders 10 days in advance.

Refunds: yes, offending bottle should be returned. Breakages should be retained with packing and reported immediately.

Specials: Christmas gift cases.

Lay & Wheeler This wine merchant's catalogue is a book in itself, 136 pages long. The wines come from all over the world with strong presences from Australia, New Zealand, South Africa and California, a good selection of ports and sherries plus some new world sparkling wines. The firm is neither pompous nor over-priced though some of its descriptions of wines are beguiling – how about "imminently drinkable"?

Lay & Wheeler Ltd, Gosbecks Park, Gosbeck Road, Colchester, Essex CO2 9JT

Tel: 01206 764446 **Fax:** 01206 560002

E-mail: laywheeler@ndirect.co.uk

Website: http://www.layandwheeler.co.uk

Price range: £3.98 to £195. Catalogue free.

Payment: cheque, major credit/debit cards.

Postage & packing: £7.95 for 1-3 bottles including gift box, £5.95 for 12 bottles, free for orders over £150 in mainland UK.

Delivery: 2 working days.

Refunds: yes, on unwanted bottles if returned within a month.

Specials: gift vouchers, bespoke gift selections, corporate gifts, gift cards included.

Reid Wines Selling – and buying – wine gets more complicated by the day. This catalogue blames the Far East for the turbulence but the end result is a list which includes Lebanon, South Africa, Argentina and one from an unnamed Eastern European country "hideously presented" but impressive. As one who enjoys wine labels, I can't wait to see it. The firm sells an Italian prosecco which is curiously hard to find.

Reid Wines (1992) Ltd, The Mill, Marsh Lane, Hallatrow, Bristol
BS39 6EB

Tel: 01761 452645 **Fax:** 01761 453642

Price range: £4 to £4,000 exc. VAT. Catalogue free.

Payment: major credit cards, subject to 3% surcharge.

Postage & packing: free in central London and for orders of 6 cases or more, otherwise from £1.50 to £6 plus VAT per case in mainland UK. Datapost delivery by following day from £17.

Delivery: normally within 3 days. Last Christmas orders 7 working days in advance.

Refunds: yes.

Sharpham Wines and Cheeses

Based in South Devon, this is one of the up-and-coming English wineries. They produce three white wines, one fermented in oak barriques, and a light red with a hint of oak and intended to be drunk cold. Their cheeses comes from their own herd of 50 Jersey cows grazing on 100 acres of permanent pasture beside the river Dart.

Sharpham Partnership Ltd, Sharpham House, Totnes, South Devon, TQ9 7UT

Tel: 01803 732203 **Fax:** 01803 732122

Price range: £5.95 to £9.99 per bottle. Send sae for catalogue.

Payment: cheque.

Postage & packing: £5 for 1 bottle, £6 for 6, £10 for 12 to 24, free for 3 dozen or more.

Delivery: normally within 7 days. Next day delivery at extra cost.

Refunds: by arrangement.

Specials: mixed cases available.

Somerset Cider Brandy

A very popular company which uses traditional cider apples – Brown Snout and Somerset Red Streak – in 120 acres of orchards to create a British version of Calvados in two French stills, called Josephine and Fifi. A new product this year is the Kingston Black Apple Aperitif in which cider brandy is blended with pure apple juice from the Kingston Black. It is 18% proof and should be drunk on the rocks. Its charming label, reminiscent of Matisse, is by Hilary McManus. The firm's five-year-old cider brandy featured this year at Tony Blair's EC presidency dinner.

FOOD AND DRINK

The Somerset Cider Brandy Company Ltd, Burrow Hill, Kingsbury
Episcopi, Martock, Somerset TA12 5BU
Tel/Fax: 01460 240782
Price range: £6.90 to to £24. Send sae for catalogue.
Payment: cheque, major credit cards.
Postage & packing: 1 bottle £3.94, 4 bottles £1.50 each.
Delivery: allow 7 days. Last Christmas orders by 18 December.
Refunds: no.

The Sussex Tea Company The firm sells our best-loved
teas both loose and in tea bags of which my favourite must be
Lapsang Souchong which combines the punch of a black, tarry
tea with the elegance of the Chinese teas. It's a good breakfast
tea and, says the firm, ideal with cucumber sandwiches. They
also do a range of fruit infusions including a berry fruit cocktail of bilberries and black and red currants, peach and apple or
passion fruit and orange. They have no additives, caffeine or
tannin and should be sweetened with honey rather than sugar.

The Sussex Tea Company Ltd, P O Box 66, Uckfield, East Sussex
TN22 3ZR
Tel: 01825 732601 **Fax:** 01825 732730
E-mail: tony.walker@btinternet.com
Price range: £1.20 to £15. Send A4 sae for catalogue.
Payment: cheque, postal order.
Postage & packing: £1.20 for 375g, £2.40 for 750g, £3.60 for
1250g, £5.50 thereafter. Overseas rates on application.
Delivery: next-day delivery at extra cost. Last Christmas orders
by first week December.
Refunds: never had a dissatisfied customer but would willingly
be given.

Tanners Specialists in finding wines from small producers all
around the world, this list is full of surprises and interests.
There are sparkling wines from Bombay, South Africa and
California, sparkling rosés and reds too, white ports and dry
Madeiras. In the spirit section there's an excellent whisky list
and a gin – Pulling's Hereford Dry – which I've never heard of
but which won the gin trophy in the International Spirit
Challenge (nothing to do with the ghost of Christmas Past).

244   MAIL ORDER MADE EASY

Tanners Wines Ltd, 26 Wyle Cop, Shrewsbury, Shropshire SY1 1XD
Tel: 01743 234500/234455 **Fax:** 01743 234501
E-mail: sales@tanners-wines.co.uk
Price range: £3.50 to £350 per bottle. Catalogue free.
Payment: cheque, major credit /debit cards or customers can open a credit account.
Postage & packing: included for orders over £75, otherwise £6.
Delivery: normally within 3 days. Last Christmas orders 15 December.
Refunds: yes, including opened bottles.

Three Choirs Vineyards The vineyard offers self-guided tours to be followed by a tasting in the shop and a meal in their restaurant. This is an excellent excuse to try their dozen wines (including one, made from Phoenix grapes and not approved by the EC, at £4.99) then go home and order a few cases. English wines get better by the year and this is a good one.

Three Choirs Vineyards, Newent, Gloucestershire GL18 1LS
Tel: 01531 890223 **Fax:** 01531 890877
Price range: £3.99 to £9.99.
Payment: cheque, major credit/debit cards.
Postage & packing: included.
Delivery: allow 7 days.
Refunds: by arrangement.

Torz & Macatonia London is leading a revolution in Britain whereby people demand real coffee rather than nasty brown flaky bits. Not only do Londoners now expect their beans to be ground on demand, they want to know where they have come from and what variety of coffee bush. T & M offer 24 different varieties or blends of coffee from Guatemala or Mexico in the west to Papua New Guinea and Malabar in the East. There are blends for espresso, decaff and French coffee. Their teas come in the same smart brown paper pack and include both China (rose congou, lapsang and jasmin yin hao), India (Darjeeling and Assam), Ceylon and English blends. Jeremy Torz and Steven Macatonia's stylish catalogue is evidence enough of how seriously they take the subject.

FOOD AND DRINK

Torz & Macatonia Gourmet Coffee Roasters, 12 Blackwall Estate, Lanrick Road, London E14 0JP

Tel: 0171 515 7770 **Fax:** 0171 515 7779

E-mail: torzmacatoniacoffee@compuserve.com

Price range: £3.55 to £8 for 250g. Catalogue free.

Payment: cheque, major credit cards.

Postage & packing: £2 for 250g, £3.50 for 750g to 1kg, £4.50 over 1kg.

Delivery: normally despatched within 2 working days. Last Christmas orders 5 working days in advance.

Refunds: yes.

Specials: gift packs from £15.70.

Valvona & Crolla

The famous Edinburgh Italian grocery started by Valvona in the 1860s and still run by Crolla's grand-children has a hugely impressive 600-strong wine list (pity it doesn't mail the other bits like Italian vegetables and food) of Italian wines and a few grown with Italian grapes elsewhere. There is a decent list of estate-bottled olive oils.

Valvona & Crolla Ltd, 19 Elm Row, Edinburgh EH7 4AA

Tel: 0131 556 6066 **Fax:** 0131 556 1668

E-mail: sales@valvonacrolla.co.uk

Price range: £4 to £400. Catalogue free.

Payment: cheque, major credit/debit cards.

Postage & packing: from £7.90 per carton. Small orders at cost plus £3.00 handling charge for orders under £30.

Delivery: guaranteed next day delivery available. Last Christmas orders by 15 December.

Refunds: by arrangement.

Specials: gift-wrapping and vouchers.

Vintage Roots

Organic wine is produced without synthetic fertilisers, pesticides and preservatives like sulphur dioxide. This company specialises in pure wine made like it used to be from all the usual countries, including two whites from Sedlescombe in Sussex and one from Chudleigh Vineyard in Devon. There are also organic liqueurs like Cassis and Crème de Mûre, Cognac and Calvados. There is a small selection of organic beers from Germany and Scotland, cider and perry and fruit juices.

246 MAIL ORDER MADE EASY

Vintage Roots Ltd, Farley Farms, Bridge Farm, Reading Road, Arborfield, Berkshire RG2 9HT

Tel: 0118 976 1999 **Fax:** 0118 976 1998

E-mail: roots@ptop.demon.co.uk

Price range: £1.35 to £29.95. Catalogue free.

Payment: cheque, major credit/debit cards.

Postage & packing: 1 case £4.95, 2-5 cases £5.95, 6 or more cases free. Overnight add £2.50. Free delivery within 30 miles of Reading.

Delivery: within 7 days.

Refunds: yes, within 3 days for breakages.

Specials: gift vouchers, mixed cases of wine for vegetarians and vegans, hampers for vegans, chocolates and gifts.

Waitrose Direct The big supermarkets have unrivalled pulling power to get prices down which means that their wines are among the best value around. But, because they must buy in large quantities, they cannot go for the small and quirky. Waitrose has one of the best reputations for quality and thoughtfulness among the giants and its wine list reflects that. It puts together cases of oaked reds, of wines from the southern hemisphere and a case of 24 half bottles. You can get your British beer by region, too. There's a home counties case from Kent and London, a midlands and northern case and a continental case with beers from Belgium, Italy, Germany and the Czech republic. There's also a Christmas selection with hampers and foodie presents.

Waitrose Direct, Deer Park Road, Merton Abbey, London SW19 3TU

Tel: free 0800 188881 **Fax:** free 0800 188888

Price range: £2.75 to £250. Catalogue free.

Payment: cheque, major credit/debit cards, plus Waitrose card.

Postage & packing: £3.95 per case, free for 2 cases or more.

Delivery: allow 21 days. Last Christmas orders by 7 December.

Refunds: yes.

Whittard of Chelsea Buy "the world's rarest wild tea" Ti Kuan Ying Monkey Picked Oolong (actually picked by people) at £12 for 50g, or Lapsang Formosa Alligator, Black Dragon

FOOD AND DRINK

Oolong or the "suave" Kalej Valley First Flush from this marvellous list. The brochure gives tasting notes and tips on teamaking. The coffee list is less dramatic but offers Sumatra Blue Lingtong, Guatemala Elephant and Old Brown Java. The firm will offer suggestions and advice too.

Whittard of Chelsea, 73 Northcote Road, London SW11 6PJ
Tel: 0171 924 1888 **Fax:** 0171 924 3085
Price range: from £6.40 for 500g. Catalogue free.
Payment: cheque, postal order, major credit/debit cards.
Postage & packing: £3.95.
Delivery: 10 days.
Refunds: by arrangement.
Specials: gift service.

See also: Charlton Orchards for apple juice, Graig Farm for organic wine, beer and cider, Vigo Vineyard Supplies for cider.

Chapter Five

LUXURIES

SCENT, AROMATICS, COSMETICS.

If gardens are the currently fashionable area for designers, scent is the currently fashionable area of cosmetics. We've discovered, recently, that the sense of smell has been greatly undervalued. It can not only evoke memories or desire but can be adapted to create moods, to cure ailments or be used as therapy for stress, worry or sleeplessness. Firms in my list will provide solutions to life's worries in the form of scented candles, pillows and drawer liners along with the newest perfumes of the hour. At the same time, we are beginning to rebel against the rule of the big cosmetic companies which insist that their goods can only be bought, at vast expense, from supercilious girls in department stores. Instead of being humiliated by them, we can now browse through the catalogues and buy after careful reflection. As experiments prove that £50 a gram creams may be no more efficacious than those at 50p a gram, we can shop without pressure, at home.

SCENTS, AROMATICS, COSMETICS - LISTINGS

Aromatherapy Associates Beautifully packaged – in matt black with gold – essential oils for the body, mind and spirit. Juniperberry and grapefruit combine for a stimulating bath oil, pine and eucalyptus spice up winter baths. Petitgrain and camomile are designed to restore the spirit while deep relaxing bath oil – camomile and vetiver – calms a confused mind. All smell wonderful.

LUXURIES 249

Aromatherapy Associates, P O Box 14981, London SW6 2WH
Tel: 0171 371 9878 **Fax:** 0171 371 9894
Price range: £5.95 to £29.95. Catalogue free.
Payment: cheque, major credit cards.
Postage & packing: £2 for 1 or 2 items, £3 for 3 or 4, £4 for 5 or 6, £6 for more.
Delivery: allow 3 weeks.
Refunds: yes, for breakages if notified within 24 hours.

Aromatique
It's not enough today to spray scent behind your ears and face the world with confidence. You have to scent your entire house – and in ways which will variously soothe, stimulate or evoke your moods. Aromatique takes this seriously with collections which include gardenia, summer sorbets and Amazon ("the vibrant colours of exotic botanicals..."). Collections may have pot pourri, room spray, burning candles and refreshers. There are also special candles and pot pourri holders to suit, gift hampers and a range for the bath.

Aromatique, 154 Brompton Road, London SW3 1HX
Tel: 0171 591 1950 **Fax:** 0171 591 1951
Price range: £7 to £25. Catalogue free.
Payment: cheque, major credit/debit cards.
Postage & packing: from £6 depending on weight.
Delivery: 5 days. Express delivery available.
Refunds: by arrangement.
Specials: customised gift baskets, gift-wrapping.

Arran Aromatics
I can never be sure if aromatherapy is anything more than enjoying pleasant scents – but what's wrong with that? Arran operates from the Scottish island and California with a large range of stockists in Britain. Try their huge range in your nearest then get top-ups via the post. As well as scent mixtures to wake you up and send you to sleep and so on, there are some good soaps, cosmetics and shampoos.

Arran Aromatics Ltd, The Home Farm, Brodick, Isle of Arran, KA27 8DD
Tel: 01770 302595 **Fax:** 01770 302599

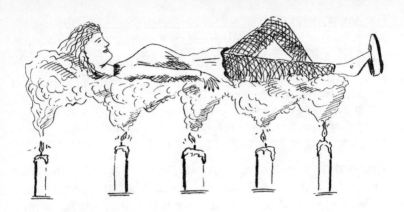

E-mail: info@arran-aromatics.co.uk
Website: http://www.arran-aromatics.co.uk
Price range: 90p to £5.99.
Payment: cheque, major credit/debit cards.
Postage & packing: £4 in UK. Overseas rates on application.
Delivery: allow 28 days.
Refunds: by arrangement.

Barry M Huge selection of over 350 foundations, eye and lip gloss, blusher and eye liner and nail paints: pearlised, glittering or even fluorescent. There are 70 eye and lip colours and over 120 nail paints. Prices are extremely good value. Shock with five shades of black nail varnish (plus green, mauve and khaki metallic), black and white lipstick (plus electric blue, grape or shocking pink) and foundation shades for every ethnic group or fashion (Goths use white foundation).

Barry M Cosmetics Direct, 1 Bittacy Business Centre, Bittacy Hill, Mill Hill East, London NW7 1BA
Tel: 0181 349 2992
Fax: 0181 346 7733
Price range: Catalogue free.
Payment: cheque, Mastercard, Visa, Switch.
Postage & packing: £1.95.
Delivery: despatched within 24 hours by first class post. Last Christmas orders by 14 December.
Refunds: yes, if returned unused.

LUXURIES

Beauty Quest The place where beauty professionals go to get the latest and the best cosmetics and equipment. Makes include Aveda, L'Occitane, Face Stockholm and Ruby Hammer's range of brushes. Buys come from all over the world and are always changing.

Beauty Quest Ltd, Vestry Road, Sevenoaks, Kent TR14 5XA
Tel: 0541 505000 **Fax:** 01732 453166
Price range: 90p to £85.50. Catalogue free.
Payment: cheque, postal order, major credit/debit cards.
Postage & packing: £2.70 for orders of £20 and under, £4.80 for orders over £30 in UK, by recorded delivery.
Delivery: despatched within 5 working days.
Refunds: yes, if returned in perfect condition within 21 days.

Le Club des Créateurs de Beauté Cosmetics are an area ideally suited to mail order once you know what you want (or are willing to experiment). Do you hate as much as I do those mask-like assistants who persuade you to spend too much on what you don't want? I reckon buying blind without a dab on the back of your hand but buying thoughtfully at home will save you money and hassle. This range includes Agnes B, Cosmence and Jean Marc Maniatis hair care.

Le Club des Créateurs de Beauté, Parliament House, Harrogate HG1 5BR
Tel: 0990 902090 **Fax:** 0990 903090
Price range: £3.50 to £16.50. Catalogue free.
Payment: cheque, postal order, major credit/debit cards.
Postage & packing: £2.95.
Delivery: allow 28 days.
Refunds: yes, if returned within 15 days.

Crabtree & Evelyn A traditional perfumier which has recently branched into using modern, avant-garde scents with great success. Along with carnation, damask rose and violet, the enticing scents of vanilla, berries and eucalyptus are available. Each scent comes in a range of products from soap and massage oil to burning candles, foot scrub and pot pourri.

MAIL ORDER MADE EASY

Choose a favourite and keep adding to the range, from drawer liners to room spray. There are also bon-bons and Mason's blue and white china in the mail order catalogue.

Crabtree & Evelyn, Freepost, Customer Services Dept, 36 Milton Park, Abingdon, Oxfordshire OX14 4BR

Tel: 01235 862244

Price range: £3.95 to £36. Catalogue free.

Payment: cheque, major credit cards.

Postage & packing: £3.50.

Delivery: allow 14 days.

Refunds: telephone if damaged.

Culpeper Named after the famous early herbalist, this company was founded in 1927 when no one at all was interested in herbs. The list includes such things as comfrey cream, three flower toning lotions and rosemary shampoo along with medicinal herbs, massage oils, pomanders, pot pourri, sleep pillows and kitchen herbs. There are also books about herbs, oriental spices and various accessories.

Culpeper Ltd, Hadstock Road, Linton, Cambridge CB1 6NJ

Tel: 01223 894054 **Fax:** 01223 893104

E-mail: culpeper@dial.pipex.com

Website: http://www.culpeper.co.uk

Price range: 10p to £175. Catalogue free.

Payment: cheque, major credit/debit cards.

Postage & packing: £3.25 for orders up to £20, £3.95 to £50, free thereafter in UK. Overseas rates on application.

Delivery: by post or Parcel Force. Last Christmas orders by last posting date.

Refunds: yes.

Specials: gift-wrapping, hampers and gift baskets.

Czech & Speake Where should we put this company? Since it does everything for bathrooms, from huge shower roses, Edwardian style taps and traditional accessories, you might think in our house section. But, there are the bath oils, scents, shower gels, soaps, candles and room scents in rose, neroli, lavender and grapefruit, so we thought it should go under lux-

LUXURIES

253

uries. Everything in the range is dedicated to making bath-time the relaxing pleasure it ought to be but rarely is. The designs are old-fashioned but not boring and the packaging makes them wonderful gifts.

Czech & Speake Direct, 244-254 Cambridge Heath Road, London E2 9DA

Tel: 0800 919728 **Fax:** 0181 981 7232

Price range: aromatics £6 to £150, fittings etc up to £3,200. Boxed brochure £5, redeemable against purchase.

Payment: cheque, major credit cards.

Postage & packing: £3 for aromatics in UK, fittings etc from £10.

Delivery: allow 28 days. Priority service available. Last Christmas orders 14 days in advance or 7 days in advance with £6 delivery charge.

Refunds: credit note.

D.R. Harris Set up in 1790, the pharmacy has been selling colognes and flower perfumes ever since. There are classic lavender, rose and English bouquet toilet waters and bay rum aftershave. The skin care ranges use milk of cucumbers, roses and almond oil – all packed in Harris's characteristic Victorian bottles. The range of sponges, loofahs and top-quality shaving brushes make excellent gifts for men – the firm has long supplied diplomats, military and naval officers as well as London dandies and rakes. There is also Harris's Original Pick-Me-Up.

D.R. Harris, 29 St. James's Street, London SW1A 1HB

Tel: 0171 930 3915/8753 **Fax:** 0171 925 2691

Price range: £1.95 to £73.60. Catalogue free.

Payment: cheque, major credit cards.

Postage & packing: £1.50 for orders over £11, £6 under £100, over £100 free in UK.

Delivery: goods despatched twice a week.

Refunds: by arrangement.

Hardys It took us some time to realise that good smells are good for you but now aromatherapy is part of life. Among the smartest presents last year were numerous scented candles, chunky pot pourris which are far chicer than tiny bits of dust and all sorts of bags for scenting linen, drawers, wardrobes and rooms. Hardys makes them all as well as less usual essential oils to throw on log fires (pine needle and cedar for instance). This is part of their special Christmas collection, which also includes spicy candles and pot pourri. It's amazing how a subtle touch of scent can create a mood (think of the supermarkets and their fresh baked bread). Other collections are Botanicals and Jewels.

Hardys, Crown Point, Waterside, Ely, Cambridgeshire CB7 4AU
Tel: 01353 664432 **Fax:** 01353 663371
Price range: £3.50 to £20. Catalogue free.
Payment: cheque, major credit cards.
Postage & packing: £2.50 to £4.50. Free for orders over £50.
Delivery: despatched within 7 days of order. Last Christmas orders 18 December.
Refunds: yes.
Specials: gift-wrapping, hand delivery by arrangement.

Jo Malone Princess Diana used to give thank-you presents from Jo Malone not least because they are so beautifully packed in black and cream surrounded by black tissue and scented wood shavings. The products are both simple and stylish. I use her gels and creams myself and note that many beauty editors swear by her Protein Skin Serum. Her fragrances are based on leaves, fruit and flowers like grapefruit, nutmeg and ginger, verbenas of Provence and, one of the favourites, lime, basil and mandarin. There are versions for shampoos, body lotion, soap plus pot pourris and scented candles. Special gift ideas are filigree glass bottles, a travelling cologne case and – at one time with a three-month waiting list – her In-flight Bag full of all necessities for jet travel.

Jo Malone Ltd, The Old Imperial Laundry, Warriner Gardens, London SW11 4XW
Tel: 0171 720 0202 **Fax:** 0171 720 0277
E-mail: info@jomalone.co.uk
Price range: £8.95 to £110. Catalogue free.
Payment: cheque, major credit/debit cards.

LUXURIES

Postage & packing: £3.50 for one item, £5 for two items or more. Overnight delivery £6. Overseas rates on request.

Delivery: 5 working days. Last Christmas orders 18 December.

Refunds: only if damaged or faulty through fault of Jo Malone Ltd.

Specials: all products are gift-wrapped. Personal delivery service in London area.

L'Artisan Parfumeur

As you might guess, this range of scents, room and drawer scents, candles and soaps tends towards the floral, the natural and the green range of scents. A new scent has been added for the World Fair in Lisbon: Navegar is inspired by the Portuguese sailors who discovered the spice routes and mingles red berries, ginger and lime with black pepper, anise and cachaca and, say the creators, reminds us of the caravels sailing East in the salt spray. I must say, it's a delicious and lively scent well worth trying. This year, too, to celebrate the 20th anniversary of their Mûre et Musc scent, there is a charming glass bottle shaped and coloured like a blackberry, full of the scent.

L'Artisan Parfumeur, 17 Cale Street, London SW3 3QR

Tel: 0171 352 4196 **Fax:** 0171 610 5317

Website: http://mkn.co.uk/help/perfume/info

Price range: £6.50 to £79.50. Sample pack containing five scents £5 inc. p&p, (£8.50 overseas). Catalogue free.

Payment: cheque, Access, Visa, Amex.

Postage & packing: £2.50 for orders up to £33.50, £4.50 thereafter in UK. Overseas rates on application.

Delivery: orders despatched three times a week.

Refunds: yes, if defective, exchange if unused.

Specials: gift-wrapping free on request.

Les Senteurs

Though many perfume departments in stores seem dauntingly huge, they all offer the same scents. This firm was founded 14 years ago on the idea that people might prefer to wear an unusual scent which was harder to find. The list includes Parfums de Nicolai, founded by the grand-daughter of Pierre Guerlain, and Annick Goutal, once a concert pianist.

Other scents are created specially for the firm, come from Diptyque, of scented candle fame and the Italian firm, Borsari di Parma. Also collections for men (and women should think of these for daytime) and for the home.

Les Senteurs-Specialist Perfumery, 227 Ebury Street, London SW1W 8UY

Tel: 0171 730 2322 **Fax:** 0171 259 9145

Price range: £8.50 to £145. Catalogue £3 refundable against order, samples £1 up to a maximum of 6.

Payment: major credit cards.

Postage & packing: £3.75 for up to 2kg by recorded delivery. Guaranteed next day delivery add £3. Overseas at cost plus £2 handling charge.

Delivery: usually next day. Courier service within Greater London by quotation. Last Christmas orders by 23 December.

Refunds: credit note or exchange if goods are suitable for resale. Sample vial included so that scent may be tried without opening packaging.

Specials: complimentary gift-wrapping service.

Molton Brown Wonderful cosmetics which use no animal extracts except those, like honey or milk, which don't harm the animal concerned. Much of the range is concerned with bath therapies, shower gels, shampoos and oils. The range of make-up brushes is superb and the variety of colours for lipstick, gloss and eyeshadow huge. The colour chart gives a very good idea of the shades but, failing that, there is a shop in South Molton Street, London.

Molton Brown by Mail, P O Box 2514, London NW6 1SR

Tel: 0171 625 6550 **Fax:** 0171 624 0737

Price range: £1.50 to £25. Catalogue free.

Payment: cheque, major credit/debit cards.

Postage & packing: £3.75 per order.

Delivery: allow 7 days. Last Christmas orders by 18 December.

Refunds: yes, if broken.

Specials: trial sizes at £1 for 3 if 1 full-size product is bought.

Officina Profumo-Farmaceutica di Santa Maria Novella The pharmacy founded by Dominican monks in

LUXURIES 257

1221 in Florence is probably the oldest in the world and has had plenty of practice in creating soaps, scents, medicines and tonics. There are wonderful shampoos based on lavender, iris and pomegranate from the Italian countryside, aromatics to calm or revive you, one called the Vinegar of the Seven Thieves, and soaps including a strong minty one, seasoned for sixty days, which repels flies. Everything is packed in old-fashioned paper and exudes quality.

Officina Profumo-Farmaceutica di Santa Maria Novella, 117 Walton Street, London SW3 2HP

Tel: 0171 460 6600 **Fax:** 0171 460 6601

Price range: £7 to £150. Catalogue free.

Payment: cheque, Mastercard, Visa.

Postage & packing: by arrangement.

Delivery: allow 28 days. Last Christmas orders by end November.

Refunds: by arrangement.

Penhaligon's In 1975 Sheila Pickles rescued the ailing company, "experts in the toilet and cosmetic arts", which had been founded in 1870 and has not put a foot wrong since, mingling the old company's designs and scents with carefully-considered new ones. The bottle design is 120 years old and the old day books and formulae are still in use. But scents like Hammam, invented in 1872, have been joined by the luscious Bluebell, created in 1978; Blenheim Bouquet, created in 1902 and used by Churchill and Quercus, created in 1996, and already becoming a worldwide favourite. The range also includes soaps, sprays, shampoos, gels and a whole series of luxuries such as marble based shaving brushes and razors, silver brushes and boxes and enamelled lipstick cases and flacons. The catalogue is worth sending for alone.

Penhaligon's By Request Postal and Gift Service, P O Box 2888, London N4 1NH

Tel: 0800 716108 (UK), 1 800 588 1992 (USA), 44 181 880 2050 (overseas) **Fax:** 0181 800 5789

E-mail: penhaligons@compuserve.com

Website: http://www.penhaligons.co.uk

Price range: from £7. Catalogue free.

Payment: cheque, major credit/debit cards.

Postage & packing: UK £2.50, or £5 next working day, Europe/USA £12.50, elsewhere £30.

Delivery: despatched within 2 days, or next day on request.

Refunds: by arrangement.

Specials: gift-wrapping, engraving.

The Perfumers Guild

A small family firm, established 1981, offers scents which you can find nowhere else. They are for women and men and for houses, via scented candles, burners and pot pourris. People can be perfumed with lavender, chypre, citrus or spice while the house is offered pretty much the same – lavender, green apple or English rose among others. The firm sends out a scented card (25p) for you to try.

The Perfumers Guild Ltd, 61 Abbots Road, Abbots Langley, Hertfordshire WD5 0BJ

Tel: 01923 260502 **Fax:** 01923 268200

Price range: £3.50 to £15. 10% discount on orders of £50 and over. Catalogue free.

Payment: cheque, postal order, major credit/debit cards.

Postage & packing: included.

Delivery: normally despatched within 3 days by first class post.

Refunds: by arrangement.

Potions & Possibilities

Julie Foster is a qualified aromatherapist who sells scents to heal and to please. There is, for example, a cushion to keep you alert while driving, a gel of lavender and mint for headaches and protection for chapped lips and cracked fingers. Julie offers gift boxes for relaxation (yes, yes) and for soothing baths. Other goodies are essential oils of bois de rose, green mandarin and cinnamon leaf, handmade soaps to invigorate or uplift and shampoo for jetlag.

Potions & Possibilities, The Aromatherapy Practice, Stable Court, Martlesham Heath, Ipswich, Suffolk IP5 3UQ

Tel: 01473 611922 **Fax:** 01773 631774

E-mail: potions@btinternet.com

Website: http://www.btinternet.com/~potions/

Price range: £1.25 to £25. Catalogue free.

Payment: cheque, postal order, major credit cards.
Postage & packing: free in UK. Overseas at cost.
Delivery: allow 10 days. Next day delivery at extra cost. Last Christmas orders 18 December.
Refunds: yes.
Specials: gift-wrapping, personalised gift baskets.

Space NK The cult make-up company which has at long last produced a mail order range. This includes the fashionable Philosophy, which gives you pause for thought while you cleanse your skin; Kiehl's, which have been making skincare since 1851, Laura Mercier, the make-up artist's range and Nars, whose cosmetics are worn by so many supermodels. All come in chic but not ridiculously gilded packaging.

Space NK, P O Box 18025, London EC2A 3RJ
Tel: 0870 607 7060 **Fax:** 0171 454 1153
Price range: £3 to £135. Catalogue free.
Payment: cheque, major credit/debit cards.
Postage & packing: £4 in UK.
Delivery: normally within 5 working days.
Refunds: yes, if returned unopened.

FLOWERS

Of course, it has always been possible to send flowers as a thank-you gift from city to city. But what arrived? All too often, the far-away florist would bundle up a sheaf of nasty chrysanths and wilting evergreen and send it round, knowing that the customer would never see it and the recipient never complain. Now flower bunches are big business, with fashions changing every year and we, the clients, want to know exactly what our money will buy. There are firms which specialise in sending the first scented flowers from the Channel Islands, giving mainlanders a brief foretaste of spring, while others deliver deliciously exotic bunches on request. People, especially in cities, especially out of season, enjoy the short luxury of flowers.

260   MAIL ORDER MADE EASY

FLOWERS - LISTINGS

Groom Bros Guarantee a touch of spring in mid-winter with a box of thirty fresh daffodils delivered to your door. Thirty daffodils fill three vases and cheer up rooms no end. Also bouquets of carnations and roses can be delivered in winter along with amaryllis for spring flowering.

> **Groom Bros Ltd**, Peck's Drove Nurseries, Spalding, Lincolnshire PE12 6BJ
>
> **Tel:** 01775 722421/766006   **Fax:** 01775 712252
>
> **Price range:** £9.60 to £35. Catalogue free.
>
> **Payment:** cheque, Access, Visa.
>
> **Postage & packing:** included.
>
> **Delivery:** by return if available. Last Christmas orders by 18 December.
>
> **Refunds:** yes.

Scent from the Islands The islands in question are the Scillies which have a sub-tropical warmth and can grow scented blooms much earlier than the rest of the UK. The firm will send boxes of up to 60 flowers or a seasonal bouquet.

> **Scent from the Islands**, Churchtown Farm, St. Martin's, Isles of Scilly TR25 0QL
>
> **Tel:** 01720 422169   **Fax:** 01720 422800
>
> **Price range:** £6.50 to £25. Catalogue free.
>
> **Payment:** cheque, postal order, major credit/debit cards.
>
> **Postage & packing:** included.
>
> **Delivery:** by first class post. Last Christmas orders 16 December.
>
> **Refunds:** no, but dissatisfied customers would be offered a replacement.

CIGARS.

I'm told that, in politically correct America, the fastest growing fashion is for cigars. It's also beginning to happen over here. If you are a cigar smoker, or want to give a colleague a present, get it sent by mail. There is a huge variety on offer, all the more so now that Cuba can trade with us. I confidently expect this sector to grow.

CIGARS - LISTINGS

Cigar Connoisseur Cigar smoking has come back and so have Havanas. At their peak, a box of 25 Montecristo cigars will cost you £640 which is serious money to go up in smoke. Others come from Dominica, Brazil, Honduras, Nicaragua and Burma. The catalogue has a full range of cigar accessories and there's a Cigar of the Month club which sends six selected smokes every month.

Cigar Connoisseur, Freepost ANG4570, Bungay NR35 1YZ
Tel: 01986 895551 **Fax:** 01986 896669
E-mail: cigars@connoisseur.demon.co.uk
Website: http://www.connoisseur.ltd.uk
Price range: £10 to £640. Catalogue free.
Payment: cheque, major credit/debit cards.
Postage & packing: £2.75 in UK.
Delivery: allow 10 days. Last Christmas orders 23 December. Goods are sent by special delivery during Christmas week.
Refunds: yes, for accessories. Goods damaged in transit will be replaced.
Specials: selection packs available. Club members are entitled to 5% discount.

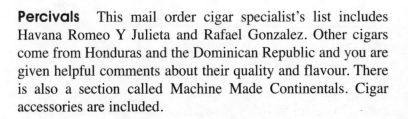

Percivals This mail order cigar specialist's list includes Havana Romeo Y Julieta and Rafael Gonzalez. Other cigars come from Honduras and the Dominican Republic and you are given helpful comments about their quality and flavour. There is also a section called Machine Made Continentals. Cigar accessories are included.

Percivals Fine Cigars, Moorside Cottages, Pott Shrigley, Cheshire SK10 5RZ

Tel/Fax: 01625 572090

Price range: £32 to £304. Catalogue free.

Payment: cheque.

Postage & packing: £2.95 in UK.

Delivery: allow 10 days. Last Christmas orders by 12 December. Havanas can be in short supply.

Refunds: yes.

See also: Candlesby Herbs, Ciel Decor, Cologne & Cotton, Hambleden Herbs and Norfolk Lavender for fragrances; Janet Reger and Agent Provocateur for sexy underwear; Marks & Spencer Home Delivery Service and Secretts for flowers; The Christmas Barn & Farmhouse Flora for dried flower arrangements, Red Letter days for visits to top health farms and hotels; entries under Drink for fine wines, brandies etc.

Chapter Six

BOOKS, CDs, CASSETTES, VIDEOS, STATIONERY

BOOKS, CDS, VIDEOS, STATIONERY.

All these goods are ideal by post: they are unbreakable, don't need to fit, can be easily described in a catalogue and, generally, not too heavy. They also make excellent presents, even as thank-yous. Why send a bottle of wine when you can send a video of M. Hulot, for instance, or a copy of the latest cookbook or biography? Stationery is, for me, a particular passion. I love interesting papers, designer pens and pencils, folders and even rubber stamps. Again, a fine, leather-bound, marbled paper notebook makes a luxurious present, whether for a diary, recipe book or general observations.

BOOKS, CDs, VIDEOS, STATIONERY - LISTINGS

Alastair Sawday Publishing If you know people who care about holidays and hotels, this publisher offers ideal gifts. Their six books select special places to stay in Britain, Paris, Spain and Portugal and Ireland along with French b&bs (which should be exciting). This is a small publisher which takes great care in its recommendations.

> **Alastair Sawday Publishing,** 44 Ambra Vale East, Bristol BS8 4RE
> **Tel:** 0117 929 9921 **Fax:** 0117 925 4712
> **Website:** www.globegate.com/sawdays
> **Price range:** £10.95 to £12.95. 20% discount and free delivery on orders of 3 or more books. No catalogue.
> **Payment:** cheque.
> **Postage & packing:** £1 per book in UK.

Delivery: normally by return. Last Christmas orders 5 days ahead.

Refunds: yes.

Barefoot Books

Two mothers, with seven children between them, started this publishing business five years ago and have built it up to top £1m turnover in that time. Their books centre around children – lots of bright, intelligent picture books for children from one to 12 plus books on fairies, eastern religions and books celebrating new babies. Though their works can be found in traditional shops, they deliberately encourage mail order direct.

Barefoot Books Mail Order Department, Colchester Road, Frating Green, Colchester, Essex CO7 7DW

Tel: 01206 256099 **Fax:** 01206 255914

E-mail: sales@barefoot-books.com

Website: http://www.barefoot-books.com

Price range: £3.99 to £12.99. Catalogue free.

Payment: cheque, postal order, major credit/debit cards.

Postage & packing: UK £3 or free for orders over £100, Europe £7, elsewhere £10.

Delivery: within 10 days if in stock.

Refunds: yes, if returned in original condition within 14 days.

Dillons

This bookshop reckons it has five miles of bookshelves and over 250,000 titles in stock at any time. It can trace rare and out-of-print books for you, produce signed first editions or giftwrap books and send them to another address as presents. There are also gift vouchers, which may be boring to receive but are very useful thereafter.

Dillons Mail Order Dept, 82 Gower Street, London WC1E 6EQ

Tel: 0171 636 1577 **Fax:** 0171 580 7680

E-mail: msc@dillons.org.uk

Website: http://www.thebookplace.com

Price range: general book prices with occasional promotional offers. Small charge for certain catalogues.

Payment: cheque, Access, Visa, Amex, Dillons/Hatchards cards.

Postage & packing: 10% of order value to £50, 5% thereafter in UK.

BOOKS, CDs, CASSETTES, VIDEOS, STATIONERY 265

Delivery: normally despatched following day.
Refunds: by arrangement.

Garden Books by Post Gardeners can never have too many books, from the inspirational to the severely practical. This firm offers a small list but one which highlights the most recent publications that you may have missed on the shelves. The list has special offers, books for the specialist and new titles. Also books on garden design, ones on ornamental grasses and some gardening classics by the likes of William Cobbett and Robinson. As well as this, the firm can supply any gardening book in print and will search for out-of-print books.

Garden Books by Post, 8 Ann Street, Worthing, West Sussex BN11 1NX
Tel: 01903 205895 **Fax:** 01903 213438
E-mail: optimusbooks@easynet.co.uk
Price range: £5 to £40. Catalogue free.
Payment: cheque, major credit/debit cards.
Postage & packing: included in UK. Overseas rates on application.
Delivery: allow 5 to 14 days. Last Christmas orders by 15 December.
Refunds: yes, if returned within 14 days.

Gosh A specialist in comics worldwide including such titles as Batman, Bastard Bunny, Humongous Man and Zombieworld. They say that the list is highly eclectic but, around Christmas, people buy compilations of Wallace and Gromit and Doonesbury. But you may know comic enthusiasts or those who want to become comic artists.

Gosh, 39 Great Russell Street, London WC1B 3PH
Tel: 0171 636 1011 **Fax:** 0171 436 5053
E-mail: gosh-com@easynet.co.uk
Price range: £5 to £15. Catalogue free.
Payment: cheque, postal order, major credit/debit cards.
Postage & packing: £3 in UK.
Delivery: allow 5 days.
Refunds: yes.

Green Books What you would expect – a smallish range of books for the eco warrior. You can learn how to grow hemp, how to save seeds plus how to make shelters and buildings of cob or straw bales. Other books are intended to inspire rather than educate.

> **Green Books Ltd**, Foxhole, Dartington, Totnes, Devon TQ9 6EB
> **Tel:** 01803 863260 **Fax:** 01803 863843
> **E-mail:** greenbooks@gn.apc.org
> **Website:** http://www.gn.apc.org/books
> **Price range:** £2.50 to £120. Catalogue free.
> **Payment:** cheque, Mastercard, Access, Visa, Switch.
> **Postage & packing:** £1 in UK, elsewhere 15% of order value (minimum £1.50).
> **Delivery:** normally by return.
> **Refunds:** by arrangement.

Neat Ideas Actually a catalogue for office equipment but real people also like to get their stationery cheap and in bulk. The bliss of having six rolls of packaging tape (£2.94) or 10 reporter's notebooks (£2.99) or an extension lead with four sockets for all those wretched computer, fax, printer leads. And life has been so much easier since I ordered 100 bubble envelopes instead of re-using old ones torn at the corners.

> **Neat Ideas Ltd**, Sandall Stones Road, Kirk Sandall, Doncaster DN3 1QU
> **Tel:** free 0800 500192 **Fax:** free 0800 600192
> **Price range:** 12p to £329. Catalogue free.
> **Payment:** major credit/debit cards.
> **Postage & packing:** £3.95 for orders under £30, free thereafter in mainland UK.
> **Delivery:** overnight for most areas.
> **Refunds:** by arrangement.

The Old Stile Press In the tradition of the small art press, Frances and Nicolas McDowall design and handprint limited edition books intended for collectors and enthusiasts. I particularly like those using Robin Tanner's delicate sketches, some only discovered after his death, while another book is of 20 of his original patterned paper designs and a personal memoir by Nicolas McDowall. Poems by Ted Hughes and stories by George Mackay Brown are also on this list.

The Old Stile Press, Catchmays Court, Llandogo, near Monmouth, Gwent NP5 4TN

Tel/Fax: 01291 689226

Price range: £25 to £300. Catalogue free.

Payment: cheque.

Postage & packing: £3 for first book, £2 for each further book in parcel in UK. Overseas delivery at cost.

Delivery: normally within 4 days. By overnight carrier by arrangement.

Refunds: yes, if returned promptly undamaged.

Periwinkle Productions Gardening is an ideal subject for videos and this firm has a dozen – and the list is growing – to help with garden tasks like pruning and propagation, as well as with specific plants. These include clematis, roses, soft and tree fruit and notoriously difficult pot plants like African violets. Also how to create hanging baskets and look after the lawn.

Periwinkle Productions, Dept B1, Old Bank House, Shore Road, Warsash, Southampton SO31 9FS

Tel: 01489 885645 **Fax:** 01489 571017

Price range: £14.99, discount for larger orders.

Payment: cheque, postal order, major credit cards.

Postage & packing: included in UK.

Delivery: within 14 days, 48-hour delivery available on request.

Refunds: yes.

The Red House Books for children (with a sideline on alternative therapies like Feng Shui and Reflexology for all the family). I really love the "horrible" series at £3.99 each teaching horrible histories of the Vicious Vikings, Angry Aztecs and Gorgeous Georgians and horrible scientific facts on bugs, digestion and chemistry. Just what children adore.

The Red House, Witney, Oxford OX8 5YF

Tel: 01993 779959

Price range: from £1.50.
Payment: cheque, postal order, Mastercard, Visa.
Postage & packing: £1.50.
Delivery: usually within a week.
Refunds: yes.
Specials: discounts of up to 50% on books.

Shepheard-Walwyn

A small publisher which specialises in calligraphy but has not been able to resist publishing other works as well. These include "Who's Who" books for historical periods from Roman times, works about Scottish tartans and the country's history and the beautifully illustrated Consider England by Linda Proud which tries to answer the question, What does it mean to be English?

Shepheard-Walwyn (Publishers) Ltd, Suite 34, 26 Charing Cross Road, London WC2H 0DH

Tel: 0171 240 5992 **Fax:** 0171 379 5770

Price range: £4.95 to £45. Catalogue free.

Payment: cheque, major credit cards.

Postage & packing: £1 for orders under £10, £2 for orders under £20 and £3 for orders over £20.

Delivery: allow 10 days. Next day delivery at extra cost. Last Christmas orders 17 December.

Refunds: yes.

Specials: special greetings in calligraphy can be included. Quotation on request.

Smythson of Bond Street

The ne plus ultra of stationers with a catalogue to lust over. There are ranges of diaries, cellar, golf and address books printed on their special featherweight paper which manages to be both light and opaque; silver pens and pencils hand-engraved copperplate cards, airmail paper and 17 different writing papers. Their desk accessories in buffalo calf or pigskin are impeccable. Though these are luxury goods, the prices are not silly.

Smythson by Post, 40 New Bond Street, London W1Y 0DE

Tel: 0990 211311 **Fax:** 0171 318 1500

Website: http://www.website@john-menzies.co.uk

BOOKS, CDs, CASSETTES, VIDEOS, STATIONERY 269

Price range: £10.50 to £1,400. Catalogue free.

Payment: cheque, major credit/debit cards.

Postage & packing: from £3 in UK. Overseas rates on application.

Delivery: despatched within 5 days. Express delivery available. Last Christmas orders by 12 December.

Refunds: yes, if returned within 14 days. Diaries may not be returned after 1 January.

Specials: most items are boxed and gift cards can be enclosed.

Software Partners

A software distribution house specialising in musical and educational CDs and floppy discs which began with Capella which, they say "does for music what a word processor does for text." Another package teaches how a music studio works. Other fascinating packs teach maths, how to create a business and how colour works.

Software Partners, Oak Tree House, Station Road, Claverdon, Warwick CV35 8PE

Tel: 01926 842998 **Fax:** 01926 842384

E-mail: information@softpart.co.uk

Website: http://www.softpart.co.uk

Price range: £39 to £189. Catalogue free. Demos £5, or they can be downloaded from the website.

Payment: cheque, major credit cards.

Postage & packing: included in UK.

Delivery: normally by return. Christmas orders by last posting date.

Refunds: yes.

Specials: free helpline available.

Sotheby's Bookshop

Based in the auction house's Bond Street premises, the book department sells what you would expect – the best art and antique books available. Some they publish themselves, some come from overseas publishers and some from British specialists. The catalogue is an excellent source and, as you see from the price range, covers the very top end of the market.

Sotheby's Bookshop, 34-35 New Bond Street, London W1A 2AA

Tel: 0171 293 5404/5164 **Fax:** 0171 293 5909

Price range: £10 to £600. Catalogue free.
Payment: cheque, major credit cards.
Postage & packing: included.
Delivery: allow 28 days. Last Christmas orders by end November.
Refunds: yes, if undamaged and valid.

Tadpole Lane The place to find videos for country lovers. There are four from the National Trust including two of gardens, a series from the RHS including Chelsea Flower Show and Wisley at all seasons plus others of England's stately homes. Perfect for gifts abroad, there's even one in Japanese.

Tadpole Lane Ltd, 13 Winnall Valley Road, Winchester, Hampshire SO23 0LD
Tel: 01962 841100 **Fax:** 01962 840004
Price range: £9.95 to £12.95. Catalogue free.
Payment: cheque, postal order, major credit cards.
Postage & packing: UK and Europe £2 per video, free in UK for 3 or more. Elsewhere £4 per video by airmail.
Delivery: allow 7 days. Last Christmas orders by last posting date.
Refunds: yes, if damaged or faulty.

The Talking Book Club Hardly has a book appeared in print before someone has produced a cassette version. Some are read by the authors – such as Tony Benn's diaries (he's an excellent reader), Dickie Bird on cricket or Dirk Bogarde (though his fine novels are read by others). Joining the writer with the reader is a skilled business but how about Eleanor Bron reading Nina Bawden, Jeremy Sinden on P.G. Wodehouse or Tony Britton reading Dick Francis? Talking books are a boon for long-distance travellers, for workers at repetitive occupations, for the blind or handicapped and for those who just prefer it spoken. This catalogue is huge, comprehensive and clearly laid out. Members may rent any title and there is no annual commitment, alternatively you can buy any of the tapes listed.

The Talking Book Club, P O Box 993, London SW6 4UW
Tel: 0171 731 6262 **Fax:** 0171 736 0162

BOOKS, CDs, CASSETTES, VIDEOS, STATIONERY

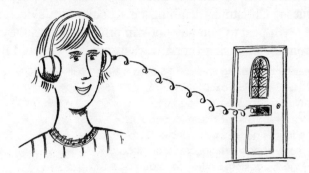

Price range: £7.99 to £58. Enrolment fee £7.50. Information pack free. Members' catalogue free on enrolment, £3.50 for non-members, refundable if you join.

Payment: cheque, postal order, Eurocheque, major credit/debit cards.

Postage & packing: at cost. Next-day delivery add £2.70. Free in UK for orders over £20.

Delivery: by second class post. Courier delivery at cost in London. Last Christmas orders 14 days in advance. Last gift memberships by last posting date.

Refunds: not applicable.

Video Plus Direct & Talking Tapes Direct

Whenever I'm faced with a catalogue which claims to be comprehensive – as this does – I test it by asking for something obscure. The catalogue won. It seems to have everything the video enthusiast would want from old films to tourist guides and teach yourself balti cooking. The Talking Tapes catalogue is equally good.

Video Plus Direct & Talking Tapes Direct, 19-24 Manasty Road, Orton Southgate, Peterborough PE2 6UP

Tel: 01733 232800 **Fax:** 01733 230618.

Price range: £6 to £30. Catalogue £2.99, redeemable against purchase.

Payment: cheque, major credit cards.

Postage & packing: £1.75 per video.

Delivery: allow 14 days.

Refunds: yes, if faulty.

Waterstone's Dedicated to good books, the firm puts out a catalogue at Christmas detailing new books available but in fact they will post to you any book in print as long as they can get it from the publisher (not always as easy as it should be).

Waterstone's Mailing Service, 4-5 Milsom Street, Bath BA1 1DA
Tel: 01225 448595 **Fax:** 01225 444732/420575
E-mail: bath-mail@easynet.co.uk
Website: http://www.waterstones.co.uk
Price range: general book prices. Catalogue free.
Payment: cheque, major credit/debit cards.
Postage & packing: £3, free for orders over £45 in UK.
Delivery: allow 2 weeks, or a month for non-catalogue orders. Last Christmas orders from catalogue 14 December. Non-catalogue orders add a month.
Refunds: by arrangement.

WCP Video This is an independent company with a strangely mixed selection of instructional videos but all are good entertainment too. There is Beth Chatto talking about gardening, Jane Packer on flower arranging, Carolyn Warrender explaining stencils and – this is the surprise – bird of prey expert Jemima Parry-Jones on owls and falconry.

WCP Video, Stone House, Main Street, Seaton, Rutland LE15 9HU
Tel: 01572 747692 **Fax:** 01572 747693
Price range: £10.99 to £19.99. Catalogue free.
Payment: cheque, money order, Eurocheque.
Postage & packing: £2.
Delivery: despatched within 24 hours.
Refunds: in case of technical problems. Exchanges possible.

See also: Anytime Records, Bird Guides, Culpeper for books, The National Trust for video of its first hundred years, Past Perfect, Samuel French, Squires Kitchen for cake-making videos.

Chapter Seven

MOTHER AND BABY
by Pat Jacobs

Many of the ideas in this section have been conceived (along with their babies) by parents in response to their own needs, rather than in the marketing department of a large corporation – and there can be no better source of inspiration.

Shopping during pregnancy can be exhausting, particularly for those with morning sickness, backache, varicose veins or swollen ankles. Maternity wear in the High Street is restricted by the limited market – as a glance round the waiting room of any antenatal clinic will show – whereas dedicated mail order catalogues offer a terrific choice of casual clothes and office wear and, as the fit is generous, sizing is not a problem. Happily the days of smocks with neck interest are past and there's no reason nowadays for pregnant women to change their style.

Once the baby's born, shopping has to be fitted in between feeds and, pressed for time, it's tempting to buy what's on offer in the nearest shop rather than comparing goods and making an informed choice. It's much easier to have bulky items delivered to the door and one big advantage of ordering children's clothes by mail is that, unlike the shops, they normally have all the sizes. Most firms have a 24-hour answering service, handy for new mothers who keep strange hours, and will despatch goods by return if they're in stock.

Finally, after shopping for the baby's arrival, women shouldn't forget themselves. For sleep-deprived new mothers time is a precious commodity and things once be taken for granted – a bath for example – become a luxury and should be as therapeutic as possible. There are now aromatherapy ranges especially for use before and after birth and, as a mother's well-being is important for the whole family, these are worth every penny.

MOTHER AND BABY LISTINGS

Anytime Records Described by composer Stephen Stapley as "a parents' album which children will love", *Angel on your Pillow* features 14 "original family songs of love and reassurance" initially written as lullabies for his two sons. It recently won an award for its contribution to children's entertainment and is available on CD or cassette.

> **Anytime Records Ltd**, P O Box 18908 London W14 9WL
> **Tel:** 0171 935 0717
> **Website:** http://www.angelpillow.com
> **Price range:** cassette £7.99, CD £11.99. Leaflet free.
> **Payment:** cheque, postal order.
> **Postage & packing:** included in EU.
> **Delivery:** allow 28 days.
> **Refunds:** by arrangement.

Babyface For those lucky enough to give birth to a photogenic baby, this company will supply embossed birth announcement cards including a photo (from negative supplied). Envelopes come in pink, blue or white and for an extra 15p per card plus first class postage your cards can be addressed and mailed directly. The firm will also supply invitations, christening and thank you cards with photographs.

> **Babyface**, Mole End Cottage, 7 Bridge Road, Chertsey, Surrey KT16 8JH
> **Tel/Fax:** 01932 570726
> **Price range:** £1.25 per card, or £1.40 plus first class postage for direct mailing (minimum order 25).

MOTHER AND BABY   275

Payment: cheque, postal order with order.
Postage & packing: £3.50.
Delivery: despatched within 10 working days.
Refunds: by arrangement.

Bagadele The three-way 'Piggyback' bag was devised by Australian designer Adele Stewart when she became a mother. Containing numerous pockets plus a fold-out changing mat, it converts easily from back-pack to shoulder bag or attaches to a pram or pushchair. Fabrics range from florals and tartans to plain dark colours and it's robust enough to last through several babies and beyond (with its mat and pockets to keep bottles upright it would be handy for a school trip or picnic). The range also includes playmats, holdalls and insulated bottle bags.

Bagadele, Holly Cottage, Kings Lane, Cookham Dean, Berkshire SL6 9AY
Tel: 01628 481952 **Fax:** 01628 475553
E-mail: bagadeleuk@compuserve.com
Price range: bags £21.95 to £90, accessories from £5. Catalogue free.
Payment: cheque, major credit/debit cards.
Postage & packing: 95p for orders under £17.50, £3.95 thereafter in UK. Express delivery add £3. Overseas rates on application.
Delivery: normally despatched within 7 working days. Last Christmas orders by 14 December, or 18 December via express service.
Refunds: yes.
Specials: Christmas gift-wrapping £3.

Bambino Mio The average baby gets through 4,500 to 6,000 disposable nappies and 8 million are added to landfill sites each day. The long term effects are unknown and it is thought they may take up to 500 years to decompose. The cost per baby is around £1,000, and it was this which persuaded me to use traditional nappies. The pinless Bambino Mio nappies are easier to use than terries, and I would imagine more comfortable for the baby. They are made of layers of tightly woven cotton, either shaped or prefold for maximum absorbency, and fit inside a waterproof cover with Velcro fastening. The company recommends buying a total of 48 nappies with 16 covers, and these should last for at least two babies. Their range also includes trainer pants and swim nappies.

Bambino Mio, 50 Cedar Road, Northampton NN1 4RW
Tel: 01604 458999
Price range: from £12 for 6 nappies, trial packs from £7.95. Catalogue free.
Payment: cheque, postal order, major credit/debit cards.
Postage & packing: included in UK.
Delivery: normally despatched within 14 days, but allow 28.
Refunds: yes, if returned unused, in new condition within 3 months.
Specials: special offers for 'birth to potty' packs.

The Bed-Side-Bed Company When Waldek Tobolewski's first child was born he and his wife felt it natural she should sleep with them but, like most parents, found it too disruptive. As a solution they devised the Bed-Side-Bed, a three-sided, finely adjustable bed with locking castors which fits flush to the parents' mattress. The baby is within easy reach but sleeps safely in her own space without risk of overheating and can be fed with minimal disturbance, as the mother doesn't even need to get out of bed. Anyone who's gingerly tried to return a baby to her cot without waking her, or shared a bed with a wriggling infant will appreciate the advantages of this system. As the baby grows the Bed-Side-Bed can be converted into a conventional cot or junior bed and, once outgrown, it's strong enough to be used as a sofa.

The Bed-Side-Bed Company, 9 Fitzgerald Road, London E11 2ST
Tel: 0181 989 8683 **Fax:** 0181 530 4792
Price range: £299. Leaflet free.
Payment: cheque, major credit/debit cards with handling charge.
Postage & packing: included.
Delivery: allow 2 weeks.
Refunds: yes.

MOTHER AND BABY

Blooming Marvellous Judy Lever and Vivienne Pringle, who boast six children between them, started this company fifteen years ago and their experience shows in this catalogue of well-designed clothes and equipment for mothers-to-be, babies and toddlers. Maternity wear includes suits and dresses as well as casuals, and is designed for wear during those waistless weeks after birth as well as before. There are clothes with concealed openings for easy breastfeeding plus underwear and swimsuits. Babywear includes a baby welcome set of animal print playsuit, bib and hat and there are big brother/big sister T shirts, which would make a tactful present for a jealous sibling. Equipment includes the ultimate potty complete with paper, a slot for books and an 'I'm done' button plus a device to rock a cradleseat – presumably invented by someone like me who spent many hours cooking on one leg and kicking the seat with the other.

> **Blooming Marvellous,** P O Box 12F, Chessington, Surrey KT9 2LS
> **Tel:** 0181 391 0338 **Fax:** 0181 397 0493
> **Price range:** £2.99 to £99.99. Catalogue free.
> **Payment:** cheque, postal order, Access, Visa, Switch.
> **Postage & packing:** £2.95 in UK, £4.95 in Eire, £15 in Europe, £30 elsewhere.
> **Delivery:** normally despatched within 48 hours, but allow 10 days if in stock, otherwise allow 28.
> **Refunds:** yes, if returned in perfect condition within 14 days.

Bobux Charming soft leather shoes for under-twos which, while brilliantly coloured, are safe for toe-sucking. They have pretty motifs on the uppers – dots, stars, flowers and boats or teddies, helicopters and kiwis. Though they are stocked in shops, the firm helps mothers with a mail order service. They're ideal, too, for presents from grandmothers who can't knit bootees, at christenings or on a first birthday.

> **Bobux,** Raynor Marketing Ltd, 48 Abbotswood Road, London SW16 1AW
> **Tel:** 0181 677 9468 **Fax:** 0181 696 0902
> **E-mail:** bobux_uk@compuserve.com

Price: £16 for all styles and sizes. Catalogue free.

Payment: cheque, major credit cards.

Postage & packing: included in UK. £2 overseas.

Delivery: allow 10 working days. Last Christmas orders by 14 December.

Refunds: yes.

Specials: goods can be sent direct to recipient with gift tag.

Cabbage Leaf Company

This firm specialises in presentation baskets to welcome new babies and is proud to number such corporate clients as Barclays Bank and Coca Cola/Schweppes among its customers. Baskets come wrapped in cellophane and festooned with ribbons in blue, pink, or unisex lemon, white or mint. Contents include playsuit, bib, socks, bootees and a teddy. More expensive versions add deluxe playsuits and, in the 'Precious Baby Basket', a bathrobe, plus a framed watercolour of the baby's initial. Baskets are available in three sizes: newborn, up to 3 months and 3-6 months.

Cabbage Leaf Company, Panther House, 38 Mount Pleasant, London WC1X 0AP

Tel: 0171 837 5662/3

Price range: £31.50 to £51.50. Leaflet free.

Payment: major credit/debit cards.

Postage & packing: included.

Delivery: next working day in mainland UK for orders received before 5.30 pm. International orders by post.

Refunds: yes, although they have never been asked.

Specials: gift-wrapping as standard.

Charlotte

Charlotte is a one-woman craft business supplying beautiful hand-framed cot blankets in wool or cotton. Blankets come in cream, mid-blue, sage or old rose and can be personalised with a baby's name and birth date. Personalised hats in wool/Alpaca are also available.

Charlotte, 11 Heigham Road, Norwich, Norfolk NR2 3AT

Tel: 01603 627448

Price range: hats £10.50 to £14.50, blankets £44 to £49. Catalogue free.

MOTHER AND BABY

Payment: cheque.
Postage & packing: hats £2, blankets £3.45.
Delivery: 2-3 weeks.
Refunds: yes.

Cheeky Rascals Selina Russell started her family while living in France. On her return to England she discovered that many products were not available here so she was inspired to compile this catalogue sourced from around the world. Ideas from France include long-sleeved body suits and the Dorelot, a cotton sleepsuit which wraps around the baby, fastening with Velcro, so there is nothing to slip over the head or arms. From Finland there are waterproof over-trousers and from Sweden a splash-proof potty plus the Kiddy Board, a platform which attaches behind a pram or buggy to let a flagging toddler hitch a ride.

Cheeky Rascals, The Briars, Petworth Road, Witley, Surrey GU8 5QW
Tel: 01428 682488 **Fax:** 01428 682464
E-mail: sales@cherascals.win-uk.net
Price range: £1.45 to £99.95. Catalogue free.
Payment: cheque, postal order, major credit/debit cards.
Postage & packing: £2 for orders up to £9.99, £2.50 to £24.99, £5 thereafter.
Delivery: allow 14 days.
Refunds: yes, if returned unused within 14 days.

Favourite Things A range of "nursery accessories" which include pretty cot quilts and hand-stitched mobiles along with fabric books, such as a finger puppet book complete with ten animal puppets, and toys like a squashy toadstool house or Noah's ark. For older children there are pyjama cases and swimming bags and for Christmas personalised stockings and sacks plus an advent calendar wall hanging.

Favourite Things, 1 Carrigshaun, Old Avenue, Weybridge, Surrey KT13 0PG
Tel: 01932 843720 **Fax:** 01224 862055
Price range: £3.50 to £135. Phone or send A4 sae for catalogue

Payment: major credit cards.

Postage & packing: £2.50 for one item, 90p per additional item. Larger items £3.99.

Delivery: allow 14 days. Extra fast delivery at additional cost. Last Christmas orders by 20 December.

Refunds: yes.

Specials: monogramming on Christmas sacks and stockings.

Flairpath

This company's catalogue is small, but includes some useful ideas, such as the Gadabout baby carrier which converts to a push or pull stroller, a waterproof toddler sunscreen from Australia with an SPF rating over 30, a vest top swim belt and the Aspinvenin, a mini vacuum pump to aspirate the poison from insect bites and stings.

Flairpath Ltd, 6 Dunedin Drive, Caterham, Surrey CR3 6BA

Tel: 01883 382636 **Fax:** 01883 341172

Price range: £8.99 to £59.99. Catalogue free.

Payment: cheque, postal order, major credit/debit cards.

Postage & packing: 80p to £4.75. Free for orders of £75 to same address. Overseas rates on application.

Delivery: normally about 5 days, but allow 28.

Refunds: yes, if returned in original condition within 14 days.

Formes

If you are working through pregnancy and your colleagues are accustomed to seeing you in sharp suits, they'll assume you've taken leave of your senses if you suddenly turn up in a flowery smock. This collection of French maternity wear, including trouser suits, shifts with matching jackets and simple evening wear, is perfect for work or special occasions, and is designed to fit from the first to the last month. Although pricier than most ranges, (and investment dressing can be hard to justify when it comes to maternity wear) the classic styling and clean lines ensure the clothes won't date.

Formes Catalogue, Frant Road, Thornton Heath CR7 7JY

Tel: 0181 689 1133 **Fax:** 0181 689 2233

Price range: £11 to £195. Catalogue free.

Payment: cheque, major credit/debit cards.

Postage & packing: £3 in UK. Overseas rates on application.

MOTHER AND BABY

Delivery: by first class recorded post.
Refunds: yes, if returned within 14 days.

Gordon's Production Services Fertility treatment has led to an increase in multiple births, and while double buggies are readily available, triples and quads are not so easy to find. This company supplies pavement-clearing triple buggies, plus a tandem style quad (the mystery is how anyone can get four small children ready and loaded into a buggy and still have the energy to go out). There is also a triple which converts to a twin, for a toddler and twin babies.

Gordon's Production Services, 58 Cavendish Road, Salford, Manchester M7 4NQ

Tel: 0161 740 9979 **Fax:** 0161 740 4219

E-mail: triples@arfam.demon.co.uk

Website: http://www.arfam.demon.co.uk

Price range: £235 to £500. Catalogue free.

Payment: cheque, Access, Visa, Amex, Switch.

Postage & packing: included in mainland UK and Northern Ireland.

Delivery: about 4 weeks, but sooner if urgent.

Refunds: by arrangement.

The Great Little Trading Company A comprehensive range for babies and toddlers from clothing and toys to off-road pushchairs plus enough safety equipment to induce paranoia in most mothers – for example a handle cover to prevent your child ingesting germs from a supermarket trolley. Good ideas include an artwork portfolio – an ideal halfway house between fridge door and dustbin for those endless playgroup daubings, and a portable all-in-one folding booster seat and high chair which straps to a dining chair.

The Great Little Trading Company, 124 Walcot Street, Bath BA1 5BG

Tel: 0990 673008 **Fax:** 0990 673010

E-mail: cat@gltc.co.uk

Website: http://www.gltc.co.uk

Price range: £2.99 to £349. Catalogue free.

Payment: cheque, postal order, Mastercard, Access, Visa.

Postage & packing: £3.95, free for orders over £75 in UK. Overseas, including Channel Islands and Eire, at cost plus £5 administration fee.

Delivery: normally within 5 working days, but allow 28. Last Christmas orders by 17 December.

Refunds: yes, if returned in perfect condition within 14 days.

Specials: gift-wrapping £2 per item.

Index Extra

Index Extra If you find it inconvenient to carry bulky packs of disposable nappies Index will deliver Pampers to your door within 48 hours. They guarantee their price is the lowest in home shopping and will refund the difference if you find goods cheaper elsewhere on similar terms.

Index Extra, Index Extra House, Kershaw Avenue, Crosby, Liverpool L72 1SL

Tel: Orders 0345 552211, Helpline 0345 979797

Price range: £6.99 to £23.50. Catalogue free.

Payment: cheque, credit account, major credit/debit cards.

Postage & packing: £2.95 for orders under £60, free thereafter.

Delivery: 48 hours in most of UK.

Refunds: yes.

JoJo Maman Bébé

JoJo Maman Bébé A catalogue for pregnant mothers and children up to five including 120 "brilliant ideas" for presents, toys and generally to make life easier. The women's clothes make few concessions to maternity – slimline trousers, gabardine jackets, big tops in neutrals, black and checks while the children's clothes are cute but not yukky. "Brilliant ideas" cover every necessity from breastfeeding to potty training and include everything you need for travelling with small children from travel sterilisers to portable potties.

JoJo Maman Bébé Ltd, 134 Lots Road, London SW10 0RJ

Tel: 0171 351 4112, catalogue request line: 0171 352 5156

Fax: 0171 352 7089

E-mail: info@jojomamanbebe.co.uk

Website: http://www.jojomamanbebe.co.uk

Price range: £2.99 to £59.99. Catalogue free within UK and Europe. Elsewhere £5.

Payment: cheque, major credit/debit cards.

Postage & packing: UK £1.95 to £2.95, Eire £3.95 to £4.95, Europe £6.95 to £9.95, elsewhere £7.95 to £14.95. Extra charges may be made on overseas orders if the parcel is overweight.

Delivery: normally within 5 working days in UK. Last Christmas orders by 21 December.

Refunds: yes.

Kiddycare Baby sleeping bags, recommended for babies from four months, are used by 9 out of 10 mothers on the Continent. This company supplies bags in summer and winter weights including a 100% cotton bag suitable for children with eczema or sensitive skin. The bag replaces conventional bed-clothes, which often get kicked off in the night, and stops the baby sliding under the covers and overheating. They are ideal for night feeds since the baby stays warm even when returned to a cold bed.

Kiddycare, Easter Lawrenceton Farmhouse, Forres, Scotland IV36 0RL

Tel: 01309 674646 **Fax:** 01309 676007

Price range: £3.90 to £49.95. Catalogue free.

Payment: cheque, postal order, major credit/debit cards.

Postage & packing: £3 per order, free for orders over £50. £1 extra for first class delivery.

Delivery: normally within a week. Last Christmas orders by 21 December.

Refunds: yes.

Specials: gift-wrapping £1.50.

Kids in Comfort Babies are more settled carried close to their mothers, particularly in the early weeks – though having painted a window frame with a baby on one hip, I know how inconvenient this can be. A baby sling is one solution for mothers who need both hands free (the other being a pram at the far end of the garden) and they are handy for country walks or journeys by public transport where a buggy would be too cumbersome. The Sling-Easy will carry a child up to 35lb and the even spread of the baby's weight avoids strain on the back or neck. It comes in plain or patterned cotton, or custom-made in your own fabric, with thick padding over the shoulder and along the top and bottom. There are four sizes (to fit the parents) plus child size replicas, to carry a doll or teddy. The design allows mothers to breastfeed discreetly, even when walking.

Kids in Comfort, 172 Victoria Road, Wargrave, Reading, Berkshire RG10 8AJ

Tel/Fax: 0118 940 4942

E-mail: klloyd@mcmail.com

Price range: £24.99 to £34.99. Catalogue free.

Payment: cheque, postal order, Switch, Delta.

Postage & packing: £2 to £2.50 for 1 sling, £3 for 2 or more. Next day delivery £5.50. Overseas rates on application.

Delivery: normally despatched within 72 hours.

Refunds: 21 day money back guarantee from purchase or birth of baby (not more than 4 months from purchase).

Lavender Blue This aromatherapy range for mothers and babies was developed by Sally Robinson when she was expecting her son Sam. Antenatal products include stretch mark cream containing vitamin E and relaxing bubble bath with mandarin, geranium and lavender. Post birth there is toning body lotion, stimulating bubble bath with grapefruit, spearmint, lemon and lime and a 'Beat the Blues' essential oil. The babies' range includes soothing bubble bath with lavender and chamomile, plus an Easybreathe version with added eucalyptus and mandarin, a barrier cream with tea tree oil and a massage oil. The oils contain no artificial colours or fragrances and can be used straight from the bottle.

Lavender Blue, Blue Tiles, Parkway Drive, Sonning, Berkshire RG4 6XG

Tel/Fax: 0118 969 3148

Price range: £4.99 to £14.95. Catalogue free.

Payment: cheque.

Postage & packing: at cost.

Delivery: 24-48 hours by post or Parcel Force.

Refunds: by arrangement.

Specials: gift packaging.

MOTHER AND BABY

Metro Products Not strictly for babies, but this brochure of child restraints and car tidies could be useful in the years to come or for an older sibling. The company sells seat belt adjusters to make an adult seat belt safe and comfortable for a child and there is a clever booster seat which repositions a safety belt so it lies over the hips rather than the abdomen. Other products include neck supports and pillows which convert to travel blankets. All come in blue with jolly yellow elephants.

Metro Products (Accessories & Leisure) Ltd, Eastman House, Fleming Way, Crawley, West Sussex RH10 2UY
Tel: 01293 533663 **Fax:** 01293 534500
Price range: £7.49 to £24.99. Leaflet free.
Payment: cheque, major credit/debit cards except Amex.
Postage & packing: included.
Delivery: allow 14 days.
Refunds: yes.

Mother & Toddler Fashions It's surprising how quickly you grow out of your underwear during pregnancy and how uncomfortable it can be. This company specialises in maternity underwear by Emma Jane, which is endorsed by the Royal College of Midwives. The range includes two styles of maternity bra with wide straps, plus a sleep bra, over/under bump briefs, maternity tights in seven colours. They also supply drop-cup bras, including a black lace number. Since the best time to buy a nursing bra, i.e. the final month of pregnancy, happens to be the worst time to go shopping, buying from a specialist supplier by mail seems a good idea. Swimsuits and button front nightshirts are also available.

Mother & Toddler Fashions, 82 Stonelaw Road, Rutherglen, Glasgow G73 3ED
Tel: 0141 647 8106 **Fax:** 0141 613 3479
Price range: £1.50 to £19.99. Catalogue free.
Payment: cheque, postal order.
Postage & packing: £1.75.
Delivery: average 48-72 hours.
Refunds: yes.

286 MAIL ORDER MADE EASY

Mothernature This firm supplies underwear and swimsuits for pregnant women and nursing mothers, as well as breast-feeding aids such as electric breast pumps and freezer bags for breast milk. Underwear is available up to size 22, and bras from size 32 to 48 with A to H cup. They also offer aromatherapy blends for pregnancy and childbirth such as stretch oil containing lavender, neroli and frankincense and clary sage, along with jasmine and frankincense labour relief oil and natural remedies including raspberry leaf tea, recommended for toning the uterus in preparation for birth, and arnica tablets which are noted for reducing bruising.

Mothernature, Acorn House, Brixham Avenue, Cheadle Hulme, Cheshire SK8 6JG
Tel: 0161 485 7359
Price range: £1 to £69. Catalogue free.
Payment: cheque.
Postage & packing: 70p to £3.50. Overseas rates on application.
Delivery: allow 10 working days.
Refunds: yes, if returned in original condition within 7 days.

Natalys This French chain has branches as far afield as Australia and Taiwan, though not yet in Britain. However with a little French you can buy by mail order for delivery to your home address, or collection at one of their stores (they have shops in Calais and Boulogne). They offer an unfussy selection of maternity wear plus a fairly traditional range of clothing for babies and toddlers. There are knitted layettes for newborns, and a large collection of dresses and rompers, many with appliqué and embroidery. By contrast the nursery furniture is simple, in natural wood, or painted white, with fabrics in chambray, yellow stripes or, for minimalists with clean children, écru. There is a cot which transforms into a desk, and safety equipment includes a harness to stop a child falling out of bed as well as a padded helmet – every toddler should have one.

Natalys, BP 714, 92007 Nanterre Cedex, France
Tel: 00 331 47 25 62 62 between 9 and 12.30 French time.

MOTHER AND BABY

Price range: FF19 to FF4890. Tax deducted for exported goods. Catalogue free.

Payment: with order by Eurocheque with card no. or international money order, credit cards for purchases collected from stores only.

Postage & packing: packing free, overseas by quotation.

Delivery: prompt delivery, or collect from store.

Refunds: yes.

Natures Gate Most women hope for a drug-free birth, and the non-invasive TENS (transcutaneous electrical nerve stimulation) system supplied by this company is said to reduce labour pain in 70-80% of mothers. Used extensively in Sweden, it sends electrical pulses through electrodes placed over the nerve centres, blocking pain signals to the brain and stimulating the body to produce natural painkillers. Settings can be adjusted so the system can be used after birth, to relieve afterpains or post-operative pain following a caesarean section. The company loans machines for a six week period, normally from the 37th week of pregnancy.

Natures Gate, P O Box 371, Basingstoke, Hampshire RG24 8GD
Tel: 01256 346060 **Fax:** 01256 346050

Price range: rental for 6 weeks £22 to £26, then £1 per day. Catalogue free.

Payment: cheque, postal order.

Payment: included. Priority service £1.50.

Delivery: normally by second class recorded delivery at least three weeks before due date, or by return if necessary.

Refunds: not applicable.

Physical State The first night my daughter came home from hospital I lay awake all night listening to her breathing (by the second night I was too exhausted) and this is very common among new parents. This company sells or hires the portable RM25 baby monitor which uses an under-mattress pad or body sensor to monitor the baby's breathing. It offers peace of mind and is especially reassuring for parents whose babies have health problems or who have lost a baby through cot death.

Physical State Ltd, St. Margarets House, Bromley Green Road, Ashford, Kent TN26 2EF

Tel: 01233 733399 **Fax:** 01233 733608

Price range: £165, or rental £29.90 per month plus £40 deposit. Catalogue free.

Payment: cheque, Mastercard, Access, Visa, Eurocard.

Postage & packing: £7.50.

Delivery: within 48 hours.

Refunds: by arrangement.

Silver Fern Some families hand down christening gowns through generations. However if yours isn't one of them, this company will supply gowns and rompers in broderie anglaise, polycotton, cotton lawn, crêpe de chine, satin or silk. As these are hand-made to order, they are happy to comply with any special requests regarding finishing touches such as trimmings, or your baby's name inside the bodice at no extra charge. Accessories include bibs, bonnets, bootees and shawls, and sizes range from newborn to 12 months, or larger on request.

Silver Fern, 1 Bedale Avenue, Rastrick, Brighouse, Yorkshire HD6 3JP

Tel: 01484 713975

Price range: Gowns £39 to £140, accessories from £3. Catalogue free, sae appreciated.

Payment: cheque, postal order.

Postage & packing: £2 in UK, £5 overseas by airmail.

Delivery: normally 14 days, but allow 4 weeks.

Refunds: 10-day money back guarantee.

Snug as a Bug These babies' sleeping bags come in a range of bright tartans (though Tania Chamberlain can't match your own child's clan) and are of cotton with a fleece interlining. They are designed to open at the bottom with a zip so that nappies can be changed without undressing entirely. Side tags are sewn beneath the arms for extra warmth.

Snug as a Bug, 72A Madeira Street Edinburgh EH6 4AU

Tel: 0131 553 4191

Price range: £24 to £35. Catalogue free.

MOTHER AND BABY

Payment: cheque, major credit cards.
Postage & packing: £2 in UK.
Delivery: within 1 week. Extra fast delivery available.
Refunds: yes.

Snuggle Nap

Snuggle Naps are shaped fabric nappies available as all-in-ones or a two part system using a breathable·outer cover and absorbent cotton pads. All-in-ones come in two sizes, while the two part Easy-Gro Supreme is designed to grow with your baby for use from birth to potty. The advantage of the two part system is that the cotton pads can be washed at maximum temperature, and up to three can be used for extra absorbency. Silk pads are available for babies with sensitive skin as well as disposable pads for travelling. The company also supplies shaped and prefold terries plus trainer and swim pants.

Snuggle Nap, 123 Valley Road, Sherwood, Nottingham NG5 3BL
Tel: 0115 953 6604 **Fax:** 0115 955 5690

Price range: £1.50 to £29.90. Packs of 21 all-in-ones £236.25 (small), £246.75 (large), or 9 Easy-Gro Supremes with 21 pads £161.75. Catalogue free.

Payment: cheque, postal order, Mastercard, Visa.

Postage & packing: 80p for orders up to £10, £1.80 to £20, £2.80 to £30, £5 thereafter.

Delivery: allow 28 days.

Refunds: by arrangement.

Stork Talk

There are now a bewildering number of options for transporting your baby, and this firm offers them all, from a traditional Silver Cross pram to a range of all-terrain buggies, plus matching car seats and accessories. Which you choose will depend on where you live and your lifestyle – living in the country, I didn't have much use for a coach-built pram nor, on the lifestyle front, a jogging pushchair. The company also supplies cots and will quote for other nursery items, as they can obtain almost anything.

Stork Talk, Birkdale Close, Manners Industrial Estate, Ilkeston, Derbyshire DE7 8YA
Tel: 0115 930 6700 **Fax:** 0115 930 4700

Price range: £67 to £750. Catalogue free.
Payment: cheque, postal order, major credit/debit cards.
Postage & packing: £5 per box (maximum £10) in mainland UK.
Delivery: within 48 hours.
Refunds: by arrangement.

The Wilkinet Baby Carrier

As a mother of eight, Sally Wilkins knows a thing or two about baby carriers, and by baby number four she had perfected the Wilkinet. It can be worn in four positions and the wide padded shoulder straps and cushioned head, back and leg support ensure that the carrier is comfortable for both parent and baby. The range also includes books, videos and tapes as well as a showerproof cape to fit over the carrier, dungarees and soft shoes.

The Wilkinet Baby Carrier, P O Box 20, Cardigan, SA43 1JB
Tel: 01239 831246 **Fax:** 01239 841390
E-mail: wilkinet@btinternet.com
Price range: from £4.50 for baby shoes to £31.50 for carriers. Catalogue free, swatches available. 15 min demonstration video £4.50 inc p&p or for hire.
Payment: cheque, postal order, major credit/debit cards.
Postage & packing: included.
Delivery: 48 hours, or 5 working days if paying by cheque.
Refunds: yes, if returned in brand new condition. Baby carriers should be returned within 4 months, other items within 7 days.
Specials: gift-wrapping.

See also: Cotton Moon, Dream Team Design, Farmer John Quilts, Graig Farm, The Green Shop, Karrimor International, Little Badger, Rachel Riley, Shetland Knitwear Associates, Thiz Bag, The White Company.

Chapter Eight

SPECIAL INTERESTS AND SPORT

SPECIAL INTERESTS AND SPORTS

While football, tennis, cricket and running gear can easily be found in the high street, the more arcane sports and hobbies are not represented. But there are plenty of people whose passion is croquet or lacrosse, bridge or chess. There are mail order firms for all of them; there are companies who will deliver classic cars to your door, give you a ride in an old aeroplane or kit you up with the latest equipment for mushroom hunting or star spotting.

ENTHUSIASMS - LISTINGS

Archers Addicts Can't go on holiday without taping affairs in Ambridge? This is the catalogue for such fanatics. There are mugs, T-shirts, a Grey Gables towelling robe, the official map of Ambridge, a replica of The Bull and there's now a weekly synopsis of the soap for ex-pats who need to keep tabs.

Archers Addicts, P O Box 1951, Moseley, Birmingham B13 9DD
Tel: 0121 773 0111 **Fax:** 0121 753 3310
Price range: £2.50 to £50. Send C4 sae for catalogue.
Payment: cheque, major credit/debit cards.
Postage & packing: £2.95 to £5.95. Express delivery add £5.
Delivery: allow 28 days. Last Christmas orders by 12 December.
Refunds: yes.

Specials: annual membership of Archers Addicts £15.50 (UK), £19 (EU), £22 (elsewhere). Christmas gift membership includes Christmas card signed by the cast. Members receive 10% off all merchandise.

The Barometer Shop

Not only do they look decorative, they're extremely useful for gardeners, sporting folk and anyone working outdoors. What's more, it's fun to see them drop as foul weather approaches. They were invented in Italy in 1643 and the firm reproduces the elegant 18th century versions as well as Victorian and ship's barometers. The barograph, which plots pressure on graph paper, is a real luxury.

The Barometer Shop, New Street, Leominster, Herefordshire HR6 8BT

Tel/Fax: 01568 610200

Price range: £65 to £6,000. Catalogue free.

Payment: cheque, Mastercard, Access, Visa.

Postage & packing: £6 or £12 depending on size.

Delivery: usually ex stock.

Refunds: yes.

Bird Guides

A twitcher's treasury of videos and CD-roms to help identify wild birds. Five videos and 10 hours are devoted to British birds alone with recordings, maps and commentary. There are also books on birds from Austria to Turkey.

Bird Guides Ltd, Jack House, Ewden Valley, Bolsterstone, Sheffield S30 5ZA

Tel: 0800 919391/0114 283 1002 **Fax:** 0114 283 1003

E-mail: dave@birdguides.com

Website: http://www.birdguides.com

Price range: £19.95 to £129.95. Catalogue free.

Payment: cheque, major credit/debit cards.

Postage & packing: £1.50 for first video/CD, and 90p for subsequent video/CD. Free for orders over £100. Next day delivery £5 extra. Overseas by Swiftair at cost.

Delivery: allow 14 days.

Refunds: yes, if returned within 7 days.

SPECIAL INTERESTS AND SPORTS

Brian Jarrett A member of the International Guild of Knot Tyers (yes, really), Jarrett specialises in the old craft of displaying the more complex nautical knots mounted and framed. Each of his designs incorporates white cotton cord in several ordinary knots and the more difficult ones, know as plaits and sinnets displayed against a navy blue backing. Each knot has a small brass plate engraved with its name. More complex boards can include a central photograph of a famous or decorated sailor or ship. One allows personal insignia to be included.

Brian Jarrett, Villa Rosa, Oakfield Lane, Dartford, Kent DA1 2TE
Tel/Fax: 01322 227725
Price range: £12.50 to £85. Catalogue free.
Payment: cheque, postal order.
Postage & packing: £1 to £6.25.
Delivery: allow 28 days. Last Christmas orders by last week November.
Refunds: by arrangement.

Classic Car Art Miniature classic car models are set in an old garage with Shell posters on the wall, the engines on the block, tools scattered around the floor and the whole thing is then framed. Charming gifts for anyone interested in old cars and eminently hangable. Women tend to buy them for men. Cars range from AC to Volkswagen and include Bugatti, Ferrari and Chevrolet Bel Air.

Classic Car Art, Two Hill End Cottages, Hatfield Park, Hatfield, Hertfordshire AL9 5PQ (correspondence only).
Tel/Fax: 01707 270308
Website: http://www.classic-car-art.com
Price range: £130 to £350. Catalogue free.
Payment: cheque, Eurocheque.
Postage & packing: around £20 apiece.
Delivery: by courier. Allow 4-6 weeks. Last Christmas orders by early November as only 900 made per year.
Refunds: no, look at goods first at the venues listed in the brochure.

MAIL ORDER MADE EASY

The Clivedon Collection Are you a badge freak or are you so serious about your car or aeroplane that you must wear a miniature on your lapel? This is the list for you. Motoring pin badges go from a Cobra to a Willys Jeep, there are over 50 different helicopter badges, more than 100 planes from the Wright Flyer to a space shuttle along with balloons, hand guns, tanks, shooting dogs, wildlife and even pigs. They come as keyrings, cufflinks, paperclips or, surprisingly, earrings. If you want a pair of Lancaster bombers in your ears, you can.

The Clivedon Collection, Witham Friary, Frome, Somerset BA11 5HH

Tel: 01749 850728 **Fax:** 01749 850729

Price range: £4.50 to £35, minimum order £10 . Catalogue free.

Payment: cheque, Mastercard, Visa, Switch.

Postage & packing: £2 for orders up to £25, £4 to £50, £6 to £100, £10 thereafter. Overseas rates on application.

Delivery: 2 days after cleared payment.

Refunds: yes, if damaged and reported within 7 days. No refund on earrings and pendants for health reasons.

Cornelissen Absolutely the best for artists' materials. They supply the top painters, gilders and print makers and their range is so vast that you need to talk to them first before getting a list of what's available. For this they employ experts who will guide you through the maze – so if you want to give a present, you'll get help.

L. Cornelissen & Son Ltd, 105 Great Russell Street, London WC1B 3RY

Tel: 0171 636 1045 **Fax:** 0171 636 3655

Price range: 50p to several hundred pounds. Price list free.

Payment: cheque, major credit/debit cards, Eurocheque and travellers cheque.

Postage & packing: at cost.

Delivery: allow 14 days. Faster delivery available at extra cost. Last Christmas orders preferably two weeks in advance.

Refunds: yes, faulty goods will be collected from customers.

SPECIAL INTERESTS AND SPORTS

The Cricketer Actually, the firm also sells special gifts for golf and rugby fanatics though mostly in the jokey line. There are gifts for umpires, that misunderstood breed, and flasks shaped like balls and bats. Also mugs, plates, teddy bears, jewellery and hats for sportsmen. I admit I can't understand why anyone should want a teapot shaped like a cricketer on the loo, but apparently they do.

The Cricketer, Beech Hanger, Ashurst, Kent TN3 9ST
Tel: 01892 740697 **Fax:** 01892 740588
E-mail: info@cricketer.co.uk
Price range: £1.99 to £150. Catalogue free.
Payment: cheque, major credit/debit cards.
Postage & packing: included in UK.
Delivery: allow 28 days. Last Christmas orders 5 working days in advance.
Refunds: yes.

The Dinosaur Society What is it about dinosaurs that make them so cuddly when the reality was far different? Joining this society plugs you into current research on dinosaurs and how they lived via DinoTimes, DinoMite and DinoReport while you help the charity fund further projects. The society says a new dinosaur is discovered every seven weeks and half of all known dinosaurs were found since 1978.

The Dinosaur Society UK, P O Box 329, Canterbury, Kent CT4 5GB
Tel: 01227 700116 **Fax:** 01227 700743
Price range: membership: junior £8 to £16, standard £24, family £40, overseas add £10 to these rates.
Payment: cheque, major credit cards, standing order, covenant.
Postage & packing: included.
Delivery: allow 28 days for initial membership processing.
Refunds: not applicable.

Dolphin Enterprises We all know that golfers get obsessional and that their wives feel more like widows. This firm has a set of cartoon table mats that make the point. I particularly like the rainy scene with fishermen sitting glumly on the bank while a wet but smiling golfer says "Look at those idiots – fishing in this weather". The present for the golfer with everything.

Dolphin Enterprises, 68 Tremadoc Road, Clapham, London SW4 7LP
Tel/Fax: 0171 498 7465
Price: £25. Catalogue free.
Payment: cheque.
Postage & packing: included.
Delivery: allow 10 days.
Refunds: yes.

The Faerie Shop

Need a pair of rainbow wings, a spangled wand or pair of pixie slippers? Yes, you can dress little girls as fairies and little boys as gnomes with the aid of this mail order catalogue. Also fairy books, cushions, cards and ornaments.

The Faerie Shop Catalogue Ltd, P O Box 604, Marlborough, Wiltshire SN8 1XS
Tel/Fax: 01672 516017
Price range: £2 to £32.50. Send stamp for free catalogue.
Payment: cheque, major credit/debit cards.
Postage & packing: £2.95, free for orders over £75.
Delivery: generally 10 days but allow 28. Some goods in short supply at Christmas.
Refunds: yes, if returned within 14 days.

Globes

This firm has been selling globes since 1930, ranging from those huge ones on wooden stands that are found in country house libraries to a 4.7-inch diameter globe of the world to be held in the hand. There are star map globes which light up to show pin-point stars against the heavens and a 12-inch globe showing features of the moon. The globes are fine without exception but in my view some of the stands are less so. Pick those which are least obtrusive. There are also colour prints of the world seen by satellite.

SPECIAL INTERESTS AND SPORTS

Globes, Thanet Globe Emporium, 2-3 Orange Street, Canterbury, Kent CT1 2JA
Tel: 01227 781111 **Fax:** 01227 760548
Price range: £5 to £7,900. Catalogue free.
Payment: cheque, major credit cards.
Postage & packing: from £3.25 for orders under £25 to £12.50 for orders up to £999, free thereafter.
Delivery: normally within 72 hours by carrier. Check availability as some globes are in short supply.
Refunds: by arrangement.

John Jordan A catalogue for motoring enthusiasts and those who have to travel a lot, from high-powered torches, tyre wrenches and chamois leathers to snow chains, roof boxes and picnic kits. Motoring today isn't fun any more but with these ideas it can be made tolerable.

John Jordan, Unit 1, Toll Bar Estate, Sedbergh, Cumbria LA10 5HA
Tel: 01539 621885 **Fax:** 01539 621886
E-mail: john.jordan@roofbox.co.uk
Website: http://www.roofbox.co.uk
Price range: £5 to £500. Catalogue free.
Payment: cheque, major credit/debit cards.
Postage & packing: £2.50 for orders under £30, £3.50 thereafter, free for orders over £200. Next day delivery £5.50. Overseas rates on application.
Delivery: most items despatched within 24 hours. Last Christmas orders by 22 December.
Refunds: yes, if notified within 10 working days.

The Leading Edge Specialising in the latest or greatest technology you can buy retro GI clocks or travel alarms, those maddening lava lamps or copies of army field phones. There are also pinball machines, fitness gadgets and weighing scales and goods already celebrating the millennium. A fair old mixture but, basically, toys for grown ups.

The Leading Edge, 23-43 Longford Street, London NW1 3NY
Tel: 0171 383 3756 **Fax:** 0171 383 7759
Price range: £4.99 to £3,500. Catalogue free.
Payment: major credit/debit cards.

Postage & packing: according to weight.
Delivery: 14 days. Last Christmas orders by 12 December.
Refunds: yes, if returned with receipt within 28 days.

Magic by Post

Magic by Post If you're looking for all the gadgets that let you push pencils through coins, pull red hankies through transparent tubes and chop off your own fingers or arms (adults only), then this is the company to get in touch with. You can set your hands on fire, do the three-card trick and make rabbits appear in hats. The range is for both beginners and professionals.

Magic by Post, 167 Winchester Road, Bristol BS4 3NJ
Tel/Fax: 0117 977 4334
E-mail: magic.by.post@cableinet.co.uk
Website: http://www.marketsite.co.uk/magic
Price range: £2 to £60. Catalogue free.
Payment: cheque, Mastercard, Access, Visa, Eurocard.
Postage & packing: £1.60 to £3.60.
Delivery: allow 28 days.
Refunds: yes.
Specials: join the Magic Club for an extra £5.

The Maritime Company

The Maritime Company Seafaring and yachting objects make great presents and are currently highly fashionable indoors – just look at the prices paid for antique pond yachts. This mail order catalogue comes from the Past Times stable and has all the hallmarks of its efficiency and smart service. Ideas vary from practical torches and pocket knives to ornamental ships' models, barometers and bird boxes shaped like colourful lighthouses.

The Maritime Company, Witney, Oxfordshire OX8 6BH
Tel: 01993 770450 **Fax:** 01993 770477
Price range: £5 to £600. Catalogue free.
Payment: cheque, postal order, major credit/debit cards.
Postage & packing: £2.95 for orders under £30, £3.50 thereafter. Next day delivery add £4.95.
Delivery: within 7 days, next day delivery available.
Refunds: yes.

SPECIAL INTERESTS AND SPORTS 299

The Musical Gift Catalogue If your hero is Handel or Haydn, you can wash up with a tea-towel printed with his portrait, or you can buy notelets like grand pianos or mugs with a bar or two of Tchaikovsky printed around their sides. There are maestro jigsaws, cleaners for musical instruments and the instruments themselves, from clarinets to penny whistles.

> **The Musical Gift Catalogue**, 51 Fortess Road, London NW5 1AD
> **Tel:** 0990 275124 **Fax:** 0171 284 1404
> **Price range:** 99p to £165. Catalogue free.
> **Payment:** cheque, postal order, major credit/debit cards except Amex and Diners.
> **Postage & packing:** £2.95, free for orders over £50 to same address.
> **Delivery:** allow 28 days. Last Christmas orders by 12 December.
> **Refunds:** yes, if returned in perfect condition within 14 days.

Mycologue The list for the fungi fanatic, this includes special brushes with compasses so you don't get lost (surprisingly easy to do), baskets which don't break up the fragile pieces and various books, posters, cards and wrapping paper on the subject. More recently, oyster mushroom kits, oak logs impregnated with shi-itake fungus have been added to the list along with drying machines for mushrooms and other foods, truffle slicers, truffle oil and dried mushrooms. There is, too stationery with Beatrix Potter's fungi illustrations.

> **Mycologue**, 47 Spencer Rise, London NW5 1AR
> **Tel:** 0171 485 7063 **Fax:** 0171 284 4058
> **E-mail:** mycologue@lewy.force9.net
> **Website:** http://www.mycologue.co.uk
> **Price range:** £5 to £40. Catalogue free.
> **Payment:** cheque, postal order, Access, Visa.
> **Postage & packing:** £2 for orders up to £20, free thereafter.
> **Delivery:** 7 days. Last Christmas orders by last posting date.
> **Refunds:** yes, for faulty goods, otherwise credit.

Nauticalia Everything for the sailor, some serious and some jokey. There are excellent hand-held spotlights, binoculars,

MAIL ORDER MADE EASY

wrist navigators and barometers on one hand, along with splendid pond yachts and other model boats, brass-bound boxes and trays (more suitable at home than on a racing yacht), Guernseys and Breton caps. The nautical theme progresses to lobster claws, bottles of champagne for launching new ships and pirate T-shirts. It's surprising how many nautical objects look extremely good in the house – brass coathooks, chronometers and bulkhead lamps, for example.

Nauticalia Ltd, The Ferry Point, Ferry Lane, Shepperton-on-Thames, Middlesex TW17 9LQ

Tel: 01932 253333 **Fax:** 01932 241679

Website: http://www.nauticalia.co.uk

Price range: £2.95 to £995. Catalogue free.

Payment: cheque, postal order, Switch, major credit cards except Amex.

Postage & packing: £2.95, 3-day service £7, 24-hour £9.65.

Delivery: allow 14 days but normally sooner.

Refunds: yes.

Specials: some items can be personalised.

The Owl Barn Gift Catalogue No, not for the owls but for owl lovers. Coasters, placemats, doormats, jewellery and ties are illustrated with owls and there are cuddly owl toys. My only complaint is that owls are not as cuddly as portrayed.

The Owl Barn Gift Catalogue, Old School House, Wortham Ling, Diss, Norfolk IP22 1ST

Tel: 01379 640363 **Fax:** 01379 644753

E-mail: owl.barn@btinternet.com

Price range: £1.99 to £140. Catalogue free.

Payment: cheque, postal order, major credit/debit cards. Catalogue free.

Postage & packing: £2.95.

Delivery: allow 21 days.

Refunds: yes, if returned within 14 days.

A Pack of Cards A fine selection of playing cards and bridge accessories. The cards are backed with Florentine or tartan patterns, portraits of Elizabeth and Essex, old-fashioned cricketers

SPECIAL INTERESTS AND SPORTS

and golfers and can be personalised. There is even a set of children's cards to get them hooked early. Also score cards, pencils and recipe books of meals to serve at bridge parties.

A Pack of Cards, Hollins Hill House, Utkinton, Tarporley, Cheshire CW6 0JP
Tel/Fax: 01829 760549
Price range: £1.75 to £147.50. Catalogue free.
Payment: cheque, Mastercard, Access, Visa.
Postage & packing: £1.75 for orders up to £15, £2.75 up to £25, £3.50 thereafter.
Delivery: usually within 7 days, longer for personalised cards.
Refunds: by arrangement.

Past Perfect Recordings to revive the music of the 20s, 30s and 40s, using the original sound but with more clarity. Cole Porter, Fred Astaire, Irving Berlin, Charleston to Jive, and lots of jazz. New releases include The Andrews Sisters, the Ink Spots and a sampler from Louis Armstrong to Al Bowlly. This is a gift ideal for old people to remember and young people with an interest in 20th century music.

Past Perfect, Lower Farm Barns, Bainton Road, Bucknell, Oxfordshire OX6 9LT
Tel: 01869 325052 **Fax:** 01869 325072
E-mail: clarity@pastperfect.com
Website: http://www.pastperfect.com
Price range: cassettes £6.99, CDs £10.99. Catalogue free.
Payment: cheque, major credit cards.
Postage & packing: £2.50.
Delivery: credit card orders received before 3.00 pm despatched same day.
Refunds: by arrangement.

Reel Times If you feel nostalgic about long-ago films, this firm can arrange showings of cinema classics to be seen through a video projector onto a giant screen. It's great for parties, special occasions (like a golden wedding when a forties film brought a couple together). The firm also offers information on casts, credits, reviews and advertisements for any film you care to suggest.

Reel Times, 26 North Gate, Upper Hopton, Mirfield, West Yorkshire WF14 8ET

Tel: 01924 494259

Price range: from £1. No catalogue send sae for list.

Payment: cheque, Eurocheque.

Postage & packing: included in UK. Overseas £1.

Delivery: by arrangement.

Refunds: by arrangement.

Samuel French London's theatre bookshop with three lists: a guide to selecting plays for amateurs, a catalogue of musical plays and lists of books about theatre. These are divided into, for instance, writing for TV and radio, makeup, costume, criticism and acting. The guides also offer a paragraph or two summing up each play which is useful in itself.

Samuel French Ltd, 52 Fitzroy Street, London W1P 6JR

Tel: 0171 387 9373, shop 0171 255 4300 **Fax:** 0171 387 2161

E-mail: theatre@samuelfrench-london.co.uk

Website: http://www.samuelfrench-london.co.uk

Price range: from £2.50. Theatre Books list and Mailing List free, The Guide to Selecting Plays £7.50, The Musical Plays catalogue £3.

Payment: cheque, postal order, major credit/debit cards, international money order or bank transfer.

Postage & packing: 5% of order value, minimum 50p, maximum £4. Priority service: 10% of order value up to £80, minimum 50p, and 7.5% of order value over £80.

Delivery: by second class post. Priority service by first class post. Courier service rates on application. Overseas rates on application. Last Christmas orders by last posting dates.

Refunds: by arrangement.

Scavenger Diving Services The Scilly Isles were once both a danger and a graveyard for ships, such was the quantity of rocks and reefs around the islands. This firm is run by a salvage diver, Mac Mace, and his wife, Tracy. He recovers silver pieces of eight (shades of Long John Silver and his parrot) from the wreck of the Hollandia, a Dutch East Indiaman which foundered in 1743, and sells them mounted. It's a romantic idea and good for presents for those who enjoy the great years of sailing ships.

SPECIAL INTERESTS AND SPORTS

Scavenger Diving Services, Bryher, Isles of Scilly, Cornwall TR23 0PR
Tel/Fax: 01720 422612
Price: £99. No catalogue.
Payment: cheque.
Postage & packing: included in UK.
Delivery: despatched as soon as cheque has cleared.
Refunds: yes.

Word Out T-shirts and magnets for poets. The Ts have a portrait of the poet on one side and a famous work on the other. The eight are e.e.cummings, W.B. Yeats, Dylan Thomas, Lewis Carroll with Jabberwocky, Christina Rossetti with Remember, Emily Dickinson and Lord Byron – by far the most dashing – and Stevie Smith's Not Waving but Drowning. The magnets include 440 different words and can be arranged on a metal surface or fridge. They were designed by a poet for poetry makers and come in two sizes, smallish magnet words for adults and larger ones for children.

Word Out, Freepost MID16770, Nottingham NG9 1BR
Tel/Fax: 0115 903 1845
Price: £16.95. Catalogue free, sae appreciated.
Payment: cheque, major credit cards.
Postage & packing: £1 per item.
Delivery: 7 days. Last Christmas orders by last posting date.
Refunds: yes.

See also: Alastair Sawday, Annie Cole Traditional Hand Knitting, Annie Sloan, Aviation Leathercraft, Pollock's Mail Order, The Dolls' House, The Dolls House Emporium, Elizabeth Bradley Designs, Glorafilia, Gosh, Mrs Pickering's Dolls Clothes, The Singing Tree, Software Partners, Squires Kitchen, Susan Lethbridge.

ACTIVITIES - LISTINGS

Acorne All sorts of derring-do by voucher. You can have a balloon ride, a sky-dive, or a parachute jump. You can give people the chance to have a go at piloting a plane, gliding a glider or hovering in a helicopter. Give them twenty minutes of Biggles in a Tiger Moth or commanding a jumbo (in a simulator, thankfully) or alternatively a 2-4 hour training session in a racing or rally car. Acorne also offers a voucher where the recipient picks his (or her) own peril and, as over 140 locations accept these vouchers, it shouldn't be too hard to find something of interest.

> **Acorne Sports Ltd**, Wycombe Air Park, Booker, Marlow, Buckinghamshire SL7 3DR
> **Tel:** 01494 451703 **Fax:** 01494 465456
> **Price range:** £51 to £361. Catalogue free.
> **Payment:** cheque, major credit cards.
> **Postage & packing:** included.
> **Delivery:** usually by return. Last Christmas orders by last posting date.
> **Refunds:** can be exchanged.
> **Specials:** gift presentation packs available.

Castle Combe Skid Pan & Kart Track Gift vouchers from this company which does exactly what it says. Children over ten and over 4ft 6in tall are eligible for the kart-track practice sessions; the kart racing proper is for anyone over fifteen. Skid pan driving is for driving licence holders only.

> **Castle Combe Skid Pan & Kart Track**, Castle Combe Circuit, Chippenham, Wiltshire SN14 7EX
> **Tel:** 01249 782101 **Fax:** 01249 782161
> **Price range:** £29.50 to £59.50. Catalogue free.
> **Payment:** cheque, Access, Visa, Switch.
> **Postage & packing:** postage of voucher included.
> **Delivery:** normally despatched by first class post the same day. Last Christmas orders by last posting date.
> **Refunds:** not applicable.

SPECIAL INTERESTS AND SPORTS

Delta Aviation Dressed up in goggles, leather and sheepskin flying jackets as the chocks are knocked away from your Tiger Moth, then it's up and away, over and out as the Biggles experience takes over. You can spend an entire day being a WWII air ace with this firm, either in the 128 mph Tiger Moth or the faster Harvard, a big beefy fighter pilot trainer, max speed 242 mph.

> **Delta Aviation**, 2 South View, Maunby, Thirsk, North Yorkshire YO7 4HF
> **Tel/Fax:** 01845 587507
> **Price range:** £79 to £399. Catalogue free.
> **Payment:** cheque, Access, Visa, Amex.
> **Postage & packing:** included.
> **Delivery:** first class post. Good choice of dates available. Last Christmas orders by fax up to Christmas Eve for faxed voucher.
> **Refunds:** no.

Great Central Railway This company gives you the chance to be an engine driver of a steam train (under supervision of course) on the main line between Loughborough and Leicester. Gift vouchers are also available for lunch and dinner in the first-class restaurant cars of the Master Cutler and Charnwood Forester trains.

> **Great Central Railway plc**, Great Central Road, Loughborough, Leicestershire LE11 1RW
> **Tel:** 01509 230726 **Fax:** 01509 239791
> **Website:** http://www.gcrailway.co.uk
> **Price range:** "Drive a Train" £195 to £1,250, "Dining Trains First Class Fare" £19 to £50. Leaflets free.
> **Payment:** cheque, major credit cards.
> **Postage & packing:** postage of vouchers included.
> **Delivery:** allow one week.
> **Refunds:** sometimes exchanges.

Peter Gethin Goodwood has a historic motor racing circuit, in the process of being revived, as well as a horse racecourse. Peter Gethin, winner of the 1971 Italian Grand Prix, teaches both performance driving and racing driving. The ultimate course, a full day with three hours or circuit driving and an afternoon on the road is called The Nurburgring. I thought it was an opera.

Peter Gethin Driving Courses Ltd, The Gate House, Goodwood Motor Circuit, Chichester, West Sussex PO18 0PH

Tel: 01243 778118 **Fax:** 01243 533498

Price range: from £125 for a weekday trial racing course. Catalogue free.

Payment: major credit cards.

Postage & packing: included.

Delivery: voucher sent by return.

Refunds: no.

Specials: personalised gift vouchers.

Red Letter Days A sort of mail order Jim'll Fix It. If you know someone who wants to train with Arsenal and Liverpool greats, fly a jet fighter, race a JCB (it has its attractions) or, more calmly, stay at a top hotel, go to a health spa, visit the theatre or take a trip on the Orient Express, this firm will organise it. You can even learn Chinese cooking or how to mix a cocktail.

Red Letter Days Ltd, Melville House, 8/12 Woodhouse Road, North Finchley, London N12 0RG

Tel: 0800 634 5555/0181 343 8822 **Fax:** 0181 343 9030

E-mail: sales@redletterdays.co.uk

Price range: £29 to £5,000. Catalogue free.

Payment: cheque, major credit/debit cards.

Postage & packing: included. Next day delivery £10.

Delivery: despatched within 48 hours.

Refunds: exchange.

Specials: supplied in personalised presentation pack.

EQUIPMENT - LISTINGS

Bugwear If you have ever been in the Highlands in June, you'll know about the midges. The Highland firm, Bugwear, has come up with lightweight insect-proof clothing which is also showerproof and ideal for all kinds of outdoor sports, especial-

SPECIAL INTERESTS AND SPORTS

ly fishing. The cotton-polyester blend has areas of fine mesh for ventilation and the sleeves, jacket bottoms and trousers are elasticated. For extreme situations there's a kind of beekeeper's mesh hood which zips onto the jacket front over the face.

Bugwear Ltd, Drummond Street, Comrie, Perthshire PH6 2DS
Tel: 01764 670033 **Fax:** 01764 670958
Price range: £29.99 to £49.95. Catalogue free.
Payment: cheque, Mastercard, Access, Visa.
Postage & packing: included.
Delivery: allow 28 days. Last Christmas orders by 1 December.
Refunds: yes, if returned within 14 days.

John Jaques The firm has been selling top quality sports and games equipment since 1795 and is the oldest such in the world. Their croquet sets are the highest quality and there are also now golf driving ranges, clock golf, petanque and badminton sets. They have snooker tables and table tennis, table football, cricket bats and balls, darts and chess. In fact, every kind of sport which individuals can enjoy.

John Jaques & Sons Ltd, 361 Whitehorse Road, Thornton Heath, Surrey CR7 8XP
Tel: 0181 684 4242 **Fax:** 0181 684 4243
Price range: approx £15 to £500. Catalogue free.
Payment: cheque.
Postage & packing: by arrangement.
Delivery: 2-3 days.
Refunds: yes, with agreement.

Pedometers International For the uniniated, says the firm, pedometers are precision instruments which record any distance walked or run. They were invented over 2000 years ago by a Roman architect. With the enthusiasm for marathons, jogging and walking for exercise, they are very much in demand. You could even strap one on to find how many miles you walk on a shopping bout – and decide that mail order is better!

Pedometers International Ltd, 13/14 James Watt Close, Drayton Fields, Daventry, Northamptonshire NN11 5RJ

Tel: 01327 706030 **Fax:** 01327 871633
E-mail: malcolmpayne@pedometers.co.uk
Website: http://www.pedometers.co.uk
Price range: £2.75 to £175. Catalogue free.
Payment: cheque, Mastercard, Visa, Switch, Connect.
Postage & packing: £2.50 for orders under £50, £5.95 thereafter.
Delivery: first class post by return.
Refunds: by arrangement.

Riders and Squires of Kensington

This company specialises in all forms of riding equipment and clothes but focuses particularly on polo and children, exporting to over fifty countries worldwide. The firm has no catalogue but works through personal contact, sending high-quality tack to enthusiasts. Knowing the number of small girls who pass through the pony phase – some never leaving it – a good riding equipment supplier is invaluable.

Riders and Squires of Kensington Co. Ltd, 8 Thackeray Street, London W8 5ET
Tel: 0171 937 4377 **Fax:** 0171 937 7335
Price range: from £10. No catalogue, all arrangements by phone.
Payment: cheque, major credit cards.
Postage & packing: by arrangement.
Delivery: by arrangement.
Refunds: by arrangement.
Specials: overseas and export orders. Helpful advice.

Sam de Teran

A choice of highly fashionable ski outfits, lined with Goretex Windstopper, which are windproof and water resistant as well as warm and soft can be bought here. Some are trimmed with artificial fur, like black beaver on the red and black outfits or cream mink on the cream. All, except those with fur, are fully washable. As well as full suits, jackets and pants, there are wool hats plus polo necks for warmth underneath. The items can also be seen at the London shop which operates the mail order side.

SPECIAL INTERESTS AND SPORTS

Sam de Teran, 151 Fulham Road, London SW3 6SN
Tel: 0171 584 0902 **Fax:** 0171 589 9906
Price range: £7 to £550. Catalogue free.
Payment: cheque, major credit cards.
Postage & packing: £6 per item.
Delivery: allow up to 4 weeks.
Refunds: exchange or credit.

Sherwoods

Mail order for the astronomer with a range of Konus telescopes, telescope accessories such as sun and moon filters, focusers, finders and image rectifiers. Also ranges of binoculars, night vision instruments, compasses and thermometers.

Sherwoods Photo Ltd, 11-13 Gt. Western Arcade, Birmingham B2 5HU
Tel: 0121 236 7211 **Fax:** 0121 236 0612
E-mail: sherwoods.photo@virgin.net
Website: www: http://freespace.virgin.net/sherwoods.photo
Price range: £100 to £3,000. Send A4 first class sae for catalogue.
Payment: cheque, major credit/debit cards.
Postage & packing: £10 per box.
Delivery: by overnight courier. Last Christmas orders by 23 December for most of UK.
Refunds: yes, notify the company by phone.

Skyview

An interesting range for all sorts of outdoor hobbyists. There are hand-held wind speed and temperature indicators for golfers and sailors, high quality binoculars and magnifiers for anyone from birdwatchers to jewellers, varios and radios for people who hang-glide and go up in balloons and for gardeners, the Weather Wizard which can monitor temperature, windspeed and direction, high wind speed and a modem for constant updates.

Skyview Systems, Skyview Centre, Churchfield Road, Chilton Industrial Estate, Sudbury, Suffolk CO10 6GT
Tel: 01787 883138 **Fax:** 01787 883139
E-mail: skyview@rmplc.co.uk
Website: http://www.skyview.co.uk
Price range: £5 to £500. Catalogue free.

310 MAIL ORDER MADE EASY

Payment: cheque, Mastercard, Access, Visa, Switch.
Postage & packing: £5 to £7.50.
Delivery: allow 28 days. Extra fast delivery available.
Refunds: by arrangement.

Snow + Rock

Everything for the skier, snowboarder, climber and walker plus roller blades and street hockey gear. The catalogue changes every year to mirror the latest fashions so there is up-to-the-minute clothing including a range of casual and surf wear.

Snow + Rock Hi Energy Sports, 99 Fordwater Road, Chertsey, Surrey KT16 8HH
Tel: 01932 569569 **Fax:** 01932 569589
E-mail: sales@snowandrock.co.uk
Website: http://www.snowandrock.com
Price range: £1 to £1,000. Catalogue free.
Payment: cheque, major credit/debit cards.
Postage & packing: £2.25 for orders under £30, £4.50 thereafter in UK, £10 for orders over £30 in Channel Islands. Express delivery £10. Overseas rates on application.
Delivery: by insured delivery service Monday to Friday. 24-hour delivery available. Last Christmas orders by 14 December.
Refunds: yes, if returned in new condition with original packaging and receipt within 14 days. Videos and books may not be returned or exchanged.
Specials: gift vouchers.

The Sports Motive

The company sells merchandise for various sporting associations: British Judo, British Gymnastics, The Grand National, British Athletics and Netball. In the latter case, the catalogue is large and offers netball kit and equipment as well as badges, rule books and luggage. The others are smaller and offer ranges of sweats, T-shirts and souvenirs with the appropriate logo. The firm also sells, under a separate list, sports bottles of Lucozade to keep up energy levels.

The Sports Motive Ltd, TSM Building, Harriot Drive, Warwick CV34 6TJ
Tel: 01926 888832 **Fax:** 01926 887447
E-mail: netball@thesportsmotive.co.uk

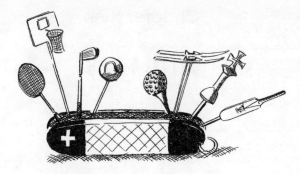

Website: http://www.thesportsmotive.co.uk
Price range: £3 to £65. Catalogue free.
Payment: cheque, postal order, major credit/debit cards.
Postage & packing: 95p to £3.95.
Delivery: same day despatch. Last Christmas orders by 19 December.
Refunds: yes.

William Powell An excellent range of country clothes, fishing and shooting tackle and gifts from a firm established in 1802. These are pieces for the serious sportsman from Maglite torches and Swiss Army knives to Barbour and Musto weather wear, Le Chameau and Hunter boots, shooting socks and thermal underwear. William Powell also makes superb shotguns which is why the firm's price range goes up to £28,000. They probably made guns during the Napoleonic wars and certainly supplied soldiers during the American Civil War.

William Powell & Son Ltd, 35-37 Carrs Lane, Birmingham B4 7SX
Tel: 0121 643 0689/8362, 0121 633 0800 **Fax:** 0121 631 3504
Price range: £5 to £28,000. Catalogue free.
Payment: cheque, postal order, major credit/debit cards.
Postage & packing: £2 for orders up to £20, £4 thereafter. Next day delivery: £5 to £10.
Delivery: allow 5 days.
Refunds: by arrangement.
Specials: gift-wrapping, monogramming.

See also: L.L. Bean, Orvis.

Chapter Nine

ANIMALS

ANIMALS

In America, the smart pooch already has his Gucci bed and in Switzerland, he has a wonderful collar decorated with silver cows. Here, we can offer mail order dog picnic baskets for the voyaging mutt or vet-like cat scratches for the vengeful moggy. There are special towels to soothe the dampened fur, throws to keep the animals comfy on journeys and even toys for parrots. I buy all my dog food delivered to the door, in mixed cases of turkey, chicken, tripe and vegetables which turn up with stainless steel bowls, psychologically-correct toys and hide chews for stressful moments. Both I and my dog find mail order a great stress-buster.

ANIMALS - LISTINGS

Bones Dog and Catalogue A marvellous catalogue featuring real dogs and cats sampling the wares. There are leopard print cat collars and flea patrol bandannas for smart if lousy dogs, raised feeding bowls for elderly dogs, all sorts of toys like kongs, buster cubes and a crackling bag which keeps cats endlessly amused. In addition there are pet beds, cataerobic columns, grooming aids and even personalised bowls and throws. They recommend pet hotels and even have a pet birthday service. What I particularly like is that it's all great fun.

Bones Dog and Catalogue, The Upper Mill, Coln St Aldwyns, Cirencester, Gloucestershire GL7 5AJ
Tel: 01285 750007 **Fax:** 01285 750100

ANIMALS 313

Price range: £3.50 to £89.99. Catalogue free.

Payment: cheque, postal order, major credit/debit cards except Amex and Diners.

Postage & packing: £3.25, beds £6.50. Overseas at cost.

Delivery: normally within a week, but allow 28 days. Urgent deliveries by arrangement.

Refunds: yes, if returned unused in original packaging within 14 days.

Specials: monogramming on bowls, collars, beds and throws.

Cantelo Cat Collars

Cantelo is actually a cattery, so they know all about collaring cats. These are at the luxury level being either in English leather or wild silk. You can add to this gold and silver fittings, a satin-lined display box for your cat's dressing table and a heart-shaped identity tag. Silly? Some people give their pets diamond necklaces.

Cantelo Cat Collars, The Lodge, Chilton Cantelo, Yeovil, Somerset BA22 8BE

Tel: 01935 850543

Price range: £59 to £175. Leaflet free.

Payment: cheque, postal order.

Postage & packing: £4 including insurance.

Delivery: allow 30 days.

Refunds: by arrangement.

The Company of Animals

Dr. Roger Mugford specialises in training difficult pets and, to this end, he has invented a raft of aids. Most famous is the Halti collar which really does stop dogs pulling. Now there are Kongs which, when thrown, bounce unpredictably and Boomer balls for macho dogs and, says Mugford, elephants, pigs or polar bears "or any other bored, manipulative animal." So if you have a bored polar bear, this is your catalogue. The toys really are indestructible as claimed. My dog has proved it.

The Company of Animals, P O Box 23, Chertsey, Surrey KT16 0PU

Tel: 01932 566696 **Fax:** 01932 565979

E-mail: drmugford_coofanimals@compuserve.com

Price range: £2.75 to £120. Catalogue free.

Payment: cheque, Mastercard, Access, Visa (minimum credit card order £10).
Postage & packing: included in UK.
Delivery: within one week. Christmas orders by last posting date.
Refunds: yes if faulty, otherwise at company's discretion.

Natural Friends This company proudly claims to be the first to offer a range of natural pet remedies such as multi-vitamin supplements and homoeopathic treatments. All products contain Spirulina, an algae described as "the food of the future", which is rich in nutrients and promotes self-healing. There is also a selection of books on alternative and complementary veterinary medicine.

> **Natural Friends,** P O Box 103, Robertsbridge, East Sussex TN32 5ZT
> **Tel:** 01580 881222 **Fax:** 01580 881444
> **Price range:** £5 to £40. Catalogue free, first class stamp appreciated.
> **Payment:** cheque, Mastercard, Visa.
> **Postage & packing:** £1 for orders up to £10, £1.50 up to £30, free thereafter.
> **Delivery:** orders normally despatched within 24 hours.
> **Refunds:** yes, if returned within 14 days.

Northern Parrots Everything for the parrot (even southern ones) from gigantic cages to parrot gymnasiums (no, I'm not

ANIMALS 315

making it up), ladders and toys. There's also an "Avian Speech Instruction Disc" which plays your chosen phrases to the bird at different intervals to keep its attention and a large selection of parrot books.

Northern Parrots, 51/53 Bridge Street, Ramsbottom, Bury, Lancashire BL0 9AD

Tel: 01706 822133 **Fax:** 01706 823820

E-mail: nparrots@pobox.com

Website: http://pobox.com/-nparrots

Price range: under £1 to £400. Catalogue free.

Payment: cheque, postal order, major credit cards.

Postage & packing: up to £5 in UK.

Delivery: normally within 10 days, next day delivery at extra charge.

Refunds: by arrangement.

The Nuttery The Nuttery makes handsome bird feeders: some, like little iron parrot cages, are designed to be squirrel proof (which means large birds and magpies are also put off), others are like small hanging flower baskets designed for the suet cakes which the tits love. Bird feeders make a lovely present for friends, the elderly – and the birds.

The Nuttery, High Barn, Pinner Hill Road, Northwood, Middlesex HA5 3YQ

Tel: 0181 429 4400 **Fax:** 0181 429 3366

Price range: £5.95 to £29.95. Catalogue free.

Payment: cheque, Mastercard, Access, Visa.

Postage & packing: £2.95.

Delivery: allow 14 days. Last Christmas orders by 18 December.

Refunds: yes, if returned undamaged within 28 days.

Petsafe Collars and Leads Stylish collars for dogs and cats which are personalised to include their names and telephone numbers embroidered onto nylon webbing collars and matching leads. The collars have strong brass buckles and D-rings and the leaders have brass-plated clips. There are five different webbing colours and seven shades of embroidery, so you can also colour-code your pets.

Petsafe Collars and Leads, Green Farm, Monewden, Woodbridge, Suffolk IP13 7DH
Tel: 01473 737877 **Fax:** 01473 737742
Price range: £12 to £27.50. Catalogue free.
Payment: cheque, Mastercard, Visa, Switch.
Postage & packing: £1.50 to £2.50 for collars in UK. Faster delivery £5.
Delivery: allow 28 days.
Refunds: yes, or replacement.

Waggers

A small catalogue dedicated to the comfort of our pets and the cleanliness of our cars and sofas. There are dog duvets, bean bags, basket liners and car back seat covers, dog coats in fetching waxed cotton and corduroy dog beds which the animal gets into (I wonder if it does). Also a sort of bag that you zip a dirty animal into so it cleans itself. Personally, I cannot imagine my dog putting up with this but the spaniel in the picture looks very content.

Waggers, Comfy Pet & People Products, 2-4 Parsonage Street, Bradninch, near Exeter, Devon EX5 4NW
Tel: 01392 881285 **Fax:** 01392 882188
Website: http://www.comfy-pet.co.uk
Price range: £3.50 to £60. Catalogue free.
Payment: cheque, major credit/debit cards.
Postage & packing: from £1.50.
Delivery: 5 days. Last Christmas orders 2 weeks in advance.
Refunds: yes, if returned by registered post.

Winna

The firm makes beds and rugs for pets. The beds are filled with a hollow fibre duvet with an outer cover of tough poly-cotton designed so the hairs don't stick. They close with Velcro and are easily washed. There are also flatter rugs for car seats and sofas plus a waterproof-backed picnic rug. The colours are very smart: Black Watch or Lindsay tartan, or dark blue and green with red piping.

Winna Pet Beds, Henley Old Farm, Henley, Dorchester, Dorset DT2 7BL
Tel/Fax: 01300 345210

Price range: £18 to £65. Catalogue free.
Payment: cheque, major credit cards.
Postage & packing: £6.50 per order.
Delivery: allow 21 days. Last Christmas orders by 7 December.
Refunds: yes, if returned unused.

See also: Bird Guides, The Blue Cross, The Owl Barn Gift Catalogue, Peoples Trust for Endangered Species, Royal Society for the Protection of Birds, R.S.P.C.A. Trading.

Chapter Ten

PRESENTS

GENERAL

There are some catalogues whose mission is to provide nothing but presents. There's nothing wrong with that: how often do we need to send a gift for a wedding, anniversary, Christmas or thank-you which is luxurious, not expensive but carefully thought out and quite impersonal? The bunch of flowers fulfils this perfectly, but you may want to send something more unusual. Current favourites are objects like champagne bottle stoppers in silver, pretty trays, initialled notebooks or diaries and ranges of scented candles or pot pourri. Our dedicated catalogues offer most of these, along with arrangements for putting on monograms, adding greetings cards or otherwise saying you care.

GENERAL PRESENTS - LISTINGS

Beckett & Graham This catalogue includes presents which are very much 'smart London' taste – ideal for townies. Leopardskin, découpage, faux ivory and tortoiseshell brushes and Italian silver corkscrews are featured, as are glass vases, china decorated with old garden tools, and glitzy ice buckets.

> **Beckett & Graham,** P O Box 95, Wantage DO, Oxfordshire OX12 9PT
>
> **Tel/Fax:** 01235 751389
>
> **Price range:** £1.30 to about £400. £1.75 to join mailing list and receive catalogues.
>
> **Payment:** cheque, Access, Visa, Switch.
>
> **Postage & packing:** £4.95.

Delivery: allow 21 days, but probably less.
Refunds: yes, if returned in perfect condition.

Coriander's

Anything from faux leather-bound books to charm bracelets feature in this catalogue dedicated to adult presents. These are both clever, tasteful and fairly impersonal. It's often a problem to give to people you don't know – distant relatives, brides, company thank-yous – and this catalogue fills the role admirably. There are elegant lamps, cushions, croquet sets, crockery and trays.

Coriander's Presents by Post, The White House, Leighton, Shrewsbury, Shropshire SY5 6RN
Tel: 01952 510885 **Fax:** 01952 510884
Price range: £5 to around £300. Catalogue free.
Payment: cheque, Mastercard, Visa, JCB, Switch.
Postage & packing: £4.75 in mainland UK. Elsewhere at cost.
Delivery: despatched next working day by 48-hour service.
Refunds: yes.
Specials: engraving, gift-wrapping £2. Free reminder service for birthdays and anniversaries.

The Finishing Touch

A very varied range of presents – not what you'd ever buy yourself but which make nice finishing touches, as the name suggests. Sconces like topiary (a highly popular theme at present), bridge accessories, little china and leather boxes, scented candles and spill vases. They make ideal presents to give to your hosts.

The Finishing Touch, P O Box 97, Grove, Wantage, Oxfordshire OX12 9YY
Tel: 01235 772353 **Fax:** 01235 772341
Price range: £1 to £100. Catalogue free.
Payment: cheque, major credit/debit cards except Amex and Diners.
Postage & packing: £3.35 per order. Overseas at cost.
Delivery: normally within a week, but allow 28 days. Last Christmas orders by last posting date, or second week of December for personalised items.
Refunds: yes, except personal items unless faulty.
Specials: gift-wrapping £2.50. Many items can be personalised.

320 MAIL ORDER MADE EASY

Flights of Fancy This catalogue seems to have an overall 'green' bias. There are plenty of 'bird' presents such as whistles which imitate bird calls, decoy geese and puffins which stand up in mud and move in the wind, plus parrot and owl fridge magnets. There are also twig whistles and pencils, whistling walking sticks (in case you lose each other) and scented logs.

> **Flights of Fancy**, 15 New Street, Leamington Spa, Warwickshire CV31 1HP
> **Tel:** 01926 423436 **Fax:** 01926 311925
> **E-mail:** mail@flightsoffancy.co.uk
> **Price range:** 99p to £17.50, minimum order £10. Catalogue free.
> **Payment:** cheque, Visa, Eurocard.
> **Postage & packing:** £2.50 for orders up to £25, free thereafter.
> **Delivery:** normally within a week.
> **Refunds:** by arrangement.

Gifts from the Grange The Grange takes products from Liberty, Lalique, Royal Doulton and many of the interesting food companies that you will find in this book. It's a catalogue designed for present-givers who may not know the recipients too well and that's immensely useful. New this year is a selection of foods chosen by Henrietta Green.

> **Gifts from the Grange Ltd**, The Grange, Hafod Farm, Goytre, Port Talbot SA13 2YR
> **Tel:** 01639 895249 **Fax:** 01639 895114
> **Price range:** £3.95 to £1,000. Catalogue free.
> **Payment:** Mastercard, Visa, Switch, Delta, JCB.
> **Postage & packing:** £3.50, free for orders over £65.
> **Delivery:** normally despatched within 7 days but allow 28.
> **Refunds:** yes.
> **Specials:** gift-wrapping.

H.L. Barnett A catalogue for corporate gifts or for people whose tastes you don't know too well. None the worse for that: there are hampers from Canada and New Zealand, a hamper of "family comestibles" ideal for an expat longing for his custard

PRESENTS

creams and rice pudding, baskets of fruits, shortbread and cakes plus flowers, toys and cosmetics.

H. L. Barnett, 31 Norwich Road, Strumpshaw, Norwich, Norfolk NR13 4AG

Tel: 01603 715242 **Fax:** 01603 713220

E-mail: barnett@paston.co.uk

Price range: £8 to £275. Catalogue free.

Payment: cheque, postal order, major credit/debit cards.

Postage & packing: included in UK, overseas by airmail £8.50.

Delivery: allow 14 days, less with surcharge. Last Christmas orders by 8 December.

Refunds: yes, if damaged or not delivered.

Initial Ideas Not, as it suggests, presents with initials but gifts, perhaps, for new people you've met. Chocolate quails' eggs, for instance, wine funnels, a dispenser for Coke tins and a David fridge magnet with added kilt or Y-fronts. You get the idea.

Initial Ideas, Chene Court, Poundwell Street, Modbury, Devon PL21 0QJ

Tel: 01548 831070 **Fax:** 01548 831074

Price range: £2.50 to £150. Catalogue free.

Payment: cheque, major credit/debit cards.

Postage & packing: £3.50, next day delivery £8.

Delivery: allow 28 days. Last Christmas orders by 6 December in UK. Some goods in short supply near Christmas.

Refunds: yes, but contact office.

Objets Extraordinaires Remember the Duchess of Windsor's pug cushions? This is the catalogue to find jokey cushions with smug cats and cracker mottos. There are also photo frames, clocks, silk ties and pink piggy cufflinks. Sloaney but good for gifts.

Objets Extraordinaires, 79 Walton Street, London SW3 2HP

Tel: 0171 589 8414 **Fax:** 0171 225 1935

Price range: £6 to £140. Catalogue free.

Payment: cheque, major credit cards.

Postage & packing: £3.95.

Delivery: 21 to 28 days. Last Christmas orders by 10 December.
Refunds: yes, if returned in good condition within 7 days.

Out of the Earth A new firm which specialises in birthday and Christmas presents chosen for their wit, beauty and quirkiness. Under beauty you can put the silver and gold plated jewellery made up of wings and hearts; quirky includes address books listing "liars, cheats, thieves, riffraff, phonies and friends." And witty are the games of cards with titles like "52 things to try once in your life." It's a very London-cool collection.

Out of the Earth, 83 Church Road, Barnes, London SW13 9HH
Tel: 0181 563 9991 **Fax:** 0181 948 4036
Price range: £4.95 to £89.50. Catalogue free.
Payment: cheque, major credit/debit cards.
Postage & packing: £4, express delivery £9. Overseas rates on application.
Delivery: despatched within 15 days. Last Christmas orders by 15 December.
Refunds: yes, if damaged or incorrect and returned within 14 days.
Specials: gift-wrapping.

Presents for Men I don't actually see why only men should have a good gardening pocket knife or a rosewood pepper mill or even gadgets like a combined calculator and measure tape. But this is an excellent catalogue for stocking fillers at under £3, under £5 and under £10 plus lots of good ideas.

Presents for Men, P O Box 16, Banbury, Oxfordshire OX17 1TF
Tel: 01295 750100 **Fax:** 01295 750800
Price range: 65p to £105. Send large sae and 2 first class stamps for catalogue.
Payment: cheque, Mastercard, Visa.
Postage & packing: £3.50.
Delivery: allow 28 days. Last Christmas orders by 6 December.
Refunds: no.

Purple Pom-Pom Well, not a name you are likely to forget. The firm sells good gift notions at the chic edge of design. As such, it will probably change items frequently but the first catalogue has funky clocks, cutlery and lighting, lots of faux leopard and zebra skin, children's toys and bootees, neat objects like dried flowers and old manuscripts in aluminium frames. Also jewellery, crockery, frames and cushions. They make a special effort at organising presents for all occasions.

Purple Pom Pom, Pom Pom HQ, Dunfield House, Dunfield, near Fairford, Gloucestershire GL7 4HE

Tel: 01285 810659 **Fax:** 01285 810692

Price range: £2.99 to £199. Catalogue free.

Payment: cheque, postal order, Access, Visa, Delta, Switch.

Postage & packing: £3.50 per address, free for orders over £150 in UK. Overseas at cost.

Delivery: normally despatched within 14 days, but allow 28. Next day delivery at extra cost. Last Christmas orders by 18 December subject to availability.

Refunds: yes, if returned unused within 14 days except earrings for health reasons.

Rosie Nieper When did the first T-shirt message arrive on the planet? So long ago that it's now part of the heritage. This firm has got the jokey T down to a fine art. There's a pun-T with, say, a dalmatian dog and the slogan "Hell and Dalmatian" or a cross parrot in a Mexican hat entitled "Tequila mocking bird". There are Archers Ts, Ts for feminists and lots of Ts with attitude. They are by a variety of artists and can be chosen to suit any mood.

Rosie Nieper, 12 Munster Road, Teddington, Middlesex TW11 9LL

Tel: 0181 255 9926 **Fax:** 0181 255 9927

E-mail: rosie.nieper@btinternet.com

Price range: £7.99 to £29.99. Catalogue free.

Payment: cheque, major credit/debit cards.

Postage & packing: £1.95. Overseas rates on application.

Delivery: if required for a specific date they will try to deliver on time or advise otherwise. Last Christmas orders by 16 December.

Refunds: yes.

TOYS

Are toys ever bought except as presents? As bribes, perhaps, or as a way of keeping a child quiet over a crisis. But, generally, the many catalogues dedicated to children's games are there for birthdays and Christmas or for doting relations to bring on visits. Buying toys is quite tricky because children's tastes vary so much and so many crazes sweep the country, only to die a sudden death. My view is that, before getting a present for a child, you should consult the parents or an expert. Many of these mail order firms offer just that expertise and people happy to talk over the problems with you. One certainty is that, if you make a mistake and get a fluffy bear for a grown-up six-year-old, you may never be forgiven. It's worth taking the trouble to find out.

TOYS - LISTINGS

A.P.E.S. Rocking Horses As well as making the traditional rocking horses either on bow rockers or Victorian pillar stands, the firm designs realistic horses – notably Mordjana, an Arab which won an award from the British Toymakers Guild in

PRESENTS   325

1996. She is a splendid beast with a dramatic mane and tail and will take an adult. Others are a fairground galloper, a unicorn and a miniature unicorn with gold-plated horn.

> **A.P.E.S. Rocking Horses**, Ty Gwyn, Llannefydd, Denbigh, Denbighshire LL16 5HB
>
> **Tel/Fax:** 01745 540365
>
> **Price range:** £300 to £2,750. Catalogue free.
>
> **Payment:** cheque, international money order.
>
> **Postage & packing:** £55 for UK delivery.
>
> **Delivery:** by arrangement. Last Christmas orders by end of September.
>
> **Refunds:** by arrangement.
>
> **Specials:** horses made to commission, restoration of old horses.

AVM Concepts Children are programmed to learn language at an early age, so it seems logical to teach them a foreign language while they're still young. This company has French cassettes to suit beginners from four up to GCSE revision level. As children enjoy listening to tapes this is a painless way to learn and parents can revive their rusty French at the same time. I used to run a French Club at the local primary school and it was surprising how quickly even the youngest children learned their numbers, colours etc and this early teaching gave them a real advantage when they started formal French classes. PJ

> **AVM Concepts Ltd**, P O Box 263, Haywards Heath, West Sussex RH16 3YS
>
> **Tel/Fax:** 01444 457227
>
> **E-mail:** enquires@avmconcepts.co.uk
>
> **Website:** http://www.avmconcepts.co.uk/avm
>
> **Price range:** £7.75 each, £23 for three. Catalogue free.
>
> **Payment:** cheque, Mastercard, Visa.
>
> **Postage & packing:** included.
>
> **Delivery:** allow 28 days.
>
> **Refunds:** by arrangement.

Babes in Wood Primary coloured, simple in outline and undeniably perky, the range covers wall clocks, book ends and room decorations. The subjects are chosen to appeal to very young children – dolphins, mice, hedgehogs, dinosaurs and teddies – though why mice are more child-friendly than ferrets or bears than wolves is anyone's guess.

Babes in Wood, Rignals House, 33 Rignals Lane, Galleywood, Chelmsford, Essex CM2 8QT

Tel: 01245 475499

Price range: £4.50 to £12.50. Catalogue free.

Payment: cheque, postal order.

Postage & packing: included in UK.

Delivery: allow 28 days, but normally 14. Last Christmas orders by 10 December.

Refunds: yes.

Baby Basics

The introduction to this catalogue is signed by Ashiya Mahdi who is, she says, the founder and mother and her range is based on good sense. Each page has a soundbite like "from birth, infants respond to bright colours" and "from 5 years teach them the secrets of space". The catalogue consists of virtually nothing but toys for children from nought to nine though it has been so successful that new ideas are introduced all the time. Prices are very sensible and this is a one-stop for stocking fillers.

Baby Basics Ltd, Suite 215, 535 Kings Road, London SW10 0SZ

Tel: 0171 823 3030 Catalogue request line: 01793 697300
Fax: 0171 823 3044

Price range: £1.99 to £50. Catalogue free.

Payment: cheque, major credit/debit cards.

Postage & packing: £3.95 in UK.

Delivery: goods despatched within 48 hours. Last Christmas orders 22 December.

Refunds: yes, if returned in perfect condition within 14 days.

Specials: gift-wrapping.

Billie Bond Designs

Children love fantasy and this imaginative painted furniture makes good use of it. The idea is to offer them small, secretive and stylish spaces of their own as well as personalised toy boxes which, I'm reliably assured, actually encourage tots to be tidy.

PRESENTS 327

Billie Bond Designs, 2 Warners Farm Cottage, Howe Street, Great Waltham, Essex CM3 1BL

Tel: 01245 360164 **Fax:** 01245 362678

Price range: £7.50 to £1,000. Catalogue £2.50.

Payment: cheque, major credit/debit cards.

Postage & packing: £3.50. Furniture from £10.

Delivery: allow 28 days. Furniture 6-8 weeks.

Refunds: not on items made to order.

The Children's Cottage Company

The cover of one catalogue shows a little red cottage set in a romantic beechwood and that's what it's all about. It's like children walking into their own house, where everything is scaled to suit them and not adults (though an adult can stand inside one). And it's their very own house, to be furnished (from the same catalogue) as they wish. They are intended to stay outside and the firm finds children play in them more in winter than summer. Though most are cottages with a central stable door, the firm actually does a castle for those with grand ideas.

The Children's Cottage Company, The Sanctuary, Shobrooke, Crediton, Devon EX17 1BG

Tel: 01363 772061 **Fax:** 01363 777868

Price range: cottages £1,275 to £2,850. Catalogue free.

Payment: cheque.

Postage & packing: at cost.

Delivery: allow 6 to 8 weeks. Give as much notice as possible as cottages are manufactured from scratch.

Refunds: by arrangement.

Specials: special requests accommodated where possible.

David Plagerson

This painter, who started making a Noah's Ark for his children, now makes two wooden versions with lift-off roofs. He also makes a range of over 100 animals which you can choose from (everyone wanted different ones). They include crocodiles, hippos, flamingos, Galapagos tortoises and koalas and obviously come in pairs. You can buy just the ark and get a set of animals every month. Arks are either painted or in mixed woods and can have a name painted on the hull.

David Plagerson, 28 Bridgetown, Totnes, Devon TQ9 5AD
Tel: 01803 866786
Price range: £14 to £1,280. Send A3 sae for catalogue.
Payment: one third deposit with order. Balance by cheque.
Postage & packing: £9.80 by 48-hour Datapost in UK.
Delivery: by arrangement: average 4 months.
Refunds: yes, if returned in perfect condition within 7 days.
Specials: commissions accepted for special arks and animals, e.g. pets, rare breeds. Arks can be inscribed with name.

Direct to your Door

Toys are the hardest objects both to carry around the shops and to post so it's a boon to find a firm who'll save you the trouble. The ranges are Playmobil with 257 products and Brio Railways.

Direct to your Door Ltd, P O Box 40, Middlesbrough, Cleveland TS8 9YG
Tel: 01642 324544, Free 0800 137880 **Fax:** 01642 324545
Price range: £1.99 to £200. Catalogue free.
Payment: cheque, Mastercard, Access, Visa, Switch, Delta.
Postage & packing: phone for quotation.
Delivery: within 3 working days. Last Christmas orders despatched 24-hour delivery but supplies might be limited.
Refunds: yes.

The Dolls' House

In a way, this is not a catalogue of toys, unless you count the fact that adults play too. It is a fine collection of anyone who enjoys life in miniature. Though some dolls' houses could be fitted with a modern Aga from here or a deck chair, it is extraordinary how little the dolls' world has changed since their houses first appeared in the 17th century.

The Dolls' House, Market Place, Northleach, near Cheltenham, Gloucestershire GL54 3EJ
Tel/Fax: 01451 860431
Price range: 50p to £1,500. Catalogue £3.50.
Payment: cheque, major credit cards.
Postage & packing: £1 to £5.
Delivery: allow 2 weeks. Some items are in limited supply.
Refunds: yes, if returned in perfect condition.

PRESENTS

The Dolls' House Emporium Aficionados of dolls' houses range from two to 90-year-olds and from this huge list you can buy and decorate the house of your choice. There are cottages and London town houses, stately homes and manors, even a conservatory (though nothing designed by Richard Rogers of the Millennium Dome). It's also extraordinary what is made for the interiors – lights which can be wired up, cactus plants and walking sticks, "Ming" porcelain and a curled-up cat called Curtis.

The Dolls House Emporium, Victoria Road, Ripley, Derbyshire DE5 3YD

Tel: 01773 513773 **Fax:** 01773 513772

E-mail: enquiries@dollshouse.co.uk

Price range: 40p to £1,760. Catalogue free.

Payment: cheque, Visa, Mastercard, Switch.

Postage & packing: £2.50 for orders under £35, free thereafter. Overseas rates on application.

Delivery: despatched following day. Last Christmas orders by 18 December. Order built dolls' houses as early as possible.

Refunds: yes, post paid label enclosed.

Early Learning Centre Despite a fairly idiotic name, this is a hugely successful high street chain. Now they've gone mail order with a big bright catalogue. There's a special section devoted to Teletubbies alone as well as electronic toys like alphabet keyboards and a talking computer. Many items are cheap enough for little gifts or stocking fillers, such as the 69p plastic animals, like cicadas, long horn beetles and tarantulas. More cuddly are elephants, cows and basset hounds. The descriptions are most helpful and suitable ages given alongside.

Early Learning Centre, South Marston Park, Swindon, Wiltshire SN3 3TJ

Tel: 0990 352352 **Fax:** 01787 881939

Price range: 69p to £499. Catalogue free.

Payment: cheque, Mastercard, Visa, Switch.

Postage & packing: £4. Overseas rates on application.

Delivery: within 7 working days in most areas. Last Christmas orders by 11 December.

Refunds: yes.

Emma Jefferson

Emma Jefferson Height is endlessly fascinating to both growing children and their proud parents and was so into antiquity (there's a scrawled height chart at Pompeii). Emma Jefferson makes a range of different wooden height charts shaped and painted like dinosaurs, knights, ballerinas and tigers which are full of charm. There are also wooden nursery lamps with similar figures and shades.

> **Emma Jefferson**, 16 Cross Bank, Great Easton, Market Harborough, Leicestershire LE16 8SR
>
> **Tel/Fax:** 01536 772074
>
> **Price range:** height charts £19.95, lamps £29.95, or £39.95 with shade. Catalogue free.
>
> **Payment:** cheque, Mastercard, Visa.
>
> **Postage & packing:** £4.75 for 1 item, £7.50 for 2 or more.
>
> **Delivery:** normally within a week. Last Christmas orders 4 working days in advance.
>
> **Refunds:** yes.

Expressly Children

Expressly Children A small catalogue which has been carefully chosen for children from toddlers to 12 year olds. Virtually everything in it can be personalised: there are named table mats and coasters, stationery, plates, teddy bears and clothes. Children can be very territorial and giving them cutlery or luggage can encourage them to use things properly.

> **Expressly Children**, The Business Village, Broomhill Road, London SW18 4JQ
>
> **Tel:** 0171 978 5005/6006 **Fax:** 0171 585 2161
>
> **Price range:** £4.95 to £54.95. Send A5 sae for catalogue.
>
> **Payment:** cheque, postal order, Mastercard, Visa, debit cards.
>
> **Postage & packing:** £2.95. Express delivery £4.50.
>
> **Delivery:** allow 28 days. Last Christmas orders by 30 November. Certain items can be ordered up to 14 December.
>
> **Refunds:** yes, if returned unused within 10 days.

The Green Board Game Company

The Green Board Game Company The games are intended to be both educational and fun for all the family. They teach about the natural world by getting children to name ani-

PRESENTS

mals by alphabet, answer geographical questions or questions about how our bodies work. Many are multi-lingual.

The Green Board Game Co Ltd, 34 Amersham Hill Drive, High Wycombe, Buckinghamshire HP13 6QY
Tel: 01494 538999 **Fax:** 01494 538646
Price range: £1 to £17.50. Catalogue free.
Payment: cheque, major credit cards.
Postage & packing: 1 game £3.50, 2 £4.50, 3 or more £5.50.
Delivery: 10 days. Last Christmas orders 5 postal days ahead.
Refunds: yes.

Haddon Rocking Horses The modern rocking horse is subtly different from his 19th century ancestor, as this range demonstrates. He has much longer hair on his mane and a serious forelock. His tail, by contrast, is less evident. The faces are more friendly and snort less. Haddon has also had the good idea to use laminates to give a saucy dapple on its Relko range.

Haddon Rocking Horses Ltd, 5 Telford Road, Clacton-on-Sea, Essex CO15 4LP
Tel: 01255 424745 **Fax:** 01255 475505
Price range: £500 upwards. Catalogue free.
Payment: cheque, Access, Visa.
Postage & packing: £12 to £40.
Delivery: 4 weeks. Last Christmas orders by 30 November.
Refunds: by arrangement.

Hamleys This world-famous children's store doesn't offer a catalogue of its 40,000-plus toys, games and gifts but it will mail order anything in stock to you and will also send gift vouchers for children's presents. This is very useful when you don't know what they want. Experts – and Hamleys are certainly that – will advise on suitability too.

Hamleys of London Ltd, 188-196 Regent Street, London W1R 6BT
Tel: 0171 734 3161 **Fax:** 0171 494 5858
Price range: 10p to £2,000. No catalogue.
Payment: cheque, postal order, major credit cards.
Postage & packing: £5. express delivery £10. Overseas rates on application.

332 · MAIL ORDER MADE EASY

Delivery: allow 14 working days. Express delivery 2 working days.
Refunds: yes, if returned in original condition.
Specials: gift-wrapping, gift vouchers.

The Hill Toy Company

Real children, clearly delighted with the toys, with real names and ages, fill the pages of this most cheerful catalogue. They are photographed playing with dolls' prams and hobby horses, stacking building bricks and putting up a medieval fort. But the happiest faces of all are on the dressing-up page where gangs of Santa Clauses, prides of tigers and families of dalmatians are cavorting together. The list is nicely balanced between the old-fashioned toys which parents like and the monster kit of teeth and claws that delight children.

The Hill Toy Company, P O Box 100, Ripon, North Yorkshire HG4 4XZ
Tel: 01765 689955 **Fax:** 01765 689111
Price range: from 99p.
Payment: cheque, Mastercard, Access, Visa, Switch.
Postage & packing: £4.50. 48-hour delivery add £4.
Delivery: normally despatched within 7 working days, but allow 28 days if out of stock.
Refunds: yes, if notified within 7 days.
Specials: gift-wrapping.

Hopscotch Dressing-up Clothes

Marvellous selection of clothes which will keep children happy for hours and are suitable for children from 18 months to nine. Characters such as witches, pirates, crusaders and Robin Hood jostle with fairies, rabbits, dalmatians and tigers. There are also hats without outfits for leopards, teddies, rabbits, donkeys, pigs and chickens and accessories. Where would an Indian be without his headdress or Biggles without his helmet? Plus sparkly shoes and bags, clown noses, magic wands and a range of swords, shields and the like.

Hopscotch Dressing-Up Clothes, 61 Palace Road, London SW2 3LB
Tel/Fax: 0181 674 9853

Price range: 50p to £28. Catalogue free.

Payment: cheque, Mastercard, Visa.

Postage & packing: £3.50, Special Delivery £7.50. Overseas rates on application.

Delivery: within 10 working days if in stock, otherwise allow 28 days. Special Delivery: allow 3 working days. Last Christmas orders by 11 December, or 18 December by Special Delivery.

Refunds: yes.

Specials: outfits are delivered in white boxes lined with tissue.

Kiddiewise

Outdoor toys for adventurous children. There are trampolines, slides, swings and ladders, a mobile sandpit. There is small-size furniture and three structures including little rooms and slides – Peter Pan's Hide-a-way, Captain Hood's Deck and Teddy's Lookout.

Kiddiewise, Katella Ltd, P O Box 433, Leek, Staffordshire ST13 7TZ

Tel: 01538 304235 **Fax:** 01538 304575

E-mail: jumpking@btinternet.com

Price range: £14 to £2,155. Catalogue free.

Payment: cheque, postal order, Mastercard, Access, Visa, Switch.

Postage & packing: included.

Delivery: allow 14 days.

Refunds: yes, if notified within 14 days.

Laurel Designs

Little girls are famously horse-mad and this range offers eight different hobby horses and donkeys in fur fabrics with wooden poles and wheels. There are also model Shetland ponies, made of the same materials, which arrive with their own stable box. These are eight inches high.

Laurel Designs, P O Box 192, Eastleigh, Hampshire SO53 5ZJ

Tel: 01703 253273 **Fax:** 01703 251611

Price range: £30 to £40. Catalogue free.

Payment: cheque, major credit cards.

Postage & packing: included.

Delivery: allow 14 days. Last Christmas orders by mid-December.

Refunds: by arrangement.

MAIL ORDER MADE EASY

Letterbox When you buy toys as presents it's worth thinking of the parents as well as the children – and Letterbox's catalogue is in impeccable good taste. There are plenty of toys in hand-painted wood such as a pullalong daisy cow and a steam train with a letter on each carriage so you can make a name. There are such things as a painted hand mirror for vain little girls, plus easy jigsaws. Older children can have small gardeners' tools and plants, a mini guitar and binoculars for trekking. There's also a good stocking-filler collection of toys for under £5. A few ideas – a Harley Davidson pen, cassette, CD and video boxes – are good for teenagers.

Letterbox, P O Box 114, Truro, Cornwall TR1 1FZ
Tel: 01872 580885 **Fax:** 01872 580866
Price range: £1.99 to £90. Catalogue free.
Payment: cheque, major credit/debit cards.
Postage & packing: £2.25 for orders up to £19.99, £3.75 up to £99.99, free thereafter.
Delivery: allow 28 days. Last Christmas orders by 14 December, or 23 November for personalised items.
Refunds: yes, if notified within 7 days and returned in resaleable condition.

Little Issues The secret of making children tidy, I've been told, is to make them interested in storage. Wendy Pinney makes toy boxes and chests which include a child's initials (or name) and which can be customised with themes like wild animals or transport. She will also make specials on commission and match colours to decor. She's happy to make clocks, mirrors and gifts for weddings or Christenings on the same themes.

Little Issues, Bristol Craft and Design Centre, 6 Leonard Lane, Bristol BS1 1EA
Tel: 0117 929 1234 **Fax:** 0117 929 7890
Price range: £15 to £245. Catalogue free.
Payment: cheque.
Postage & packing: from £2 for smaller items to £25 for chests.
Delivery: normally within 1 month. Last Christmas orders by mid-November.
Refunds: by arrangement.

PRESENTS 335

Mrs Pickering's Dolls' Clothes Mrs P will make clothes to fit any doll (there's a measurement checklist in her brochure) so you can kit out Barbie or Sindy with a wedding dress or dungarees, or Action man in an anorak. Teddies get clothes too – you can even kit him out in your school uniform.

> **Mrs Pickering's Dolls' Clothes**, Dept C, The Pines, Decoy Road, Potter Heigham, Great Yarmouth, Norfolk NR29 5LX
> **Tel:** 01692 670407
> **Price range:** 20p to £10. Send 9" x 4" sae for catalogue.
> **Payment:** cheque or postal order with order.
> **Postage & packing:** 60p, free for 8 or more items.
> **Delivery:** allow 28 days. Last Christmas orders in November.
> **Refunds:** yes, if resaleable.

The Mulberry Bush Collection A collection of high quality and interesting toys which parents will love to buy. There are beechwood toys from Czechoslovakia such as a pull-along cement mixer and a pull apart work bench complete with vices, spanners, nuts and bolts which I bet girls love to play with too. I love Noah's Arks and little farms with animals and they are here, too. There are games I used to play, like Jacks and lots of floppy toys.

> **The Mulberry Bush Ltd**, The Old Coach House, Marlands, Itchingfield, Horsham, West Sussex RH13 7NN
> **Tel:** 01403 734714 **Fax:** 01403 733085
> **Price range:** £1.95 to £99.95. Catalogue free.
> **Payment:** cheque, Mastercard, Visa.
> **Postage & packing:** £1.50 for orders up to £10, £3.50 up to £99.99, free thereafter. Next-day delivery add £3.
> **Delivery:** 5 days. Last Christmas orders by 16 December.
> **Refunds:** yes, if returned within 14 days.
> **Specials:** gift-wrapping £1.50 per item.

Orchard Toys All the toys in this range are "rigorously tested by children for durability and play value" which is a hard test to pass. Many are clever, such as the combined jigsaw and alphabet game composed around teddy bears and Slug in a Jug which teaches children rhyming. Their big floor jigsaws are terrific – London buses, cement mixers and dolls' houses.

Orchard Toys, Debdale Lane, Keyworth, Nottingham NG12 5HN
Tel: 0115 937 3547 **Fax:** 0115 937 6575
Price range: £1.68 to £9.50. Catalogue free.
Payment: cheque, major credit cards.
Postage & packing: £3.50 for orders up to £20, £5 up to £70, free thereafter.
Delivery: allow 28 days. Last Christmas orders by 14 December.
Refunds: ring Customer Services on the above number.

Pappa Geppetto's Toys

These are brilliantly coloured puzzles for young children which will occupy them for hours. There are interconnected loops, gyroscopes, a series of sticks and rods called skwish and flexible worms, dinosaurs and bugs. The age range goes from birth to about four.

Pappa Geppetto's Toys, Mail Order Express, 39 Sherrard Street, Melton Mowbray, Leicestershire LE13 1XH
Tel: 01664 483838 **Fax:** 01664 850011
E-mail: sales@arbon-watts.demon.co.uk
Price range: approx £4.50 to £45. Send sae for free catalogue.
Payment: cheque, postal order, major credit/debit cards.
Postage & packing: £2 administration charge for orders under £15, otherwise free. Next day delivery £3.
Delivery: 5 working days in mainland UK. Last Christmas orders by 21 December.
Refunds: yes, if returned in original packaging.
Specials: gift-wrapping at extra charge.

Pintoy and Plan Toys

Hobby horses, three-wheel scooters and trikes, rocking dolphins and aeroplanes make up half the range. The rest are some cleverly designed desks, chairs, shelves, clothes hangers and benches for small children. The pieces are made especially safe, with hinges that won't trap fingers. The range also includes a series of wooden games, from solitaire to chess.

Pintoy and Plan Toys, Mail Order Express, 39 Sherrard Street, Melton Mowbray, Leicestershire LE13 1XH

PRESENTS

Tel: 01664 483838 **Fax:** 01664 850011
E-mail: sales@arbon-watts.demon.co.uk
Price range: £1.99 to £89.99. Send A4 sae for free catalogue.
Payment: cheque, postal order, major credit/debit cards.
Postage & packing: £2 adminstration charge for orders under £15, otherwise free. Next day delivery £3.
Delivery: 5 working days in mainland UK. Last Christmas orders by 21 December.
Refunds: yes, if returned In original packaging.
Specials: gift-wrapping at extra charge.

Benjamin Pollock's Toyshop

Mr P was born in 1856 into a family of toy theatre makers in London's East End. The firm was kept going by enthusiasts and is now run by the Baldwin brothers, one an actor, with a new shop in Covent Garden. Now there is a mail order catalogue including 19th century toy theatre replicas from Britain and Europe, simpler ones for young children and all sorts of cut-out toys, puppets, clowns and visual illusions. There are dolls, tin flats, miniature figures and nativity scenes for Christmas. A lovely, nostalgic collection with some nice stocking-fillers.

Pollock's Mail Order, 44 The Market, Covent Garden, London WC2E 8RF
Tel/Fax: 0171 636 0559
Price range: 50p to £200. Catalogue £3.50.
Payment: cheque, major credit/debit cards.
Postage & packing: £3.50, larger items £7 in UK.
Delivery: allow 28 days.
Refunds: yes, if returned in perfect condition within 14 days.
Specials: gift vouchers.

Robert Mullis

Rocking horses probably originated as a way to teach children to be at ease with horses as well as through the circus. Mullis, a jolly grey-haired craftsman, makes new horses in the old tradition along with his own designs of Arab horses with especially kindly faces. His miniatures will seat dolls. He also repairs and restores old horses.

Robert Mullis, 55 Berkeley Road, Wroughton, Swindon, Wiltshire SN4 9BN

Tel/Fax: 01793 813583

Price range: £390 to £1,575. Catalogue free.

Payment: 10% deposit with order. Balance by cheque, Access or Visa.

Postage & packing: at cost.

Delivery: all made to order taking 6-8 weeks. Order as early as possible.

Refunds: by arrangement.

The Rocking Sheep Centre

Unusual breeds of sheep make up the skins which are used for these charming and different rockers. There are blackface sheep and Jacob rams, a black Welsh ram and a fluffy white ewe. The sheep are all child friendly and provide a warm and comfortable seat for toddlers.

The Rocking Sheep Centre, Penllyn Workshops, Plasey Street, Bala, Gwynedd LL23 7SW

Tel: 01678 521232 **Fax:** 01678 521111

Price range: £190 to £380. Catalogue free.

Payment: cheque, major credit cards.

Postage & packing: included in UK.

Delivery: allow 28 days in UK.

Refunds: yes, if returned within 28 days.

Spottiswoode Trading

It's amazing what you can do with stuffed cotton. Soft skittles, for example, or a large carrot. There are mobiles of circus animals and sheep to send babies to sleep, primary coloured pram strings of animals and even a big, bright horsey toy. Presents for young children only.

Spottiswoode Trading, P O Box 3009, Littlehampton, West Sussex BN17 5SJ

Tel: 01903 733123 **Fax:** 01903 713777

Price range: £10 to £30. Catalogue free.

Payment: cheque, Mastercard, Visa, Switch.

Postage & packing: £2.95 per item.

Delivery: allow 14 days. Last Christmas orders by 15 December, later orders may pay extra to ensure delivery.

Refunds: yes, if returned unused within 7 days.

PRESENTS

Stuart Lennie Specialises in dolls' houses made of pine and matching furniture. There are rocking cradles, bunk beds for full-sized dolls, nativity scenes and toy stables. He's won several awards since he started making toys in 1996 and his range is constantly extending.

> **Stuart Lennie**, 44 Bisley Road, Stroud, Gloucestershire GL5 1HF
> **Tel:** 01453 750791
> **Price range:** £3 to £350. Send sae for catalogue.
> **Payment:** cheque.
> **Postage & packing:** 50p to £20 depending on item.
> **Delivery:** within 28 days. Christmas orders as early as possible.
> **Refunds:** yes.
> **Specials:** commissions undertaken.

Super Tramp A range of trampolines to give fun and exercise for all from the Frog to the Super Kangaroo designed for gymnasts, stuntmen and high divers. The firm also sells the large range of slides, ladders, swings and huts made by *hout-land* which can be put together to make a whole adventure playground.

> **Super Tramp Trampolines**, Langlands Business Park, Uffculme, Cullompton, Devon EX15 3DA
> **Tel:** 0800 074 7040 or 07000 BOUNCE **Fax:** 01884 841319
> **Price range:** £34 to £1,389. Catalogue free.
> **Payment:** cheque, major credit/debit cards.
> **Postage & packing:** included.
> **Delivery:** by 24-hour carrier. Last Christmas orders by midday 22 December.
> **Refunds:** yes, within 10 days.

Teddy Bears of Witney Teddies must be Britain's most popular and enduring toy for adults as well as children. This catalogue, which shows the staff all hugging a bear, features Baby Alfonzo, a small version of the bear belonging to a Russian princess bought for a record price at auction, a new version of Aloysius from Brideshead and a new Pooh bear not in captivity in New York.

340 MAIL ORDER MADE EASY

Teddy Bears of Witney, 99 High Street, Witney, Oxfordshire
OX8 6LY
Tel: 01993 702616/706616 **Fax:** 01993 702344
Price range: £35 to £425. Catalogue £5.
Payment: cheque, Mastercard, Visa, Eurocard.
Postage & packing: £5 per bear worldwide.
Delivery: within 2 working days on request.
Refunds: please discuss your order before buying.

Traditional Toys This is the first mail order catalogue from the Chelsea shop which sells such delightful toys – not old-fashioned but ones which never go out of fashion. There are lots of furries and fluffies including Muffy (a bear) and Hoppy (a hare) who have separate clothes, their own birthday parties and a whole hospital of accessories for them to care for including a sick pup.

Traditional Toys, 53 Godfrey Street, Chelsea Green, London
SW3 3SX
Tel: 0171 349 9604, shop 0171 352 1718 **Fax:** 0181 671 9988
E-mail: trad toys@aol.com
Price range: £4.99 to £127.99. Catalogue free.
Payment: cheque, major credit cards.
Postage & packing: £2.95.
Delivery: normally 3-4 days. Overnight at additional cost. Last Christmas orders by 23 December.
Refunds: yes.
Specials: gift-wrapping.

Treasure Chest The helpful catalogue shows where this team gets its expertise about children: the staff work with their children all around them and are clearly proud of the fact. The list is pretty comprehensive, including games, puzzles, wall-hangings, dolls and dolls' houses plus books and outdoor chutes and swings. As well as mail order, the firm has a shop where you can look at the full range.

Treasure Chest, The Old School, 1 High Street, Tattenhall, Chester
CH3 9PX
Tel: 01829 770787 **Fax:** 01829 770312

Price range: £1.50 to £89. Catalogue free.

Payment: cheque, postal order, major credit/debit cards.

Postage & packing: £3.95 for orders up to £50, 2.95 up to £75, free thereafter. Overnight delivery £8.95.

Delivery: 10-14 days. Last Christmas orders by 18 December.

Refunds: yes, if returned with covering letter within 14 days.

Tridias!

I wonder if children would really take to the little cleaning kit – bucket, mop, shovel and brushes – in this catalogue. Probably, but not to clean up the mess they make. Other notions balance education with fun like a crystal radio set, a chemistry set with 100 experiments designed not to blow your house down, and an ant farm where real insects can colonise and be seen. There's a special section on party presents and stocking fillers.

Tridias! Toys, 124 Walcot Street, Bath BA1 5BG

Tel: 01225 469455 **Fax:** 01225 448592

Price range: 90p to £160. Catalogue free.

Payment: cheque, postal order, Mastercard, Visa.

Postage & packing: £2.95. Priority service add £4.

Delivery: normally 14 working days, but occasionally 28. Priority delivery 4 working days. Last Christmas orders by 17 December.

Refunds: yes, if returned within 28 days.

Specials: gift vouchers.

Wild Wood

I have always loved the best building bricks and this is what David Cartwright produces (he also makes model yachts). The bricks are in a range of 19 different woods, with different hues and characteristics. All are grown in Britain and include yew and box, apple, cherry, sweet chestnut and cedar of Lebanon. Holly, willow and plane will also soon feature. The shapes are cubes, rectangles, cylinders, arches and triangles which can construct an entire basilica. They can be ordered in high-quality wooden boxes.

Wild Wood, 37 Lion Street, Hay on Wye, Hereford HR3 5AA

Tel: 01497 831561/821377 **Fax:** 01497 820996

Price range: standard set (60 bricks) £55. Catalogue free.

Payment: cheque with order.

Postage & packing: £5.50 for standard set.

Delivery: usually within a few days. Special requests may take longer. Last Christmas orders by 15 December.

Refunds: yes, if damaged.

Specials: sets and boxes can be personalised.

See also: Dream Team Design, Ends, The Faerie Shop, Favourite Things, Frog Hollow, Goslings, Hawkin, Homecrafts Direct, Kantara. Layden Designs, Magic by Post, Panduro Hobby, Plainfeather, Sasti, The Singing Tree.

STOCKING FILLERS

It's not so much what is in the stocking which matters – it's the fact that Santa has brought it at all. I don't think there's much point in exhausting yourself getting the perfect 97 presents to put at the end of the bed when a rough assortment of goodies will do. Some firms specialise in huge lists of entertainments, games, jokes, balloons, all under £1. They'll send the whole caboodle to Santa in time for Christmas Eve. The only advice I would give is to choose a large variety, cheap and gaudy, and stuff a nice tangerine in the toe.

PRESENTS

STOCKING FILLERS - LISTINGS

Frog Hollow Though most toy catalogues have some cheap and cheery stocking fillers, this one has more than most – even special packs of goodies for stockings. These might include a bag of chocolate coins, jumping beans, a whoopee cushion and a croaking sponge (for any age or sex) or a little girl's pack of fan, purse, silk notebook and teddy. You can get personalised pencils and little leather boxes along with personalised stockings and a jumbo Victorian one.

> **Frog Hollow**, 91 High Street, Markyate, Hertfordshire AL3 8JG
> **Tel:** 01582 842117 **Fax:** 01582 842113
> **Price range:** £3 to £30. Catalogue free.
> **Payment:** cheque, postal order, Mastercard, Visa, Switch, Delta.
> **Postage & packing:** included in UK. Overseas at cost.
> **Delivery:** normally 14-21 days. Ring first if urgent. Christmas orders despatched up to last posting date.
> **Refunds:** yes.

Goslings A catalogue of presents intended to cause hysterics in a party or family get-together. There are adult stocking fillers verging on the naughty such as nipple warmers and chocolate body paint, a range of jokey T-shirts, aprons and "probably the silliest game in the world" which consists of two velcro hats, three fluffy balls and a booklet.

> **Goslings**, Spring House, The Clementines, Blockley, Moreton-in-Marsh, Gloucestershire GL56 9ER
> **Tel:** 01386 701529 **Fax:** 01386 701531
> **Price range:** £1.99 to £49.95. Catalogue free.
> **Payment:** cheque, Mastercard, Access, Visa.
> **Postage & packing:** £2.95 for orders under £20, £4.50 under £50, £5.50 under £100, free thereafter.
> **Delivery:** allow 28 days. Last Christmas orders by 11 December.
> **Refunds:** yes, if returned undamaged within 28 days.

Hawkin & Co Toys for all the family: wind-up penguins and monkeys, Edwardian mini masks, snake in the box which springs out, finger puppets and kazoos. The firm produces a large catalogue of objects which anyone from a toddler to an ancient would enjoy. There are over seventy items at less than £1 each, plus lots of old-fashioned toys like slithery snakes and tiny carved nuts with insects inside. Great for the child in all of us.

Hawkin & Co, St. Margaret, Harleston, Norfolk IP20 0PJ
Tel: 01986 782536 **Fax:** 01986 782468
E-mail: sales@hawkin.co.uk
Website: http://www.hawkin.co.uk
Price range: 12p to £519. Catalogue free.
Payment: cheque, postal order, major credit/debit cards except Amex.
Postage & packing: £2.95 for orders under £25, free thereafter. Express delivery £6.50.
Delivery: normally despatched within 5 working days. Allow 10 working days if paying by cheque.
Refunds: yes.

See also: Baby Basics, Early Learning Centre, The Hill Toy Company, Letterbox, Minh Mang, Pollock's Mail Order, Presents for Men, Tridias!

TEENAGERS

Does anyone know what a teenager wants for Christmas? Do teenagers themselves? Teenagers are by far the hardest people to buy presents for but, nevertheless, cannot be ignored. One tip from numerous parents is not to bust a gut thinking of pleasing teenagers in general but try to find out what pleases any one in particular. It may seem hard to buy them black lipstick or skull-and-crossbones jewellery but if that's what they want, that's what you will have to do. Otherwise clothes and accessories are the safest bet, especially for girls. The suppliers below include designers and buyers who are still young enough to be on the right wavelength.

PRESENTS

TEENAGERS - LISTINGS

Johnny Loves Rosie Maryrose Monroe named her firm after her mom and dad, who still gives his wife little presents. The range is a delightful collection of accessories from America. These are tiger lily hairclips and others made from popcorn or sweeties (coated in plastic), there are lovely holiday buys like floral flipflops, bright shoppers and cufflinks made from bottle tops. The range is always changing – maribou scrunchies and feather clips are hot this year – and among the clients are top celebs like Nicole Kidman.

> **Johnny Loves Rosie Ltd**, 3rd Floor, 32-38 Osborn Street, London E1 6TD
> **Tel:** 0171 247 1496 **Fax:** 0171 247 3166
> **E-mail:** jlrltd@aol.com
> **Price range:** £2 to £29.95. Catalogue free.
> **Payment:** cheque, major credit/debit cards.
> **Postage & packing:** £1.95, express delivery £5.
> **Delivery:** allow 3-4 weeks. Items may be in limited supply.
> **Refunds:** yes, if returned within 14 days.

Tyrrell Katz James T and Julia K are fabric designers who create overall patterns with marching animals, beetles, dancers riders. Each drawing is a little cartoon, usually jokey. You might find a group of frogs, from bull frogs and trees frogs alongside a chap called Jean Paul or, in among the landrace and Tamworth pigs, a Wild Bore asking if you've seen his new anorak. The fabrics make up T-shirts, drawstring bags, bed linen, pyjamas and notebooks for every age.

> **Tyrrell Katz**, The Old Coach House, 25 Dunster Gardens, London NW6 7NG
> **Tel:** 0181 537 6757 **Fax:** 0181 537 6760
> **Price range:** £1.95 to £62.95. Catalogue free.
> **Payment:** cheque, postal order, major credit/debit cards.
> **Postage & packing:** see order form.
> **Delivery:** normally within 7 days but allow 21.
> **Refunds:** yes.

346   MAIL ORDER MADE EASY

See also: Barry M Cosmetics, Castle Combe Skid Pan & Kart Track, Drive it all, The Iron Bed Company, Letterbox, Purple Pom Pom, Racing Green, Red Letter Days, Word Out.

PROBLEM PEOPLE

Problem people divide into two categories, there are those who can't help it and those who can. Those who can't are people who have chronic conditions such as diabetes, asthma, eczema, or allergies to additives or ingredients which mean that presents must fulfil special needs (see the end of this section for firms which help). The second category of problem people are those who have everything – or want nothing. For those who are satisfied with life, give them the chance to adopt an animal at the zoo (even if it's a gerbil) or have a star of their very own. Give them tickets to a concert and a meal afterwards, arrange a red-letter day at a posh hotel or the chance to fly an old aeroplane.

PROBLEM PEOPLE - LISTINGS

Adopt an Animal Depending on the size and cuddliness of your choice, you can sponsor an exotic beast from Hilary, a giraffe, at £1,500 to a nameless piranha for £20. Some people feel that cockroaches and rats need a cuddle and here's their chance. When you become an adoptive parent to a pangolin, you get a certificate, a picture of a similar beast, a car sticker, a free ticket to the zoo and a magazine subscription. You also help the zoo itself.

Adopt an Animal, London Zoo, Regent's Park, London NW1 4RY
Tel: 0171 449 6262
Price range: from £20 for a dormouse to £6,000 for an elephant. Leaflet free.
Payment: cheque, major credit cards.

PRESENTS 347

Postage & packing: not applicable.
Delivery: allow 28 days to process.
Refunds: no.

Anything Left-Handed

Just what it says and if, like me, you've struggled with a right-handed potato peeler for years, even this is a present worth having. Other implements include pens, knives, secateurs and scythes, nail scissors and tin openers. There are also books to help people cope with being sinister.

Anything Left-Handed Ltd,18 Avenue Road, Belmont, Surrey SM2 6JD
Tel: 0181 770 3722 **Fax:** 0181 715 1220
Price range: £1.15 to £56.95. Catalogue free.
Payment: cheque, Mastercard, Visa.
Postage & packing: £1 for orders up to £7.50, £2 thereafter.
Delivery: allow 28 days.
Refunds: by arrangement.

International Star Registry

There are a limitless number of stars and more are being found the whole time. About 15m have so far been identified and this company can have one named after you which is entered and copyrighted in the official listings lodged in the British Library and Library of Congress. You get a certificate and an idea of where your star is. Stars have been named after Marilyn and Elvis, Pavarotti and John Lennon, Richard Branson and Oprah Winfrey. Now over to you.

International Star Registry, Freepost, 24 Highbury Grove, London N5 2BR
Tel: 0171 226 6886, free 0800 212493 **Fax:** 0171 226 8668
E-mail: orion@starregistry.co.uk
Website: http://www.starregistry.co.uk
Price range: £55 for registration and commemorative gift pack. Leaflet free.
Payment: cheque, postal order, major credit/debit cards.
Postage & packing: included in UK. Overseas including Channel Islands and Isle of Man £8. Express delivery £10.

Delivery: allow up to 28 days. Last Christmas orders by 18 December.
Refunds: yes.

Theatre Tokens A good gift, whatever the occasion. They can be exchanged for tickets at over 160 theatres nationwide, including all of London's West End. Theatre Tokens are well presented, saving the hassle of gift-wrapping and can also be sent direct to the recipient with a personal, hand-written message. You can include a drink and programme voucher, Godiva Belgian chocolates, champagne or a meal for two at a selection of wine bars and restaurants in London.

> **Theatre Tokens, Tokenline:** 0171 240 8800 **Fax:** 0171 557 6799
> **E-mail:** helen@solttma.co.uk
> **Price range:** £1, £5, £10 and £20.
> **Payment:** cheque or postal order payable to West End Theatre Managers Ltd., Virgin vouchers, major credit/debit cards.
> **Postage & packing:** included.
> **Delivery:** posted first class by return. Last Christmas orders by last first class posting date.
> **Refunds:** no, but no expiry date on tokens.

See also: Birkenstock for sandals for vegetarians and vegans, Soled Out for shoes for difficult feet, Devon Fudge Direct for people with allergies, vegetarians and vegans, Doves Farm Foods for gluten-free breads and cakes, Jenkins & Hustwit for cakes for diabetics, Vintage Roots for organic wine and hampers for vegetarians and vegans plus entries under Special Interests.

PERSONALISED

Once a monogrammed shirt had to be stitched by hand. Now there are all sorts of new techniques which sew, print or otherwise stick initials where they're needed. Other machines will print up T-shirts, table mats, prints and luggage with names, pictures or cartoons. Then you can buy, for very little money, name tags for bedrooms or duvet covers, for toy boxes or furniture. There are firms which will make videos of magic moments or compile jigsaws from family snaps. It's a growing area, with prices tumbling.

PERSONALISED - LISTINGS

Arty-Zan This company will turn your photograph – any size, black and white or colour – into a jigsaw although, if it's a bad or fuzzy photograph, the jigsaw will be the same (could make solving it even harder). They will also make jigsaws from children's drawings, postcards or any other picture you care to send them. Jigsaws come in four sizes, the cheapest a doddle of thirty pieces; the most expensive a fiend of 280.

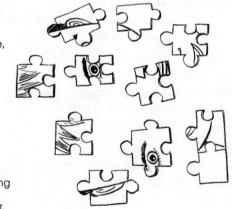

Arty-Zan, Fairholme Farm, 14 Croydon Lane, Banstead, Surrey SM7 3AN
Tel: 01737 379342
Price range: £9.99 to £13.99. Details free.
Payment: cheque or postal order.
Postage & packing: included in UK.
Delivery: within 7 working days. Last Christmas orders by 18 December.
Refunds: yes.

Ends (UK) Ltd Generously, they sent me a personalised doorplate saying Leslie's Room (spelling the name right for once) with a Noah's ark full of cheerful rabbits, lions and elephants. I didn't hang it up because I'm too old for that kind of thing. But lots of children like to put up the equivalent of a do not disturb sign and I'm all for encouraging a sense of possession in children. Another personalised idea is a crocodile jigsaw where each piece has a letter from the child's name. This should make it easy to complete.

Ends (UK) Ltd, Unit 5, Lynderswood Farm, Upper London Road, Braintree, Essex CM7 8QN

Tel: 01245 362444 **Fax:** 01245 362888

Price range: £2.50 to £35. Catalogue free.

Payment: cheque, Mastercard, Access, Visa.

Postage & packing: included.

Delivery: by return. Last Christmas orders by 18 December.

Refunds: yes.

Specials: personalised birthday or greetings card included for small additional charge.

Kingston Collection This company was founded in 1879 to make bagpipes and now uses the skills acquired to create watches, clocks, hip flasks and cases for calculators and cards in highly polished stainless steel, mostly for corporate gifts. These, however, translate well into personalised presents beautifully engraved. I particularly like the Voyager clock which is designed like an old-fashioned compass.

Kingston Collection, Suite 10, The Old Railway Station, Elgin, Morayshire IV30 1RH

Tel: 01343 540053 **Fax:** 01343 540032

Price range: £10.95 to £65. Catalogue free in UK, £3 overseas refunded on first order.

Payment: cheque, major credit cards.

Postage & packing: £2.95 per order.

Delivery: despatched within 3 days, engraved may take an extra day. Last Christmas orders by 20 December.

Refunds: not when engraved.

The Magic Calendar Company The product after which they are named is a personalised calendar using your own best family snaps month after month, from holiday haunts or sepia pictures of relatives to your favourite pet. Now you can also order your favourite photos on T-shirts, on Teddy Bears' T-

PRESENTS 351

shirts and on your mouse mat. The way I treat my mouse mat, I should have a shot of my best enemy.

The Magic Calendar Company Ltd, P O Box 6, Manchester M60 3EL

Tel: 0161 236 8009 **Fax:** 0161 236 5404

Price range: calendars from £9.99, mouse mats/T shirts £12.

Payment: cheque with order.

Postage & packing: included.

Delivery: 1 week. Last Christmas orders by 14 December.

Refunds: yes.

Papers Past The company has over 100 tons of old newspapers – I know the feeling – but they use them to send out on birthdays or other special dates so you can see what was happening in previous years. Could your date mirror the introduction of the zebra crossing or the day Christine Keeler revealed all?

Papers Past, Longstone Heritage Centre, St. Mary's, Isles of Scilly, Cornwall TR21 0NW

Tel/Fax: 01720 422924

Price range: £19.95 for 1 date, £35 for 2, £45 for 3 Leaflet free.

Payment: cheque, postal order, Mastercard, Visa.

Postage & packing: included in UK. Overseas at cost.

Delivery: normally despatched within 24 hours. Last Christmas orders 2 days before last posting date.

Refunds: yes.

Specials: gift-boxed as standard.

Remember When The cleverness of sending somebody a newspaper of the same date as their birthday, wedding, christening etc (or one from the same day but a different year) is that it is quite fascinating to read what was happening at the time. The firm holds about two million newspapers from the 17th century to the present.

Remember When, The Tithe Barn, 520 Purley Way, Croydon, Surrey CR0 4RE

Tel: 0181 688 6323 **Fax:** 0181 781 1227

Price range: £19.50 to £34.50 for most daily newspapers, other prices may vary. Catalogue free.

Payment: cheque, major credit/debit cards.
Postage & packing: included.
Delivery: despatched same day by post.
Refunds: no.

Roger Alsop Lucky is the man who owns a special old car, since it costs about as much to buy and keep as a racehorse. Roger Alsop is, therefore, a modern Stubbs who will paint your old car in flowing watercolours with lots of highlights. Each is set against a suitable background and, obviously, the more interesting the car the better it works.

Roger Alsop, 4 St. John's Villas, London N19 3EG
Tel: 0171 263 8067
Price range: £200 a painting. No catalogue, but photos of earlier paintings sent on request.
Payment: cheque.
Postage & packing: included in UK.
Delivery: by arrangement. Last Christmas orders by 15 December, but not if he's already working.
Refunds: yes.

What's in a Name! The brochure for this firm shows just how many variations there can be in personalised, jokey wine labels. Château Stag Night, mis en bouteille au King's Head; Château Hayes, mis en bouteille au Golf Club or Château Liz 'n Bob, mis en bouteille au vestry gives the flavour. You can order anything from a single label to – their record – 15,000 or more and supply your own picture and sense of humour. Labels are self-adhesive – just soak off the genuine one and apply your own.

What's in a Name!, St. Julians, Sevenoaks, Kent TN15 0RX
Tel: 01732 743501 **Fax:** 01732 741091
Price range: £4.75 for 1 to £1 each for 60 plus.
Payment: cheque.
Postage & packing: included.
Delivery: 2-3 days if pushed.
Refunds: no.

PRESENTS

Wright and Logan Based in Portsmouth, the firm has been taking portraits of Royal Navy ships which dock there since 1924 and has built up an archive of over 50,000 negatives. Surely one of them will fit the sailors in your life, especially if they have sailed in more than one ship. A whole group (even for landlubbers) would make a most decorative wall.

Wright & Logan, 20 Queen Street, Portsea, Portsmouth
PO1 3HL
Tel: 01705 829555 **Fax:** 01705 861694
Price range: £29.95 to £41.95. Catalogue free.
Payment: cheque, postal order, major credit cards.
Postage & packing: included.
Delivery: 7-10 days.
Refunds: yes.

See also: Billie Bond Designs, Bridge House Design, Charlotte, David Plagerson, Dream Team Design, Expressly Children, Little Issues, A Pack of Cards, Petsafe Collars and Leads.

CHARITIES

It's almost de rigueur to buy Christmas cards from the charity of your choice and there is now a very good selection of high quality versions. Charities are now moving in on a whole range of present ideas, with varying success. Too many, in my view, are in the hands of marketing men who fail to appreciate the charity's purpose. Thus, a charity devoted to improving the quality of life, should take trouble to find gifts which enhance this while one to help old people should have a list which does the same. The area is improving, but you still have to pick carefully among the catalogues to find something exceptional.

MAIL ORDER MADE EASY

CHARITIES - LISTINGS

The Blue Cross If you, like me, are an animal lover, you'll be keen to support the charity through their imaginative catalogue. They treated over 60,000 ill or injured pets last year and rehoused another 8,000 unwanted animals. Obviously, the catalogue homes in on animal ideas – mainly cats and dogs – though you can get horsy and piggy items, those which support hedgehogs and, for Christmas, robins.

The Blue Cross, Shilton Road, Burford, Oxfordshire OX18 4PF
Tel: 01993 822651 **Fax:** 01993 823083
Price range: 75p to £39.95. Catalogue free.
Payment: cheque, postal order, Access, Visa, Switch.
Postage & packing: £1.95 for orders up to £8.99, £3.25 thereafter. Overseas rates on application.
Delivery: allow 21 days. Last Christmas orders by 15 December.
Refunds: yes.
Specials: personalised Christmas cards.

Countrywide Workshops The company is in business to create work for disabled people and much, therefore, can be made to your own specification. Charles Cragg, for instance who is deaf, dumb and blind can make almost anything of turned wood and once produced a matching set of pulls for a bathroom lavatory, light and blinds. Other craftsmen can engrave on glass, mix pot pourri, create woven dolls' cradles or full-scale furniture. It's a general catalogue of great usefulness.

Countrywide Workshops Charitable Trust, Brynteg, Llandovery, Carmarthenshire SA20 0ET
Tel: 01550 720414 **Fax:** 01550 720525
E-mail: countryww@aol.com
Price range: £1.70 to £585. Catalogue free but donations wecome.
Payment: cheque, major credit/debit cards.
Postage & packing: £1.50.
Delivery: allow 28 days.
Refunds: yes.

PRESENTS 355

The Gardeners' Royal Benevolent Society As you would expect, full of useful objects for gardeners. Some pieces are simply patterned with fruit and flowers, others are hand-cream, pruning saws and midge repellent.

G.R.B.S. (Enterprises) Ltd, Bridge House, 139 Kingston Road, Leatherhead, Surrey KT22 7NT
Tel: 01372 372266 **Fax:** 01372 362575
Price range: £2 to £25. Send sae for catalogue.
Payment: cheque, Mastercard, Access, Visa, Switch.
Postage & packing: £2 for orders up to £12, £3.50 thereafter.
Delivery: allow 28 days.
Refunds: yes.

Help the Aged All the profits of the charity go to the elderly with problems, and the catalogue has a bias towards their comforts. There are pill organisers, special pillows, a gadget to help pull on tights, walking sticks and wheeled shopping baskets. There's a clever selection of cassettes from the BBC with old favourites like Joyce Grenfell, Round the Horne and Alistair Cooke's Letter from America. General items include cards, calendars, food and children's toys.

Help the Aged (Mail Order) Ltd, St. James's Walk, Clerkenwell Green, London EC1R 0BE.
Tel: 0171 253 0253 or 0171 250 1907 **Fax:** 0171 250 4485
Price range: £1.95 to £550. Catalogue free.
Payment: cheque, Mastercard, Access, Visa.
Postage & packing: £2.95 for orders under £25, free thereafter.
Delivery: allow 21 days. Last Christmas orders by 10 December.
Refunds: yes.

The National Trust A distillation of what you find in National Trust shops: calendars, NT's own books which are getting better and better, country clothes, heritage Christmas puds and the like. I would really like this catalogue to be less self-consciously 'heritage' and give us some really interesting replicas plus furniture, lighting and garden plants inspired by its wonderful properties.

The National Trust (Enterprises) Ltd, P O Box 101, Melksham, Wiltshire SN12 8EA
Tel: 0117 988 4747 **Fax:** 01225 792269
Price range: £3 to £95. Catalogue free.
Payment: cheque, postal order, major credit/debit cards.
Postage & packing: UK £3.50, Europe £12.49, elsewhere £18.49.
Delivery: normally within 10 days but allow 28. Last Christmas orders by 9 December UK and Europe; 18 November USA, Canada, Far East, Australasia; 25 September elsewhere.
Refunds: yes, except personalised items unless faulty.

Peoples Trust for Endangered Species
This charity, working to help wildlife, has a small catalogue. T-shirts, aprons, bags and so on are printed with animals; there are some good books on the subject plus items such as hedgehog boxes, seeds for butterfly-attracting plants and cards to help children identify animals' tracks. Cards and gift-tags are also available.

Peoples Trust for Endangered Species, 15 Cloisters House, 8 Battersea Park Road, London SW8 4BG
Tel: 0171 498 4533 **Fax:** 0171 498 4459
Price range: 75p to £19.99. Catalogue free.
Payment: cheque, Mastercard, Visa, Eurocard.
Postage & packing: included.
Delivery: a few days, but allow longer at Christmas.
Refunds: yes.

Royal Horticultural Society
This charity has a nicely chosen general catalogue with some connection with gardening. There is crockery patterned with flowers, gardening books and videos, pot pourri and small garden tools such as secateurs and pruning knives. Simple but charming cards are available.

RHS Enterprises, RHS Garden, Wisley, Woking, Surrey GU23 6QB
Tel: 01483 211320
Price range: £3 to £45. Send sae for catalogue.
Payment: cheque, major credit cards.
Postage & packing: approx £2.95 per order.
Delivery: allow 28 days.
Refunds: yes, if returned as new within 14 days.

Royal Society for the Protection of Birds This charity is very smart when it comes to marketing – you can find their approved bird table mix in most supermarkets. The catalogue offers a huge range of bird tables, nest boxes and even a house martin's nest along with cds to identify bird song, books on identifying the birds in your garden and various household items decorated with birds. I'd like to see them, however, concentrate on serious books, cds and foods for birds and drop some of the twee T-shirts and sweats with gooey owl motifs.

Royal Society for the Protection of Birds, The Lodge, Sandy, Bedfordshire SG19 2DL

Tel: 01767 680551
Fax: 01767 682118
Website: http://www.charity-gifts.com
Price range: 50p to £99. Catalogue free on request to RSPB Sales Ltd, Queensbridge Works, Queens Street, Burton on Trent DE14 3LQ
Payment: cheque, postal order, major credit/debit cards.
Postage & packing: £3.45 in UK, 30% of order value in Europe.
Delivery: normally within 14 days. Personalised items may take up to 28.
Refunds: yes, if returned within 14 days.

RSPCA Sensibly, this charity is turning its merchandising towards the pets it serves. There will be a special pets' pizza and birthday cake for those special occasions along with a happy cat kit of seeds that your cat will love to play in. You can get sticky address labels with silhouettes of 32 different dogs and cats (I bet they don't have my Weimaraner). There is a stripey sisal mouse for the cat's claws and a personalised pet towel if your dog can read its name. It looks to me as though this charity has stepped out of the rut to find some really useful ideas.

358 MAIL ORDER MADE EASY

R.S.P.C.A. Trading Ltd, P O Box 46, Burton upon Trent, DE14 3LQ
Tel: 01283 506125, catalogue request line 01283 506122
Price range: £1.99 to £59.99. Catalogue free.
Payment: cheque, Mastercard, Visa, Switch, Delta.
Postage & packing: £3.45.
Delivery: normally within 14 days but allow 28. Last Christmas orders by 11 December.
Refunds: yes, if returned within 14 days.

Shelter
This important charity does what it can for the homeless and, though its book of London's young street dwellers is hardly festive, it's salutary. Other gifts have little to do with the roofless but they are carefully thought out, friendly and stylish. Give your support.

J. Arthur Dixon (Shelter Trading Ltd), Forest Side, Newport, Isle of Wight PO30 5QW
Tel: orders 0990 539102, enquiries 0990 539162, catalogue request line 0171 505 2071
Price range: £1.95 to £25. Catalogue free.
Payment: cheque, Access, Visa, Switch, Delta.
Postage & packing: £1.75 for orders up to £10, £3.50 for orders over £10 in UK. Europe £6.75. Elsewhere £11.50 by surface mail, £13 + 25% order value by air mail.
Delivery: 7-21 days, 28 days for personalised Christmas cards. Last Christmas orders by 12 December.
Refunds: yes.

Soil Association
This charity, dedicated to good farming practice, has a list including masses of books from Goat Husbandry to Story of the Potato. There are a few cards, shopping bags and labels for re-using envelopes. You can also buy copies of their directory of farm shops and vegetable box schemes.

Soil Association Trading, Bristol House, 40-56 Victoria Street, Bristol BS1 6BY
Tel: 0117 929 0661 **Fax:** 0117 925 2504
E-mail: soilassoc@gn.apc.org
Price range: 50p to £50. Catalogue free.
Payment: cheque, Mastercard, Access, Visa, Switch.
Postage & packing: 50p for orders up to £3, £1.50 to £10, £3 to £20, £4 thereafter.

PRESENTS 359

Delivery: Last Christmas orders by 4 December. Ring after this date for last minute availability.
Refunds: by arrangement.

Traidcraft

This company, which encourages fair trade with the Third World, sells nativity sets from Peru and Tanzania, decorative seagrass stars from the Philippines and gilded moon and star baubles from Bali. The gift range includes marbled and batik covered stationery and jewellery from Asia, plus a good selection of Christmas cards and wrapping papers. Good for unusual ideas.

Traidcraft plc, Kingsway, Gateshead, Tyne and Wear NE11 0NE

Tel: orders 0191 491 0855, catalogue request 0191 491 1001
Fax: 0191 487 0133

Price range: £1 to £80. Catalogue free.

Payment: cheque, Mastercard, Visa, credit account.

Postage & packing: £3.50.

Delivery: allow 7 days. Last Christmas orders by 18 December, or 21 December by express delivery.

Refunds: yes, if returned within 14 days.

WaterAid

The charity is devoted to getting safe water to Third World country communities. Its catalogue is a curious mix of goods connected with water: a wavy silver-plated photo frame, water bug T-shirts and floating candles. Bathroom ideas include soapdishes and beakers patterned with fish, sparkling bath crystals with a brass scoop and hippo wash mitts. Nicely chosen.

WaterAid Trading Ltd, P O Box 220, 14-20 Eldon Way, Paddock Wood, Kent TN12 6BE

Tel: 01892 837800

Price range: £2.95 to £35. Catalogue free.

Payment: cheque, Mastercard, Access, Visa.

Postage & packing: £1.95 for orders up to £15, £2.95 thereafter.

Delivery: Last Christmas orders by 18 December.

Refunds: yes if returned within 14 days.

Chapter Eleven

CELEBRATIONS

CARDS AND WRAPPINGS.

Thank God for the jiffy bag, in which almost anything unbreakable will travel. And, thank Him too for masking tape, Sellotape and that wide brown stuff which, when it's not curling in on itself, makes parcels impenetrable. If the outer shell looks pretty pedestrian, the interior can still shine. Take a leaf from Jo Malone, whose cosmetics by post arrive in forests of wood shavings, subtly scented, with each individual item packed in black tissue paper. As in many mail order areas, new ideas are arriving all the time, so it's worth looking at the packaging catalogues for new labour-saving products.

CARDS AND WRAPPINGS - LISTINGS

Bridge House Design Lorette Roberts, a watercolour artist, draws and paints cards exclusively for this family firm. Though she does greetings cards of garden flowers for all occasions, the best are her funny combinations of little clowns and children in Heath Robinson like situations. Many of these can be personalised with the child's name, address, birthday and so on.

> **Bridge House Design**, Lemsford Village, Hertfordshire AL8 7TN
> **Tel:** 01707 323741 **Fax:** 01707 332536
> **Price range:** 50p to £15.50. Send A5 sae for catalogue.
> **Payment:** cheque.
> **Postage & packing:** £1.50 for orders up to £5, £2.90 thereafter.
> **Delivery:** within 14 days. Last Christmas orders 18 December.
> **Refunds:** by arrangement.

CELEBRATIONS 361

Paperchase From the shop which really understands about paper, there now comes a mail order catalogue. It has a selection of cards chosen from charities, beautiful wrapping paper in the latest fashions and excellent tree decorations, plus a stylish range of stationery and gifts.

Paperchase, 213 Tottenham Court Road, London W1P 9AF
Tel: 0171 323 3707 **Fax:** 0171 637 1225
E-mail: paperchase@paperchase.telme.com
Price range: £1 to £50. Catalogue free.
Payment: cheque, major credit/debit cards.
Postage & packing: £4.95, orders over £100 free in UK. Express delivery £10. Overseas rates on application.
Delivery: allow 21 days.
Refunds: yes, if faulty.

Sophie Allport Cards Sophie's designs are both funny and decorative and, in general, are multi-images tightly packed on the paper. They're always changing but recent ideas show rows of strawberries and one jar of cream, a host of green wellies with one flirting and groups of helicopters entitled "Spot the Poseur." Designs might be suitable for golfers, drinkers and teddy bear freaks. She also does highly decorative limited edition prints of flowers, fruit and vegetables.

Sophie Allport Cards, Friars Orchard, Nocton Road, Potterhanworth, Lincoln LN4 2DN
Tel: 01522 791435 **Tel/Fax:** 0181 780 0419
Price range: 40p to £89. Catalogue free.
Payment: cheque.
Postage & packing: £1.50 for orders up to £25, £2 up to £50, free thereafter.
Delivery: allow 5 days. Last Christmas orders 19 December.
Refunds: yes if returned within 7 days.

See also: Babyface, Bond & Gibbins, Lakeland and entries under Charities.

DECORATIONS

I am not a fan, at all, of paper chains, bunches of balloons or seedy Christmas trees brought out every year for generations. I accept that, when children are about, tasteful celebrations go out of the window – and so they should. But for adult parties, the modern craze for scented candles is a winner, as are subtle crystal baubles, silver rather than gold and, at Christmas, a large bunch of evergreens plus ivy swags is better by far than a potted poinsettia. The glossy magazines, bless and curse them, provide constant ideas and an ever-present feeling of guilt that you didn't do even better.

DECORATIONS - LISTINGS

Balloons by Breeze Open your mystery present and, from the box, floats out a helium-filled balloon with a special message for you. It may be "You're special" or "Get Well" or, useful this, a balloon illustrated with a very hangdog pooch saying "I'm sorry". Then the box might also hold a bottle of champagne, a teddy bear or a box of chocolates. An effective way of getting a last minute message with a difference.

Balloons by Breeze, 2 Railway Approach, East Grinstead, West Sussex RH19 1BP
Tel: 01342 315592 **Fax:** 01342 317839
Price range: £17.25 to £46. Catalogue free.
Payment: cheque, Access, Visa, Amex, Switch.

Postage & packing: included. Special delivery £2.70.

Delivery: by first class post, allow 2 days. Last Christmas orders by 21 December.

Refunds: yes, if damaged.

Chatsworth

A complete selection of Christmas decorations originally intended for the restaurant trade. They stock fake but natural-looking fir wreaths and swags which you can add to, crackers, tinsel and shimmer garlands, realistic fake Christmas trees and flickering lights. There are 22-inch high Father Christmas and snowman balloons with feet and 36-inch high Santa Bear and Banana Face as well as hats, masks, blow-outs and streamers. These are neither elegant nor beautiful but they're good for a party.

Chatsworth, 31 Norwich Road, Strumpshaw, Norwich, Norfolk NR13 4AG

Tel: 01603 716815 **Fax:** 01603 715440

E-mail: chatsworth@paston.co.uk

Price range: £2 to £200. Catalogue free.

Payment: cheque, postal order, major credit cards.

Postage & packing: £7.95 for orders under £300.

Delivery: allow 28 days, less with surcharge.

Refunds: yes, if damaged or not delivered.

Specials: 10% discount on orders paid for by 30 September for Christmas products.

Cherie Colman Designs

This company makes ready-made card hangers with scrunchy tartan bows at the top and a fall of ribbon on which to attach the cards. Cherie Colman initially made them for herself but went into business after finding that others wanted a way to make their cards look good (and not fall over). They look splendid and make instant decorations all the year round.

Cherie Colman Designs, 23 Calbourne Road, London SW12 8LW

Tel: 0181 675 9847 **Fax:** 0181 265 3775

Price range: £10 to £18. Send A4 sae for catalogue.

Payment: cheque.

Postage & packing: £2.50 for orders up to £50, £5.50 thereafter.

Delivery: within 1 week. Last Christmas orders by 18 December. Supplies may be limited.
Refunds: yes.

The Christmas Barn and Farmhouse Flora

New to mail order, this small family business, run by Anne Ballard who trained at Constance Spry, specialises in home-grown freshly dried flowers. The Christmas Barn supplies modern and traditional Christmas decorations including table centres, garlands, wreaths and tree ornaments based on dried flowers and foliage, nuts, berries, fruits and spices. Its sister company, Farmhouse Flora, offers stylish dried arrangements all year round, as well as silk flowers, containers and accessories.

The Christmas Barn and Farmhouse Flora, Church Farm, Shrawley, Worcester WR6 6TS
Tel: 01905 620283 **Fax:** 01905 621608
Price range: £5 to £35, or more for specially commissioned work.
Payment: cheque, major credit/debit cards.
Postage & packing: varies according to weight and destination.
Delivery: by arrangement as goods are made to order. Express delivery available. Last Christmas orders by 10 December.
Refunds: yes.
Specials: gift-wrapping, courses, workshops and demonstrations, private commissions undertaken.

Designer Crackers

Very smart crackers wrapped in chic paper may include a cotton bandanna, a mulled wine sachet, Belgian chocolates or a teddy bear along with the inevitable paper hat and motto. The firm can do a huge single cracker over two meters long and needing 12 people to wield it, party parcels which are much the same as crackers but you don't need to pull and what they call "party bombs" which are indoor fireworks which throw out balloons, streamers, confetti and gifts when you light the blue touch paper.

Designer Crackers, East Morden, Wareham, Dorset BH20 7DW
Tel: 01929 551001 **Fax:** 01929 459511
Price range: 42p to £35. Catalogue free.

CELEBRATIONS

Payment: cheque, postal order, Mastercard, Access, Visa, Delta.

Postage & packing: from £2 for orders up to £15 to £5.50 over £40.

Delivery: by arrangement.

Refunds: by arrangement.

Homecrafts Direct
This company's huge catalogue is a good source for glues, modelling kits, paper and board (if you want to make your own cards and decorations) and figures for the tree or around the home. There are candle-making kits, glitter kits and masses of different paints – from acrylic to fluorescent. Also a good source of presents for children with hobbies like finger painting or photography.

Homecrafts Direct, P O Box 38, Leicester LE1 9BU

Tel: 0116 251 3139 **Fax:** 0116 251 5015

E-mail: post@speccrafts.demon.co.uk

Website: http://www.speccrafts.co.uk

Price range: a few pence to £700. Catalogue £3.75 refundable against orders over £30.

Payment: cheque, postal order, Mastercard, Visa.

Postage & packing: from £1 for orders under £5 to £5 over £50. Over £130 free.

Delivery: usually within a few days. 24-hour service at extra charge.

Refunds: by arrangement.

Panduro Hobby
A huge catalogue of over 10,000 items which, apart from food, virtually does Christmas for you. There are tree decorations, spray paints, labels and stickers of Santa Claus, angels, wreaths, advent calendars and Christmas cards, wrapping paper, string, gift boxes and sealing wax. Then you can get the necessary materials to make your own Christmas figures – from mice in bed to little match girls – or sprays of dried flowers and berries and so on. This Scandinavian company has some slightly strange products (very few robins, for instance) and the sheer quantity is boggling but there's a helpful index.

Panduro Hobby, Freepost, Transport Avenue, Brentford, Middlesex TW8 8BR

Tel: 0181 847 6161 **Fax:** 0181 847 5073
E-mail: pandurohobby@compuserve.com
Price range: 85p to £195. Catalogue £2.95.
Payment: cheque, postal order, major credit/debit cards.
Postage & packing: generally £2.95 a parcel.
Delivery: allow 28 days. Last Christmas orders by 12 December.
Refunds: yes, if damaged and returned within 14 days.

Plaid Tidings It seems slightly ironic that these tree decorations, stockings and Santa Claus hangers are actually made in the far East where Christmas is simply a way of making money. Lynn Royce, however, says that her decorations and ideas are a cut above the High Street and, certainly, they are more unusual. She also does a range for babies – or, rather, proud parents.

Plaid Tidings, Sudpre, Perry Hill, Worplesdon, Surrey GU3 3RB
Tel: 01483 232684 **Fax:** 01483 237062
Price range: £2.95 to £58. Catalogue free.
Payment: cheque, Mastercard, Visa.
Postage & packing: £2.50 for orders under £40, £3.50 thereafter.
Delivery: usually 10 days, but allow 2-3 weeks for personalised items. Last Christmas orders by 10 December or 1 December for personalised items.
Refunds: yes, if returned unused and in original packing within 10 days.

Worton Cottage Industry Petronella Ballard has invented The Ultimate Cardhanger which, with a bit of thought by people as unhandy as me, can hold around eight cards in a neat line. Hang these from nails about the place and not only will they stay tidy but won't blow over the whole time. Ideal for Christmas but they can be used for birthdays, invitations, photographs and for children who have a special range of their own.

Worton Cottage Industry, Over Worton, Chipping Norton, Oxfordshire OX7 7EP
Tel: 01608 683419 **Fax:** 01608 683519
E-mail: cottage.industry@worton.demon.co.uk
Price range: cardhangers £4.90, gifts/toys £1 to £45. Catalogue free.
Payment: cheque, Mastercard, Visa, Delta.

CELEBRATIONS

Postage & packing: cardhangers 40p each, free for orders of over 10, gifts/toys £1 to £4, free for orders over £50.
Delivery: usually within 2-3 working days, but allow 6.
Refunds: only if faulty.

See also: Lakeland, Kirker Greer for candles, Fortnum & Mason for candles and crackers, Meat Matters for wreaths, Tobias and the Angel for decorations, WCP Video for Jane Packer's video on Flowers for Christmas, Terrace and Garden for twig Christmas trees and glass decorations. Virtually all the charity catalogues offer crackers and decorations.

CHRISTMAS

A subject in itself which took up all of my last book. I have the feeling that soon commonsense will prevail and we will stop giving up six months of the year to planning a three-day holiday. That's not to say that we shouldn't do our utmost to enjoy it – but we shouldn't be driven by the perfectionism implicit in so many magazine articles. I'm a journalist and I know the effort expended on the glossy pages of the magazine is often in inverse proportion to the effort the writer actually spends on his or her own home. If it's at all possible, Christmas should be treated as a great, big party where anything goes. Better the Lord of Misrule than a tight-lipped tantrum.

Refer to: all suggestions in Celebrations, plus entries under Food and Drink.

CREATING AN ATMOSPHERE.

Much of the success of a party lies in its preparation. I have, in the past, hired a caterer who hands round party food on plates decorated with shells, minute wrapped parcels and swathes of

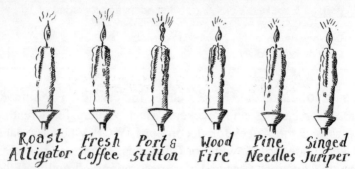

dried leaves; the food is tiny and exquisite. This gains compliments out of all proportion to the effort involved, just as a scented log fire will do at a dinner party or the production of a whole sea trout decorated with leafy fronds of dill at a summer lunch. It's all a question of theatre, illusion, making all the senses work. The prime sense to be pampered is, in my view, smell. Whether it's the aroma of new baked bread or lilies of the valley wafting in the hall, scent creates a subliminal feeling of enjoyment. There are plenty of scented candles, oils to drop on heated light bulbs or modern versions of the joss stick to help in this. Otherwise, decide what atmosphere you want to purvey and go for it. Freshness – spray your fruit and flowers so there are tiny drops of water glinting on their skins; romance – add soft lights from polished silver and cut glass; luxury – try a full orchestra playing Mozart or Haydn on the turntable and a vase full of deep purple flowers. Best of all, steal ideas from the stylists whose job it is to make a pair of pyjamas, a dish of pasta or the corner of a summer house look infinitely desirable.

Refer to: Aromatherapy Associates, Aromatique, Crabtree & Evelyn, Culpeper, Czech & Speake, D.R. Harris, Hardys, L'Artisan Parfumeur, The Perfumers Guild and Kirker Greer for scented candles, oils and room sprays; Groom Bros, Scent from the Islands, Secretts and Farmhouse Flora for flowers.

YOUR LEGAL RIGHTS

If you buy goods by mail order, you are automatically protected by the laws and rights that cover normal shopping. The most important of these is the Sale and Supply of Goods Act of 1994 which toughens earlier Sale of Goods Acts.

The first right you have is that goods must be or do what they say they will. If the sheets you order are described as linen, they must be 100% linen, and the cheese grater must adequately grate cheese. Further any goods must also be of 'satisfactory quality' – that is durable, safe and free from faults. The description given in a mail order catalogue should be accurate though you should allow for a bit of purple prosery. If, however, it's downright misleading you have the right to reject anything and get your money back as long as you do so in a 'reasonable' time. However 'reasonable' is not defined.

You can also claim compensation if a tool or toy breaks down after too short a time because, again, it is not 'satisfactory.' You are entitled to a full refund of your money – not a credit note or exchange – if that's what you want. This protection also covers mail order sale goods, unless they are clearly called seconds. Sale goods also have to be 'satisfactory.'

If you just don't like what you have bought, you do not have these legal rights but many mail order firms will still help because it is important to them to encourage the use of mail order for shopping. I must add that the public clearly does not always treat firms well. This is why so many insist that returned goods must be clean, unworn or undamaged and that broken bits or faulty parts must be returned. They have found that some people order an expensive shirt, wear it to a party then try to send it back. Or claim breakages when there are none. If we find some companies wary or brusque to deal with, or cautious when we report faults, this may be the reason.

It is, obviously, far harder to return objects which have been made to commission or engraved with initials or special greetings. If you are especially concerned, it should be possible to see a similar piece – before it is customised – so that you can appreciate its quality and how it feels. Always discuss arrangements before you make a firm agreement.

A further problem about giving presents is that the legal protection covers only the buyer, not the recipient and firms often insist on seeing a receipt, probably, once again, because the public cannot always be trusted. Recipients are often unwilling to own up that they are unhappy with their present and this makes getting the receipt a problem. But this is what you will have to do before you can legally claim your rights.

There is a code of mail order practice (though the firm you are dealing with may not belong to it) which suggests that all goods should arrive in 30 days and that, if returned in 7 days, money will be refunded. You will see that many of the firms in this guide ask for 28 days for delivery while adding that it's

YOUR LEGAL RIGHTS

usually within a week. When timing is important, whether because you are sending a birthday or wedding present or simply want the object before you go on holiday, make it a condition of contract with the seller by writing the vital delivery time onto your order. A further precaution is to add, in writing, 'Time is of the essence' on the order form.

If you return an item because it is not 'satisfactory' under law, then your postage costs should be refunded along with the price; if you return because you don't like it, then you'll probably have to pay postage.

There is not much protection if companies go out of business and they are not likely to tell you if they are on their last legs. But, if you pay a bill of over £100 by credit card (and this is a major reason for doing so) you can be compensated by the card company which is 'jointly and severally liable' with the mail order company under the Consumer Credit Act.

If you buy goods direct from an advertisement, check that the company's name and address is written somewhere outside the coupon, so you can retain it for your reference. If it isn't, or if on receiving your goods you feel that the advertisement was misleading, your first port of call is the Advertising Standards Authority. Write to their Complaints Department at 2 Torrington Place, London WC1E 7HW, or phone 0171 580 5555.

One side effect of using mail order is that your details may be passed on to other companies, and you could end up with a collection of catalogues you didn't ask for. Companies use what they know about your lifestyle to determine what to send you, so what you receive should normally be relevant, but if it isn't you can tailor it to your needs. You can get on or off any mailing list simply by writing to the company concerned. You can tick the box on the coupons and order forms if you don't want to receive unsolicited mail. Further help is available from the Mailing Preference Service, Freepost 22, London W1E 7EZ. They can arrange for you to be sent information on whole categories that interest you, like kids' clothes or travel. Alternatively, they can get your name removed from the mailing lists of all companies registered with them, which should stop nearly all unsolicited mail for five years. Personally I enjoy a degree of unsolicited mail and only ask for privacy if a firm becomes too intrusive.

Which? magazine has given advice on how to complain successfully. Relevant points were these:

- Be clear about the problem.

- Keep your receipt.

- Decide whether you want a refund, exchange or repair.

- Return the goods as soon as possible.

- If the goods are too big to return, write or ring saying why you are rejecting them.

- Speak to the manager and state your case firmly.

- Follow up your complaint in writing and set a reasonable time limit for their response. If you are still dissatisfied, seek advice from a consumer advice centre, Citizens' Advice Bureau or trading standards department.

INDEX OF SUPPLIERS

A J Trading Co, The 58
A.P.E.S. Rocking Horses 324
Abbotsbury Oysters 195
Abbott & Holder 80
Acorne Sports 304
Adopt an Animal 346
Aero Clothing Co 43
After Noah 92
Agent Provocateur 58
Air de Provence 92
Alba Smokehouse 195
Alastair Sawday Publishing 263
Alpaca Collection, The 23
Ancestral Collections 81
Ancient Art 81
Andrew Crace Designs 143
Andrew Martin 93
Andrew Ransford 73
Annie Cole 93
Annie Sloan 94
Anta 94
Anything Left-Handed 347
Anytime Records 274
Archers Addicts 291
Architectural Plants 143
Archival Fine Art Print
  Collection, The 82
Arne Herbs 144
Aromatherapy Associates 248
Aromatique 249
Arran Aromatics 249
Art Guild, The 94
Art Room 82
Artifex 95
Artigiano 24
Artisan 95
Arty-Zan 349

Ashfield Traditional 83
Australian Wine Club, The 235
Aviation Leathercraft 43
AVM Concepts 325
Avon Bulbs 145

Babes in Wood 325
Baby Basics 326
Babyface 274
Bagadele 275
Baileys Architectural Antiques 96
Balloons by Breeze 362
Bambino Mio 275
Barclay & Bodie 15
Barefoot Books 264
Barnett, H.L. 320
Barnsbury Collection, The 59
Barometer Shop, The 290
Barrow Boar 209
Barry M Cosmetics 250
Bates Gentlemen's Hatter 59
Bathrobe Co, 24
Bear Essentials 50
Beardmore 96
Beauty Quest 251
Beckett & Graham 318
Bed-Side-Bed Co, The 276
Beer Cellar, The 235
Bel Frames 97
Bennett & Green 97
Betty's and Taylors of
  Harrogate 176
Billie Bond Designs 32
Bird Guides 290
Birkenstock 60
Black Dog of Wells 98
Black Sheep Brewery 16

374 — MAIL ORDER MADE EASY

Blooming Marvellous 277
Blooming Things 145
Blue Cross, The 354
Bobbins 98
Bobux 272
Boden 44
Bombay Duck 98
Bon Goût 168
Bond & Gibbins 99
Bones Dog and Catalogue 312
Born for Loden 25
Bouchon 99
Bow Art 83
Brett Payne 74
Brian Jarrett 293
Bridge House Design 360
Brigade Designs 74
Brillbury Hall Farm Food Co 209
British Museum Co 84
Brora 25
Bryson's of Keswick 177
Bugwear 306

Cabbage Leaf Co 278
Calange 51
Candlesby Herbs 223
Cantelo Cat Collars 313
Carden Cunietti 100
Cargo 100
Caribbean Hamper Co, The 204
Carluccio's 169
Carol Mather 75
Carpet Bags Plus 60
Carrier Co, The 101
Cartmel Village Shop 178
Cashmere Co, The 26
Castle Combe Skid Pan
  & Kart Track 304
Cath Kidston 101
Cavendish Chocolate Co,
  The 190
CCA Galleries 84
Celestial Buttons 61
Champagne Select 236

Charbonnel et Walker 191
Charlotte 278
Charlton Orchards 202
Chatsworth 363
Chatsworth Farm Shop 169
Cheeky Rascals 229
Cheese Hamlet, The 186
Chelsea Collections, The 27
Cherie Colman Designs 363
Children's Cottage Co, The 327
China Beasts 102
Choc Express 191
Chocolate Club, The 192
Chocolate Society, The 192
Christmas Barn, The 364
Christopher Simpson 75
Ciel Decor 102
Cigar Connoisseur 261
Claire Sowden 103
Clark Trading Co, The 170
Classic Car Art 293
Classic Garden 146
Claudio Vanelli 223
Cleo 27
Clivedon Collection, The 294
Cloakrooms 103
Club des Créateurs de Beauté,
  Le 251
Cobra & Bellamy 76
Cocoon 27
Collin Street Bakery 178
Cologne & Cotton 104
Colour Blue 104
Company of Animals, The 313
Connolly 61
Conservas Rainha Santa 231
Contemporary Artworks 85
Cool Chile Co 224
Cordings 44
Coriander's Presents by Post 319
Cornelissen 294
Cottage Garden Roses 146
Cotton Comfort 51
Cotton Moon 51

INDEX OF SUPPLIERS 375

Country Traditionals 105
Country Victualler, The 210
Countrywide Workshops 354
Crabtree & Evelyn 251
Cricketer, The 295
Crucial Trading 105
Culpeper 252
Curry Sauce Co, The 224
CXD - Cashmere by Design 28
Cyrillus 29
Czech & Speake Direct 252

Damask 106
David Austen Roses 147
David Mellor 106
David Plagerson 327
Delta Aviation 305
Denewear 45
Denner Cashmere 29
Denny Andrews 29
Designer Crackers 364
Devon Fudge Direct 193
Devon Hamper Co, The 204
Di Gilpin 30
Dickinson & Morris 178
Dillons 264
Dinosaur Society, The 295
Direct Import 107
Direct to your Door 328
Divertimenti 107
Dolls' House, The 328
Dolls' House Emporium 329
Donald Russell Direct 210
Dophin Enterprises 295
Doves Farm Foods 179
Dream Team Design 108
Dromedary Trading 52
Dukeshill Ham 211

Early Learning Centre 329
Eastbrook Farms Organic
    Meat 212
Elizabeth Bradley Designs 108
Emma Jefferson 330

Ends (UK) 349
England at Home 109
English Garden 147
English Home Collection - see
    Sussex House 137
English Hurdle 148
English Picnic Basket Co 109
English Stamp Co, The 110
Espresso Warehouse 236
Eurolounge 110
Exclusive Brandy Club, The 237
Expressly Children 330

Faerie Shop, The 296
Farmer John Quilts 111
Farmhouse Flora – see The
    Christmas Barn 364
Favourite Things 279
Feast of Frames, A 111
Felicitous 171
Fine Cheese Co, The 187
Fine Food Club 171
Finishing Touch, The 319
Fired Earth 112,
First Impressions 16
Flairpath 280
Flavell & Flavell 62
Fletchers of Auchtermuchty 212
Flights of Fancy 320
Flower Plots 148
Food Ferry, The 172
Formes 280
Fortnum & Mason 17
Franchetti Bond 62
Fresh Food Co, The 172
Fresh Olives Direct 231
Friars Goose 112
Frog Hollow 343
Future Foods 149

G.R.B.S. (Enterprises) 355
Garden Books by Post 365
Garden Factory, The 149
Garden Systems 150

MAIL ORDER MADE EASY

General Trading Co, The 17
Gifts from the Grange 320
Gilly Forge 63
Glazebrook & Co 113
Glendevon Smoked Salmon 196
Globes 296
Glorafilia 113
Glover & Smith 114
Gluttonous Gardener 205
Goodman's Geese 213
Goodwood Festival of Speed
  Collection 18
Goodwood Racecourse
  Collection 18
Gordon's Condiments 225
Gordon's Production
  Services 281
Gosh 265
Goslings 343
Graham, J & J 173
Graig Farm 213
Great Central Railway 305
Great Little Trading Co,
  The 281
Great Northern Wine Co,
  The 237
Great Western Wine Co 238
Green Board Game Co,
  The 331
Green Books 266
Green River Panamas, 63
Green Shop, The 19
Grenadier Firelighters 114
Groom Bros 260

Haddon Rocking Horses 331
Halcyon Days 85
Halzephron Herb Farm 226
Hambleden Herbs 226
Hamilton & Inches 76
Hamleys of London 331
Handmade Wooden Tray Co,
  The 115
Hansel & Gretel 52

Happy Flannelies 53
Hardys 253
Harris, D.R. 253
Harrods 19
Hawkin & Co 343
Hay Hampers 205
Heal Farm 214
Hebridean Seafoods 196
Help the Aged 355
Hereford Duck Co 214
Heveningham Collection,
  The 150
Higginbotham 30
Higgins, H.R. 239
Highfield Nurseries 151
Hill Toy Co, The 332
Hitchcocks' by Post 20
Hobbs House Bakery 179
Holding Company, The 115
Holland & Holland 45
Homecrafts Direct 365
Hopleys Plants 151
Hopscotch Dressing Up
  Clothes 332
Hortus Ornamenti 151
House 115
House Nameplate Co, The 116
House of Bruar. The 20
House of Henry, The 21
Howels of Sheffield 152
Hughes Butchers 215
Humphreys Exclusive
  Confectionery 193

If Only... 116
Imperial War Museum 86
Index Extra 282
India Shop. The 117
Indian Ocean Trading Co 152
Initial Ideas 321
International Star Registry 347
Inthebag 117
Inverawe Smokehouses 197
Iron Bed Co, The 118

INDEX OF SUPPLIERS

J. P. Promos 63
J.G.S. Metalwork 153
Jack Joseph Designs 77
Jack Scaife 215
James Baxter & Son 198
James Nicholson Wine
  Merchant 239
James of Pershore 198
James Smith & Sons 64
James White Apple Juices 240
Jane Hogben Terracotta 153
Janet Reger 65
Jenkins & Hustwit 180
Jeremy Law 65
Jeroboams 187
Jo Malone 254
Joanna's 119
John Halifax 65
John Jaques 307
John Jordan 297
John Pimblett 180
Johnny Loves Rosie 345
JoJo Maman Bébé 282
Judith Glue 31
Justerini & Brooks 240

Kantara 119
Kari Mix 227
Karin Hessenberg 154
Karrimor International 66
Katharine Goodison Millinery 66
Katie Eastaugh Ceramics 120
Katie Mawson 53
Keith Metcalf's Garden
  Heritage 154
Kelly Turkey Farms 216
Kiddiewise 333
Kiddycare 283
Kids in Comfort 283
Kids' Stuff 54
Kileravagh Smoked Foods 198
Kingshill 31
Kingston Collection 350

Kirker Greer 120
Kootensaw Dovecotes 155
Kynes Feather Bed Co 121

L'Artisan Parfumeur 255
L.L. Bean 21
Lakeland 121
Lands' End 32
Latham & Neve 77
Laurel Designs 333
Lavender Blue 284
Lay & Wheeler 241
Layden Designs 22
Leading Edge, The 297
Les Senteurs 255
Letterbox 334
Lewin, T. M. 48
Little Badger 54
Little Issues 334
Little Red Barn, The 181
Little Treasures 54
Liz Cox 67
Loch Fyne Oysters 199
Loch Ruray House 46
Lochengower 200
Lodge, R & J 218
Long Tall Sally 32
Loon Cartoons 86
Louise Bradley 122
Lovers of Blue & White 87
Low Sizergh Barn 206

MacGregor's Galloway
  Oatcakes 182
Mackenzies Smoked
  Products 200
Macsween 217
Made in America 173
Madeleine Trehearne
  & Harpal Brar 33
Magic by Post 298
Magic Calendar Co, The 350
Mamble Foods 227
Manx Loaghtan Produce Co 217

378   MAIL ORDER MADE EASY

Margaret Anne Gloves 67
Maritime Co, The 298
Marks & Spencer 122
McCord 123
Meat Matters 218
Meg Rivers Cakes and Gifts by
  Post 182
Melin Tregwynt 123
Mercator 77
Metro Products 285
Millers 33
Mills' Farm Plants 155
Minh Mang 123
Mini Boden 55
Molton Brown 256
Monte's 174
Morel Bros Cobbett & Son 174
Morgan Bellows 124
Mother & Toddler Fashions 285
Mothernature 286
Motley Crew 55
Mrs Gill's Country Cakes 183
Mrs Pickering's Dolls'
  Clothes 335
Muchen Silk 34
Mulberry Bush, The 335
Mulberry Hall 124
Musical Gift Catalogue, The 299
Mycologue 299

Natalys 286
National Trust for Scotland,
  The 87
National Trust (Enterprises),
  The 355
Natural Collection 22
Natural Fabric Co, The 125
Natural Friends 314
Natural Knitwear 34
Nature's Gate 287
Nauticalia 299
Neat Ideas 266
Neptune Classics 156
Nether Wallop Trading

Co, The 126
New Quay Honey Farm 232
Newell Glass 126
Nice Irma's 127
Nisbets Chefs Choice 127
Noël Productions 78
Nordic Design 127
Nordic Style 128
Norfolk Lavender 156
Norfolk Provender, The 206
Northern Parrots 314
Northumberland Cheese
  Co, The 188
Nuttery, The 315

Obelisk Collection, The 88
Objets Extraordinaires 321
Ocean 128
Office 68
Officina Profumo-Farmaceautica
  di Santa Maria Novella 256
Oil Merchant, The 228
Old Stile Press, The 266
Oliver Brown, 35
Olives Et Al 232
Orchard Toys 335
Organic Gardening Catalogue,
  The 157
Organics Direct 175
Original Celtic Sheepskin
  Co, The 68
Original Orkney Hamper Co,
  The 207
Orvis 35
Out of the Earth 322
Outhwaite, W. R. & Son 140
Owl Barn Gift Catalogue,
  The 300

P S Polos 37
Pack of Cards, A 300
Pajama Box, The 46
Panduro Hobby 365
Panzer's 207

INDEX OF SUPPLIERS

Paperchase 361
Papers and Paints 129
Papers Past 351
Pappa Geppetto's Toys 336
Past Perfect 301
Past Times 88
Paxton & Whitfield 188
Pedlars Clothing 35
Pedometers International 307
Penhaligon's 257
Penkridge Ceramics 129
Peoples Trust for Endangered
   Species 356
Peppers by Post 228
Percivals Fine Cigars 261
Perfumers Guild. The 258
Period House Group, The 130
Periwinkle Productions 267
Peruvian Connection 36
Peta Flint 47
Peter Gethin Driving Courses 305
Petsafe Collars and Leads 315
Physical State 287
Pickett Fine Leather 68
Pier Direct 130
Pintoy and Plan Toys 336
Plaid Tidings 366
Plainfeather 130
Planta Vera 157
Pollock's Mail Order 337
Polo Neck Designs 36
Potions & Possibilities 258
Presents for Men 322
Prickly Pear 131
Prizma Embroidery 69
Purple Pom Pom 322

Quicke, J .G. 189
Quintessentials Europe 175

R.S.P.C.A. Trading 357
Rachel Riley 56
Racing Green 37
Rainforest Clothing Co 38

Ramsay of Carluke 219
Rannoch Smokery 219
Real Cakes 183
Real Meat Co, The 220
Real Pyjamas Co, The 47
Red House, The 267
Red Letter Days 306
Reel Times 301
Reid Wines 241
Remember When 351
Riders and Squires 308
Robert Mullis 337
Robert Smith 131
Robert Welch 132
Robinson, W. 163
Rocking Sheep Centre 338
Roger Alsop 352
Rosebud Preserves 235
Rosie Nieper 323
Rowan Prints 89
Royal Horticultural Society 356
Royal Society for the Protection
   of Birds 357

Salar 200
Sam de Teran 308
Samuel French 302
Sarah Broadhead-Riall 132
Sarah Hamilton 133
Sarah Meade's Special Occasion
   Cakes 184
Sarah Parker-Eaton 78
Sarah Raven's Cutting
   Garden 158
Sasti 56
Scavenger Diving Services 302
Scent from the Islands 260
Scotland's Larder 208
Secret People 57
Secretts 202
Seriously Smart 79
Shaded Candle Co, The 133
Shaker 134
Sharpham Wines & Cheeses 242

Shelter 358
Shepheard-Walwyn 268
Sheridan & Hunter 158
Sherwoods Photo 309
Shetland Knitwear
  Associates 38
Shilasdair 39
Shirt Press, The 47
Silken Robes 39
Silver Direct 134
Silver Editions 134
Silver Fern 288
Silver Moon 69
Simon Charles 70
Singing Tree, The 89
Sitting Pretty 135
Skyview Systems 309
Smythson by Post 268
Snow + Rock 310
Snug as a Bug 288
Snuggle Nap 289
Software Partners 269
Soil Association Trading 358
Soled Out 70
Somerset Cider Brandy
  Co, The 242
Soo San 89
Sophie Allport Cards 361
Sotheby's Bookshop 269
Space Appeal 135
Space NK 259
Spencers Trousers 48
Spice Shop, The 229
Sports Motive, The 310
Spottiswoode Trading 338
Squires Kitchen 184
Stork Talk 289
Stroffs Speciality Sausages 220
Stuart Buglass 136
Stuart Lennie 339
Suffolk Gardens 159
Suffolk Herbs 159
Super Tramp Trampolines 339
Susan Lethbridge 136

Susie Thomson 137
Sussex House 137
Sussex Tea Co, The 243
Swaddles Green Farm 221

Tadpole Lane 270
Taillissime 40
Talking Book Club, The 270
Tank Exchange, The 160
Tanners Wines 243
Teddington Cheese, The 189
Teddy Bears of Witney 339
Terrace & Garden 160
Thai Shop, The 40
Theatre Tokens 348
Thiz Bag 71
Thomas Goode & Co 138
Thompson & Morgan 160
Three Choirs Vineyards 244
Toast 41
Tobias and the Angel 138
Toffee Shop, The 194
Tombuie Smokehouse 222
Torz & Macatonia 244
Touch Design 139
Tracklements 229
Traditional Farmfresh
  Turkeys 222
Traditional Garden
  Supply Co, The 161
Traditional Toys 340
Traidcraft 359
Treasure Chest 340
Tridias! Toys 341
Truffles 184
Truggery, The 161
Two Wests and Elliott 162
Tyrrell Katz 345

Up Front Designware 71

Valvona & Crolla 245
Video Plus Direct & Talking
  Tapes Direct 271

INDEX OF SUPPLIERS

Vigo Vineyard Supplies 163
Village Bakery, The 185
Vintage Roots 245
Volga Linen Company 139

Waddesdon Manor 90
Wadham Trading Company, The 163
Waggers 316
Waitrose Direct 246
Walcot Reclamation 140
WaterAid Trading 359
Waterstone's 272
WCP Video 272
Weald Smokery, The 201
Wealth of Nations 41
Wells & Winter 164
Welsh Mountain Garden 230
Wendy Brandon 233
What's in a Name! 352
Wheelie Bin Cover Co 164

Whichford Pottery 165
White Company, The 141
Whittard of Chelsea 246
Wiggly Wigglers 165
Wild Seeds 166
Wild Wood 341
Wilkinet 290
William Powell & Son 311
William Yeoward Crystal 142
Windrush Mill 166
Winna Pet Beds 316
Wiseman Originals 90
Wolford 72
Woollons Brothers 141
Woolshed, The 41
Word Out 303
Worton Cottage Industry 366
Wright & Logan 353

Yeoward South 142

Readers' Report Form

Future editions of this book will be improved if you write with your comments, letting us know (i) if any mail order suppliers are not included which you think should be and (ii) if you have any comments on a supplier listed in the Guide. Please print your name clearly.

Send your comments to:

**Columbine Press Ltd
42 Canonbury Square
London N1 2AW**
E-mail:dovebooks@aol.com
Website: www.g-vis.co.uk/MailOrderMadeEasy

Mail Order Made Easy - Report form

To the author

From my own experience the following supplier should/should not be included:

SUPPLIER'S NAME: ....

Address: ....

....Tel: ....

Comments:...

....

....

YOUR NAME: ....

Address: ....

....

....